THE BYZANTINE SAINT

THE
BYZANTINE SAINT

edited by

SERGEI HACKEL

ST VLADIMIR'S SEMINARY PRESS
CRESTWOOD, NEW YORK
2001

Library of Congress Cataloging-in-Publication Data

Spring Symposium of Byzantine Studies (14th: 1980: University of Birmingham)
    The Byzantine saint / edited by Sergei Hackel.
        p. cm.
    Originally published: London: Fellowship of St. Alban and St. Sergius, 1981, as learned
    papers presented at the 14th Spring Symposium of Byzantine Studies.
    Includes index.
    ISBN 0-88141-202-3
    1. Christian saints—Byzantine Empire—Congresses. I. Hackel, Sergei. II. Title.
BX380.S64 1980b
270'.092'2—dc21   2001041985

THE BYZANTINE SAINT

ST VLADIMIR'S SEMINARY PRESS

575 Scarsdale Road, Crestwood, New York, 10707-1699
1-800-204-2665

First published in 1981 by the
Fellowship of St Alban and St Sergius, London.
Learned papers presented at the
Fourteenth Spring Symposium of Byzantine Studies,
University of Birmingham.

ISBN 0-88141-202-3

PRINTED IN THE UNITED STATES OF AMERICA

THE MARTYRDOM OF ST THEKLA

Contents

ILLUSTRATIONS

Frontispiece
Martyrdom of St Thekla. Detail from the Menologion of Symeon Metaphrastes. BM Add MSS 11870 f 174ᵛ, c.early 12th century. Photo by courtesy of the Courtauld Institute of Art. On the panēgyris *of St Thekla see 200-2 below.*

Flyleaf
The Forty Martyrs of Sabaste.

Acknowledgements

In the preliminary stages of this project I received invaluable help from members of the *Sobornost/ECR* editorial board: Dr Sebastian Brock, the Revd Dr Robert Murray SJ, the Revd Norman Russell and the V Revd Dr Kallistos Ware. The Secretary of the Fellowship of St Alban and St Sergius (our publisher), the Revd Gareth Evans, gave guidance on the business side of the publication. Professor Anthony Bryer made the original proposal that we should consider it, participated in the planning of it, and provided willing and effective help on a number of occasions as the work proceeded. Dr James Shiel and the Revd Norman Russell offered advice on problems of transliteration. The Revd Norman Russell also generously shared in the work of proofreading and compiled the index. But in the end, the editor's is a lonely task, and his remains the responsibility for editorial deficiencies. Their number will have been augmented by the brave/foolhardy decision to make these papers available well before the year is out in which they were delivered.

Abbreviations

In virtually every case periodicals and serials are cited in accordance with the list of abbreviations given in *Dumbarton Oaks Papers* 27 (1973), 329-39. Works not listed there are usually cited in full. Recurrent citations of articles or books has led to an uneasy mixture of short titles, op.cit. (where the previous mention of the title was in close proximity) or op.cit. with reference to the antecedent note (where this was further off). There may be some inconsistency, but there should be no lack of clarity. Where page references have been followed by references to paragraphs or lines the subordinate reference is preceded by a full stop. *Synopsis* 527.28-528.1 thus brings one from page 527 line 28 to the first line of the following page. But if paragraphs rather than lines are at issue, reference to the work itself will immediately reveal it. For the same reason there has been no attempt to distinguish references to page or column from each other.

Introduction

SERGEI HACKEL

T HE building of Pachomios' wall at Tabennisi, with which this symposium opens, speaks of the monastic's intention to withdraw from the world;[1] the setting up of the stylite's pillar involves withdrawal even from such a *koinobion* as the wall was set up to safeguard. Yet the ascetic's very separateness made an impact on the society with which he parted ways.[2] In the evaluation of this separateness the innocent Byzantine might occasionally be misled or manipulated by charlatans, who did their best to blur the distinction between the physical incidentals of ascesis and its ultimate aims.[3] But in general Byzantine society was not to be disenchanted by that part which Gibbon thought to be the whole. The holy man had his accepted role in high and low society alike.[4]

For some holy men it was a role which was more or less coterminous with their lives. For others it was to be adapted and extended far beyond death. Their reputation as members of the Kingdom was to outlive the Empire itself. Hagiographers,[5] hymnographers,[6] iconographers,[7] pilgrims[8] and patrons of *panēgyreis*[9] helped to

1. Henry Chadwick, 'Pachomios and the Idea of Sanctity', 11-24. This reference like most of those that follow, is to a paper published below.

2. So much is implicit in many of the contributions to this volume, but see in particular Han J.W. Drijvers, 'Hellenistic and Oriental Origins' and Susan Ashbrook Harvey, 'The Politicisation of the Byzantine Saint'.

3. Paul Magdalino, 'The Byzantine Holy Man in the Twelfth Century', 51-66. As is noted by Lennart Rydén, 'The Holy Fool', 111-12, there were also spurious *saloi.*

4. On high society see in particular Rosemary Morris, 'The Political Saint in the Eleventh Century'; Ruth Macrides, 'Saints and Sainthood in the Early Palaiologan Period'; and Evelyne Patlagean, 'Sainteté et Pouvoir'. On low society see Robert Browning, 'The "Low Level" Saint's Life in the Early Byzantine World' and Speros Vryonis Jr, 'The *Panēgyris* of the Byzantine Saint: A study in the nature of a medieval institution, its origins and fate'.

5. The work of hagiographers is variously treated by Robert Browning, 'The "Low Level" Saint's Life'; Michael van Esbroeck, 'Le Saint comme Symbole'; Anna Crabbe, 'St Polychronius and his Companions – but which Polychronius?'; Flor Van Ommeslaeghe, 'The *Acta Sanctorum* and Bollandist Methodology'.

6. Hymnography was not separately treated at the Symposium and the subject plays no significant part in any of the papers given below.

7. Nicholas Gendle, 'The role of the Byzantine Saint in the Development of the Icon Cult'; also summaries of the papers by David Buckton, 'The Mass-produced Byzantine Saint' and Vera Likhacheva, 'The Iconography of the Byzantine Saint in Illuminations of the Eleventh and Twelfth Centuries' (together with illustrations 1, 2, 4, 7-11, and the frontispiece and endpapers).

ensure that their memory would be perpetuated. Those who gained recognition as saints[10] are not forgotten in those parts of the world which harboured them or their relics.[11] To a greater or lesser degree they are commemorated by the Orthodox world at large. Some have gained acclaim in both East and West.

Such acclaim is now tempered by the scrutiny to which (largely Western) scholarship has subjected Lives and reputations. The heritage bequeathed by Rosweyde and Bollandus is a weighty one.[12] Both Bollandists and their admirers continue to enrich it.[13] The pious lay observer may be outraged and dismayed by the consequences of their work.[14] But in the end it can only be someone like the dreadful Blemmydes[15] or the fake holy man[16] who might be interested in the maintenance of spurious reputations.

Scholarship is committed to the establishment of truth. The Church, for her part, should be willing to accept nothing less. This was already the burden of Bollandus' title page of 1643, where ERVDITIO and VERITAS are prominently displayed and juxtaposed.[17] There is always a need to distinguish and to preserve Tradition from traditions.

At the same time traditions, superstitions and myths are justly valued by historians. They provide a vital – often the principal – gauge for a study of the popular mind. A *panēgyris*,[18] a memento[19] or a mass-produced image[20] of a saint is likely to reveal more of this mind than the most stylish Life or mosaic. The Bollandist's chaff may thus prove to be the social historian's grain. And the study of the Byzantine saint may become (as often in this volume) the study of his clientele.

---

8. E. D. Hunt, 'The Traffic in Relics; some Late Roman Evidence'.
9. Vryonis, *'Panēgyris'*.
10. As is noted by Ruth Macrides, aspects of the Byzantine canonisation procedure remain to be explored (83-7). Constantinopolitan methods were never to match those of Rome, though in the early Palaiologan period the established practice of local canonisation was to lose favour in preference to canonisation by synodal decree. Whether or not this was under Western influence remains an open question.
11. See the map, 'Hagiogeography of the Byzantine World', 228.
12. A survey of this heritage is given by Van Ommeslaeghe, *'Acta Sanctorum'*.
13. See for example the papers of Michel van Esbroeck and Anna Crabbe.
14. Considerable changes in the Roman General Calendar were legitimised by the motu proprio *Mysterii Paschalis* of 14 February 1969 (*Acta Apostolicae Sedis* 61 [1969], 222-6) and defined in *Notitiae* 5 (1969), 159-202. Justification for the changes (which came into effect 1 January 1970) is provided in *Calendarium Romanum* (Vatican 1969), 63-149. I am grateful to Fr Norman Russell for these references.
15. See Joseph A. Munitiz, 'Self-canonisation: the "Partial Account" of Nikephoros Blemmydes'.
16. See n.3. above.
17. Reproduced below, 159.
18. Vryonis, *'Panēgyris'*.
19. Hunt, 'Traffic in Relics'.
20. Buckton, 'Mass-produced Saint'.

Even the superannuated saint may therefore have a humble function to perform; while the dignity of his authentic counterpart ('in whose companionship the heaven exults; in whose guardianship the earth rejoices; by whose triumphs holy Church is crowned')[21] can never be impugned or diminished.

21. Bede, Sermon for All Saints Day, *PL* 94.450 (tr. J.M. Neale in *Famous Sermons by English Preachers*, ed. D. Macleane [London 1911], 2).

'The Byzantine Saint':
The XIVth Spring Symposium of
Byzantine Studies

ANTHONY BRYER

S INCE 1967 the University of Birmingham's Committee for Byzantine Studies
(which became a graduate Centre in 1976)[1] has held an annual course on a
Byzantine topic for the University's Department of Extramural Studies, usually
during the last weekend of the spring term. Over the last decade this meeting has
assumed the trappings of an international conference under the aegis of the British
National Committee of the International Byzantine Association (which meets at it).
So it attempts to serve British Byzantinists in a peculiarly international field and regularly attracts participants from over a dozen countries. Up to 250 people (the limit
of the Symposium's capacity) come to take part in it. But the Centre has not forgotten that its spring symposia are essentially no more than night schools, open to
all who apply in time: furthermore it is recognised that their quality (and the
XIVth was regarded as a particularly good meeting) does not depend only on the
designated speakers. It is a pleasure also to acknowledge the Centre's debt to an
anonymous benefactor, without whom the symposia could not be held with such
gusto.

Papers given at earlier symposia are scattered in various journals. Videotapes
were made at the VIIth (1973), VIIIth (1974), XIth (1977) and XIIth (1978)
symposia; publication of their proceedings as a whole began with the IXth (1975).[2]

1. See G. Every, 'Byzantium at Birmingham', *ECR* ix (1977), 109-10. Philip Howard contri-
buted 'A positively Byzantine affair in Birmingham' to *The Times*, 22 March 1980.
2. The following are available on application to the Secretary, Centre for Byzantine Studies,
University of Birmingham, Birmingham B15 2TT:
   One hour Videotapes (at price of tape, for bona fide teaching purposes): *The Ceremonies
   of Constantine Porphyrogenitus* (1973); *Byzantine Society and Economy* (1974); and
   Mark Antonios Foskolos, *Fourtounatos* (1976).
   Papers and catalogues: H.A.L. Lidderdale, *The (Greek) War of Independence in Pictures*
   (1976); P.D. Whitting, *Catalogue of an Exhibition of Coins from the 'Mardin' hoard*
   (1977); W. Farag, *The truce of Safar A.H. 359 – December-January 969/970* (1977); S.
   Karpov, *The Empire of Trebizond in Venice in 1374-76* (1978) and A. Bryer, *A Cadaster
   of the Great Estates of the Empire of Trebizond* (1978).
   Of *collected papers* given at Symposia, *Iconoclasm* (IXth, 1975), ed. A. Bryer and J.
   Herrin (reviewed in *ECR* x [1978]165-9), is out of print. *Byzantium and the Classical
   Tradition* (XIIth, 1979), ed. M. Mullett and R. Scott, will be published by the Centre in
   late 1980. *The Byzantine Black Sea* (XIIth, 1978) was published as a special volume of
   the *Archeion Pontou* 35 (1979) and is available at $22/£10 from the General Secretary,
   Epitropē Pontiakōn Meletōn, Kolokotronis 25, Athens 125, Greece.

The Centre is most grateful to Dr Sergei Hackel and the editorial board of *Sobornost/ Eastern Churches Review* for publishing a selection of papers from the XIVth Symposium (22-25 March 1980) in this volume.

The XIVth Symposium

The 1980 Conference was directed by a committee of the Centre's staff and students: Susan Ashbrook, Dr J. Neville Birdsall, Mary Cunningham, Dr John Haldon and Dr Frances Young, with Professor Anthony Bryer, its Director, as Symposiarch. It took up the theme of the Vth (1971) Symposium, on 'Asceticism in the early Byzantine World', at which Peter Brown raised the question of 'The Role of the Holy Man in the Early Byzantine World'.

Since 1971 the posthumous career of the Byzantine holy man has flourished mightily, not least at the hands of Professor Brown, and it seemed high time to take stock.[3] But the committee was anxious to open out the topic to the whole phenomenon of 'The Byzantine Saint' by calling upon speakers as various as the Byzantine saint himself. Among visitors, two Bollandists, guardians of an awesome tradition of hagiographical scholarship, were especially welcome; but it was intriguing to find that all participants spoke much the same scholarly language. A consensus emerged at the Symposium which is equally recognisable in these pages. The only thing which all Byzantine saints have in common is the source of their spiritual power. But the strength of their authority is marvellously demonstrated by the manner in which the Byzantine saint used it in the world; and it is on this demonstration that these papers concentrate.

Origins and Lives

The first day of the symposium, which was opened by *Dr John Ferguson,* the new President of Selly Oak Colleges, discussed **The Origins and Lives of the Byzantine Saint.** *The Revd Professor Henry Chadwick* (Cambridge) spoke on 'Pachomios and the Idea of Sanctity'*. This is published below (together with other papers which are asterisked). *Dr Sebastian Brock* (Oxford and Birmingham)[4] chaired a session on the pre-Christian origins of the Byzantine saint at which *Dr Geza Vermes* (Oxford) concluded that principal of 'Jewish Origins' was Christ himself; *Professor Han Drijvers* (Groningen) spoke on 'Hellenistic and Oriental Origins'*; and *Garth Fowden* (Washington, now Cambridge) on 'Pagan Asceticism'. *Sam Lieu* (Warwick) gave a communication on 'Buddhist Influence in early Christian Asceticism?' which will be published as part of a larger work.

A session on the Lives of the Byzantine saint (which was all too brief) was chaired by *Dr J. Neville Birdsall* (Birmingham). *The Revd Flor Van Ommeslaeghe SJ* (Bollandist) spoke on 'The *Acta Sanctorum* and Bollandist Methodology'*.

---

3. Cf. P.R.L. Brown, 'The Rise and Function of the Holy Man in Late Antiquity', *JRS* 61 (1971), 80-101; also H. Mayr-Harting, 'Functions of a twelfth-century recluse'; *History* 60 (1975), 337-52.
4. See Sebastian Brock 'The Byzantine Saint', *Sobornost/ECR* 2:2 (1980), 75-6.

Professor Robert Browning (London) considered ' "Low-style" Saints' Lives'*, while *Professor Ihor Ševčenko* (Harvard and Oxford) gave a paper on ' "High-style" Saints' Lives' which is to be published (with a textual appendix) in the *Analecta Bollandiana*. *Dr Anna Crabbe* (Belfast) spoke on 'Hagiography and the Narrative Straightjacket'. But it has been agreed this might be more appropriately published with the papers of the XIIIth (1979) Symposium (*Byzantium and the Classical Tradition*), while the paper which she gave then ('Polychronius and his Companions – but which Polychronius?')* would be most at home in this volume. In addition *Jelizaveta Allen* (Dumbarton Oaks) gave a communication on the 'Author Index of Byzantine Literature' which she is preparing.

The Byzantine Saint in the World

The second day of the symposium concentrated on **The Byzantine Saint in the World**. *Professor Evelyne Patlagean* (Paris) gave the main paper on 'Sanctity and Power'*. *Dr John Haldon* (Birmingham) chaired a discussion on the Byzantine Saint in Politics, with contributions by *Susan Ashbrook [Harvey]* on 'The Politicisation of the Byzantine Saint'*; *Professor George Huxley* (Belfast) on 'The Byzantine Saint in Iconoclasm'; and *Dr Rosemary Morris* (Manchester) on 'The Political Saint in the Eleventh Century'*. The theme was taken up in communications by *Nicholas Couchman* (Durham) on 'The Attitude of Facundus, Bishop of Hermionas, towards Emperor Justinian I in his "Three Chapters Controversy" '; *Dr Lowell Clucas* (Munich) on 'John Italos and John of Damascus'; *Dr Paul Magdalino* (St Andrews) on 'The Byzantine Holy Man in the Twelfth Century'*; and *Dr Ruth Macrides* (St Andrews) on 'Anti-Palaiologan Saints' (since revised and renamed)*.

The variety of the Byzantine saint was further demonstrated in a session chaired by *Rowena Loverance* (Birmingham). *The Revd Michel van Esbroeck SJ* (Bollandist) spoke on 'The Symbolic Saint'*; and *Dr Lennart Rydén* (Uppsala) on 'The Holy Fool'*.

Communications were offered on texts. *Michael Whitby* (Oxford) spoke on 'The Greek Hagiography of the Emperor Maurice' (a communication which will form part of a larger work). *Dr Warren Treadgold* (Munich) discussed 'The deservedly unpublished Life of St Eirene the Empress' – unpublished for it does not exist. *The Revd Dr Joseph A. Munitiz SJ* (Leuven) presented 'Self-canonisation: the "Partial Account" of Nikephoros Blemmydes'*, which he is editing. *Dr Hans-Veit Beyer*, the editor of Nikephoros Gregoras, spoke on 'References to the Bible, Patristic Tradition and Religious Experience in a discourse of Gregory the Sinaite'. *Mary Cunningham* (Birmingham) spoke on 'The Manuscript Tradition of Andreas of Crete's Homily on Lazaros'; and *George Every* (Oscott and Birmingham) on 'The Lives of the Virgin in *PG* 120'. *Dr David Balfour* followed his recent edition of *Politico-Historical Works of Symeon, Archbishop of Thessalonica (1416/17 to 1429)* with a communication concerning new data on Symeon. *Professor Anthony Bryer* (Birmingham) described 'The Hagiogeography of Chaldia', followed a series of Pontic Group Passions (beginning with the Forty Martyrs) to St Eugenios of

Trebizond, and asked why the latter's companions were not found sites for their cult in the mountain villages of Chaldia until the fourteenth century, when local lords, coastal emperors and Türkmen emirs were competing for control of the region.

Cult and Art

The Forty Martyrs were taken up again in a session on the final day which was devoted to **The Cult and Art of the Byzantine Saint.** This was chaired by *Dr Frances Young* (Birmingham). *Patricia Karlin-Hayter* (Birmingham, Dumbarton Oaks, and now Belfast) argued for the authenticity of the Testament of the Forty ('The Forty in History'), while *Zaga Gavrilović* (Birmingham) discussed the significance of the 'Forty in Art' ** [=summarised below].

The saint in art was widely discussed. There was a main paper by *The Revd Dr Christopher Walter* (Paris) on 'Iconodule Saints in the Madrid Skylitzes' (to be published in *Revue des études byzantines*). Another main paper was delivered by *Dr Vera Likhacheva* (Leningrad) on 'The Iconography of the Byzantine Saint in Illuminations of the Eleventh and Twelfth Centuries'**. Dr Likhacheva illustrated her paper with slides of miniatures in manuscripts which are located in the USSR; one of these miniatures is reproduced below.

Communications were given by *Dr Nicholas Gendle* (Oxford) on 'The Role of the Ascetic in the development of the Icon Cult, 4th-7th centuries' (since renamed)*; *Dr Robin Cormack* (London and Birmingham) on a newly-identified icon of 'St George seen through the eyes of Crusader painters' (to be published elsewhere); and *Robin Milner-Gulland* (Sussex) on 'The Oxford *Lazaros:* some new considerations'.

Finally the symposium examined **The Cult of the Byzantine Saint.** *Lucy-Anne Hunt* (Birmingham) chaired papers by *Dr E.D. Hunt* (Durham) on 'The Traffic in Relics'*; by *David Buckton* (British Museum) on 'The Mass-produced Byzantine Saint'**; and by *Dr Nancy Ševčenko* on 'The St Nicholas Cycle' (which she is to publish in a larger work on the subject). *Professor Speros Vryonis Jr* (UCLA, Athens and Dumbarton Oaks) concluded the symposium with a lively festival, ' The *Panēgyris* of the Byzantine Saint'*.

Although symposiasts regretted that *Dr Vladimir Vavřinek* (Prague) was unable to come and speak, as he and they had hoped, on Sts Cyril and Methodios, the Byzantine saint was celebrated in other ways. *David Buckton* brought an exhibition of 54 rarely shown Byzantine ivories, steatites, crosses and gems depicting the Byzantine saint from the British Museum, and *Nubar Hampartumian* displayed 146 seals and coins showing Byzantine saints in the Barber Institute of Fine Arts. Catalogues of both exhibitions were given to participants. Through the kindness of *the Very Revd Milenko Zebić* of St Lazar's, Bournville, a film of the monastery of Chilandari, Athos, was shown. There were two receptions; and a final feast concluded with a performance of Dufay's *Lamentatio Sanctae Matris Ecclesiae Constantinopolitanae* of 1454.[5]

---

5.   By way of a postscript it may be added that the XVth Spring Symposium of Byzantine Studies is concerned with 'Byzantium and the Slavs': it will be held in Birmingham on 21-24 March 1981, when the Centre is collaborating with the Medieval Studies Group of the British Universities' Association of Slavists. The XVIth Spring Symposium (1982) on 'The Byzantine Family' will move from Birmingham for the first time. It will be held at Edinburgh, where it will be directed by Dr Michael Angold.

ORIGINS

Pachomios and the Idea of Sanctity

HENRY CHADWICK

T
O talk of saints is hardly free of controversy. The subject of sanctity and of the means by which it is normally achieved, namely asceticism and renunciation, cannot be altogether a suitable topic for an urbane dinner-party conversation. We have decided that it is all right for an academic symposium, since historically the ideal is of vast consequence; but it may be well if we begin with some recognition that the topic can be divisive.

To most men and women life is beset by noise; and the possibility of chosen silence comes to be felt as a divine gift, at least to that large number of us whose daily round is a succession of trivialities punctuated by frustration, rage, envy, and the rest. ('Telegrams and anger', as E.M. Forster put it.) The pain of ascetic renunciation lies in the forgoing of natural goods, in a deliberate choice that puts the normal activities of human society on the far side of a wall.

But the shining portrait is also felt to have a dark shadow, which we can see depicted in eloquent prose in the pages of Gibbon's chapter on the monastic movement.[1] To Gibbon and the Enlightenment all monkery is synonymous with superstition of which, if not the creator, it is a fanatical fosterer — fanatical in the sense that it requires a devotion that is impervious to rational consideration. For Gibbon the ascetic life is a religion of 'children and females', a refuge for those who have failed or blundered in this world and seek solace for their misfortune and healing for their remorse. As monasteries came to be recruiting grounds for the episcopate, so the profession was entered by ambitious men hungry for power, who realised how celibacy enhanced their authority. The discipline of the monasteries, Gibbon thinks, is one of repellent, inhuman austerity — the disgraces, confinements, fastings, and bloody flagellations, executed in the name of a religious obedience which is tyranny. 'A cruel unfeeling temper has distinguished the monks of every age', writes Gibbon (in a surely dreadful and gross sentence), a stern indifference inflamed by religious hatred, a merciless zeal put to the service of intolerance and the Holy Office. With all this goes the resentment of lay people when popular monks insinuate themselves into noble households, and vast public and private wealth becomes absorbed in the maintenance of unproductive persons useless to society and enjoying a sacred indolence in the name of holy poverty; a body whose

1. *The Decline and Fall of the Roman Empire*, ch.37.

11

aggressive and useful military spirit is suppressed in the cloister but then reemerges to fight bitter, futile ecclesiastical controversies with implacable hostility. To monks pleasure and guilt are synonymous; and, as for their style of life, 'every sensation offensive to man is acceptable to God'. But for Gibbon they do not falsify the Christian spirit; rather do they supremely exemplify it by acting out the ultimate logic of 'the preaching of patience and pusillanimity'.

Gibbon evidently enjoyed writing his savage indictment. One recalls Porson's famous review of the *Decline and Fall:*

> An impartial judge, I think, must allow that Mr Gibbon's History is one of the ablest performances of its kind that has ever appeared [. . .]. Nor does his humanity ever slumber, unless when women are ravished or the Christians persecuted [. . .]. He draws out the thread of his verbosity finer than the staple of his argument [. . .]. A less pardonable fault is that rage for indecency which pervades the whole work, but especially the last volumes.[2]

Even when one has discounted Gibbon's vehement prejudices, which add such power to the elegance of his mannered prose, modern studies of the Byzantine saint have to recognise that for us modern men the subject can be one of peculiar complexity. Whatever our personal standpoint, we of 1980 do not share many of the assumptions that produced their manner of setting themselves on the road to sanctity. In consequence we are tempted either to tell the stories of their mortifications and then, as was said of Lytton Strachey, ostentatiously refrain from laughing, or we go in search of trendy non-religious explanations of the social needs that created them. It is of course certain that Byzantine saints fulfilled social needs, and it is a proper question to ask how that worked out. I am also sure that a stripping away of their religious motivation will leave the historian with a distorted picture. So in this paper opening the conference, I venture to put some initial questions about the religious presuppositions that underlie the saintly man's role.

Early Christian attitudes

The early Church was a tiny, persecuted body, and the experience sharpened its sense of having different values from the surrounding society. Its ideal was the martyr whose allegiance to his crucified Master was so strong that he preferred death to apostasy. But the second- and especially the third-century churches enjoyed long periods of peace during which their numbers grew to an extent that embarrassed those concerned to maintain standards. Many texts of Origen comment on the to him appalling fact that the churches are packed out with passengers, who come from a mixture of motives, who sit in dark corners of the building reading secular literature while the preacher seeks to expound the word of God, who prefer bishops to be easygoing in the discipline of the laity. In large cities bishops are becoming persons of social consequence cultivated by ladies of wealth and refinement, so that the office comes to be sought for non-religious reasons. Several third-century texts disclose strong debate about the compatibility of office and power

---

2.   *Letters to Mr Archdeacon Travis [. . .]* (London 1790), preface.

with the Christian profession. On the one side, there stand the biblical examples of Joseph and Daniel, holding high office, yet keeping their conscience undefiled. On the other side, a Roman magistrate cannot escape idolatrous pollution and punitive duties; and to Tertullian (*On Idolatry,* 17-18) the exercise of power and authority is simply incompatible with humility; that is the axiom which already in the fourth century led many 'secular' clergy to withdraw to monasteries and a quiet life. In the seventies of the second century the pagan Celsus was calling the Christians to shoulder public office and to serve in the army (Origen, *C. Cels.* viii.75). The third-century Christians did just that, and the more they did so, the greater the pagan apprehension that they aroused.

Already by the middle of the third century two ethical standards were being if not advocated, at least acquiesced in. Origen's 26th homily on Numbers (26.10) distinguishes within Christ's army the front-line troops who fight Satan hand to hand and the many camp followers who support the combat forces but do little or no fighting themselves. A generation later Eusebius of Caesarea (*Dem.Evang.* i.8. 29-30) marks a distinction between (a) those who keep the moral commands of the Decalogue while pursuing trade, farming, soldiering, political life, marriage, and attend church services on special occasions, and (b) those who go beyond what is commanded to keep themselves unencumbered by marriage ties, practise poverty, renounce the world of Vanity Fair, and devote their whole life to God's service.

So the Christians even before Constantine's revolution provide a blueprint for the scene realised after Constantine's conversion, both for the world-renouncing ascetics and for the world-affirming ethic which identifies the *res Romana* with God's purpose at work through the Church. In either case they are operating with a basic contrast between the Church and the *kosmos* or *saeculum,* the earthly city under the dark god of this world (even if only temporarily so), standing in antithesis to the heavenly city of God's Kingdom. Thereby the ascetic Christians create the concept that this world, in its daily business of getting and spending, of political power and social organisation, is a 'secular' entity apart from and perhaps hostile to the true calling of God; certainly going on its way in indifference to and independence of the divine purpose.

'Secularisation' is a complex word for a complicated and ambiguous idea. Its modern use comes from the mid-seventeenth century to apply to the transfer of property from clerical to lay hands; then from being first used for the expropriation of property, it comes to be used of a deeper attempt at expropriation of minds: *non licet esse vos,* Tertullian quotes the pagans as saying.[3] We should be on our guard against suggestions that secularisation is a modern concept. Both the concept and the vocabulary stem from the ascetic drive in quest of holiness in the pre-Constantinian Christian tradition, which sought to erect an invisible wall between the Church and the world.

---

3. *Apol.* iv.4.

Pachomios' wall

If we ask who first made this invisible wall into a visible entity, we are brought to Pachomios.[4] To him more than to any other single man we owe it that the word 'monk', literally a 'solitary', is one we naturally associate with a community and not with a hermit withdrawn in isolation. Everyone knows that this ex-soldier peasant Copt from upper Egypt, converted from paganism by the impression made on him by Christian charity without regard to membership of the Church, created the *koinobion* or community of monks and the concept of an 'order' with many monks in several linked houses living under rule. His houses were mainly located in or around the loop of the Nile in the neighbourhood of Dendera (ancient Tentyra). To say 'created' is not actually quite true, of course. From the earliest of the Greek Lives of Pachomios we know that, at the time when he first became a Christian and put himself to school with the laconic hermit Palamon, there were already little groups of semi-anchorites living near one another or together, mainly in twos, though we also hear of a group of five and another of ten. There is high probability that all these were groups of disciples gathered round some master of the path to sanctity. In the earliest Greek Life of Pachomios (cited below as G^1) we learn of an otherwise unknown Aotas, remembered for his unsuccessful attempts to form a *koinobion*, his failure being contrasted with Pachomios' success (G^1 120). The Coptic tradition recalls how Pachomios too had his initial setback.

But Pachomios is differentiated from all contemporaries and predecessors by the sheer scale of his operations, designed to incorporate large numbers of monks within his society and to subject them to strict discipline. So far as our information goes, Pachomios first makes the enclosure wall of the monastery a physical and not merely a mental fact. The wall was the first building operation to be undertaken; and we learn that his brother John disapproved of it and tried to dismantle it, since he could see that it spelled the end of anchoritic life as hitherto understood.

---

4. The earliest Greek Lives with the letter of Ammon and *Paralipomena* are edited by F. Halkin, *Sancti Pachomii vitae graecae* (SubsHag 18 [1931]), the Coptic translated into French by L.T. Lefort (1943), the Arabic into French by E. Amélineau (*Annales du Musée Guimet* 17 [1889]); Jerome's Latin version of the Rule and Letters edited by A. Boon, *Pachomia Latina* [Bibliothèque de la Revue d'histoire ecclésiastique Fasc. 7] (Louvain 1932); Dionysius Exiguus' Latin version of the Life, akin to the second Greek Life, by H. van Cranenburgh (1969). Pachomios' *Catechesis*, Coptic text edited and translated by Lefort (CSCO 160 [1956]). New material in Hans Quecke, *Die Briefe Pachoms* (Regensburg 1975) . See also his lecture 'Ein Handvoll Pachomianischer Texte', *XIX Deutscher Orientalistentag 1975* (Wiesbaden 1977), 221-9, promising yet further Coptic texts from the Chester Beatty library. H. Bacht edits with commentary the *Liber Orsiesi* in *Das Vermächtnis des Ursprungs* (Würzburg 1972). Pachomian scholarship has not welcomed A. Veilleux, *La liturgie dans le cénobitisme pachômien au quatrième siècle* (*Studia Anselmiana* 37 [1968]); Veilleux summarises his argument in *Bibliotheca Sanctorum* x (1968), 10-20, and meets rejection from A. de Vogüé, *RHE* 69 (1974), 425-63, and D.J. Chitty, *JTS* 21 (1970), 195-9. Cf. J. Vergote, 'La valeur des vies grecques et coptes de S. Pachôme; *Orientalia Lovaniensia periodica* 8 (1977), 175-86. Much of the recent bibliography is in Philip Rousseau, *Ascetics, Authority, and the Church in the Age of Jerome and Cassian* (Oxford 1978).

The wall had evident consequences for the development of the community.[5] It greatly facilitated the control of the monks within at the same time as it limited access to outsiders, such as members of their families and members of the opposite sex who might distract them from their high purposes. No doubt the wall also served to mark out the frontiers of the monastery in face of encroaching farmers. Above all the wall made a very visible, public statement not merely about the division from the pagan world outside but also about the compromises besetting the normal life of the churches lived out in a pagan world.

One cannot assume that life in the Thebaid in 320 A.D. was so untroubled by Blemmyes or other nomadic marauders that the wall was not intended to serve any defensive purpose. But the Pachomian texts give no hint of this. The likelihood is that Pachomios' wall was simply a self-evidently natural thing for him to build, familiar as he was, after his pagan upbringing, with the walled *temenos* characteristic of unnumbered Egyptian temples going back to Zoser's funerary complex at Saqqara early in the third millennium B.C. Within his wall Pachomios planned buildings to serve various purposes: houses for groups of monks (each with their distinctive marks), a chapel, a guest house near the gate for visitors, a bakery and cookhouse for preparing food, a depository for the library of codices, another store for clothing. It can hardly be accidental that this general type of organisation is exemplified by pagan complexes in the Nile valley, such as the marvellously preserved Ptolemaic temple at Edfu. So nothing could have seemed more obvious to Pachomios than that his community should be enclosed, and that the wall should be provided with gates and door-keepers to control ingress and egress. If not intended as a fortification wall against marauding tribesmen, the barrier was evidently of sufficient height to deter anyone from going in and out without due authority; and before many years had passed its merits as a defence against barbarian raiding parties seeking prisoners to sell in the slave-markets must have been evident.

The Pachomian Lives

In this paper I shall not discuss at length what everyone knows, namely the sharp controversies of modern scholarship concerning the complex sources for the history of the Pachomian foundations. The Greek, Coptic, and Arabic Lives have each in turn enjoyed zealous advocates of their primacy. After consideration and comparison of the various documents and of the writings of their respective advocates, I believe we ought to conclude that the Arabic tradition and its advocate Père Veilleux have the least claim to be held in awe, though there are assuredly places where the Arabic text includes good matter. As for the old battleground between the Greek and the Coptic, the subject of hard jousting between Derwas Chitty and L.T. Lefort, scholars to whom all students of the Pachomian texts owe a large debt, there is no very simple choice to be made. Both sets of texts draw on the same

5. H. Torp, 'Murs d'enceinte des monastères coptes primitifs et couvents-forteresses', *Mél Rom* 76, 1964), 173-200, has seen the disciplinary, juridical, and *temenos* significance of the wall.

pool of tradition, which was originally Coptic and oral, but I do not think it likely that the Greek *Vita Prima* drew on a prior written Coptic Life. It is composed from a very Greek and Alexandrian viewpoint. Of the Greek and Coptic Lives each preserves good tradition neglected in the other strand. Lefort was evidently right in urging that the Coptic merits deep attention. The Coptic biographers offer early strata in the transmission for which we look in vain in the Greek Lives.

The consensus of sensible men is that the Greek *Vita Prima* is a priceless witness from within the Pachomian monastic tradition, but naturally from its Greek speaking minority, perhaps from the Pachomian house at Canopus (Metanoia) mentioned by Jerome in the preface to his Latin version of the *Praecepta*. The *Vita Prima* may be dated with reasonable confidence in (or very soon after) 390-400 A.D. The name of Origen is a bogy (G^1 31). Moreover there is an emphatic statement (G^1 94) that the incomparable honour of the patriarchate of Alexandria, whose occupant the Pachomian monks see as Christ's representative, is not actually personal to Athanasius himself but, by virtue of office, belongs to his successors. This looks like a reflection of Theophilos' well known struggle to retain archiepiscopal authority in relation to the many monasteries within his jurisdiction, where offence had been caused by his initial indications of sympathy for Origen and Evagrios and of hostility towards 'anthropormophites' who wanted to picture God in human form in their prayers.

The *Vita Prima* is of course more than a Life of Pachomios (though that is the simple title of the manuscript tradition). It includes also the story of his first three or four successors. In particular it is at least as much interested in a biography of his devoted pupil and eventual (perhaps to the regret of the *Vita Prima*, not immediate) successor Theodore. Pachomios' death may be confidently assigned to 9 May 346 (G^1 114-16 and 120), that of Theodore to 27 April probably of either 368 or 371. Much of the dramatic force of the Life turns on the contrast between these two superiors of the order, and on the assertion of an ultimate harmony triumphing over a succession of painful episodes between them.

The author of the *Vita Prima* is acutely conscious that things are not now what they used to be; in his time there is moral and spiritual decline, and the readers need warnings of the perils of negligence (G^1 118). Some monks have an open ambition to be higumen or even to be promoted to the episcopate (G^1 126, 118). The old discipline requiring a stern renunciation of family ties has evidently undergone some relaxation (G^1 24, 67-8, 74, 80). The portrayals of the intense severity of Pachomios and of the self-extinguishing humility of Theodore are sermons addressed to a generation where discipline has fallen off, so that monks now actively seek posts of honour and leadership which, in the earlier period, they would have accepted only as an act of obedience to their superior.

There are also other indications of the post-Pachomian concerns of the biographical tradition. The author of the *Vita Prima* is anxious that Pachomios' *koinobion* (his name for the entire order of monasteries) be ranked on a par with the achievements of Anthony, so sweetly sung by Athanasius. This biography of

16

Pachomios is intended to do for the founder what the *Vita Antonii* had done for Anthony. Moreover, the Pachomian houses, it is stressed, had a warm place in Athanasius' heart. How widely known this love was is shown by the fact that the refugee archbishop was vainly sought in the monasteries by the dux Artemius (G[1] 137-8). In 346 Pachomian monks called upon Anthony who expressed warm approbation of the *koinobion* as a re-creation of the apostolic *koinōnia,* and added how much he himself would have liked to enter a *koinobion* had such a thing existed when he began to follow the ascetic life (G[1] 120). Again, Pachomios once says that 'the three most important things in Egypt are Athanasius, Anthony, and this *koinobion'* (G[1] 136). It is stressed that Pachomios and especially Theodore act constantly in reverence for and in harmony with the bishops (G[1] 27, 29-30, 135, 144), and indeed that when Athanasius came up the Nile on his visitation of the Thebaid Theodore (not at that time superior) laid on a noble reception for him from the monks (G[1] 144).

Twice the author of the *Vita Prima* seeks to explain why no contemporary of Pachomios wrote a Life at the time (G[1] 46 and 98), and is clearly aware of sceptics who will ask how authentic his portrait is, so that he must assure them of the valued traditions from the old fathers he has consulted. These two texts appear to assume that the earliest Greek biographer has no written material before him in either Coptic or Greek. On the other hand, the oral tradition has surely shaped the portrait in important directions; and in recent times the question has been increasingly put whether in the tensions between Pachomios and Theodore depicted in the *Vita Prima* and in the Coptic Lives there may have lain some fundamental conflicts of principle about the nature of the Pachomian ideal and its attachment to the Church. In particular does Theodore represent, in contrast with Pachomios, a tightening of the disciplinary rules (necessitated perhaps by the increasing size of the community), a stronger insistence on obedience within the *koinōnia* in antithesis to an older anchoritic freedom? And is there any possible link with a greater theological freedom in the earlier stage of development?

Pachomios' orthodoxy

The so-called gnostic library of Nag Hammadi was found in the mountain within sight of the Pachomian monastery nearby. John Barns thought that letters and receipts used as filling for the bindings of some of the codices are likely to have come from the Pachomian houses.[6] His suggestion has not yet been either vindicated or disproved, but in principle it has obviously inherent probability. Athanasius' Festal Letter announcing the date of Easter for 367 lists the books of the Bible canon, and forcibly forbids the reading of secret books. Perhaps the cache was made in consequence of this or some similar later 'crackdown' by authority. That

6. John Barns, 'Greek and Coptic papyri from the covers of the Nag Hammadi Codices', in *Essays on the Nag Hammadi Texts in honour of Pahor Labib,* ed. M. Krause [Nag Hammadi Studies vi] (Leiden 1975), 9-18. See the preface to the recent volume of the Nag Hammadi Codices in Facsimile (on the cartonnage) by J.M. Robinson (1979).

the codices were read in the nearby monastery is surely as good as certain. Several Nag-Hammadi texts are not so much gnostic (though many may be so labelled) as encratite: they are to justify celibacy, and hence the presence of a piece from Plato's Republic (588-9), and a Coptic version of the Sentences of Sextus. On the other hand, the libertine wing of gnosticism is virtually unrepresented (other than in ambiguous allusions such as logion 61 of the Coptic Gospel of Thomas, where the couch of Salome on which Jesus is said to have rested is more naturally located in her dining-room than in her bedroom).

It is not inherently probable that Pachomios was interested in the niceties of orthodox doctrine as a theological system. Except for the Origenists, early monks are seldom concerned with theological refinements which they regard as having intellectual pretensions conducive to pride and as generating dissensions. Pachomios' links to the ordinary life of the Church may have gradually grown as local bishops either came to assert jurisdiction over his houses or, as at Panopolis, saw how useful monks could be in a missionary situation and encouraged them to build a monastery as an assertion of a Christian presence in a predominantly pagan city (G^1 81). But initially such links will have been few and weak. It is worth asking whether the various early strands of tradition attest any tendencies to sympathise with doctrinal themes that could have aroused alarm in an orthodox bishop's breast. This is not a matter of naively setting out to 'discover' Pachomios to have been a heretical ascetic subsequently covered in orthodox plasterwork, but rather of asking to what extent it is reasonable to think the early Pachomian tradition largely indifferent where dogma is concerned, content to make use of a diversity of gifts so long as they all encourage renunciation of the world.

In the *Vita Prima* the resurrection of Christ is first affirmed as a historic redemptive fact; and nothing can be less gnostic than that. But when the theme is reinterpreted of the 'spiritual resurrection' which means that we should exercise patience and not revile others (G^1 57), such language is reminiscent of the dualistic heretic Hierakas, a Greek-speaking Copt of Leontopolis in the Delta about 300, whose influence provoked Epiphanios of Salamis in 375 to compose some pages of refutation (*Panarion* 67).

According to one Pachomian narrative (Letter of Ammon 12), when Pachomios desired to become a monk, he was first invited to join the schismatic Melitians and the heretical Marcionites; but a vision assured him that Christ stands with the bishop of Alexandria. The same source (26) speaks of an influential monk in one Pachomian monastery, named Patchelphios, who taught a young man to disbelieve in the resurrection of the flesh but was brought to conform to the teachings of the Church.

In the second Greek Life there is mention of demonic assaults on Pachomios' orthodoxy,[7] but without success since he hated Arians, Melitians, and Origen.[8]

7. G^2 17; Halkin, 183.
8. G^2 27 and 88; Halkin, 268.9-10.

On one occasion (*Paralipomena* xiv.33) heretics in hairshirts challenged Pachomios to walk on the water of the Nile, a charism attributed to several holy men, and once in the *Vita Prima* credited to Pachomios himself.[9] But Pachomios angrily rejected the suggestion as being both foreign to God and also thought ill of by secular persons; in other words as a well known trick of sorcery. (Lucian, *Philopseudes* 34, tells us that in the caverns of Memphis sorcerers professed to teach one how to do this trick.)

In all our texts Theodore appears as a pillar of orthodoxy explicitly attached to the authority of the episcopate. That there was tension between Pachomios and Theodore over the succession is certain (G^1 106). One can only speculate (and therefore go beyond the authority of the texts), but it seems inevitable to ask whether or not the tension between the two heroes originated in Theodore's wish to link the *koinōnia* more closely with the local churches and their clergy, whereas Pachomios represented the desire to keep the old independence and freedom of the initial colony of anchorites.

When the news came that Athanasius was coming south on his visitation of the Thebaid, Theodore was responsible for hastily rushing monks north to meet him before he reached Hermopolis (on the left bank opposite Antinoopolis). A hundred monks lined the banks of the great river, with Theodore holding the bridle of the ass on which Athanasius rode when he came to visit the Pachomian houses, honouring the primate with a torchlight procession and chanting. Theodore, we are told, won Athanasius' approval for the internal arrangements of the monasteries, the chapel, refectory, cells with the little stools on which the monks rested (it was not their way to lie down for sleep) − everything evoked the primate's praise. But Horsiesios, still in office as superior of the *koinonia,* did not appear, and Athanasius was persuaded to send him a letter by Theodore's hand (G^1 144).

The Pachomian Rule

According to one strand of the Coptic tradition, Pachomios' first attempt to establish a community of disciples under his personal direction was a failure. He gave a rule to the brothers gathering round him, namely to share all their earnings for a common purse to supply the group's material needs and for food. Pachomios acted as treasurer. But they would not accept his authority and insulted him, indulging in mockery and laughter. After five years he abandoned his efforts and dissolved the community. The dissident monks in vain complained to the bishop of Dendera, Saprion, who, after listening to them stating their complaints, decided that Pachomios was getting it right (VC 68-9).

The Greek *Vita Prima* suppresses or ignores this false start in which the founder is insulted, and reports that the scheme for founding the *koinōnia* was formed in response to an angelic message calling Pachomios to a life of service to the human race, evidently in contrast to his personal and private interest. Then follows an

9. G^1 21; Halkin, 13.21.

account of Pachomios' Rule for the community laying down that dress, food, and sleeping arrangements are all to be uniformly observed by every monk without distinction. All recruits are to be admitted after a test of some kind; then they are clothed in the habit, required to make formal renunciation of the world and of any contact with their kinsfolk. They are set to learn parts of the Bible, especially the psalter and the gospels. If illiterate, they are to be taught letters.

The mature Rule translated from Greek into Latin by Jerome at the end of the century shows how many permanent monastic customs originate in the Pachomian houses: the weekly roster of duty in church, refectory and kitchen (*Praecepta* 13); the weekly catechism; the reckoning of seniority from the date of profession, not by age or dignity (31). Monks should act with consideration for their brothers, not entering another's cell without express leave (112), never physically touching another (95).

Neither Greek nor Coptic tradition knows of expulsions for homosexual practices (the Coptic has dark allusions that might be so construed but do not require this interpretation).[10] On the other hand the Rule forbids joking or playing games with young boys in the monastery.[11]

Pachomios' initial rule was not to admit any clergy to his *koinōnia*, on the ground that ambition for office produces envy, strife, and faction (G^1 27). The community in each monastery attended the liturgy on Saturdays and Sundays; on Saturdays at the nearest village church, on Sundays in the monastery itself, the local presbyter being invited to come and celebrate. Attendance at the synaxis is compulsory (G^1 74; *Praecepta* 22). The communities meet for prayers in the evening and at dawn. The monks have a duty of service to one another and to the weak, the old, the sick, the young (G^1 28; cf. 24). Their employment is to weave baskets and spin ropes for sale, and to cultivate vegetables on adjacent land belonging to the monastery.

Expansion of the koinōnia

Pachomios' community rapidly grew in numbers, and this came to require the division of each monastery into constituent houses, each ruled by a housemaster and his assistant or second. Soon other monasteries beside the upper Nile were impressed and asked to be incorporated into the *koinōnia.* Although a number of bishop of the pagan stronghold Panopolis (Akhmîm) actually invited the Pachomian synod of Latopolis c.344 (below), he was vindicated; and as we have seen, the bishop of the pagan stronghold Panopolis (Akhmîm) actually invited the Pachomian monks to come to his diocese to found a house At first local opposition dismantled by night whatever walls were erected by day, but eventually, with miraculous aid and angelic fire, the monks succeeded in constructing their enclosure wall as a fortress of Christian protest in a militantly pagan environment (G^1 81).

10. VC 156 f,185, 397.
11. *Praecepta* 166; Boon, 66.10-15.

By the year 345 the federation of the *koinōnia* numbered no less than nine houses. The great monastery at Pbau had 600 monks in 352 (Letter of Ammon 2), twenty of them being Greek-speaking (ibid. 7). The figures given by the fifth century writers seem to be rounded up to an impressive size without any reliable precision, and one can conclude only that the total numbers continued to grow in the second half of the fourth century. Jerome's figure of 50,000 seems a wild exaggeration, Sozomen's 500 a grave underestimate. John Cassian speaks of 5,000. Palladios offers both 3,000 and 7,000.[12]

Pachomios' successors

A crisis of leadership occurred on Pachomios' death. The support for Theodore had been set aside by Pachomios himself, who designated Petronios to succeed him (G^1 114). But plague was removing many of the brothers by death, and Petronios was soon among them. Before death he nominated Horsiesios as superior, despite Horsiesios' protests that it was beyond his powers. This proved to be the case. The monasteries were so growing in numbers that they could put more land under cultivation with their large labour force. Already in Pachomios' time it was the rule for the superior to summon the heads of all his monasteries twice a year, at the August meeting going carefully through the accounts (G^1 83). They acquired numerous boats for transporting their produce (G^1 146), in contrast to the early days when the entire *koinōnia* possessed only two boats (G^1 113). Apollonios the abbot of Monchosis (Temouschous) was among those who had associated his house with the Pachomian *koinōnia*. Apollonios wanted the agricultural industry of the monks to increase still further, probably by the taking on of additional labour from lay persons, perhaps even women, outside the monastery. At the parent house of Pbau, Horsiesios agreed with Apollonios' expansionist economic policy. But Theodore saw in it a serious threat to Pachomios' overriding religious purpose. A dramatic crisis ensued in which Horsiesios suddenly retired by night to Chenoboskeia, and Theodore succeeded him as superior. For a time Apollonios wholly withdrew his monastery from association with the *koinōnia* but was eventually won back by Theodore's diplomacy with some compromise formula of which we are not given the text. Even Horsiesios who had moved outside Theodore's jurisdiction to join Apollonios at Monchosis was eventually charmed by Theodore to move back to Pbau, a transfer that Theodore stage-managed with an evident sense of high dramatic style (G^1 145). But the disagreements certainly went deep. Both the Greek and the Coptic traditions seek to gloss over them, and only the Arabic Life frankly explains the essence of the matter.

Theodore, in a word, feared the secularisation of Pachomios' ideal. It is no doubt true that the Pachomian monasteries were solving a social and economic problem for many peasants in the Nile valley, put out of work by the inflation of the second

12. Jerome's preface, Boon, 8; Cassian, Inst.iv.1; Sozom.iii.14; Palladius, HL VI.6.xxxii. Cf. G.M. Colombás, *El monacato primitivo* i (Madrid 1974), 97, whose pages on Pachomios are particularly well done.

half of the third century so well attested in the papyri. Both Tabennisi and Pbau are described as deserted villages.[13] A peasant was more secure economically inside the monastery than outside.[14] Inside his life would be simple and frugal. The food would not be rich, but sufficient for life without any temptation to excess (G^1 53, 55). Wine and meat would be very infrequent unless one were to fall sick. Except for the two nunneries (134), there was virtually no contact with women, which spared the monks emotional stress, and no doubt contributed something to the common achievement of great longevity among the old men. The dilapidations of old age were cared for by the young recruits. All this is enough to explain why the monasteries attracted large numbers. But the magnetic attraction seems to have been Pachomios himself and his unconditional obedience to his own uncompromising ideals.

The call to obedience

The Greek *Vita Prima* once contrasts Theodore's gentleness and charm with the 'mournful and fierce austerity' of Pachomios (G^1 91) who never allowed himself to forget the souls in torment and felt himself responsible for seeing that his monks did not join them. It is easy to think of Pachomios as resembling the Pantokrator at Daphni. He inspired fear in his flock — in contrast to Samuel, who combined abstemiousness with characteristic cheerfulness of character (G^1 81). The founding father of the *koinōnia* expected his monks to give him that unconditional obedience that a disciple wished to give an anchorite in the desert.

Pachomios' discipline is hostile to all excessive mortifications (G^1 69) and especially to ostentatious proposals such as ordeal by fire (G^1 8). The monk who proposed to him this test of faith ended, by a terrible irony, in throwing himself on the hot coals of the furnace of the bathhouse at Panopolis. Perhaps he was trying his luck at fire-walking once too often rather than committing suicide. (G^1 96 mentions suicides among the Pachomian ascetics.) Excess, however, is a relative term. Laughter and gossip in the bakery (cf. *Praecepta* 116) or working during an hour appointed for meditation brought unpleasant consequences.[15] An ex-actor Silvanos began his novitiate by strenuous mortifications. But he then relaxed his rigour until one day his conversation suddenly reverted to entertaining his brother monks with the old indecent jokes of the stage.[16] Before all the brothers Pachomios demanded that he remove his habit, resume his lay clothing, and submit to expulsion. 'Forgive me, just this once more', pleaded Silvanos. 'But how much have I tolerated and rebuked already, how many beatings have you received and ignored?' (a reply which is important evidence for monastery discipline).[17] But

13. G^1 12; Halkin, 8.1 and $G^1$54; Halkin 36.4.
14 *Liber Orsiesi* 47; Boon, 140.5 ff.
15. G^1 89 of Tabennisi; cf. 121 of Pachoum near Latopolis=Esna.
16. Cf. *Praecepta et Inst.* 10 (Boon 56.5): *'qui [. . .] plus ioco quam honestum est deditus'.*
17. Cf. *Praecepta* 163; Boon, 65.6.

then senior monks took the evidently high risk of speaking on behalf of the delinquent Silvanos, an act of intercession which, as the *Liber Orsiesi* shows, could easily land one in as much trouble as the delinquent himself, making one a partaker of his sins.[18] Pachomios relented, Silvanos stayed. His weeping was so uncontrollable as to make him distressing company in the refectory. After eight years of the severest penitential life he died, and Pachomios assured the community that he had heard flights of angels singing him to his rest.[19] A delinquent monk ran the risk of being refused a cortège singing psalms at his funeral as his body was borne up to the mountain caves three miles away.[20] The Rule lays down a strict control over the psalm-singing at a funeral (*Praecepta* 127).

Pachomios is a seer who is granted visions, not (he says) of his own will but when the Lord so grants (G^1 112). And some of his visions of things to come predict fearful decline after his departing, penetration of the monasteries by heresies, and lax discipline (G^1 71).[21] At the synod of Latopolis c.344 serious charges were brought against Pachomios' claim that he could see the demons (G^1 112). Happily the synod included two bishops who had at one time been Pachomian monks and who helped to defend him. Like other holy men, he can discern the hearts, and can detect innocence and guilt (G^1 42-3, 122). A bishop sends a man accused of theft to Pachomios for judgement (G^1 76; cf. 92). His diacritic power also enables him to diagnose illness (52). He possesses clairvoyant powers of knowing things happening at a distance (89). He has a criterion for distinguishing divine from demonic spirits, namely that in divinely given visions the recipient's personal thoughts wholly disappear together with any selfconsciousness of receiving the vision, whereas in demonic visions the recipient knows he is seeing it and can still retain the power to think and deliberate naturally (87). It is a criterion that has a strongly Montanist ring about it. The old orthodox complaint against Montanist prophecy protested that orthodox prophets always retain their natural rationality when delivering their prophecy, even if that may be suspended while they are receiving its revelation.

A fundamental requirement in the Pachomian *koinōnia* is obedience to the superior. Provided that the superior himself is the first to keep the rules, this principle holds the society together. The coherence of the congregation therefore depends intimately upon one man. The superior is responsible for his monks as shepherd of their souls, as their intercessor when they fall sick (G^1 132-3). Pachomios has to teach Theodore obedience by the hard way. He is arbitrary, unreasonable, jealous of his personal autocracy, at the borderline of cruelty, until Theodore has learnt that Pachomios will never share his authority with anyone else (G^1 50; cf. 126). At the same time the Lives record anecdotes of Pachomios'

18. *Liber Orsiesi* 24; Boon, 125.14-16.
19. *Paralipomena* 2-4; cf. G^1 104-5. The power to hear the angelic choir receiving a departing soul is possessed also by Theodore (G^1 93).
20. G^1 103; cf. *Paralipomena* 5-6.
21. Cf. G^1 146 on Theodore.

humility and self-effacement. I do not think much will survive of recent suggestions that in the cenobitic tradition the begetter of paternal autocracy is Theodore, and that the authentic Pachomios had much more democratic and fraternal conceptions of his role than his successors found practicable.

Pachomios communicated with the heads of his monasteries with the help of a strange alphabetical cipher whose code remains unbroken. Even though a major recent discovery by Fr Quecke has unearthed the Coptic and Greek originals of several letters hitherto known only in Jerome's Latin, it remains the case that no cryptographer has yet been able to penetrate their arcane method of communication. I venture to suggest that the cipher will never be broken because its intention is not actually to communicate in the ordinary sense of that word; it has the purpose of being obscure, and therefore of surrounding its author with an aura of mystery and authority.

The Pachomian heritage

In this paper I have tried to sketch out an outline of Pachomios' achievement. The ideal of sanctity is a noble end; the means by which it is to be realised are beset by thorns and brambles on the pathway. Pachomios realises some important Christian aims: identification with the poor, restraint of lust for power and clerical domination, creating a *koinōnia* of the Spirit bound together by the common prayers and meals and labour and by a personal obedience to the superior which is seen as a way of following the Lord himself. Simultaneously Pachomios does more than any other single person to create rules and wise customs necessary for the good order of a religious community, a remarkable number of which remain in use even now. Nevertheless, there is another side to the coin. The enclosure wall that symbolises the separateness of the community from the world also accentuates the secularisation of the created order.

To busy university teachers beset by committees and administration the monastic ideal of withdrawal and reflection can provoke to envy. And even university teachers can easily operate with a mental wall separating their college or their campus from the outside world, in some cases with a physical barrier as well. The enclosure wall fulfils several roles, some beneficial, others not so. When Pachomios created the enclosed religious community, something was lost at the same time as something was gained.

Hellenistic and Oriental Origins

HAN J.W. DRIJVERS

'THE holy men who minted the ideal of the saint in society came from Syria', so we are told by Peter Brown in his well-known article on 'The Rise and Function of the Holy Man in Late Antiquity'.[1] Brown traces the rise of the holy man back into the villages of the Syrian countryside which, especially during the fourth and fifth century, were passing through a crisis of leadership and were in need of a good patron. The holy man living on the edge of the desert and the *oikoumene* took on the role of mediator in village life and as a stranger exercised his power in the complicated network of Syrian rural society. Although his role is applicable to urban conditions, the specific characteristics of the Syrian villages surrounded by desert provide a sufficient explanation for the rise and function of the holy man who, in complete social disengagement, coming as a stranger from the desert, was able to solve the problems of life and thought of simple folk. Brown's emphasis on the Syrian countryside as the primary stage of the holy man relieved him from a closer examination of the cultural background of the saints: a sociological approach replaces a wider cultural one which also inquires after the cultural sources for the lifestyle of the holy men and asks what is specifically Syrian in it.

Does Syria have a specific cultural identity which distinguishes it from other regions in the Roman Empire? Syria as well as Mesopotamia is a thoroughly bilingual country; large groups of the population could speak and understand Greek besides their native tongue and many Lives of saints and other works were translated from Syriac into Greek or vice versa. That is why we speak of the *tréfonds oriental* of Byzantine hagiography.[2]

But is a linguistic frontier equal to a cultural frontier in the hellenized Orient? To consider the Syriac-speaking villages as untouched by Hellenistic civilization seems too simple, however attractive the idea of a barbarian saint might be. Furthermore it is misleading to consider Northern Mesopotamia as an area that was

1. P.R.L. Brown, 'The Rise and Function of the Holy Man in Late Antiquity', *JRS* 61 (1971), 80-101, esp. 82. Cf. id., *The World of Late Antiquity from Marcus Aurelius to Muhammad* (London 1971), 101: 'In villages dedicated for millennia to holding their own against nature, the holy man had deliberately chosen "anti-culture" – the neighbouring desert, the nearest mountain crags. In a civilisation identified exclusively with town life, the monks had committed the absurd – they had "made a city in the desert".'
2. See P. Peeters, *Le tréfonds oriental de l'hagiographie byzantine* (SubsHag 26 [1950]), 165.

free from contacts with the West and therefore characterized by a strong and un-broken Semitic tradition which made itself manifest in Edessene Christianity as distinct from its Antiochene hellenized counterpart in Coele-Syria. There is some-thing like Greek in Syriac disguise and a local cultural tradition in Greek dress, so that the division of languages in Syria and Mesopotamia is not identical with different cultural tradition.[3] The hellenistic and the oriental do not exclude each other and, therefore, remain to be defined. Yet it seems to be true that Syria developed a special type of saint with a lifestyle of his own, who made his appearance in towns and villages in Syria and Mesopotamia and there represented divine power.[4] In a sense his rise and function is independent of local geography which only provides a scene, but does not dictate the role. That is explicitly stated by Theodoret in a touching remark at the end of the Life of Maisymas (14): Those who practise ascesis are not hindered by a stay in towns or villages, because they prove that it is also possible to attain the summit of virtue surrounded by crowds.[5]

It is, therefore, appropriate to analyse some Lives of Eastern saints more closely, not only to analyse these images as products of the society around the holy man, but also to have a closer look at the inherent ideology of the Lives. The holy man represents the needs of the society and a religious ideology in a characteristic life-style. His life is symbolical, his actions, cures and deeds of power refer to a religious myth and make plain how religious behaviour has sociological and ideological components.[6]

The holy man of Edessa

A typical example of a Syriac life of a saint is the legend of the Man of God from Rome, who lived his holy life at Edessa.[7] It dates from the second half of the fifth century and tells the story of an anonymous nobleman from Rome, the only child of rich parents, who was born through prayers and the special grace of God, a prerogative that he shares with Isaac, Samuel, John the Baptist and other biblical prototypes of holy men. In humility he devoted himself to gain 'great science'

3. See Fergus Millar, 'Paul of Samosata, Zenobia and Aurelian: The Church, local culture and political allegiance in third-century Syria', *JRS* 61 (1971), 1-17, esp. 2ff; id., *JJS* 29 (1978), 3ff; H. Drijvers, *Aufstieg und Niedergang der römischen Welt* viii (1977), 885ff. A Vööbus, *History of Asceticism in the Syrian Orient,* (CSCO Sub 14 and 17 [1958], i.140 is of a different opinion: in his view, Mesopotamia 'had remained almost untouched by Hellenism and contacts with the West'. Cf. R. Schmidt, 'Die Sprachen im römischen Reich der Kaiserzeit', *BJb* 40 (1980), 196ff.
4. A. Vööbus, op.cit.; S.P. Brock, 'Early Syrian Asceticism', *Numen* 20 (1973), 1-19; P. Canivet, 'Le monachisme syrien selon Théodoret de Cyr', *ThH* 42 (1977), 255; A.J. Festugière, *Les moines d'Orient* (Paris 1961-5), i (= *Culture ou sainteté).*
5. Theodoret, *H.Ph.* xiv; cf. Canivet, op.cit., 248 and 263 on Maisymas.
6. See J.A. Delaunay, 'Rite et symbolique en ACTA THOMAE vers. syr. I.2a et ss', *Mémorial Jean de Menasce,* ed. P. Gignoux (Tehran 1974), 11-24.
7. A. Amiaud, 'La légende syriaque de Saint Alexis l'homme de Dieu', BEHEt 79 (1889); cf. A. Baumstark, *Geschichte der syrischen Literatur* (Bonn 1922), 96; and C.E. Stebbins, 'Les origines de la légende de Saint Alexis', *Revue Belge de Philologie et d'Histoire* 51 (1973), 497-507.

(*yd't' sgy't'*) and despised all earthly things. His parents arranged a bride for him and a wedding-feast to which the whole city was invited. But on the first day of this feast the holy man escaped his bride and his city, found a ship and sailed to Seleucia in Syria, whence he arrived at Edessa. There he used to stay in the church, fasting in the daytime and living off alms, since he gave away his riches (as well as all he got and did not need) to the poor. The night, when all were asleep, he spent praying with extended arms, that is in the form of the cross – exactly the same gesture as Symeon the Stylite took up on his column. One night the *paramonarius* saw him like that and asked him where he was from. At last after long persuasion he told him the truth. When the holy man fell ill the *paramonarius* brought him to hospital. But he was absent when he died and was buried at the special cemetery for strangers. When the *paramonarius* heard what had happened he ran to the bishop Rabbula and told him how holy a man had stayed in his city and died there. Thereupon the bishop and the *paramonarius* went to the cemetery and ordered the grave to be opened. But the holy body had disappeared and only his rags were left. Since that day Rabbula devoted himself to take care of strangers, poor people, widows and orphans and even stopped his building activities to give all his attention to these pious deeds.

The holy man as alter Christus

This tale dealing with an anonymous stranger formed the starting point for the well-known legend of St Alexis via a more elaborated version that became known in Byzantium. Leaving aside all complicated questions that are connected with the further development of this legend it can be stated that the primitive form represents some typical traits of a Syrian life of a saint. Although there are some minor deviations, the lifestyle of the Man of God is an *imago Christi.* His youth is like Jesus' youth during which he 'increased in wisdom and stature and in favour with God and man' (Luke 2:52). Like Jesus he left his glory behind at the same time as he left his bride and became a *monogenēs* or *monachos,* in Syriac an *yhydy',* living in humility (cf. Phil. 2).[8] In Edessa he lived among the poor as a completely anonymous stranger from abroad, representing Christ on earth. His nightly prayer amidst the sleeping people in the church court is a symbolic imitation of Jesus' prayer in Gethsemane, when all his disciples fell asleep, and actually an *imitatio passionis Christi.* The *paramonarius* is a kind of counterpart of Peter; this becomes completely clear after the saint's death when the *paramonarius* and bishop Rabbula went to the tomb as once Peter and John did according to the Gospel of

8. On the *yhydy'* see A. Adam, 'Grundbegriffe des Mönchtums in sprachlicher Sicht', *Zeitschrift für Kirchengeschichte* 4te Folge iii.65 (1953-4), 209ff; and E. Beck, 'Zur Terminologie des ältesten syrischen Mönchtums', *Studia Anselmiana* 38 (1956), 254-67. A. Adam criticises the views of Beck and Vööbus in *Gottingische geiehrte Anzeiger* 213 (1960), 127-45 and in *Askese und Mönchtum in der Alten Kirche,* ed. K. Suso Frank (Darmstadt 1975), 230-54, esp. 244ff. See also G. Nedungatt, 'The Convenanters of the Early Syriac-Speaking Church', *OCP* 39 (1973), 205ff.

John 20:3ff. It is not without reason that Rabbula's care of poor people and strangers is explicitly emphasized as a consequence of the saint's life and death.

In this legend the Syrian holy man has nothing in common with the good patronus, but is rather an *alter Christus* with a strong integrating function in the urban society he inhabits. Cities in Syria and Mesopotamia, especially during the fourth and fifth century, were crowded with poor and starving people and the suffering of homeless strangers was terrible in the severity of winter.[9] The holy man broke through all social boundaries and classes and represented help and justice in the merciless social structure of an ancient city, in which a stranger especially was a social outcast. In fact he did not have a position *vis-à-vis* the community, mediating between that community and the outside world, but rather worked within the population and fully belonged to it. The great emphasis laid on Rabbula's work of relief for the poor and sick is a natural consequence of the saint's actions. Rabbula indeed established permanent hospices for men and women and infirmaries for diseased and in particular for lepers.[10] The pious Euphemia did the same at Amida in the sixth century.[11] The life of the holy man of God at Edessa, therefore, does not only afford a description of his life and death, but also makes an appeal on the hearer and reader, and functions as a source of social change. It seems to me a necessary task of historical research to analyse the *Wirkungsgeschichte* of the Lives of the holy men and their influence on the society. These Lives represent not only products of the society around the holy man, but in turn exercise a certain influence on that society. They offer an ideal life that asks for imitation in exactly the same way as Christ's life is symbolically represented by the holy man in his stylized and ritualised behaviour. The empty grave of the holy man at Edessa, therefore, is not a miraculous addition to the legend meant to link it to the story of his second life after his return in his father's house in Byzantium, the New Rome, but an essential part of the original legend that highlights the role of the holy man as an *alter Christus*.[12]

Jacob of Nisibis

The second life I would draw to your attention is the *vita* of Jacob of Nisibis, with which Theodoret opens the *Historia Religiosa*.[13] This *vita* is also preserved in a

9. See J.B. Segal 'Mesopotamian Communities from Julian to the Rise of Islam', *Proceedings of the British Academy* 41 (1955), 116ff and id., *Edessa 'the blessed City'* (Oxford 1970), 147ff.
10. G.G. Blum, 'Rabbula von Edessa. Der Christ, der Bischof, der Theologe', CSCO Sub 34 (1969), 70ff.
11. John of Ephesus, 'Lives of the Eastern Saints' 12 (PO 17.1.166ff).
12. Amiaud, op.cit. (n.7 above), xlvii suggests that the empty grave was 'indispensible pour faire une histoire populaire de la vie de l'humble ascète inconnu qui fut plus tard Saint Alexis'. Cf. Stebbins, op.cit. (n.7 above), 499ff.
13. Theodoret de Cyr, *Histoire des moines de Syrie*, ed. P. Canivet and A. Leroy-Molinghen (SC 234 [1977]), i.160. Cf. P. Peeters, 'La légende de S. Jacques de Nisibe', *AnalBoll* 38 (1920), 285-373; P. Bedjan, *Acta Martyrum et Sanctorum* (Paris 1890ff), 4.262-3 (Jacob

Syriac version like that of Julian Saba, the second life that Theodoret describes. Jacob was born in Nisibis in the latter part of the third century and as a young man he chose the ascetic life in the desert. He lived in the open air on fruits and herbs, did not use fire and maltreated his body. His soul, however, received spiritual food and the holy man acquired the image of God's glory. Hence he had foreknowledge of the future and could work miracles. Theodoret tells us some of these, such as the punishment of some bold girls at a spring and of an unjust judge. Theodoret expli- citly refers to Moses and to Jesus' gentleness in telling these miracles which actually are a kind of *sēmeia*. The holy man Jacob became so well-known and famous that he was called to the bishop's see of Nisibis. Reluctantly he went there, but did not change his food or his clothes: only the place, but not his way of life, as Theodoret puts it. At Nisibis he took care of the poor and diseased, the widows and orphans; he punished the wicked and practised justice. He even raised a dead beggar, imitat- ing in everything the Lord's grace. He seems to have attended the Council of Nicaea, but his work at Nisibis culminated in his brave behaviour during a siege by Sapor. The story in the *Historia Religiosa* gives the strong impression that Jacob organised the population during that siege not only through prayer but also through hard work in the rebuilding of walls that were broken by the force of the artificially dammed waters of the local river. Like Moses, Jacob prayed to God, who sent dark- ness and fleas to disconcert the enemy. He even appeared on the walls of Nisibis dressed in purple and with the royal diadem to confuse Sapor, who had attacked Nisibis because he believed the king was not there. The enemy withdrew; and as long as Jacob lived Nisibis was not taken by the barbarians. It is not surprising that the tomb of this *promachos* became the real centre of the city, or that the people of Nisibis took his body with them when they left their city on its being ceded by Jovian to the Persians (363).[14]

Although this Life and its striking details are for the greater part legendary — Jacob of Nisibis died in 337-8 and the *vita* refers to a siege of Nisibis by Sapor in 350 — it gives quite an exact picture of what was expected of the saint.[15] His *vita* actually depicts his ideal role, which is partly the same that is played by Ephrem in Nisibis according to his legendary Syriac *vita*. The best explanation of these elements in the Syriac *vita* of Ephrem as well as in Theodoret's story of Jacob of Nisibis is that the third siege of Nisibis by Sapor (as described by a letter of bishop Vologeses of Nisibis preserved in the *Chronicon Paschale*, by the *Orationes* of Julian and possibly other texts) gave rise to these legendary *vitae* in which the dominant role

of Nisibis); ibid., 6.380-4 (Julian Saba); Ephrem Syrus, *Carmina Nisibena* ed. E. Beck (CSCO, S 92-3 [1961]), Hymns xiii-xvi; also Canivet, op.cit (n.4 above), 104.

14. See G.W. Bowersock, *Julian the Apostate* (Cambridge Mass. 1978), 118; R. Turcan, 'L'abandon de Nisibe et l'opinion publique', *Mélanges d'archéologie et d'histoire offerts à André Piganiol*, ed. R. Chevallier (Paris 1966), 875-90.

15. See Canivet, op.cit. (n.4 above), 107-8, and P. Peeters, op.cit. (n.13 above), 289, 296-312.

of the holy men was strongly emphasised.[16] That role is pre-eminently an urban one: the holy man organizes the resistance against the enemy with all means available and therefore functions as the social centre of the city even after his death. This function is even corroborated by his other social activities on behalf of the poor and diseased. That holds true for Jacob of Nisibis, for Ephrem Syrus, for the Man of God at Edessa and for many other saints whose lives are described by Theodoret or are to be found in the various Syriac sources, such as Aphraates at Edessa and Antioch (*Historia Religiosa* 8), Theodosios at Antioch, Abraham at Harran *et al.*[17]

The role of ascesis

If we have found strong indications that the role of the holy man is independent of the place where he manifests his power, so that, next to his appearance in the Syrian villages, his protecting and integrating function in the urban centres should be stressed, the question arises what forces contributed to his rise and characteristic lifestyle. Two elements are of special importance: the social disengagement of the holy man, which expresses itself in his favoured stay in the desert and other barren places, and his ascesis (often called the mortification of his body) through a remarkable diet and demanding bodily exercises. Both elements are interwoven: the desert is the place of solitude par excellence, where human existence reaches its lowest level, or in the view of the ascetic himself the summit of virtue and wisdom. 'Where did all this madness come from?', exclaims E.R. Dodds, and for lack of a satisfying answer to this desperate and intriguing question he states that contempt for the human condition and hatred of the body was a disease endemic in the entire culture of the period, of which some Christian and Gnostic manifestations are the most extreme, but which also show themselves in pagans of purely Hellenic education.[18] A. Vööbus, therefore, attributes the ascetic practice of the Syrian holy men to the strong influence of the Manichees and their anti-cosmic and anti-bodily dualism.[19] Vööbus is partly followed by P. Canivet, when he states: 'le mal réside dans la matière' and considers this to be an all-explaining ground for the ascetic practice of

16. See B. Outtier, 'Saint Ephrem d'après ses biographies et ses oeuvres' *Parole de l'orient* iv (1973), 22; Julian, *Or.* i and ii, ed. F.C. Hertlein, 22-4, 33-9, 79-80; *Chronicon Paschale, PG* 92. 724B.14-728A.8; also Canivet, op.cit. (n.4 above), 104-8.

17. Julian Saba played an important role at Antioch (Theodoret, *H.Ph.* 2). For Theodosius (*H.Ph.* 10) see Canivet, op.cit. (n.4 above), 182-5. Abraham, bishop of Harran (*H.Ph.* 17) took care of widows and strangers and played a stabilising role in social tensions. See also J.H.W.G. Liebeschuetz, *Antioch. City and Imperial Administration in the Later Roman Empire* (Oxford 1972), 234ff on the urban function of the Syrian saints and hermits.

18. E.R. Dodds, *Pagan and Christian in an Age of Anxiety. Some Aspects of religious experience from Marcus Aurelius to Constantine* (Cambridge 1965), 34.

19. Vööbus, *History of Asceticism* i.158ff. For a severe criticism of Vööbus see the works cited in n.8 above. See also A. Guillaumont. 'Perspectives actuelles sur les origines du monachisme' in *The Frontiers of Human Knowledge. Lectures held at the Quincentenary Celebrations of Uppsala University 1977*, ed. T.T. Segerstedt (Uppsala 1978), 111-23.

the Syrian saints and their mortification of the body.[20] But is the Christian ascetic practice an expression of contempt for the human condition and hatred of the body as such?

It should be emphasised that the social role of the holy men is in flagrant contradiction of such an explanation. The Manichaean *electi* are a religious elite which never interferes with the troubles of the body social, but always lives at a safe distance from the cares and worries of daily life. We never hear about their social activities or care of the poor.[21] Contrary to Christianity, Manichaeism never became a social movement: its doctrinal ideology leads away from the trivial and material aspects of human life. The Christian holy men are always ready to participate in the daily life of common people and the social elite in order to protect and integrate that life. They may cherish the ideal of virginity, but when necessary they repair a marriage and they pray for barren women. That does not agree with a general atmosphere of hatred of the body and contempt for the human condition.

It is noteworthy that often when the ascetic practice of the holy man is discussed (as by Theodoret), such discussion involves mention of his special wisdom and eventually his *apatheia*. The *vita* of Julian Saba as told by Theodoret is a good example of such a pattern.[22] These elements find their unity in the *imago Christi* which is represented by the saint in his lifestyle.[23] Actually that lifestyle is an exact replica of the essential elements in early Syrian Christology. To phrase it in a theological way: anthropology is part of christology. It might be useful therefore to sketch the main lines of early Syrian thinking on Christ before returning to our problem.

Early Syrian christology

The literary heritage of the early Syriac-speaking Church (which is essentially part of Antiochene theological traditions) comprises some apocryphal Acts of the Apostles, of which the Syriac Acts of Thomas are the most important, the Syriac Odes of Solomon (dating from the second part of the third century) and the remnants

20. Theodoret de Cyr, op.cit. (n.13 above), i.45.
21. See G. Widengren, *Mani und der Manichäismus* (Stuttgart 1961), 97ff; O. Klima, *Manis Zeit und Leben* (Prague 1962), 84 ff; K. Rudolph, *Die Gnosis. Wesen und Geschichte einer spätantiken Religion* (Leipzig 1977), 362ff.
22. Theodoret, *H.R.* ii.3. Cf. ibid., Prologue 2-3; on Theodoret's use of *apatheia*, ibid. 148 n.6. See also Canivet, op.cit. (n.4 above), 273; P. Harb, 'Les origines de la doctrine de 'la-hašūšūtā (Apatheia) chez Philoxène de Mabbug', *Parole de l'orient* 5 (1974), 227-41. The article 'Apatheia' by G. Bardy in *Dictionnaire de spiritualité* i.727-46 remains fundamental. Since asceticism in Syria was not merely a rural movement but also had strong roots in the towns and cities, philosophical influences on its very beginnings cannot be denied *a priori*.
23. Canivet, op.cit. (n.4 above), 275-9. In the Syriac *Acts of Thomas,* the apostle is depicted as Christ's earthly 'double', and each is repeatedly identified completely with the other. Cf. H. Drijvers, 'Spätantike Parallelen zur altchristlichen Helligenverehrung unter besonderer Berücksichtigung des syrischen Stylitenkultus, *Erkentnisse und Meinungen* ii, ed. G. Weissner [*Göttinger* Orientforschungen/Reihe: Syriaca 17], 77-113. The stylites in particular represent Christ and his passion in their ritualised lifestyle.

of Tatian's *Diatessaron.*[24] In all that literature Christ is considered God's eternal thought and will, incarnate in a human body in order that man might return to the original state in which he was created according to God's thought and will. Christ manifests the divine will by his obedience unto death, which means by dominating human passions and strivings, revealing in this way God's eternal thought concerning the salvation of mankind.[25] The lifestyle of the holy man is an imitation of Christ's passion, a training of his will in dominating his passions and human strivings; so he shows a certain Christ-conformity. Virginity is not the ideal of the holy man because he is filled with a deep hatred of the human body, but because Christ was an *ihidaya,* in fact the *ihidaya* or *monogenēs.*[26] The doctrine of the free will of man which can control all his passions and guide his body is therefore an essential part of all forms of theology in the Syrian area, however different these may be. The best illustration of this are the Acts of Thomas, with which the *vita* of the Man of God at Edessa has some striking literary and ideological parallels. In the hard exercise of his will the holy man gains insight into God's saving thought – asceticism and the acquirement of wisdom are two sides of the same *imitatio Christi* – and he displays this insight in his acts of power, which always aim at the salvation of men. The desert is the place of trial and hence preeminently the place for exercising the will; at the same time the desert is between servitude and slavery and the promised land. That is why the holy man is also depicted as a *Moyses redivivus,* just as Christ was an *alter Moyses.*[27]

From philosophia to apatheia

The combination of self-discipline by exercising the human will and the acquisition of wisdom is part of the hellenistic philosophical tradition. Hence Theodoret can describe the ascetic life as a *philosophia aiming at apatheia.* That does not mean that Christian asceticism in its Syrian manifestation is due to the influence of Greek philosophical tradition, as Reitzenstein and Leipoldt believed.[28] There is a

24. In general see R. Murray, *Symbols of Church and Kingdom. A Study in Early Syriac Tradition* (Cambridge 1975), 24ff. On the date of the Odes of Solomon see H. Drijvers, 'Kerygma und Logos in den Oden Salomons dargestellt am Beispiel der 23. Ode', *Kerygma und Logos. Festschrift Carl Andresen,* ed. A.M. Ritter (Göttingen 1979), 153-72, esp. 171; and id., 'The 19th Ode of Solomon: its Interpretation and Place in Syrian Christianity', *JThS* (1980), 337-55. On Tatian see M. Elze, *Tatian und seine Theologie* (Göttingen 1960). A fresh enquiry into Tatian's encratism and its influence on early Syrian asceticism seems to be required.

25. See Drijvers, 'Kerygma und Logos', 159ff. This theological concept is also found in Addai's sermons in the Syriac *Doctrina Addai,* ed. G. Phillips (London 1876), and is an essential element in the doctrinal parts of the Syriac apocryphal *Acts of Thomas.*

26. See A. Guillaumont, op.cit. (n.19 above), 114ff. As to the development of the word *monachos,* the term occurs in the Coptic *Gospel of Thomas:* cf. H.-Ch. Puech, *En quête de la gnose* ii (=*Sur l'Evangile selon Thomas*) (Paris 1978), 178, 216, 222, 236, 240.

27. See J. Daniélou, *Sacramentum Futuri* (Paris 1950), 131-200. A good example is provided by the miracle of the well in the *vita* of Julian Saba (*H.R.* 2, 7-8).

28. R. Reitzenstein, 'Historia monachorum und Historia Lausica', *Forschungen zur Religion und Literatur des Alten und Neuen Testaments* 24 (1916); J. Leipoldt, 'Griechische Philo-

common pattern, of which the Syrian holy man is a characteristic variant, formed and guided by the life of Christ as understood in Syria. Perhaps this may be related to certain philosophical trends, since Christ as thought and will of God has some relation with Middle Platonism, and this life can itself be considered a kind of philosophical life. But its main characteristic is the holy man as *imago Christi* and continuation of the incarnation, so that the divine manifests itself in human shape by transforming that shape into an instrument of God's thought and will. And that might be the ground for the combination of spiritual and ascetic life with philosophical learning which is quite common in the early and later Syrian Church.[29]

Sociology and ideology

If the rise and function of the holy man in Syrian towns and villages are determined by that ideal of *imitatio Christi* which strives for the transcendence of human existence by controlling the most fragile part of it, the body, the final question is: what is the influence of a written and preached religious tradition on human behaviour in a given historical and social situation? In other words, what is the interaction between sociological and ideological elements in a society? It seems that Christianity's most distinct ideological type, the saint, exercised the strongest influence on the society of Late Antiquity, in the Syrian villages as well as in the towns. The special character of the Syrian holy men is rooted in earlier phases of theological thinking, but it fully unfolds during the fourth and fifth centuries. His special way of functioning in the Syrian society of that period, therefore, should be explained by a fresh examination of the structure of that society and its specific needs.

sophie und frühchristliche Askese', *Berichte über die Verhandlungen der sächsischen Akademie der Wissenschaften zu Leipzig P.H.* 106.4 (1961).

29. See A. Guillaumont, 'Un philosophe au désert: Euagre le Pontique', *RHR* 181 (1972), 29-56; and P. Harb, op.cit. (n.22 above), 227. It can be assumed that at Edessa, for example, there was a strong unbroken philosophical tradition from pagan times, of which the so-called 'Letter of Mara bar Serapion to his Son' is an expression (ed. W. Cureton, *Spicilegium Syriacum* (London 1855), 43-8.

THE SAINT AND SOCIETY

The Politicisation of the Byzantine Saint

SUSAN ASHBROOK HARVEY

T HE role of the Eastern ascetic has been widely discussed by scholars of the late Roman/early Byzantine period — a role both fulfilling a socially and politically institutionalised function, and also providing an intimidating degree of popular influence. In any number of ways, the point has been made that during the early Byzantine centuries, the impact of the Eastern holy man or woman on the wider public cannot be over-estimated.[1] The key models for this basic tenet are clearly delineated. Anthony and Athanasius had left a legacy from asceticism's emergence in the fourth century, of coming forward out of the desert to re-enter the temporal world in times of religious crisis. The fifth century had seen the far-reaching temporal and spiritual power of Symeon the Stylite matched by its darker counterpart, the monastic thuggery utilised with such skill by Cyril of Alexandria; while Daniel the Stylite had commanded the policies of emperors. By the sixth century the role of the Eastern holy man and woman had become firmly established with the populace and it is this period I would like to consider. Its intriguing possibilities in the development of the ascetic's role may lead to wider questions.

The first half of the sixth century witnessed an almost unbroken period of natural and human calamity in the Byzantine East. Heralded at the century's turn by an onslaught of foreboding omens, the events of the succeeding decades followed a relentless pattern. Devastating invasions were made against the eastern provinces by both Sassanian Persians and White Huns. Famine was a chronic condition from the century's start, creating a situation both ripe for the eruption of plague and also resulting from it; while numerous local epidemics merged into the massive outbreak

---

1. In particular see P.R.L. Brown, 'The Rise and Function of the Holy Man in Late Antiquity', *JRS* 61 (1971), 80-101, and 'A Dark Age Crisis: aspects of the Iconoclastic controversy', *EHR* 88 (1973), 1-34; also W.H.C. Frend, 'The Monks and the Survival of the East Roman Empire in the Fifth Century', *Past and Present* 54 (1972), 3-24.

OPPOSITE
Daniel the Stylite. Fresco by Theophanes the Greek, Church of the Transfiguration (Spas Preobrazheniia na Il'ine), Novgorod, 1379.
Photo: A.I. Komech (G.I. Vzdornov, Freski Feofana Greka v tserkvi Spasa Preobrazheniia v Novgorode *[1976]*.

of the Great (bubonic) Plague in 542. Earthquakes were severe and relatively common; floods also took their toll. In addition to these hardships, the accession of Justin I in 518 brought a dramatic shift in the government's religious policy to one of Chalcedonian faith imposed by force; harsh persecutions against monophysite dissidents were instituted, and these were to be continued under Justinian and successive rulers. To the monophysite stronghold – the eastern provinces of the empire – the blow was yet another trial to be faced.[2]

The Chalcedonian-monophysite struggle was fierce, and hardly the concern of religious leaders alone. There can be no doubt that this controversy was an issue of popular faith, moving far deeper than questions of theological debate or ecclesiastical manoeuvring. In Constantinople, rioting Chalcedonian crowds murdered a hapless Syrian monk mistaken for the monophysite leader Severos of Antioch.[3] In the monophysite East, particularly in the Syrian Orient and in Egypt, popular fears about receiving communion from the heretical hands of Chalcedonian priests forced the monophysite leaders to take a stance much against their wills and to sanction the ordination of a separate monophysite clergy. The implications of this reluctant move were not long hidden: in a matter of decades the monophysite congregation stood as a separate Church, having an independent ecclesiastical hierarchy. Unity as one Christian body had ceased to be a possibility, whatever turn theological negotiations might take.[4]

The first half of the sixth century, then, found a situation in the eastern Byzantine provinces wherein an ascetic response was needed not only for the urgency of religious crisis, but further, for the pressing economic and social conditions created by continual tragedy. Two primary portraits, drawn by spokesmen for the opposing sides of monophysite and Chalcedonian belief, present the potency of their holy men and women in the midst of these times with disturbingly dissimilar perspectives. John of Ephesus wrote his *Lives of the Eastern Saints* in the mid-560s, both to glorify the virtues of monophysite ascetics whom he himself knew, and to inspire the hard-hit population of the Syrian Orient.[5] Almost two generations later, John Moschus wrote his *Pratum Spirituale,* a similar collection of Eastern ascetic vignettes, but told in more anecdotal form. Moschus wrote with the self-satisfied assurance of established Chalcedonian victory, but many of his stories date back to the period

2. Ps.-Zachariah Rhetor, *HE* VII-XI; Joshua Stylites, *Chron.;* John of Ephesus, *HE* (*ROChr* 2 [1897], 462-89); *Chron. Edessenum,* CSCO iii.4. lxxvi-ciii; Jacob of Edessa, *Chron.,* CSCO iii.4. 314-21; *Chron. ad annum 819,* CSCO iii.4, 7-10; *Chron. ad annum 846,* CSCO iii.4, 218-29; *Chron. ad annum 1234,* l-lxii; Michael the Syrian, *Chron.,* IX.vii-xxxii; Procopius, *Wars* i-ii; Evagrius Scholasticus, *HE* iv; John of Nikiu, *Chron.,* lxxxix-xc. On the cumulative nature of this period of crisis, see further my article, 'Asceticism in Adversity: An Early Byzantine Experience', *Byzantine and Modern Greek Studies* 6 (1980), 1-10.
3. John of Nikiu, *Chron.,* lxxxix.64.
4. See especially W.H.C. Frend, *The Rise of the Monophysite Movement* (Cambridge 1972); and W.A. Wigram, *The Separation of the Monophysites* (New York 1978).
5. John of Ephesus, *Lives of the Eastern Saints,* ed. and tr. E.W. Brooks (PO 17-19 [1923-5]) (hereafter Jo. Eph.).

covered by John of Ephesus and retain a coherent sense of sixth century tradition.[6]

Even the most cursory comparison between these works evokes a sense of tension; the vibrancy in John of Ephesus' urban asceticism and the arid stillness of Moschus' desert seem to speak of altogether disconnected matters. But for the provinces of the eastern empire, the question of religious crisis in the midst of their worldly plight must have raised just this tension in their own lives and experiences. The contrasts are major, and their implications instructive.

John of Ephesus

Anyone who has ever read John of Ephesus will recall only too well the problem of coping with his literary style. Pompous, pious, and utterly chaotic, John lumbers breathlessly through his accounts with a less than graceful ease. Still, his style is not inappropriate, and is perhaps a better mirror for his content than one might like to think. Centred on the area of north Mesopotamia, and especially on the metropolitan city of Amida,[7] John's ascetics – indeed the inspired elect who seek pure devotion to God – are not the desert anchorites so far removed from civilisation as to lose all contact with it. Quite the contrary: theirs is an asceticism defined by active ministry to an almost fanatical degree. They are found settled in the bleak villages, and in the hopeless mess of the city itself; while those more inclined to solitude are located in between, and never out of reach for people who desire their company or aid.

The reality of John's time is consistently apparent throughout his Lives. The people his ascetics seek out and care for, in chapter after chapter, are the victims of the many calamities befalling the east: they are starving, plague-stricken, violated, frightened. The sheer immediacy of John's portrait of the area, and above all, of the presence of the holy within it, is the more haunting for the shared suffering he depicts: the campaign waged against the monophysites reached its cruellest level in Mesopotamia, and it was the highly visible and influential ascetic communities who were most likely to suffer a brutal imprisonment and exile. It was thus often under hazardous or uncertain circumstances that the Amidan ascetics performed their ministry.

The seeming chaos of John's style and narrative well reflects his context, but is belied by the uniformity of the asceticism which he describes. Amida's precarious location on the eastern frontiers of Byzantium had created an ascetic heritage of strong ties between the populace of the area and the monasteries and semi-recluses.[8] The events of the sixth century evoked a response indicative of a sense of shared commitment and experience. Solitaries now exorcise demons appearing in the guise

6. Joannis Moschi, *Pratum Spirituale* (*PG* 87.iii. 2851-3112) (hereafter Jo. Mos.).
7. See the article 'Amid', *DHGE* ii. 1237-49 (Karalewsky).
8. Jo. Eph. 58 (PO 19. 206-27); A. Vööbus, *History of Asceticism in the Syrian Orient* (CSCO Sub 14 and 17 [1958-60]), i. 228-9; ii. 37-9. Cf. Dom A. Baker, 'Syriac and the Origins of Monasticism', *Downside Review* 86 (1968), 342-53.

of invading Huns or Persians.[9] In exile the Amidan ascetics run soup-kitchens and health clinics in their new locales, however brief their stay.[10] Those who had served the homeless and poor travellers in Amida perform identical work wherever their exile leads them, the same (John tells us) 'in peace or in persecution, in city or in exile'.[11] Holy men and women nursing the sick and destitute of Amida's streets also provide shelter for exiles fleeing through the city.[12] And recluses who had lived outside the settled areas return now to towns and cities, taking up the work left by those who have been expelled — organising religious services, performing baptisms, and otherwise tending the flocks.[13]

The unity of John's ascetic vision is further enhanced by the few accounts he includes of holy men and women solely devoted to spiritual practice.[14] At first appearing oddly incongruous with his emphatically urban-orientated subjects, these few virtuosos of private asceticism are in fact consistently placed in John's schema. Never appearing in isolation, they are included to verify beyond question the spiritual authority of the Amidan ascetics. They join or pass through the Amidan monastic communities during their times in exile, in affirmation of the untarnished excellence of religious devotion which these groups maintained, even under persecution — thus revitalising the spiritual potency of these communities in the eyes of the populace. Alternatively, as in the striking case of the two sisters Mary and Euphemia, the single-minded solitary practice of the one is closely tied to the immensely energetic service of the other, thereby validating and strengthening the power of both.[15]

What is most apparent in the *Lives of the Eastern Saints* is that the fundamental ascetic vision and the response to the religious crisis of monophysite persecution are identical. Neither offers a means of retreat or refuge from the plight of the eastern provinces. There is no aloofness, no distance, and despite John's zeal, little illusion. In the grim conditions of exile, the Amidan ascetics are easy prey for plague; moreover their religious status does not exempt them from massacre wrought by plundering foreign troops. Again, they can survive only so much Chalcedonian torture. In fact, these stories are notable for the standard hagiographical fare they do *not* include: the ascetic suffering the boredom of accidie or the taunting desire of lust, for there is no time for such indulgence. Most pointedly, there are no miraculous answers, no divine intervention for the hardship at hand. The ascetics may cure the sick and exorcise demons; but they cannot call forth any instant wonders to dispel reality. They can only serve.

9. Jo. Eph. 6 (PO 17. 111-18).
10. Jo. Eph. 15 (PO 17. 220-8); and 35 (PO 18. 614-17).
11. Jo. Eph. 3 (PO 17. 42-4); 33 and 34 (PO 18. 592-606).
12. Jo. Eph. 12 (PO 17. 171-86).
13. Jo. Eph. 5 and 23 (PO 17. 95-111 and 300-4).
14. Jo. Eph. 14, 17, 19, 20 (PO 17. 213-20, 248-59, 266-83); see also 28 (PO 18. 559-62) and 53 (PO 19. 179-85).
15. Jo. Eph. 12 (PO 17. 166-86).

John Moschus

Reading John of Ephesus, one has no doubt where and when the stories are set. Reading John Moschus, one might often wonder. Moschus, too, writes in a style that befits his content: spare and stark, his language easily conjures up the uncluttered world he unfolds.[16] Here the eastern desert — primarily in Palestine — is very remote indeed, both in place and time. The ascetics Moschus bring to life are also remote. These can pass years, sometimes decades, without seeing or speaking with anyone;[17] they can lie dead for as long again, unchanged, until another anchorite or traveller accidentally stumbles across them.[18] These often suffer the demons of boredom and sex, and seem to return to towns or cities only when they have fallen from their vows and must seek the debauchery tormenting their fantasies.[19] In this austerely black and white existence, miracles and prodigies are the norm, the Lord's favoured people are plainly indicated, and the divine will is quite explicit.

Moschus does include stories of worthy ascetics living in urban settings. These tend to be bishops, or holy men on business, who remain as detached in city as in desert, though an occasional glimpse of social context is provided: the women who become prostitutes because they are starving,[20] the citizens ruined by burdensome debts.[21] The ascetics themselves are untouched by the events and circumstances of their time, which penetrate the rarified desert air only for didactic purposes. If plague strikes a village, one may seek these holy men, whose prayers can save one's children and banish the epidemic.[22] If a marauding barbarian attacks, the holy men's prayers can cause the offender to be swallowed up by the earth, carried off to death by a giant bird, or even the innocent person to be instantly transported elsewhere.[23] One may notice, however, that for Moschus holy women seem solely occupied with battling Satan over the issue of fornication — in contrast to the more pragmatic treatment in John of Ephesus, where holy women, albeit few and far between, are strong and wilful, impressive as leaders who gain the respect of male and female alike, and found in roles not normally open to women in their society.[24]

Moschus' passion for Chalcedonian faith is also manifested by the same means as his ascetic vision. This is an orthodoxy revealed in thunderous signs, in terrifying dreams, in irrefutable miracles. The gates of hell are opened to reveal what punish-

16. Cf. H. Chadwick, 'John Moschus and his Friend Sophronius the Sophist', *JTS* 25 (1974), 41-74; and 'Jean Moschus', *Dictionnaire de spiritualité*, fasc. lii. 632-40 (E. Mioni).
17. Jo. Mos. 179.
18. Jo. Mos. 84, 87, 89, 120, 121, 170, 179.
19. Jo. Mos. 14, 19, 39, 45, 97, 135.
20. Jo. Mos. 136, 186, 207.
21. Jo. Mos. 186, 193, 201, 207.
22. Jo. Mos. 131, 132.
23. Jo. Mos. 20, 21, 99.
24. E.g. Jo. Mos. 39, 60, 75, 76, 135, 179, 204, 205; and Jo. Eph. 12 (PO 17. 166-86); 27 (PO 18. 541-58); 28 (PO 18. 559-62); 52 (PO 19. 164-79); 54 (PO 19. 185-91).

ment awaits the heretic in after-life,[25] holy sacraments are consumed by lightening if defiled by monophysite hands.[26] Divine apparitions prevent monophysites from worshipping in the holy places of Jerusalem;[27] evil odours are emitted by Syrian monophysite monks, however faultless their ascetic practice.[28] The question of faith is omnipresent, but this is a faith forever tested out in the intangible space found somewhere between the temporal and divine worlds. Thus two stylites, one Chalcedonian and one monophysite, bring their religious dispute to the test by exploring the miraculous qualities of their respective holy sacraments — the monophysite morsel, not surprisingly, proving unable to survive the trial.[29]

What we obviously need here are accounts of how common people perceived the Chalcedonian-monophysite rivalry, and its appearance in the work of holy men and women in the world. Instead, we are left with the biases of hagiographical proselytising. Moschus portrays in clear and even tones an asceticism of impenetrable timelessness, in which the temporal world is a place only to be shunned, while one's faith is played out between oneself and one's God. For Moschus this also is the nature and realm of religious crisis — a passionate display of divine warfare in a space far removed from the irrelevance of human time and place.

I am not suggesting that the acute situation of the sixth century provided an excuse for the monophysite ascetics of the East to turn a religious crisis into a political one. Rather, I would simply stress that there were times when the ascetics of the early Byzantine Empire held themselves accountable for the condition of the temporal world, not because a beleaguered population sought them out, but because they perceived themselves as inextricably bound to it. John of Ephesus writes with a life-affirming fervour so politically charged that his Lives border on monophysite propaganda of the most blatant kind. But if so, it is a propaganda permeated by realism. These saints of the eastern Byzantine provinces find only one answer to the calamities of their time and to the urgency of religious crisis: for them, the presence of the holy is found not outside the temporal world of human society, but manifestly within it.

25. Jo. Mos. 26.
26. Jo. Mos. 30.
27. Jo. Mos. 48, 49.
28. Jo. Mos. 106.
29. Jo. Mos. 29; cf. also 36.

The Political Saint of the Eleventh Century

ROSEMARY MORRIS

A THEME which clearly emerged from many of the papers given at the Birmingham Symposium on the Byzantine Saint was that, far from being the distant, solitary and unworldly figure of popular imagination (and, sometimes, scholarly inclination) the Byzantine saint was an active participant in the affairs of the world. He was both 'in the world' *and* 'of it'.[1] In this paper, this point of view is further developed and, in particular, the role of the Byzantine saint in the political life of the eleventh century is examined. By 'political life' is meant not only involvement in (and influence upon) imperial and governmental decisions, but also active participation in the activities of those with a somewhat lesser degree of influence within the Byzantine state.

Three saints are particularly important in this connection, not only because they themselves were interesting figures, but also because they were blessed with contemporary and lively hagiographers – a somewhat rare event after the stultifying (if elegant) hand of the Metaphrastic school had descended on the genre at the end of the tenth century.[2] The three saints and their hagiographers are, in chronological order, St Symeon the New Theologian; St Lazaros the Galesiote and St Cyril Phileotes. The Life of St Symeon the New Theologian (949-1022) was composed by Niketas Stethatos, one of his disciples at the monastery of St Mamas in Constantinople.[3] He is that same Stethatos who incurred imperial displeasure for the intemperate pamphlet published against the Latins in the aftermath of the mutual excommunications of 1054.[4] The second saint is St Lazaros of Mount Galesion (north of Ephesus) who lived 968-1054. His Life was written, in the first instance, by a disciple, Gregory.[5] St Cyril Phileotes completes the trio. His Life, covering the

1. See in particular the paper by Professor Browning, below. This view, of course, is in direct contrast to that first developed in the seminal article of P.R.L. Brown, 'The Rise and Function of the Holy Man in Late Antiquity', *JRS* 61 (1971), 80-101.

2. See Professor I. Ševčenko's Birmingham paper on ' "High Style" Saints' Lives', to be published in *AnalBoll.*

3. Nicétas Stéthatos, *Vie de Syméon le Nouveau Théologien (949-1022)*, ed. and tr. I. Hausherr and G. Horn, OC 12 (1928). For the monastery of St Mamas see R. Janin, *La géographie ecclésiastique de l'Empire byzantin* 1.iii (Paris 1949).

4. See Nicetas Stethatos, 'Against the Latins' in A. Michel, *Humbert und Kerullarius* (Paderborn 1923-30), ii. 322-42. The scandal caused by his pamphlet is described by S. Runciman, *The Eastern Schism* (Oxford 1955), 46-50.

5. *Vita S. Lazari auctore Gregorio monacho, ActaSS* Nov. III, 508-88. A second Life, by Gregory of Cyprus (d.1289) is derived from this original.

43

period 1015-1110, was again composed by a disciple, Nicholas Kataskepenos (who died sometime after 1143).[6]

The Lives of these saints cover the geographical areas of Constantinople and its environs, western Asia Minor and Thrace. They also provide a contrast between the activities of the urban and the rural saint.

The entry of these saints into political life was a lengthy process. But there can be no doubt that great social influence was ultimately achieved; the very existence of a hagiography is a mark of success. In the past, it has been argued that political or moral influence followed the acceptance of the holiness of the saint. Sanctity, as evidenced in the powers of healing, prophecy and intercession, came first. The man who was an 'outsider' was drawn into political life by the fact of consultation.[7] But there are good reasons for suggesting that successful saints never really severed their connections with the world, simply that their place within it was expressed by a different set of criteria. It is no accident that all hagiographers seek to place their subjects in the middling ranks of society. It may be a *topos* to be told that the saint was the child of parents who, though not excessively rich were 'well born' (*eugeneis*), but it must always be remembered that *topoi* are an important means of expressing the accepted and, more importantly, the *expected*.

The benefits of education

In the three cases around which this paper is centred, we learn a few highly significant details about the parentage and early life of the saints concerned. In particular, the education of the saint is often described. Symeon the New Theologian, for example, was born in Galata in Paphlagonia. He was educated at first by his parents and was then sent to his grandparents in Constantinople to be perfected in 'profane culture and rhetoric'.[8] He was taken up by an uncle who was a *koitōnitēs* – a chamberlain in charge of the *koubikoularioi*, the bodyservants of the emperors Basil II and Constantine VIII. He himself entered the imperial service and gained the post of *spatharokoubikoularios*.[9] We do not know how long Symeon remained at court, but it seems clear that he entered the monastery at Stoudion at about twenty-eight years of age.[10] By this time, however, his place in the society of

6. *La vie de S. Cyrille le Philéote par Nicholas Katasképonos*, ed. E. Sargologos (SubsHag 39 [1964]).
7. P.R.L. Brown, *JRS* 61 (1971), esp. 91-101.
8. *Vie de Syméon* 2; Hausherr-Horn, 1. The phrase *exellenisthenai ten glottan* clearly indicates a secular education. See P. Lemerle, *Le premier humanisme byzantin* (Paris 1971).
9. For the *koubikoularioi* see N. Oikonomidès, *Les listes de préséance byzantines des IXe et Xe siècles* (Paris 1972), 301. For the *spatharokoubikoularios* see ibid., 301-2. Both these posts were held by eunuchs, as was that of the *koitōnitēs* (ibid., 305). Symeon's uncle foresaw a successful career for his nephew in the imperial service 'because of his great beauty', a comment which would support the view that Symeon was already a eunuch. See *Vie de Syméon* 3; Hausherr-Horn, 4.
10. *Vie de Syméon* 4; Hausherr-Horn, 7; Symeon's first request to enter Stoudion was refused because of his age (about fourteen). According to the Life, he was finally permitted to enter some six years later, but we should probably take this date as approximate. Hausherr (*Vie de Syméon*, lxxxvii) considered that he was about twenty-eight.

44

middle-ranking court officials had been established and it is no surprise to learn that it was of such people that the saint's lay circle was later comprised.

St Lazaros was born at Magnesia on the Maeander. Again, we know that his parents were of the 'middling sort' and that their names were Niketas and Eirene. For them, too, the education of their child was a major concern. Lazaros was taught firstly by them and then by a priest, Leontios, on the instructions of the child's uncle, the monk Elias. After three further years' training with a *notarios,* Lazaros joined his uncle in the monastery *tōn Kalathōn.* [11] His education had ended at the stage before Symeon's; he had not been sent to Constantinople to be 'finished', but had probably studied the Scriptures in detail and some theology. His notarial training would have familiarised him not only with the techniques of drawing up legal documents, but also, perhaps, with basic legal terminology and financial calculation.

The last example, Cyril, had an even more basic education. But the information provided by his biographer that he was appointed to the rank of reader in his local church by the archbishop of Derkos, is clear evidence that he had risen above the ranks of the barely literate. [12] The importance of a degree of education in youth cannot be overstressed. For it enabled the saints to communicate with disciples of a higher social standing, to receive their confidences and give them advice. It is hardly conceivable that members of the Byzantine aristocracy would have entrusted their spiritual guidance to illiterates. The saints may not have been highly sophisticated — indeed, simplicity of behaviour was a much admired quality — but in the initial selection of a spiritual father or confidant, the ability of the holy man to create a rapport with his followers was an important element.

Education placed men within a particular social stratum, albeit a wide one and was an aspect of worldly contact which could never be discarded. Other early influences, however, could. The moment of withdrawal from the world is another favourite *topos* of hagiographers. Certainly, many seeking the religious life abandoned their families, their careers, their homes and their property. We have seen how Symeon the New Theologian left a promising career in the imperial service. He also renounced his rights to his landed inheritance. [13] Cyril Phileotes went even further by leaving both his work as a pilot on the Black Sea and his wife and family. [14] In many cases, the hagiographers relate the efforts of their subject's families to track them down and persuade them to return to the fold. The struggle against the ties of family affection and responsibility was part and parcel of that wrestling with the affairs of the world which these spiritual *athlētai* must undertake before their internal, religious development could properly begin.

11. *Vita S. Lazari* 2-3; *ActaSS,* 509-10. The monastery of Kalathai may have been near Magnesia, cf. R. Janin, *La géographie ecclésiastique de l'Empire byzantin* 1.iv (Paris 1975), 242 n.5.
12. *Vie de S. Cyrille* 2.i; Sargologos, 268.
13. *Vie de Syméon* 9; Hausherr-Horn, 14.
14. *Vie de S. Cyrille* 8; Sargologos, 293.

Spiritual kinship and its role

But the nexus of family relationships was replaced by a far more politically influential network — that of spiritual kinship. The relationship between the spiritual father and his children has long been of interest to historians and theologians, though the subject has still to receive the major study it deserves.[15] In particular, the process by which the choice of spiritual father was made (and the role accepted, since the affair was a two way process) has still to be elucidated.

But it is clear that it followed upon the acceptance of the saint by a large body of people, and on their respect for a sanctity associated with the qualities of curing, prophecy and asceticism.[16] This acceptance showed itself in concrete form in increased patronage of the foundations set up by the holy men concerned — and in their rising reputations as spiritual guides.

The relationship between the holy men and their spiritual children was conducted in a number of ways. The disciple could visit the holy man in his monastery, receive advice or admonition and then, perhaps, make a donation to the house. This had advantages in times of political crisis, as a visit to a remote provincial monastery might initially escape the notice of imperial informants. But there is much evidence to suggest that the rural saints themselves were in close contact with their disciples further afield and took particular interest in the affairs of Constantinople. St Lazaros corresponded with his followers in the capital and we also know that after his death letters were speedily despatched to Constantinople.[17] Doubtless these were primarily addressed to the *metochion* of the houses of Galesion in the city, but they may well have been the means of informing the saint's most influential disciples and spiritual sons of his death.

In other hagiographies, the process of contact with the capital and the highest echelons of the government is even more noticeable. The archives of Athos, and of the Lavra in particular, reveal numerous occasions upon which powerful *hēgoumenoi* seemed to have unhindered access to the emperor to put their case on disputed questions concerning the administration of the Holy Mountain.[18] St Christodoulos of Patmos similarly enjoyed access to both emperor and patriarch when he was in dispute with members of his flock on Mount Latros.[19]

15. I. Hausherr, *Direction spirituelle en Orient autrefois* (*OCA* 144 [1955]) remains the only study, as far as I know, and concentrates on the period of the desert fathers.
16. As pointed out by Professor Patlagean below.
17. *Vita S. Lazari* 221; *ActaSS*, 576.
18. See, for example, *Actes du Prôtaton* [= *Archives de l'Athos* vii], ed. D. Papachryssanthou (Paris 1975). No. 7 (972) relates how conflicts about the conduct of the spiritual life on Athos were placed before the emperor; No. 8 (1045) — the *Typikon* of Monomachos — deplores the habit of the warring Athonites of taking their grievances to lay judges, but (tacitly) exempts the emperor from these strictures.
19. See F. Miklosich and J. Müller, *Acta et diplomata graeca medii aevi sacra et profana* (Vienna 1860-90), vi. 30-1. The rather mysterious conflict between Christodoulos and his monks is reconstructed in E. Vranousses, *Ta hagiologika keimena tou hosiou Christodoulou* (Athens 1966), 90-6.

The term 'contact' has been deliberately used to cover a range of associations in person, by proxy or by letter. But what, precisely, was the nature of the exchange of information which has been postulated? This problem may best be answered by what we know of the pattern of a spiritual 'counselling-session'. Symeon the New Theologian himself wrote of the relationship and explained the process by which the choice or a spiritual father was made:

> Go and find the man whom God, either mysteriously through himself, or externally through his servant shall show you. He [the spiritual father] is· Christ himself. So you must regard him and speak to him; so must you honour him; so must you learn from him that which will be of benefit to you.[20]

The consequence of this docility and obedience would, it was hoped, be the achievement of complete self-renunciation: 'For the fact of accomplishing an act not of their own will, but of that of their spiritual father's will lead just as much to self-renunciation as to death in the world'.[21] Ideally, then, the relationship between the two parties was to be, from the first, one of complete openness and trust and an unquestioning acceptance of the advice of the spiritual father. In practice, this seems to have been very much the case.

An episode from the Life of St Cyril Phileotes will illustrate the concept of spiritual fatherhood in action. An unnamed woman, who is clearly Anna Dalassena the future empress, asks the saint to provide her with a piece of spiritual advice (*rhēma sōtērias*) which would be suited to her abilities. Cyril responds with a series of short *apophthegmata,* quoting from Basil of Caesarea on the virtues of charity, and, amongst others, John Klimakos and the desert father, Barsanouphios. At this point the penitent declares 'I wish to reveal my thoughts to your holiness but I am afraid of not staying faithful to your words and thus offending God'. Cyril assures her that the unveiling of one's innermost thoughts to spiritual fathers is the first indication of wishing to reform one's way of life and proceeds to give her a set of moral precepts which she should attempt to follow.[22]

It is clear that the nub of the relationship between spiritual father and spiritual son or daughter consisted in complete frankness on the latter's part. Spiritual fathers must, then, have received a vast amount of detailed and often 'sensitive' information. What has to be established, however, is whether the secrets of the consultations were passed on.

One reason for supposing that they might be is a consideration of the relationship between the spiritual sons of a particular saint. Did they consider themselves to be spiritual brothers *of each other?* If this was indeed the case, as the exclusivity of

20. Syméon le Nouveau Théologien, *Cathéchèses,* ed. B. Krivochéine and tr. J. Paramelle (Paris 1963-5), ii. 335.
21. Syméon le Nouveau Théologien, *Traités théologiques et éthiques,* ed. and tr. J. Darrouzès (Paris 1966-7), ii.18.
22. *Vie de S. Cyrille* 17; Sargologos, 314.

some of these circles would suggest, then an important basis for alliances beyond those of family and kin was thus established.

Social implications of spiritual kinship

Analysis of the named spiritual sons and close followers of the three eleventh-century saints provides illuminating information on the social status of those who consulted them. In all three cases, we hear of members of the imperial family and the aristocracy taking advice from the holy men. It is this activity which reveals their important role in the formulation of state policy and their position in the volatile world of secular politics.

On the highest level, St Lazaros was consulted by Maria Skleraina, the influential mistress of the emperor Constantine Monomachos and the sister of the *stratēgos* Romanos Skleros; by the *stratēgos* himself, and by a certain Makrembolites – clearly a relative of the empress Eudokia Makrembolitissa, the consort of Constantine X Doukas (1059-67) and his successor, Romanos IV Diogenes (1067-81).[23] The contacts between St Cyril Phileotes and the imperial family were even closer. He was the spiritual father of Anna Dalassena, the mother of the future emperor Alexios Komnenos (whose elevation to the purple he prophesied); of the emperor himself; and of his brother-in-law George Palaiologos. He was also consulted by the celebrated general, Eumathios Philokales and by Constantine Choirosphaktes, a scion of an eminent Byzantine family.[24]

The relationship of these spiritual fathers with the highest echelons of Byzantine society was an indication that they had reached the peak of their profession. Their fame had spread widely enough to reach the ears of the members of powerful families in the regions in which they lived and beyond. The advice given varied from encouragement to undertake a coup d'état to advice on the likely outcome of a campaign and in this sense played an important part in the evolution of imperial policy.[25]

But of far more use in plotting the possible means of access to governmental circles in Byzantium, to the professional bureaucrats who ensured the continuity of administration as emperors came and went, is the analysis of the association of holy men with what might be termed Byzantine 'middle management'. Such men were,

23. For the members of the Skleros family see *Vita S. Lazari* 245; *ActaSS,* 554 (Maria Skleraina) and ibid. 87; *ActaSS,* 536 (Romanos Skleros). For Makrembolites, ibid., 101; *ActaSS,* 539. Both families are frequently mentioned in the *Chronographia* of Psellos and in the *History* of Scylitzes. The Skleros family has been the subject of a recent study: W. Seibt, *Die Skleroi. Eine prosopographisch-sigillographische Studie* (Vienna 1976).

24. For Anna Dalassena see *Vie de S. Cyrille* 17; Sargologos, 314. For Eumathios Philokales see ibid. 35 and Anna Komnena, *Alexiade,* ed. B. Leib (Paris 1937-45), *passim.* For Constantine Choirosphaktes see *Vie de S. Cyrille* 34; Sargologos, 370. His family is known from the tenth century: cf. G. Koilas, *Léon Choerosphaktès* (Athens 1939).

25. See *Vita S. Lazari* 230; *ActaSS,* 579, where encouragement from Galesion for Constantine Monomachos' coup is mentioned, and *Vie de S. Cyrille* 17; Sargologos, 312, where the saint prophesied that Alexios would ultimately be victorious over the Norman, Bohemund, thus probably encouraging him to undertake a risky campaign.

THE POLITICAL SAINT OF THE ELEVENTH CENTURY

for example, the group of disciples of Symeon the New Theologian (and the fact that they are referred to as a *group* is of prime importance) which met at the house of a certain Christopher Phagoura in Constantinople.[26] This circle of loyal followers continued to place its faith in Symeon even after he had been strongly censured by the patriarchs Nicholas Chrysoberges and Sergios for venerating an icon of his own spiritual father, Symeon of Stoudion. This action must suggest that the group was made up of men powerful enough to risk ecclesiastical censure with equanimity. We know that Christopher Phagoura himself built a small house for Symeon on the Asiatic shores of the Bosphorus and may surmise that he and his friends were reasonably well-off members of the government élite of the capital.[27]

St Lazaros of Mount Galesion had, if anything, more interesting contacts with the local secular authorities. His circle included Nikephoros Proteuon, the *kritēs* of the Thrakesion theme;[28] John Mitas, the *dioikētēs* of Ephesus in charge of the property of the *sekrēton* of the Myrelaion in the same theme, his uncle Eustathios Mitas[29] and Leon Bazilitzes, a *prōtospatharios* from Attaleia.[30] But he also had contacts in Constantinople. He warned the eparch, Nikephoros Kampanares, of an imminent revolt against the emperor Michael V;[31] he prophesied the downfall of Constantine Barys after his abortive revolt against Constantine Monomachos, as well as the political survival of his associate, Nikephoros, son of Euthymios.[32] He received visits from the *stratēgos* Romanos Skleros and Kosmas Konidares, two of the figures who are also known from contemporary chronicles and the legal compilation of the *Peira*.

The 'politicisation' of the saint

The holy men thus played their part in the political life of both their local areas and, in some cases, the empire itself. They had an important role as formulators of policy and as the means by which like-minded men could keep in touch with one another. This had two important consequences for the spiritual and political life of Byzantium. Firstly, the advice given by holy men to those of standing and influence

26. *Vie de Syméon* 109; Hausherr-Horn, 146.
27. Ibid. 78-103; Hausherr-Horn, 106ff. The house was the small oratory of St Makrina (ibid. 100; Hausherr-Horn, 138).
28. For Nikephoros Proteuon see *Vita S. Lazari* 120; *ActaSS*, 543.
29. For John and Eustachios Mitas see ibid. 103; *ActaSS*, 539.
30. For Leon Bazilitzes see ibid. 71; *ActaSS*, 531.
31. ibid. 102; *ActaSS*. 539. The 'Kampares' of the text should almost certainly be emended to 'Kampanares'. This man is mentioned by Scylitzes in his *Synopsis Historiarum*, ed. J. Thurn (Berlin-New York 1973), 420. He could also be the *kritēs* 'Kampanarios' of *Peira* xxiii.6. Cf. 'Practica ex actis Eustathii Romani' in J. and P. Zepos, *Jus graeco-romanum* (Athens 1931), iv.
32. For the plot of Constantine Barys see *Vita S. Lazari* 105; *ActaSS*, 540. Two earlier members of the Barys family are known from the reign of Constantine Porphyrogennetos (913-59), a Constantine Barys and his son Michael: cf. Pseudo-Symeon magister, *Annales*, ed. I. Bekker (Bonn 1838), 728. Given the Byzantine habit of calling grandsons after their grandfathers, this Constantine Barys could be Michael's son. It is at present impossible to identify Nikephoros, son of Euthymios.

in public affairs often amounted to directing political action. Secondly, the links between the spiritual sons may well have provided an important basis for political alliances. Most of all, however, the direction of patronage was influenced by these links. This subject is, of course, deserving of much more detailed study, but one can indicate a very strong link between the followers of a holy man who had given sage advice and the subsequent direction of their monetary and landed gifts.

This was especially true in the imperial connection. In earlier generations, Romanos Lekapenos and Nikephoros Phokas had made grants to the houses on Mount Kyminas and in particular to that of the great spiritual leader, St Michael Maleïnos.[33] The success of St Athanasios of the Lavra in gaining generous donations for his house on Athos from his spiritual son, Nikephoros Phokas, is well known.[34] Donations to the houses of St Lazaros and St Cyril thus fell into a well established pattern and they are by no means the only examples which could be cited from the eleventh century.[35] The initial success of the holy men in attracting followers, a very real measure not only of their spiritual reputations but also of their cultural qualifications to participate in an educated milieu, was perpetuated by the increased prosperity which followed and of which the writing of hagiography was a testament.

But the 'politicisation' of the Byzantine saint was part and parcel of the changing role of such men in the society of the eleventh century. In the twelfth and thirteenth centuries, saints became almost the tools of the high aristocracy – a process already begun in the eleventh century.[36] It was associated with the popularity of a new type of monasticism, that which associated the charisma of the holy ascetic and spiritual guide with the cenobitic community, the 'monasteriasation' of the holy man to which Evelyne Patlagean referred.[37] This meant that the saints were quite literally more accessible than they had been in the past.

The encroachments of the Turks and Normans accelerated this movement and brought the holy men *geographically* into the more immediate orbit of the administrative and military élites of the empire as they moved closer to the capital for safety. The fortunes of war, however, merely accentuated an already existing involvement of successful saints in political life: an aspect of their role in a world which birth, education and personal connections had ensured that they had never completely abandoned.

33. *Vie de S. Michel Maleïnos*, ed. L. Petit, *ROChr* 7 (1902), 543-58; see also Theophanes Continuatus, *Chronographia*, ed. I. Bekker (Bonn, 1838), 418.
34. See the Introduction to *Actes de Lavra* i [=*Archives de l'Athos* v], ed. P. Lemerle, A. Guillou, N. Svoronos and D. Papachryssanthou (Paris 1970), where Athanasios' career is examined in detail.
35. One could add the examples of Nea Monē on Chios which received considerable gifts from Constantine Monomachos, and of St Christodoulos' foundation on Patmos, similarly patronised by the emperors Nikephoros Botaneiates and Alexios Komnenos. I examine the links between spiritual fatherhood and patronage in detail in my thesis 'The Byzantine Church and the Land in the Tenth and Eleventh Centuries' (unpublished D.Phil thesis, University of Oxford 1978).
36. See the fascinating papers of Dr P. Magdalino and Dr R. Macrides below.
37. See Professor E. Patlagean's study of 'Sainteté et Pouvoir' below.

The Byzantine Holy Man in the Twelfth Century

PAUL MAGDALINO

A S Peter Brown has reminded us more than once,[1] the holy man was an indispensible feature of the Byzantine scene. Whether he was a straightforward dropout in the Egyptian manner, or whether he was into eccentric Syrian fashions like columns, trees, chains, or holy foolishness, he was as integral to East Roman society as the imperial bureaucracy and the megalopolis. Indeed society needed him precisely because in his paradoxical, anti-social way, he provided a release from the tensions of too much civilisation. The Christian West could not, or would not, keep the same distinction between sanctity and social norms. The holy man, like the icon (with which he had much in common), was an Eastern institution which Latin Europe shared in principle, but in practice tamed almost out of recognition. St Francis was the exception that proved the rule.[2]

Even in Byzantium, as is well known, the icon went through a severe crisis before it became established. What about the holy man? Did he share the same troubles? This has generally been assumed. Peter Brown is not the first or the last to have seen iconoclasm as a crisis for the living ascetic.[3] There are clear indications that the monks were the social group who suffered most from the reaction against icons, and, correspondingly, gained most from their restoration. It would seem, therefore, that the holy man should have been quite as securely established as the icon after 843. But did holy men and icons really belong to the same 'package' to this extent, and was the holy man really home and dry in the mid-ninth century? Here certain observations must be made.

1. P.R.L. Brown, 'The Rise and Function of the Holy Man in Late Antiquity', *JRS* 71 (1971), 80-101; id., 'A Dark-Age Crisis: Aspects of the Iconoclastic Controversy', *EHR* (1973), 1-34; id., Eastern and Western Christendom in Late Antiquity: A Parting of the Ways', *Studies in Church History* 13 (1976), 1-24.
2. This is not to deny the presence, and influence, of solitary ascetics in Western Europe, particularly in the eleventh and twelfth centuries, and the methodology of Peter Brown has been applied to the study of one twelfth-century English holy man: H. Mayr-Harting, 'Functions of a Twelfth-Century Recluse', *History* 60 (1975), 337-52. It is nevertheless fair to state that the Western Church discouraged solitary and eccentric asceticism more consistently and successfuly than was ever the case in Byzantium.
3. G. Ladner, 'Origin and Significance of the Byzantine Iconoclast Controversy', *MedSt* 2 (1940), 127-49; H. Ahrweiler in *Iconoclasm*, ed. A. Bryer and J. Herrin (Birmingham 1977), 24.

First, it is not impossible that there were iconoclast ascetics on the traditional model.[4] Second, icons and holy men differed significantly in that icons represented saints who had made it, whereas holy men were saints in the making. Third, the holy man, unlike the icon, was not actually prescribed as a devotional aid by an ecumenical council of the Church. Fourth, cenobitic monasticism could, if necessary, survive without conspicuous heroes, especially of the more exotic kind. Together, these observations point to the conclusion that Byzantine society was still free to change its mind about the holy man. I suggest that there was at least one period, beginning in the twelfth century, when the holy man ran the risk of losing his credentials.

A decline in hagiography

Holy men are the stuff of hagiography, and Beck has written that 'the period of the Komnenoi is hagiographically a disappointment'.[5] This remark needs some qualification. The hagiography of Christodoulos of Patmos,[6] the Life of Cyril Phileotes by Nicholas Kataskepenos,[7] those of Hosios Meletios by Nicholas of Methone and Theodore Prodromos,[8] and that of Leontios of Jerusalem by the monk Theodosios:[9] these are all twelfth-century works, as, presumably, was the now lost Life of John the Faster, founder of the Petra monastery in Constantinople.[10] These texts may be disappointing to connoisseurs of the genre, but as historical sources and mirrors of holy men in action they are as interesting as any

4. See Ihor Ševčenko, 'Hagiography of the Iconoclast World', *Iconoclasm*, 113-31.
5. H.G. Beck, *Kirche und theologische Literatur im byzantinischen Reich* (Munich 1959), 271.
6. *BHG*[3], 303ff; *Auctarium*, 305; E. Vranouse, *Ta hagiologika keimena tou hosiou Christodoulou* (Athens 1966).
7. *BHG*[3], *Auctarium*, 468; *La Vie de S. Cyrille le Philéote, moine byzantin*, ed. E. Sargologos (SubsHag 39 [1964]), 39.
8. *BHG*[3], 1247-8; ed. B. Vasilevskii in *Pravoslavnyi Palestinskii Sbornik* 6.2 (1886), 1-69.
9. Makarios Chrysokephalos, *14 Logoi panēgyrikoi* (Cosmopolis [Vienna] 1794), 380-434.
10. The Life is twice mentioned by the fourteenth-century patriarch Kallistos in his encomium of the saint: *BHG*[3]. 892; ed. H. Gelzer, *ZWTh* 29 (1886), 64-89; see 67. 13-14, and 69. 13-15. The encomium, an important source for the Petra monastery, is not cited by R. Janin. *La géographie ecclésiastique de l'Empire byzantin* l.iii (Paris 1969),421;orJ.Darrouzès *TM* 6 (1976), 161. The text indicates that John the Faster, a eunuch *malgré lui* from Cappadocia, came to Constantinople and occupied the *monydrion* of Petra during the patriarchate of Nicholas III (1084-1111); his saintliness attracted the patronage of the emperor Alexios I and an unnamed empress, and by the time of his death he was head of a flourishing community (68-78). John must therefore have been the author of the unpublished and largely illegible *Testament* of the monastery's *ktētōr* preserved in *Ambrosianus* E 9 Sup., which mentions Anna Dalassena, Alexios I, and the patriarch Nicholas as benefactors: see Darrouzès, loc.cit., n.2. Kallistos also provides information that John the Faster's monastery was transformed into a much grander and wealthier foundation by its 'second *ktētōr*', John Ioalites, a civil aristocrat and *prōtasēkrētis* (81-5). It was presumably after this transformation that Manuel I (1143-80) called upon the Petra monastery to provide him with a whole range of gastronomic specialities which he needed for wedding celebrations at the Blachernae palace: ed. T.L.F. Tafel, *Eustathii Opuscula* (Frankfurt-am-Main 1832), 230-1.

saints' Lives. The saints themselves were important figures who had personal contact with the emperors of their day, and all, apart from Leontios of Jerusalem, founded monasteries.

However, Beck's point is well made. Leontios was the only one of these saints who lived his whole life under Comnenian rule. The other four were all, like Alexios I Komnenos, products of the eleventh-century, and Alexios (1081-1118) outlived all of them. Compared with earlier centuries and with the fourteenth (we shall come back to the thirteenth), the twelfth century *is* disappointing in terms of the saints and hagiography it produced, especially when we consider that this was an age when much literature was written and many monasteries were founded.

True, the list of twelfth-century Byzantine saints can be extended to include a number of figures not already mentioned, but for one reason or another these do not deserve attention as holy men of central importance to Byzantine society at the time. Cyprian of Calabria lived outside the Byzantine Empire,[11] and Neophytos the Recluse confined his activities to Cyprus which, although imperial territory until 1184, was, as Cyril Mango has demonstrated, very far from being a 'cross-roads of the Byzantine world'.[12] Hilarion of Moglena (d.1164) lived much closer to the centre of things, and he is said to have prevented the emperor Manuel I (1143-80) from lapsing into heresy.[13] However, he made his reputation not as an ascetic, but as a bishop fighting against heresy, and it is perhaps significant that he is not known from any Greek text but from a Slavonic life written by the fourteenth-century Bulgarian patriarch Evfimii of Trnovo.

There are, finally, two Greek saints who may have lived in the twelfth century, although this is not certain. One Gregory, an ascetic near Nicomedia, is said by Nikodemos Hagioreites to have died in 1240, but this cannot be verified from the fourteenth-century Life by Joseph Kalothetos, which is singularly lacking in circumstantial detail.[14] Another Gregory, bishop of Assos in the Troad and founder of a monastery on Mitylene, is the subject of a still unpublished Life, which states that he grew up under Manuel I.[15] I have not been able to consult both manuscripts of this curious document, but the evidence of the older of the two, Patmiacus 448 (15th century) does not inspire confidence. The text of the Life is preceded by a Synaxarion attributed to Nikephoros Xanthopoulos, which says that Gregory lived

11. *BHG³*. 2089.
12. *BHG³*. 1325 m-n; C. Mango-E.J.W. Hawkins, 'The Hermitage of St Neophytos and its Wall Paintings', *DOP* 20 (1966), 122-8; C. Mango, 'Chypre carrefour du monde byzantin', *XVᵉ Congrès International d'Etudes Byzantines* (Athens 1976), *Rapports* v.5.
13. Ed. E. Kalužniacki, *Werke des Patriarchen von Bulgarien Euthymius* (Vienna 1901), 52; cf. E. Turdeanu, *La littérature bulgare du XIVᵉ siècle et sa diffusion les pays roumains* (Paris 1947), 82-4.
14. *BHG³*, 709; ed. D.G. Tsames, Joseph Kalothetos, 'Letters' and 'Life' of Hosios Gregorios, *Epistēmonikē Epetēris tes Theologikēs Scholēs tou Panepistēmiou Thessalonikes* 19 (1974), 103ff.
15. *BHG³*. and *Auctarium*, 701a; cf. cod. Patmiacus 448, f34ʳ.

under Constantine Monomachos (1042-55).[16] There are other discrepancies, of which I need cite but two. According to the Life, Gregory left the bishopric because he was falsely accused of sodomy with his spiritual son; according to the Synaxarion, his accusers produced a woman to say that she had slept with him. The Life says that Gregory's mother wept bitterly at his death, while the Synaxarion says that he had to sort out the family property after her demise. One's first inclination is to trust the Life rather than the Synaxarion, which (if the work of Xanthopoulos) can not date from earlier than about 1310. But the author of the Life says that he composed it, using oral tradition and written records, 160 years after the saint's death.[17] This means that if Gregory really lived under Manuel, the author of the Life was either Xanthopoulos' contemporary, or of a later generation.

Alternative sources

If we want to meet the Byzantine holy man of the twelfth century, we have to look for him not in hagiography, but in other literature: the letters of John Tzetzes,[18] the canon-law commentaries of Theodore Balsamon,[19] certain rhetorical works of Eustathios of Thessalonica,[20] and the history of Niketas Choniates.[21] These authors reveal that Constantinople and other Byzantine cities were teeming with holy men of all imaginable kinds. They also, without exception, portray the holy men in an unfavourable light, characterising them as fraudulent, greedy, or superfluous.

Two illustrations will suffice. Firstly, a passage from a letter of Tzetzes supposedly addressed to his runaway slave Demetrios Gobinos, who had started a new life as a sausage maker in Philippopolis.[22] Why, asks Tzetzes, does he not return to Constantinople?

> For now, every disgusting and thrice-accursed wretch like you only has to put on a monastic habit, or hang bells from his penis or wrap fetters or chains round his feet, or a rope or chain round his neck — in short to dress himself up to look self-effacing in an ostentatious and highly theatrical way, and put on an artificial and highly calculated air of artless simplicity. Immediately the city of Constantine showers him with honours, and the rogue is publicly feted as a saint above the apostles, above the martyrs, and above whatever is pleasing to God. Why describe in detail the sweetmeats and delicacies and tit-

16. Fols. 8-13; *BHG*[3] *Auctarium*, 710c; on Xanthopoulos, see Beck, *Kirche und theologische Literatur*, 705ff.
17. Fol. 58[r].
18. Nos. 14, 55, 57, 104; ed. P.A. Leone, *Ioannis Tzetzae Epistulae* (Leipzig 1972) (hereafter Tzetzes, ed. Leone), 25-7, 75-7, 79-84, 150-2.
19. Commentaries on Canons 42 and 60 of the Council in Trullo: Migne, *PG* 137, 665, 716.
20. Principally the discourse 'On hyprocrisy', ed. T.L.F. Tafel, *Eustathii Opuscula*, 88-98, especially 94ff; but his 'Address to a stylite' (ibid., 182-96) is also in the spirit of a reproof.
21. J.L. Van Dieten, ed., *Nicetae Choniatae Historia* (Berlin-New York 1975), 383, 448-9, 558 (Bonn ed., 498-9, 590-1, 737-8).
22. No. 104: Tzetzes, ed. Leone, 150-2.

bits, the bags of money and the privileges with which the city regales this monster? Leading ladies, and not a few men, of the highest birth consider it a great thing to fit out their private chapels, not with icons of saintly men by the hand of some first-rate artist, but with the leg-irons and fetters and chains of these accursed villains, which they obtain from them after much supplication, and then replace with others.

Secondly, a passage in Eustathios' discourse 'On hypocrisy', citing the example of a hypocritical holy man who had been one of the sights of Constantinople in the reign of John II (1118-43).[23] This monk was a *sidērophoros*, or 'iron-wearer', and stank horribly. His act was to pretend that the irons bit into his flesh and made it come away like sawdust.

Taking animal lights or liver, and mincing it into a greenish-yellow pulp which looked like chewed meat, then smearing it on himself wherever the iron left room, he would receive his audience. After speaking for a short while he would give a slight shudder, as if he were racked by pain. Then inserting his hand where the offal was smeared, he scraped it up and brought his accursed accomplice to light. And groaning painfully, 'My flesh!', he discreetly flicked it off, so that some of the vile stuff fell to the ground, already reeking heavily of decay, while the rest remained under his nails. Washing this off in a filthy torrent, he caused great wonderment to those who were not yet wise to him — this man who really did deserve to be devoured in this world, as well as by the worms of the next.

Why were Tzetzes, Eustathios, and others so critical of contemporary holy men? Is there a connection between their criticisms and the 'disappointing' state of contemporary hagiography? If so, what was happening to the institution of the holy man?

A spiritual decline?

There is a simple answer to these questions: the Byzantine Church was in a state of moral and spiritual decline and the quality of monastic life was low. This is the picture which we get from reading Oeconomos' study of Byzantine religious life in the twelfth century, still the most comprehensive treatment of the subject.[24] According to Oeconomos, ecclesiastical government was in disarray and upset by imperial interference, which was, however, curiously unable to check abuses such as episcopal absenteeism. Monasticism was corrupted by too much wealth and too much lay patronage, with a complete breakdown of community discipline. He admits that lay piety was strong, but he sees it as riddled with heresy, astrology, magic and superstition.

Undoubtedly this picture, though dated, contains much of value, and it is relevant to our problem. There is obviously a connection (and Tzetzes indeed

23. *Eustathii Opuscula*, 97.
24. L. Oeconomos, *La vie réligieuse dans l'empire byzantin au temps des Comnènes et des Anges* (Paris 1918). Similar opinions are expressed by Charles Diehl, *La société byzantine à l'époque des Comnènes* (Paris 1929), 42ff, 56-7.

makes it) between the phenomenon of disreputable holy men and the phenomenon of monastic indiscipline, of which many contemporary sources complain,[25] and which, as Kazhdan has pointed out, stands in sharp contrast to the pattern of regulated community life prescribed by monastic typika of the eleventh and twelfth centuries.[26]

But how helpful, or correct, is it to view the disreputable twelfth-century holy man as a symptom of religious decline? Whatever our sources may tell us about the state of the Church, they tell us more immediately about the attitudes of the authors. One man's charlatans were clearly another man's saints. We should therefore consider whether standards were in fact slipping, or whether a section of articulate opinion was becoming more selective and critical in the standards it applied. This consideration is very much to our present point, since Oeconomos' picture of decadence is based largely on the writings of those authors who criticise contemporary holy men. Since we see the holy men, and the Church, through their eyes, we must be sure that we understand their point of view.

Social and professional jealousy

To some extent, the attitudes of the critics are explicable in terms of social and professional jealousy. All were highly educated by contemporary standards, and this affected the way in which at least two of them regarded the contemporary holy man. Eustathios' complaints about the ignorance of Thessalonican monks are well known,[27] and in his discourse 'On hypocrisy' he accuses the hypocritical holy men 'of cultivating silence and reticence, so as to avoid criticism, whereas wise monks — men of letters and men of virtue and initiates of useful learning — project their voices, speaking forcefully, and they adorn their speech, pouring forth inspired allusions like rivers, whose sources are a delight to the cities of God'.[28] Tzetzes complains that the pittance he makes popularising the classics for his noble patrons is nothing to the fortunes which vagrant monks can make selling fruit to noble households at extortionate prices.[29] Clearly, neither author has any time for uneducated holiness,[30] and Tzetzes is bitter that it proves more lucrative than his own

---

25. Tzetzes, ed. Leone, 27, 82; Eustathios, 'Visitations of the monastic life', ed. Tafel, *Eustathii Opuscula*, 214-67, especially 254; P. Gautier, 'Les lettres de Grégoire higumene d'Oxia', *REB* 31 (1973), 214-18. See also the dossier of the scandal of the Vlach women on Mount Athos under Alexios I, ed. P. Meyer, *Die Haupturkunden für die Geschichte der Athos-klöster* (Leipzig 1894), 163-84. Many Athonites used the scandal as an excuse to leave their monasteries and hang about in the towns, including Constantinople (ibid., 69).

26. A.P. Kazhdan, 'Vizantiiskii monastyr' XI-XIIvv. kak sotsial'naia gruppa', *VV* 31 (1971), 48-70. Kazhdan notes that the contrast between corporate ideals and individualistic practice was characteristic of other Byzantine 'microstructures'.

27. *Eustathii Opuscula*, 244-51.

28. ibid., 95.

29. Tzetzes, ed. Leone, 79-84.

30. An attitude which seems to have been at variance with one of the basic tenets of Christian hagiography, that the ascetic, however illiterate, was the true 'philosopher': cf. Theodoret of Cyrrhus, *Historia Religiosa*, ed. P. Canivet-A. Leroy-Molinghen, *Histoire des moines de*

erudition. The sentiments are similar to those of Ptochoprodromos, complaining that his education has not paid off, and that the butcher, the baker, and the candlestick maker all earn a better living.[31]

Education was commonly a means of social advancement,[32] but it was most easily accessible to those who already possessed some financial backing and social standing.[33] Although we know little about the social origins of Eustathios,[34] Balsamon,[35] and Choniates,[36] what Tzetzes tells us about his own ancestry[37] allows us to suppose that all came from comfortably established families. Social as well as intellectual snobbery is implicit in their criticisms of contemporary holy men. Denunciation of monks who did not sincerely renounce the world was probably in effect denunciation of those who had started out with little or nothing to renounce. Tzetzes suggests that the profession of holy man in Constantinople is one that will suit an escaped slave turned sausage-maker. Eustathios condemns holy hypocrites for much the same reason that he criticises banausic folk who enter monasteries in order to engage in trade or agriculture:[38] in either case, they have become monks in order to better themselves socially and economically. Tzetzes despised the holy men about town for the further reason that so many of them were provincials and foreigners. Commenting on the letter addressed to his slave, he writes, 'Cretans and Turks, Alans, Rhodians, and Chiots — all the most thieving and corrupt elements of every race and land — these are the people who are made saints in Constantinople'.[39] The implicit snobbery and explicit xenophobia of the critics

Syrie (Paris 1977-9), *passim* and esp. 297. Compare the words of Eustathios (*Opscula,* 249), 'How can anyone philosophise who has not even a modicum of learning, and has not stooped to consider *spiritual* practice?' with those which Saint Athanasius attributes to Saint Anthony: 'He whose mind is healthy has no need of learning' (*PG* 26.945). Eustathios recommends that monks should be versed in secular as well as religious literature.

31. D.C. Hesseling and H. Pernot, *Poèmes prodromiques en grec vulgaire* (Amsterdam 1910), No. 4.

32. Michael Choniates says that he was regarded as eccentric because he enjoyed learning for its own sake: S. Lampros, *Michael Akominatou tou Chōniatou ta sōzomena* i (Athens 1879), 9ff.

33. See the remarks of I. Ševčenko, 'Society and Intellectual Life in the Fourteenth Century', *XIVᵉ Congrès International d'Études Byzantines* (Bucharest 1971), 7-14; P. Lemerle, *Le premier humanisme byzantin* (Paris 1971), 255ff; R. Browning, 'Literacy in the Byzantine World', *Byzantine and Modern Greek Studies* 4 (1978), 40.

34. See P. Wirth, 'Zu Nikolaos Kataphloros', *ClMed* 21 (1960), 212-14; V. Laurent, 'Kataphloros, patronyme supposé du métropolite de Thessalonique Eustathe', *REB* 20 (1962), 218-21; H. Hunger, *Die hochsprachliche profane Literatur der Byzantiner* (Munich 1978), 428-7.

35. Cf. *In Can. Conc. Chalc.*, 28 (*PG* 137. 488); K. Horna, *WSt* 25 (1903), 166; E. Herman in *DDC* ii. 76-83.

36. J.L. Van Dieten, *Niketas Choniates. Erläuterungen zu den Reden und Briefen nebst einer Biographie* (Berlin 1971), 8ff.

37. Ed. P.A.M. Leone, *Ioannis Tzetzae historiae* (Naples 1968), 190-1; P. Gautier, 'La curieuse ascendance de Jean Tzetzes', *REB* 28 (1970), 207-20.

38. *Eustathii Opuscula,* 96, 223, 251.

39. Ed. Leone, *Ioannis Tzetzae historiae,* Chiliad xiii. 359ff.

appear all the more striking in the light of what a late twelfth-century hagiographer, Theodosios, has to say about the *patris* and *genos* of his subject, Leontios of Jerusalem, who had been a holy fool in the streets of Constantinople at about the time that Tzetzes was writing. It was, of course, a matter of form to say good things about a saint's family and birthplace, but Theodosios insists too much. He writes that the saint's birthplace, Stroumitza, 'does not have a barbarian name like a place that is *mixobarbaros*'. He could not, he says, learn the names of Leontios' parents, but he knew for a fact that they were some of the best people in the town. It is almost as if a man could not be considered holy if he was of low or barbarian origin.[40]

Finally, all our critics were more or less closely connected with the church hierarchy. Eustathios was a patriarchal rhetor then metropolitan of Thessalonica. Balsamon was chartophylax of the Great Church before becoming titular patriarch of Antioch. Tzetzes corresponded freely with bishops and patriarchal officials. Choniates was the brother of a metropolitan, and held Balsamon and Eustathios in high regard.[41] As members or close associates of the episcopate, all were likely to share episcopal misgivings about monks who ignored their bishops and set themselves up as spiritual leaders.[42] Eustathios, a practising bishop, and Balsamon, a canon lawyer, both approached the whole question of monastic abuses as men with a professional interest in the imperial and conciliar legislation which emphasised community life and gave the bishop full authority to discipline the monks in his diocese.[43]

Thus our critics can be seen to have criticised the contemporary holy man from the point of view of men with vested interests — cultural, social, and professional —

40. Makarios Chrysokephalos, op.cit. (n.9 above), 381. Base and alien origins were common material for *psogos*: cf. A. Garzya, 'Una declamazione giudizaria di Niceforo Basilace', *Epetēris Hetaireias Byzantinōn Spoudōn* 36 (1968), 92-3.
41. Choniates, ed. Van Dieten, 216, 307-8, 406 (Bonn ed., 282, 399-400, 531).
42. In a society where monks not only became spiritual fathers of novices, but also regularly heard the confessions of laymen, there was a real danger that those with a reputation for sanctity might usurp or undermine the role of the bishop. See for example the letter which Nikephoros, ex-chartophylax of the Great Church, sent to Theodosios, a recluse in Corinth, in reply to certain confessional and penitential questions which the latter had asked: ed. P. Gautier, *REB* 27 (1969), 170f. Nikephoros expresses his reluctance to pronounce on these matters without the authorisation of the local bishop, and he advises Theodosios that 'the right and proper thing for you to do is to ask the bishop of Corinth and learn from him, and do nothing for the salvation of souls without his knowledge, neither hearing confessions nor absolving penitents without his permission'. Eustathios thought that hypocritical holy men were motivated largely by the desire to acquire spiritual children (*Opuscula*, 96).
43. See in particular *Eustathii Opuscula*, 247-8, 260; Balsamon, *In Can. xlv Con. in Trullo* (*PG* 137. 674): 'It seems to me that all who violate the canons in the judgement of the local bishop are to be punished'. The principal legislation regarding the regulation and episcopal supervision of monastic communities is the following: Canons 4, 8, 24 of Chalcedon; Canons 40-7 of the Council in Trullo; Justinian, Novels 123 and 133, incorporated in *Basilica* IV.

whose value was threatened by competition from outsiders who did not play by the rules. That such complaints are heard in the twelfth century, and not earlier, is perhaps understandable if we accept that this was the age when Byzantine urban expansion reached its peak, and Constantinople was attracting immigrants as never before.[44]

The rejection of a pattern?

Having said this, we have still not explained the criticisms. Were these directed simply at the perversion of certain ascetic models, or were they aimed at the models as such?

The long eulogy of asceticism with which Eustathios introduces his 'Visitation of the monastic life' is no doubt sincere and representative, but it is clear that for him, as for Balsamon and for Tzetzes, asceticism was best practised in a strictly regulated community.[45] Eustathios pretends that he can see the point of being a stylite, but only once does he make favourable mention of solitary asceticism,[46] and among his hagiographical homilies, I know of only one celebration of an ascetic saint.[47] Balsamon and Choniates drop direct hints that they had their doubts about the value of the holy man as an institution. Balsamon, in his commentary on canon 60 of the Council in Trullo condemning 'those who simulate demonic frenzy for gain', writes as follows:[48]

> As I see many such wandering the towns and not being punished, but actually welcomed as saints by some, I want to know the reason, and I demand reform. Out of ignorance, I put the late Staurakios Oxeobaphos, who feigned foolishness for Christ's sake, among the hypocrites, because there are so many deceivers, even though he was really genuine. Such practices should be prohibited by the 'force of this canon, in order that the good may not suffer through the fault of the bad. There are many means to salvation of the soul, and one may be saved by them without scandal. I say this not as a matter of personal opinion, but on the basis of what good men have told me, who

44. D. Jacoby, 'La population de Constantinople à l'époque byzantine: un problème de démographie urbaine', *Byzantion* 31 (1961), 81, 107; P. Tivčev, 'Sur les cités byzantines aux XIᵉ-XIIᵉ siècles', *Byzantinobulgarica* 1 (1962), 145-82; M.F. Hendy, 'Byzantium, 1081-1204: 'An Economic Reappraisal', *Transactions of the Royal Historical Society* (1970), 31-52.

45. *Eustathii Opuscula*, 224, 227, 254.

46. In 'Visitation of the Monastic life', *Eustathii Opuscula*, 234. 54-9. These remarks seem to contradict what the author says in 'On hypocrisy' (ibid., 94), 'I see few pillars of ascetic fire shining among us, but myriad examples of hypocritical darkness'. It should be noted, however, that Eustathios aimed the 'Visitation' at the monks of his diocese, Thessalonica, and was trying to depict them as boorish provincials who did not live up to the standards of the metropolis. Whether he said this for rhetorical effect, or whether he believed it to be true, it is plain that he wrote the work for imperial consumption, and that the emperor of the day was Isaac II, who as Choniates tells us had great reverence for the holy men of Constantinople (ed. Van Dieten, 383). Combine *Opuscula*, 241. 60-1, with ibid., 230. 62-3.

47. Encomium of St Philotheos Opsikianos: *Eustathii Opuscula*, 145-51.

48. *PG* 137. 716.

adopted that way of life as one supposedly pleasing to God, but gave it up as dangerous and leading to perdition.[49] For this reason many holy patriarchs arrested many of the chained anchorites who squatted in the church of Saint Niketas, along with others who roamed the streets and faked demonic frenzy, and locked them up in public gaols in accordance with the canon.

Choniates, in his account of Branas' rebellion (1187) which threatened to overthrow Isaac II, says that Isaac asked the stylites and other holy men of Constantinople to pray for him. While he does not venture the opinion that Isaac was wasting his time, he implies it by pointing out that it was the practical measures advised by Conrad of Montferrat which saved the day.[50] Similarly, while indicating that Isaac's fall in 1195 was correctly prophesied by a frenzied holy man, Basil, at Raidestos, he has nothing but contempt for this man and the clientele he attracted.[51]

Even when the holy man is genuine, therefore, the critics are not impressed. Their attitude seems not unlike that of Gregory of Tours and the sixth-century Gallic bishops who put a stop to the career of a promising stylite near Trier, ordering him to come down and destroying his column, because, as Gregory has them say, 'This life you are living is not normal (aequa), nor can you, ignoble one, hope to imitate Symeon of Antioch, who sat on a pillar'.[52] Compare Eustathios: 'A few great stylites are recorded among the saints of old, sky-climbers who reached heaven by using pillars for ladders. But this generation sprouts the stylite kind like trees in a forest, and these are not trees of life or trees of knowledge, but very mean little trees indeed [. . .]'.[53] The basic assumptions seem to be the same. Saints who are larger than life belong to folklore, not the real world. Monks should live in communities, avoid extremes, and be responsible citizens. A dead holy man, whose holiness can be verified according to objective criteria, is preferable to a live one, whose eccentricities only confuse the issue.

Some twelfth-century Byzantines were thus coming close to rejecting an important part of their inherited religious tradition, and adopting a position which had long been conventional in the West. Indeed, Balsamon, although no admirer of the Latins, had to recognise that Benedictine monasticism was closer to canonical tradition than the looser patterns of monastic organisation now followed by the Greeks.[54]

49. It is likely that Leontios of Jerusalem was one of these: he had for a time been a holy fool in Constantinople and Balsamon would have had plenty of opportunity to meet him when he returned to the city later in his career: see Makarios Chrysokephalos, op.cit. (n.9 above), 383-4, 412-3, 426-31.

50. Choniates, ed. Van Dieten, 383 (Bonn ed., 498-9); cf. Hunger, *Die hochsprachliche profane, Literatur* i.440: 'Bemerkenswert scheint mir die durchaus unbyzañtinische Einstellung des Geschichtsschreibers zum Mönchtum'.

51. Choniates, ed. Van Dieten, 448-9 (Bonn ed., 590-1).

52. *Historia Francorum*, viii, 15: *MGH ScriptRerMerov* (1951), 382-3; cf. H. Delehaye, *Les saints stylites* (SubsHag 14 [1923]), cxlii-iii; Brown, 'Eastern and Western Christendom in Late Antiquity', 16.

53. *Eustathii Opuscula*, 97.

54. *In Can. xlviii Conc. Carthag.: PG* 138.176, with reference to Justinian, Novel 123 (*Basilica* IV.1.4); cr. Kazhdan, 'Vizantiiskii monastyr'', 54.

The status of the critics

It is now necessary to establish whether the critics spoke only for themselves, or whether they in any sense represented an official point of view.

In general, Byzantine ecclesiastical opinion of this period would not seem to have favoured the idea that contemporary monks could or should emulate the great ascetic saints of the past. The compilation of the Metaphrastic corpus and the Synaxarion of Constantinople, and the opposition aroused by Symeon the New Theologian in his attempt to establish a cult of his spiritual father Symeon the Studite, indicate that the official Church was tending, from the end of the tenth century, to conceive of the communion of saints as a closed society, whose numbers were now more or less complete.[55]

As we have noted, all our authors had close connections with the ecclesiastical hierarchy, and two of them can be said to have written on its behalf. Eustathios was not only metropolitan of the Empire's second city, but also Manuel I's most accomplished propagandist.[56] Balsamon, a patriarchal official and then a titular patriarch, undertook his life's work of clarifying the corpus of canon law at the request of Manuel and the patriarch Michael of Anchialos (1170-8).[57] Such authors are hardly likely to have committed to writing opinions offensive to the establishment, especially at a time when the establishment was only too ready to take offence. Their writings echo the insistence on community life to be found in twelfth-century monastic typika.[58] Their complaints about spurious holy men are in keeping with the repressive ideological climate which set in with Alexios I, and can be seen in the same context as the measures which Comnenian patriarchs and synods took to suppress heresy, intellectual speculation, and pagan survivals.[59] John Italos, Basil the Bogomil, Theodore Blachernites, Constantine Chrysomallos, Soterichos

55. Delehaye, *Saints stylites*, cxv-cxvi; Beck, *Kirche und theologische Literatur*, 271, 273; Nikétas Stéthatos, *Vie de Syméon le Nouveau Théologien*, ed. I. Hausherr and G. Horn, (*OC* 12 [1928]), 98ff.

56. Despite his disagreement with Manuel over the emperor's proposal to upgrade the Muslim deity (Choniates, 216-8), he pronounced several official speeches for Manuel, as well as his funeral oration: for references, see Hunger, *Die hochsprachliche profane Literatur*, i.126, 136, 148.

57. Preface to his commentary on the *Nomocanon*: PG 104. 976-7.

58. E.G. L. Petit, 'Typikon du monastère de la Kosmosotira', *Izvestiia Russakago Arkheologicheskago Instituta v Konstantinopole* 13 (1908), 6, 29, 31; P. Gautier, 'Le typikon du Christ Sauveur Pantokrator', *REB* 32 (1974), 63. However, as Kazhdan points out ('Vizantiiskii monastyr'', 55) the only evidence for communal dormitories in this period comes from the *typikon* of a nunnery, which confirms Balsamon's statement that in Byzantium only nuns kept to the canonically required eating and sleeping arrangements (n.54 above).

59. See, in general, R. Browning, 'Enlightenment and Repression in Byzantium in the Eleventh and Twelfth Centuries', *Past and Present* 69 (1975), 3-23. According to Anna Komnena, Alexios I and his mother introduced a new moral austerity into the palace: Anna Comnène, *Alexiade*, ed. B. Leib (Paris 1937-45), i.125; ii.37-8. The patriarch Luke Chrysoberges (1157-70) put an end to what was no doubt a long standing custom of pagan origin by forbidding the masques which accompanied the celebration of the feast of the Holy Notaries: Balsamon, *In Can. lxii Conc. in Trullo* (PG 137. 732).

Panteugenos and others;[60] the Life of a Saint Paraskeuē written by a layman —
presumably in 'low' style — which the patriarch Nicholas Mouzalon (1147-51) ordered
to be burned:[61] all had one feature in common with each other and with the un-
authorised holy man. All offered alternatives to the services provided by the sacer-
dotal hierarchy, and all therefore had to be brought in line by the bishop, the
emperor, and the law. As the patriarch Leo Stypes put it in the preface to the
synodal act condemning Chrysomallos, 'How can one excuse those who just decide,
without approval or consecration, to become healers of souls, teachers of a way of
life, exponents and authors of proper learning, or, in some cases, dogmatists?'[62]

But was there still not a case for the authorised holy man and the authorised
saint's Life? Clearly there was: Alexios I used Christodoulos as an instrument of
monastic reform,[63] and favoured the ascetic enterprises of other holy men, whose
hagiography has a highly official flavour. The biographers of Hosios Meletios were a
leading theologian and a poet laureate at the court of Manuel I; the biographer of
Cyril Phileotes was one of the monks hand picked by Manuel to staff his new model
monastery of Kataskepe, and Cyril is made to deliver a long tirade against vagrant
monks which would certainly have pleased Balsamon.[64]

The role of Manuel I

However, we should note that in the surviving literature there is no biography of a holy man whom Manuel I encouraged to found a new monastery,
and also that criticism of the contemporary holy man begins in his reign. This
may be significant in view of the fact that Manuel's religious policy differed from

60. On these and other 'dissidents' of the Comnenian period, see J. Gouillard, 'Le Synodikon
de l'Orthodoxie: édition et commentaire', *TM* 2 (1967), 183-237; 'Constantin Chrysomallos sous le masque de Syméon le Nouveau Théologien', *TM* 5 (1973), 313-7; id.,
'Quatre procès de mystiques à Byzance (vers 960-1143)', *REB* 36 (1978), 5-81: in these
last two works, Gouillard shows that the teachings of Chrysomallos regarding the suffi-
ciency of Baptism, which were posthumously condemned in 1143, did not differ greatly
from those which the orthodox, and influential, Symeon the New Theologian had ex-
pounded over a century earlier.

61. Balsamon, *In Can. lxiii Conc. in Trullo: PG* 137. 733: 'The most holy late patriarch Kyr
Nicholas Mouzalon, finding that the Life of Saint Paraskeuē, who is honoured in the
village of Kallikrateia, had been written by some villager in an amateurish way inappropriate to the angelic life-style of the saint, ordered it to be consigned to the fire'. It would
be interesting to know what made a piece of hagiography unacceptable to the church
authorities, whether in the seventh or in the twelfth century. Balsamon seems to imply
that the Life of Saint Paraskeuē was *stylistically* unsuitable, and the fact that he remarks
earlier in the same passage, 'thanks be to the blessed Metaphrastes who with much toil and
sweat adorned the martyr acts for the sake of truth', further suggests that hagiography was
authorised according to style. It is worth noting, however, that Symeon was considered to
have improved not only the style but also the content of the Lives (of ascetics as well as
martyrs) which he rewrote: Michael Psellos, *Scripta minora*, ed. E. Kurtz and F. Drexl, i
(Milan 1936), 100.

62. Ed. Gouillard, *REB* 36 (1978), 68.

63. Vranouse, *Hagiologika keimena*, 128-39.

64. Ed. Sargologos, 112-7.

that of Alexios in three important respects. Firstly, he exalted the authority of the emperor in doctrinal matters to Justinianic heights.[65] Secondly, he looked after the material interests of the empire's bishoprics to an extent for which there was no recent precedent: besides the evidence of his chrysobull *later* and imperial orations, there are specific mentions of benefactions to the sees of Athens, Thessalonica, Kroja, Corfu, Selymbria, and Stagoi in Thessaly.[66] Thirdly, Manuel made a point of going against the traditional monastic patronage of his predecessors and his family. While not ungenerous to monasteries, particularly those in the neighbourhood of Constantinople, he encouraged the restoration of old monasteries as opposed to the foundation of new ones, and he enforced the principle if not the letter of Nikephoros II's legislation limiting the growth of monastic properties. He did found one new monastery, that of Kataskepe, but according to Choniates he founded it in deliberate reaction to the type of family foundation that other Komnenoi, including his father, had favoured: it was not to be a family mausoleum, it was well away from Constantinople, and it was supported by state subsidies rather than endowments.[67]

Manuel's ecclesiastical policy was not just a matter of reform. It was part of a large effort to create an imperial image and an imperial programme, which, although they grew out of the Comnenian revival, took this one stage further.[68] The Comnenian system as created by Alexios I was essentially aristocratic, and emphasised the imperial clan rather than the person of the emperor. Manuel worked within the system, but demonstrably tried to make the person of the emperor stand out among the ever-increasing crowd of privileged and prestigious imperial relatives. His imperial image-building was carried out partly in order to steal the thunder from his international rivals, especially the Sicilian kings and Frederick Barbarossa, but it was also for domestic consumption, and aimed at overcoming the intense competition which Manuel faced from his brother, uncle, and cousins.[69] In

65. Choniates, ed. Van Dieten, 210ff (Bonn ed., 274). The style of Manuel's 'caesaropapism' is admirably conveyed by the *ekthesis* and especially the edict which he published after the council of 1166: see C. Mango, 'The Conciliar Edict of 1166', *DOP* 17 (1963), 317-30.

66. On Manuel's policy with regard to ecclesiastical landowners, see in general N. Svoronos, 'Les privilèges de l'église à l'époque des Comnènes: un rescrit inédit de Manuel Ier Comnène', *TM* 1 (1965), 329-91, reprinted in his *Études sur l'organisation intérieure, la société et l'économie de l'empire byzantin* (London 1973). For Manuel's benefactions to bishoprics, see ibid., 328-9, 360-5 and the sources cited there; also the following: John Staurakios, ed. Ioakeim Iberites, *Makedonika* 1 (1940), 368-9; P. Magdalino, 'Byzantine Churches of Selymbria', *DOP* 32 (1978), 311-3. Svoronos argues that until about 1160, Manuel pursued a policy of indiscriminate generosity to the Church, after which he tended to favour the lay establishment at the Church's expense. This analysis is useful, providing the following points are taken into consideration: (1) the evidence does not allow one to assume that *all* Manuel's benefactions to bishoprics were made early in his reign; (2) it is misleading to treat 'the Church' as a single entity, without due regard for the division of interest between bishoprics and many monasteries — a division which was in some ways deeper than that between monasteries and the laity.

67. Eustathios, *Opuscula*, 207. 85ff; Choniates, ed. Van Dieten, 206-8 (Bonn ed., 270-2); Balsamon, *In Can. ii Conc. C'pol.* (*PG* 137. 1012); Svornos, *TM* 1 (1965), 379-81.

68. I intend to deal more fully elsewhere with the question of Manuel's imperial 'style'.

69. Choniates, ed. Van Dieten, 32, 48-9, 101ff, 138-46 (Bonn ed., 42-3, 65-6, 133ff, 180-9); John Cinnamus (Bonn ed.), 26-7, 31-2, 53-4, 126-30, 265ff.

view of Manuel's great need to rise above and dominate his kin, it is perhaps possible to see in the quirks of his religious policy a consistent attempt to play up those elements in the Byzantine religious tradition where only the emperor was supreme, and to play down those others where influential laymen could dominate, and which might then become foci of disaffection.[70] If this was indeed the pattern, the urban holy man, like the endowed urban monastery, was an element to be played down. He might be an instrument of imperial policy, but since he derived his charisma independently of the imperially dominated hierarchy, and could enjoy great influence as father of a spiritual 'family', he was potentially a subversive weapon in the hands of ambitious princes of the blood, and it might be prudent to discourage him altogether.[71]

I conclude, therefore, that what Tzetzes, Eustathios, Balsamon and Choniates have to say about contemporary holy men does not reflect a qualitative change in Byzantine monasticism, nor does it merely reflect the authors' personal and professional distaste for a social phenomenon that has got out of hand; it reflects an increasing official intolerance of the holy man's kind of holiness, which became most acute in Manuel's reign. The evidence is open to other interpretations. The one I have adopted perhaps helps to make sense of the two basic contradictions which the evidence presents: the fact that the holy man was at the same time assiduously cultivated by the court aristocracy and openly criticised by establishment intellectuals, and the fact that the cenobitic ideal was so strongly encouraged and yet so consistently ignored.

70. The fourteenth-century Western crusading propagandist William Adam (Pseudo-Brocardus) remarked that private religious foundations in Constantinople tended to serve as meeting places for conspiratorial gatherings: *Recueil des Historiens des Croisades: Documents latins et français relatifs à l'Arménie* ii (Paris 1906), 475.

71. As a potentially subversive, centrifugal association, the spiritual 'family' concerned the emperor as much as it did the bishop (see n.42 above). The natural affinity between the holy man and the court aristocrat is evident not only from what Tzetzes has to say about his *bêtes-noires,* but also from the Life of Leontios of Jerusalem, who was introduced to Manuel by the *megas droungarios* Andronikos Kamateros: see Makarios Chrysokephalos, op.cit. (n.9 above), 412: D. Polemis, *The Doukai* (London 1968), 126-7. See also the dossier of the Athonite scandal of Alexios I's reign: the devil succeeded in ensnaring not only the undesirables of the mountain, but through them 'great and holy men who come near to God [. . .] and do not be amazed if some have fallen away [. . .] though they be rhetors and learned men, and even from the palace' (Meyer, *Die Haupturkunden,* 175). The importance of the holy man as a political prophet is illustrated by the case of Cyril Phileotes, who under Michael VII (1071-8) prophesied to Anna Dalassena, mother of Alexios I, that she would see 'the sons of your sons, and your children, rule cities and nations' (ed. Sargologos, 90ff). This prediction of the successful usurpation which brought the Comnenian dynasty to power adds to the quasi-official character of the work. It also demonstrates that Manuel had every reason for not wanting the holy men of his day to enjoy Cyril's reputation and success.

The relationship between the tensions in the Comnenian court and the religious movements and ideological crises of twelfth-century Byzantium remain to be explored, although a useful start has been made by D. Gress-Wright, 'Bogomilism in Constantinople', *Byzantion* 47 (1977), 163-85. On centrifugal trends in this period, see the papers of H. Ahrweiler and A.P. Kazhdan delivered at the XVth International Congress of Byzantine Studies (Athens 1976).

What is certain is that the 'brilliant, fragile, delicate and empty civilisation' of the reign of Manuel Komnenos[72] was an important stage in the development of Byzantine religious life. Of course, Manuel was only one emperor, and his imperial programme rapidly collapsed after his death. Yet the effects of a strenuous, sustained, all-embracing governmental effort such as Manuel's do not end with that government or the failure of its policies: indeed it may take a generation or even two for them to be felt. From 1180 to 1204 and even longer, the Byzantine world was dominated by rulers, intellectuals, values, and habits formed at the court of Manuel Komnenos. This is something to bear in mind when evaluating the society which was dismembered by the Fourth Crusade. As far as we are concerned that society is remarkable not only for its lack of recorded ascetic saints, but also because it has left evidence for four exemplary Byzantine bishops: Eustathios, Michael Choniates, John Apokaukos and Demetrios Chomatenos — men who combined a high degree of metropolitan refinement and worldly sophistication with a conscientious devotion to duty. They emerge from their writings as humane, balanced, effective spiritual leaders of their flocks in a difficult period when secular government was more a hindrance than a help. It says a great deal for the state of the episcopate in the aftermath of Manuel's reign that the bishop could do so much to pick up the pieces of provincial administration.[73]

The holy man below the surface

With the wisdom of hindsight, we can see that the bishop never stood a chance against the holy man, especially in a society where the two categories frequently overlapped. For every bishop who had studied law or rhetoric to a high level was at least one who had come straight from a monastery. All Byzantines had a soft spot for a holy man. Manuel I himself was responsible for appointing to the see of Jerusalem a one-time holy fool who had gone on to become a monk at Patmos, there to practise self-flagellation and a peculiar form of asceticism which involved weeping naked in the coffins of dead monks.[74] Isaac II, as we have seen, went straight to the stylites of Constantinople in time of political trouble. The holy man was only just below the surface, and when circumstances permitted he again emerged as a saint. Yet it is worth noting that this did not happen for a long time; the thirteenth century was not, on the whole, an age of Greek saints.[75] Even the

72. Browning, 'Enlightenment and Repression', 23.
73. The episcopal careers of these authors still await comprehensive, and comparative, analysis. For Eustathios, see in addition to the bibliography cited above (n.34), S. Kyriakides, ed., *La espugnazione di Tessalonica* (Palermo 1961). For Michael Choniates: Judith Herrin, 'Realities of Byzantine Provincial Government: Hellas and Peloponnesos, 1180-1205', *DOP* 29 (1975), 255-84, esp. 258-66. For Apokaukos and Chomatenos: D.M. Nicol, *The Despotate of Epiros, 1204-1261* (Oxford 1957), 217-9; id., 'Refugees, mixed population and local patriotism in Epiros and Western Macedonia after the Fourth Crusade', *XVe Congrès International d'Études Byzantines* (Athens 1976), *Rapports* i.2. On Apokaukos see also N.A. Bees (Veis) and E. Seferli-Vei, *BNJbb* 21 (1975).
74. Makarios Chrysokephalos, op.cit., (n.9 above), 390-1.
75. Beck, *Kirche und theologische Literatur*, 697; see also Dr Ruth Macrides' paper below.

events of 1204 did not, apparently, cause the Byzantines of the diaspora to turn to the holy man for comfort; instead, they got on with the job of restoring their empire. It was only after the disappointments of Michael VIII's reign, when it became apparent that the restored empire was not going to work, that the initiative passed from the bureaucratic to the ascetic elite. In the meantime, educated Byzantines had learned to live without the holy man. Not all of them wanted him back on his own terms.[76]

76. On the holy man in the Palaiologan period, see D.M. Nicol, 'Hilarion of Didymoteichon and the Gift of Prophecy', *Byzantine Studies/Études Byzantines* 5. 1-2 (1978), 186-200; id., *Church and Society in the last centuries of Byzantium* (Cambridge 1979), 31-65. Nicol rightly points out that whether late Byzantines sought the 'inner' or the 'outer' wisdom, they were alike in their elitism, but he himself cites evidence which shows that all was not well between the two elites: see *Church and Society*, 51-2; 'Hilarion of Didymoteichon', 197 n.12. The hostility became open as a result of the hesychast controversy. Demetrios Kydones criticises the extremist monks of fourteenth-century Constantinople in language reminiscent of Tzetzes and Eustathios and of contemporary Western propaganda: ed. G. Mercati. *Notizie di Procoro e Demetrio Cidone*, ST 56 (1931), 335-6; cf. Pseudo-Brocardus, op.cit. (n.70 above), 470.

Saints and Sainthood in the Early Palaiologan Period*

RUTH MACRIDES

A LONG with other aspects of pre-1204 society that Byzantium of the thirteenth century inherited was its attitude towards the holy man.[1] The 'cosmic cataclysm'[2] of 1204 did not, it seems, create an environment in which the holy man's gifts were sought. This state of affairs is reflected in the fact that the little hagiography which exists from the thirteenth century draws on figures from the distant past as its subject.[3] Two exceptions to this statement are eloquent evidence for the paucity of any real hagiography for the period. The learned monk Nikephoros Blemmydes took it upon himself to ensure that his virtues did not go unnoticed by writing his own Life.[4] His disciples in the monastery which he founded evidently were not moved to do so themselves. In the late thirteenth century Constantine Akropolites wrote an encomium for St John the Almsgiver, the Younger, a monk who had lived in the empire of Nicaea, about whom Constantine had information at second hand. According to him, John was an obscure figure and he remains so after the author has finished his work.[5] In fact, the encomium tells us more above its author's habits of 'collecting' saints to write up,[6] than it does about the practice of asceticism in the empire of Nicaea.

If these examples are representative of ascetics in the Nicaean empire then it would appear that the holy man did not occupy an important place in the society

---

* An enlarged version of the paper ('Anti-Palaiologan Saints') read at the Birmingham Symposium.

1. See P. Magdalino, 'The Byzantine Holy Man in the Twelfth Century', above.
2. J. Darrouzès, 'Les Discours d'Euthyme Tornikès (1200-1205)', *REB* 26 (1978), 82-3.
3. See H.G. Beck, *Kirche und theologische Literatur im byzantinischen Reich* (Munich, 1959), 271-2; 685-6; 698-9; 700-1; A. Guillou, 'Les Poids des Conditions materielles, sociales et économiques sur la production culturelle à Byzance de 1071 à 1261', *XVe Congrès International d'études byzantines* (Athens 1976), Rapports ii.3.
4. See J. Munitiz, 'Self-canonisation: the "Partial Account" of Nikephoros Blemmydes', below.
5. D.I. Polemis, 'The Speech of Constantine Akropolites on St John Merciful the Young', *AnalBoll* 91 (1973), 31-54..
6. See Constantine's own comment with regard to his hagiographical interests in Polemis, op.cit., 52-3; see also a list of his hagiographical works in H. Delehaye, 'Constantini Acropolitae Hagiographi Byzantini epistularum manipulus', *AnalBoll* 51 (1933), 263-8; D.M. Nicol, 'Constantine Akropolites, A Prosopographical Note', *DOP* 19 (1965), 245-6.

which was working towards the reconquest of Constantinople.[7] This situation is all the more impressive when it is compared with that of the fourteenth century, a period in which hagiography flourished and the ascetic was much in evidence as prophet, adviser and leading figure in ecclesiastical controversies.[8] The striking difference in the status of the holy man in these periods leads one to ask who, if anyone, took the place of the ascetic in the thirteenth century, and what conditions brought him back in the fourteenth.

While the reconquest of Constantinople was the raison d'être of the states which were created after 1204, and of Nicaea in particular,[9] in the more than fifty years of life in 'exile' an alternative existence was created in Asia Minor, one whose strength lay in the men who filled the imperial office, the Laskaris family.[10] But when the goal was achieved and Constantinople retaken, it was not a Laskarid but the founder of a new dynasty, Michael Palaiologos, who won the capital. He was an usurper who upset the existing order, neglecting Asia Minor and leaving behind the legitimate heir to the throne.[11]

It was during Michael Palaiologos' reign and his successors' that saints reappear. But they do not have the face of the holy man. Instead they are figures from the civil and ecclesiastical hierarchy, the emperors John III Batatzes, John IV Laskaris, and the patriarch Arsenios, men who represented the right order, as it had existed in Asia Minor before the Palaiologoi. To these names should be added those of the patriarch Joseph and the monk Meletios who defended orthodoxy in opposition to Michael VIII's policy of union with Rome. These men were not especially remembered for any ascetic qualities they may have had. More dominant and significant in the recognition of their sainthood and in the creation of their 'cults' was their use as symbols of anti-Palaiologan resistance. The histories of each of these men, how they came to be considered saints, by whom and why, are commentaries on the failure of the Palaiologoi to command the loyalty of their subjects, a failure which led to the Church's take-over in leadership and the return of the ascetic in the late thirteenth century.

7.   I exclude from discussion cases such as that of Germanos (c. 1252-1336); although he lived during the period of the Latin occupation, he belongs more to the world of his biographer, the patriarch Philotheos. See P. Joannou, 'Vie de S. Germain l'Hagiorite par son contemporain le patriarche Philothée de Constantinople', *AnalBoll* 70 (1952), 35ff. esp. 38-40; Beck, *Kirche*, 723ff.

8.   Beck, *Kirche*, 272; D.M. Nicol, 'Hilarion of Didymoteichon and the Gift of Prophecy', *Byzantine Studies/Études Byzantines* 5 (1978), 186ff; A.E. Laiou-Thomadakis, 'Saints and Society in the Late Byzantine Empire', in *Charanis Studies, Essays in Honor of Peter Charanis*, ed. A.E. Laiou-Thomadakis (New Brunswick 1980), 84ff.

9.   See H. Ahrweiler, *L'idéologie politique de l'empire byzantin* (Paris 1975), 107-11.

10.   M. Angold, *A Byzantine government in exile* [. . .] (Oxford 1975), *passim*; S. Vryonis Jr., *The Decline of Medieval Hellenism in Asia Minor and the Process of Islamization from the Eleventh through the Fifteenth Century* (Berkeley-London 1971), 219-20.

11.   H. Ahrweiler, 'L'Expérience Nicéene, *DOP* 29 (1975), 23-40; D.J. Geanakoplos, *Emperor Michael Palaeologus and the West* (Cambridge 1959), 33ff.

John the Almsgiver

Of all the thirteenth century saints, John III Batatzes (1222-54), son-in-law of the first emperor at Nicaea, Theodore Laskaris, has the longest history of veneration. Heisenberg noted that at the turn of this century his memory was celebrated in the region of Magnesia, the place of his burial, and his name still appears today in the calendar of the Greek Orthodox Church (4 November).[12] By piecing together the available sources it is possible to reconstruct the stages by which his reputation as a saint was created.

In his lifetime John was noted for his generosity; indeed, so much so that like his namesake, the seventh century patriarch of Alexandria, he was called 'the Almsgiver'. According to a late fourteenth century encomium of the emperor, John was given this epithet in his lifetime.[13] A statement by Pachymeres suggests that the people of Lydia referred to him as such by the late thirteenth century.[14]

Eleēmosynē is one of the virtues which every *philanthropōs basileus* was expected to possess. Encomia for emperors include some reference to this quality while treatises on kingship list it as a primary virtue. But the testimony of more than one source indicates that John's *eleos* went beyond the conventional. Stories about the emperor's generosity in providing for his subjects have a legendary ring to them. The emperor founded churches, hospitals, orphanages, old-age homes, and still left reserves in the treasury and piles of provisions heaped high in towers.[15] Money for these foundations was not squeezed from the people but amassed by the emperor's careful management. Pachymeres tells us that on one occasion when the emperor was ill and could not obtain help from doctors, in imitation of God's *eleos* he gave sacks of gold coins to the needy. The emperor asked the patriarch to testify to the fact that the money was not from the public treasury but from the emperor's own savings.[16]

But Batatzes' compassion for his subjects would not seem to have been enough by itself to have created his reputation as a saint. It would seem rather that events after his death kept his memory alive and were formative in the creation of his cult.

The first miracle associated with him, which occurred near his burial place almost fifty years after his death, illustrates this point. The empire was then in the hands of Andronikos II, son of Michael VIII. The lands which had formed the empire of Nicaea had been declining in prosperity under the Palaiologoi. Lydia, the heart of Batatzes' empire, was under attack from the Turks. In 1302, Andronikos'

12. A. Heisenberg, 'Kaiser Johannes Batatzes der Barmherzige', *BZ* 14 (1905), 192; S. Eustratiades, *Hagiologion tes Orthodoxes Ekklesias* (Athens n.d.), 229.

13. Heisenberg, op.cit., 231, 27-9.

14. Pachymeres, Bonn ed. (1839), ii.401.19-402. 2.

15. Theodore Skoutariotes, 'Additamentum ad Georgii Acropolitae Historiam' in A. Heisenberg, *Georgii Acropolitae Opera* i (Leipzig 1903), 284-8; Gregoras, Bonn ed. (1828-55), i.42; 44-5; Pachymeres, i.68.6-69.2; Heisenberg, 'Kaiser Johannes Batatzes der Barmherzige', 231. 231.

16. Pachymeres, i. 70-1.

son and co-emperor made an attempt to repel the enemy at Magnesia on the Hermos but he abandoned the fight, leaving the town in the hands of others. One night as the watchmen were going their rounds they saw a lighted torch on the walls and then a man dressed as an emperor who announced that he was in charge of the garrison. People identified the man in this vision as John the Almsgiver whose protection God had given them.[17] The Palaiologoi had failed them but their emperor John who had provided for them in the past returned to defend them.

Thus, events of the late thirteenth century created a situation in which subjects of a Palaiologos looked to John III as a protector and substitute emperor. His memory was kept alive in these circumstances. When the Turks took over the region, his relic was moved to Magnesia. According to the author of the 'Life of the emperor John the Almsgiver', John's relic was still in Magnesia at the time of his writing (1365-70) and was a source of healing.[18]

While the faithful of Asia Minor in the fourteenth century and later put their hopes in the emperor John and looked upon his relic as a source of miracles, for members of the ecclesiastical hierarchy in other parts of the empire John Batatzes' name came to be used to evoke an image of the ideal emperor. Thus, the patriarch Kallistos (1350-3; 1355-63), in his 'Life of Gregory of Sinai', considered it 'fitting and proper' to compare the munificence of the Bulgarian ruler Ivan Alexander to that of 'the holy emperor John Batatzes'.[19] He could find no better nor more recent imperial example.

For another fourteenth century writer, George bishop of Pelagonia, Batatzes was a model emperor to be held up as an example to rulers of his own time. In his 'Life of the emperor John the Almsgiver' which is essentially an encomium,[20] the author contrasts each virtue John III possessed with the vices of contemporary rulers. Even John's accession to the throne as a son-in-law of a reigning emperor and not as a blood heir is an advantage. The author labours the point that heirs to the throne do not necessarily make good emperors. Indeed, they are more often than not 'corrupted by luxury, servile flattery, empty bombast, moral turpitude and disgraceful indolence'.[21] It is noteworthy that even in the late fourteenth century remembrance of the emperor John's reign could be a context for expressing disapproval of contemporary rulers, descendants of Michael Palaiologos.

17. Pachymeres, ii. 400-2; A.E. Laiou, *Constantinople and the Latins* (Cambridge Mass. 1972), 90-1.
18. Heisenberg, 'Kaiser Johannes Batatzes der Barmherzige', 232-3.
19. I. Pomialovskii, 'Zhitie izhe vo sviatykh ottsa nashego Grigoriia Sinaita', *Zapiski isotoriko-filologicheskago fakul'teta imperatorskago S. Peterburgskago universiteta* 35 (1896), 41, 16-21. I wish to thank Dr. H.-V. Beyer for calling this passage to my attention.
20. On the work and its author see J. Moravcsik, 'Der Verfasser der Mittelgriechischen Legende von Johannes dem Barmherzigen', *BZ* 27 (1927), 36-9; K. Amantos, 'Ho Bios Ioannou Batatzē tou Eleēmonos', *Prosphora eis Stilpona P. Kyriakidēn* (Thessalonica 1953), 29-34; Beck, *Kirche*, 723.
21. Heisenberg, 'Kaiser Johannes Batatzes der Barmherzige', 194; 196. 19-21; 197.

Although Batatzes' veneration as a saint continued in the region of Magnesia until the twentieth century, his reputation gained wider recognition in the seventeenth, when his name was inserted into the calendar of the patriarchate of Constantinople.[22] Thus, in the emperor John's case, most of the elements one would expect to find in the recognition and celebration of a saint are present: miracles, an encomium or *vita*, liturgical celebration of the saint's memory,[23] and finally, wider acknowledgement of the cult with the insertion of the saint's name into the calendar of the patriarchate.

John Laskaris

The case of John IV Laskaris, Batatzes' grandson, exhibits few of these elements but provides another example of the way in which sainthood could be acknowledged. John IV, son of Theodore II Laskaris and the legitimate heir to the throne in 1258, was blinded by Michael VIII as a young boy and spent at least half his life in confinement in Asia Minor.[24] Although he is rarely mentioned in the sources, his name was connected with revolts and plots against Michael Palaiologos and his son Andronikos.[25] Various anti-Palaiologan parties presented pseudo-Johns to further their claims. Soon after John was blinded in 1261 the people of a village near Nicaea revolted. They found a congenitally blind child and claimed he was John Laskaris their lord, on whose behalf they would fight to the death.[26] Later, in the west, John was said to have escaped from prison and gone to the court of Charles of Anjou, Michael VIII's greatest enemy.[27]

Even after his death (*c.* 1305)[28] John's name was associated with the Palaiologoi,

22. M. Gedeon, *Patriarchikoi Pinakes* (Constantinople 1888), 587-8.

23. Evidence for the liturgical celebration of his memory comes from an unpublished sixteenth century manuscript (cod. Burney 54 f 219v) containing parts of an office for the emperor John the Almsgiver. In this work Batatzes is celebrated for his conversion of the barbarians (Cumans), the healing miracles from his relic and his *eleēmosynē*. See also D.I. Polemis, *The Doukai, A Contribution to Byzantine Prosopography* (London 1968), 108 n.8. For a later office see L. Petit, *Bibliographie des acolouthies grecques* (Brussels 1926), 121.

24. Pachymeres, i. 190.16-192.19; A. Failler, 'La Tradition manuscrite de l'Histoire de Georges Pachymere (Livres I-VI)' *REB* 37 (1979), 154ff; idem., 'Chronologie et composition dans l'Histoire de George Pachymère', *REB* 38 (1980), 74ff; Angold, *A Byzantine government in exile*, 80ff.

25. On the 'Drimys' plot see Pachymeres, ii. 592-3; I. Ševčenko, 'The Imprisonment of Manuel Moschopoulos in the year 1305 or 1306', *Speculum* 27 (1952), 149f.; A.E. Laiou, *Constantinople and the Latins*, 197f. On Glykys see A.-M. Maffry Talbot, *The Correspondence of Athanasius I Patriarch of Constantinople* (Washington DC 1975), letter 103 and commentary 430-1; see also M. Angold, review of Talbot in *JHS* 98 (1978), 220; I. Ševčenko, 'Notes on Stephen, the Novgorodian Pilgrim to Constantinople in the XIV Century' *Südost-Forschungen* 12 (1953), 173-4.

26. Pachymeres, i. 193-201; Laiou, *Constantinople and the Latins*, 22; Ahrweiler, *DOP* 29 (1975), 35.

27. For this incident see Geanakoplos, *Emperor Michael Palaeologus*, 217-18.

28. For the date see A.-M. Maffry Talbot, *The Correspondence of Athanasius I*, 204. 49-50; 262. 41-52; V. Laurent, *Les regestes des actes du patriarcat de Constantinople* (Paris 1971), iv, N. 1636.

for his remains were kept in the monastery of St Demetrios in Constantinople,[29] a Palaiologan foundation rebuilt by Michael VIII.[30] The presence of his relic there may indicate a conciliatory gesture by Andronikos II, Michael's son, to appease the anti-Palaiologan elements in the city.[31] John may even have been connected with this monastery in his life since it is known that he became a monk with the name Ioasaph[32] sometime after 1285.[33] In either case, John's presence in a Palaiologan foundation would have been equivalent to a public restoration for the wronged heir.

Furthermore, John's relic appears to have been on the 'tourist track' and to have received a great deal of attention. A fourteenth century Russian traveller to Constantinople, Stephen of Novgorod, visited the monastery of St Demetrios where he reports that he kissed the relic (*telo*) of a saint who was an emperor called 'Laskariiasaf'.[34] But the Russian pilgrim is not alone in attributing to John the status of sainthood. There is evidence that John was considered a saint among the Greeks as well.[35] Theodore Agallianos, a patriarchal official writing in the fifteenth century, includes John in a list of men and women whom God graced with divine energy by bestowing miraculous powers on their mortal remains.[36] Agallianos' reference to John is in a 'Dialogue against the Latins' and it is therefore reasonable

29. See Stephen of Novgorod: M.N. Speranskii, *Iz starinnoi novgorodskoi literatury XIV veka* (Leningrad 1934), 55, and Ševčenko, 'Notes on Stephen', 173; also, an anonymous sixteenth-century note published by P. Schreiner, *Die Byzantinischen Kleinchroniken* ii (Vienna 1977), 197 n.79.

30. For the identification of the resting place of John's relic with the Palaiologan foundation see R. Janin, *La géographie ecclésiastique de l'Empire byzantin* I.iii (Paris 1969), 93; for Michael's *typikon* see H. Grégoire, 'Imperatoris Michaelis Palaeologi de vita sua', *REB* 29-30 (1959-60), 461-74.

31. For the danger posed to Andronikos II by Laskarid supporters see Ševčenko, *Speculum* 27 (1952), 149 and notes.

32. Speranskii, *Iz starinnoi novgorodskoi literatury*, 55; Ševčenko, 'Notes on Stephen', 173; Theodore Agallianos, 'Hieromnēmonos tinos dialogou meta monachou tinos kata Latinōn' in Dositheos of Jerusalem, *Tomos Charas* (Jassy 1705), 622: '*monachou* [. . .] *Ioasaph tou Laskareos*'. The sixteenth-century note published by Schreiner (*Kleinchroniken* ii. 197 n.79) states that Michael Palaiologos' victim became a monk; it does not however imply that he became a monk in the monastery of St Demetrios as Failler would have it (*REB* 38 [1980], 77).

33. In 1285, after the second council of Blachernae, Andronikos II visited John in a prison in Asia Minor: Pachymeres, ii. 103-4; Gregoras, i. 173-4; Failler, 'La Tradition manuscrite', 156. This is the last reference to him in Asia Minor. See Ševčenko, 'Notes on Stephen', 174, for the conjecture that John died in Constantinople.

34. Speranskii, *Iz starinnoi novgorodskoi literatury*, 55. See Ševčenko, 'Notes on Stephen', 173, for the identification of 'Laskariiasaf' with John IV Laskaris and see n.32 above for confirmation of this identification from other sources.

35. See the suggestion by Ševčenko, 'Notes on Stephen', 175, that Stephen's use of the word 'saint' should perhaps be attributed to the Russian's own ideas about the status of victims of a dynastic struggle. It is now possible to take a less cautious view.

36. See Dositheos of Jerusalem, *Tomos Charas* (Jassy 1705), 622, 625. On the identification of the author of the dialogue with Agallianos, an anti-unionist writing in the 1440's, see Beck, *Kirche*, 759; J. Darrouzès, *Les regestes des actes du patriarcat de Constantinople* v (Paris 1977), 99.

to assume that this patriarchal functionary was not merely stating his personal view. Additional evidence for John's sanctity comes from an early sixteenth-century manuscript note which states that John's relic worked healing miracles.[37]

John's relic, then, like that of John Batatzes, his grandfather, must have been the object of intense devotion, since miracles are attributed to it. Refugees from Asia Minor, as well as other disaffected people in the capital, may have kept his cult alive by focussing on him their hopes and fears. Although there is no surviving hagiography for John or liturgical commemoration, the statements of the Russian traveller, Agallianos, and the author of the note, show that John was considered a saint and enjoyed considerable devotion in Constantinople.

Patriarch Arsenios

Associated with John Laskaris was the patriarch Arsenios who had defended the legitimate heir's rights, excommunicating the emperor Michael for ordering the blinding of the boy.[38] Michael's subsequent deposition of Arsenios caused a schism in the Church which proved to be the most serious internal problem Byzantium faced in the early Palaiologan period.[39] Arsenios' name was linked with plots against the regime, including the 1262 uprising in Bithynia and an attempt on the emperor's life in 1265.[40] After the patriarch's death in exile on the island of Prokonnesos in 1273[41] the Arsenites continued to stir up dissension which was only formally resolved in 1310.

The history of the Arsenite schism has been told before in various contexts. However, the role which Arsenios' recognition as a saint played in the schism has not been properly evaluated, in part because of a lack of published sources and also because of a misunderstanding of the available material.

Laurent and others following him have stated that Arsenios was 'canonised' shortly after his death in 1273 by Joseph (1266-75; 1282-3), the patriarch who absolved Michael Palaiologos of Arsenios' excommunication.[42] This idea is based on the fact that an *akolouthia* for Arsenios, an office in his memory (30 September), was included in a *mēnaion* which Joseph presented to Hagia Sophia while he was patriarch.[43] Laurent argued that this gesture on Joseph's part was an indication of the esteem in which he held his predecessor. But to consider it possible for such a

37. See P. Schreiner, *Kleinchroniken* ii. 197 n.79 and i. 191.
38. Pachymeres, i. 201-4; Gregoras, i. 93. 17-22; Arsenios, 'Testament', *PG* 140. 956 AB.
39. See I. Sykoutres, 'Peri to schisma tōn Arseniatōn', *Hellenika* 2 (1929), 267-332; ibid. 3 (1930), 15-44; V. Laurent, 'Les grandes crises religieuses à Byzance. La fin du schisme Arsénite', *Académie Roumaine. Bulletin de la section historique* 26 (1945), 225ff.
40. Arsenios, 'Testament', *PG* 140. 956 ABC.
41. Pachymeres, i. 394.19-395.2; ii. 83.10-12; J. Gill, 'Notes on the *De Michaele et Andronico Palaeologis* of George Pachymeres', *BZ* 68 (1975), 303.
42. Laurent, 'La fin du schisme Arsénite', 259 and n.6; idem., *Regestes* iv, N. 1461.
43. See A. Papadopoulos-Kerameus, *Hierosolymitikē Bibliothēkē*, v (St Petersburg 1915), 207-8 for the text of the dedicatory note.

gesture to have been made while Michael Palaiologos was reigning is to misunderstand completely the significance of the Arsenite schism. Joseph's recognition of Arsenios as a saint would have been equivalent to acknowledging Michael VIII's eternal damnation as an excommunicate of that patriarch.

The *akolouthia* has now been published and it is clear from the language and tone of the piece that it could not have been celebrated at any time while Michael was alive. The hymns hail Arsenios for exposing the 'injustice', 'the unjust deed of the emperor' and state that it was for this reason he was deposed and exiled 'like a second holy Chrysostom'.[44] Nor could the *akolouthia* have been celebrated during Joseph's second patriarchate (1282-3) after Michael's death:[45] the hymns allude to the presence of Arsenios' relic 'through which the Lord grants healing',[46] and this was not translated to Constantinople until 1284.[47]

Nikolopoulos, the editor of the *akolouthia*, notes that the text was inserted between the months of September and October, after the patriarch Joseph's dedicatory note, a position which indicates a later addition to the *mēnaion* Joseph presented to Hagia Sophia.[48] According to Nikolopoulos, the later occasion on which the *akolouthia* may have been inserted was 1310, the date of the formal end to the schism.[49] At that time the patriarch Niphon, a man acceptable to the Arsenite faction, read a formula of absolution from the ambo of Hagia Sophia, in the presence of Arsenios' relic.[50]

However, Arsenios' restoration had occurred long before the formal end of the schism. The ceremonial *adventus* of his relic in Constantinople in 1284 and its deposition in Hagia Sophia to the right of the *bēma* was the occasion of his reinstatement.[51] Andronikos II, Michael's son, had agreed to the translation in a move to satisfy the Arsenites who complained of the injustice of Arsenios' deposition and exile.[52] This was but one in a series of pacificatory acts which Andronikos and the patriarch Gregory undertook in 1283-4 in an attempt to end the schism.[53]

44. P.G. Nikolopoulos, 'Akolouthia Anekdotos eis Arsenion Patriarchēn Kōnstantinoupoleōs', *Epetēris Hetaireias Byzantinōn Spoudōn* [hereafter *EEBS*] 43 (1977-8), 376. 13ff; 377.32 ff; 378.67ff; 380. 123ff; 381. 129ff.

45. For the dates of Joseph's patriarchates see V. Laurent, 'La chronologie des patriarches de Constantinople au XIIIᵉ s. (1208-1309)', *REB* 27 (1969), 144-6.

46. Nikolopoulos, 'Akolouthia', 378. 56-62; 379. 86-93.

47. Pachymeres, ii. 83.8-86.9: after the synod of Adramyttion (April 1284); for the date see Laurent, *Regestes* iv, N. 1470.

48. Nikolopoulos, 'Akolouthia', 366-7.

49. ibid., 367-9; 373-4. Nikolopoulos argues that the *akolouthia* could not have been inserted earlier than 1310 because the patriarchate was in the control of enemies of the Arsenites until then.

50. Laurent, 'La fin du schisme Arsénite', Document v (303-4); Document vi (306-11, esp. 308. 66ff); Gregoras, i. 259-62, esp. 262.

51. This event was recorded in a verse chronicle as late as 1392: J. Müller, 'Byzantinische Analekten aus Handschriften der S. Markus-Bibliothek zi Venedig', SB Wien Phil-Hist. Klasse (1852), 56.747-9.

52. Pachymeres, ii. 83.14-84.7.

53. Laurent, *Regestes* iv, N.1463; N. 1740; Laiou, *Constantinople and the Latins*, 35.

The translation of Arsenios' relic, as described by Pachymeres, gave full honours to the patriarch's memory and could well have been the occasion for which the *akolouthia* was written.[54] The ceremony, attended by the emperor, senate, patriarch and clergy, included hymns and panegyrics for Arsenios with the coffin containing the relic standing before the altar.[55] Furthermore, provision was made for the veneration of his relic. Pachymeres states that 'every third day of the week when people went to the monastery *ton Hodegon*, as was customary, the coffin was opened and available to those who came [to Hagia Sophia]'.[56]

Evidence for the continued veneration of Arsenios' relic in Hagia Sophia comes from travellers to Constantinople in the fourteenth and fifteenth centuries. Five Russian travellers mention that they saw the relic of 'St Arsenios the patriarch' in the east end of the church, while one of them adds that a monk anointed him with the saint's oil.[57] The Castilian envoy Clavijo who visited Constantinople in the early fifteenth century claims that he was shown 'a sacred relic, namely the body of a certain patriarch, that was most perfectly preserved, with the bones and flesh thereon'. From his description of the position of the relic it is clear that he is referring to Arsenios.[58] The preserved state of Arsenios' corpse is corroborated by Greek sources and must have been an important aspect in his recognition as a saint.[59] It was a sign of holiness which may have helped the Arsenites further their demands for the full restitution of Arsenios.

Although there is ample evidence for Arsenios' cult until the fifteenth century, with the power of healing attributed to his relic, his liturgical commemoration appears to have been short in duration. Nikolopoulos has pointed out that the *akolouthia* for Arsenios survives only in one manuscript.[60] Moreover, Arsenios is not commemorated in the Orthodox Church today.

What has been presented so far with regard to Arsenios is the public aspect of his recognition as a saint — the liturgical celebration of his memory, however short-lived

54. This date is more acceptable than 1310 from a codicological point of view as well. Nikolopoulos himself admits ('Akolouthia', 367) that the *akolouthia* is in the same hand as the text for the months September and October between which the *akolouthia* is inserted. The period from the 1260s (Joseph's patriarchate) to 1310 is rather long for the same scribe to have been employed.

55. Pachymeres, ii. 84.18-85.14.

56. Pachymeres, ii. 85. 17-19. At a later time the relic was moved to the monastery of St Andrew in Krisei by request of Theodora Raoulina, where it was kept until 1310: Pachymeres, ii. 85.18-86.9; Gregoras, i, 262. 1-4; Laurent, 'La fin du schisme Arsénite', Document vi (308. 66-71).

57. G. Majeska, 'St Sophia in the Fourteenth and Fifteenth Centuries: The Russian Travelers on the Relics', *DOP* 27 (1973), 83-4.

58. ibid., 84.

59. Theodore Agallianos in Dositheos of Jerusalem, *Tomos Charas*, 625. 25ff; Laurent, 'La fin du schisme Arsénite', Document vi (308. 71-5); Manuel Kalekas, *Contra Graecorum Errores*, PG 152. 211 A. See Pachymeres, ii. 480. 5-7, for the Arsenites' belief in the sanctity of the monk Kouboukleisios whose body had 'remained uncorrupted for many years'. The Arsenites 'considered him a saint and venerated him'.

60. Nikolopoulos, 'Akolouthia', 375.

that may have been, and the veneration of his relic. But it is now possible to add to the above hagiographical literature by reference to an unpublished encomium, included among the collection of works written and owned by Philotheos, metropolitan of Selymbria in the second half of the fourteenth century.[61] This 'Encomium for St Arsenios' gives some idea of the kind of Arsenite literature which may have been circulating from the time of the patriarch's death, if not earlier. The encomium was perhaps based on a Life of the patriarch which has not survived. In any case, it is of interest both for the biographical material it provides and for the attitudes its author expresses concerning patriarchal-imperial relations.

The encomium, which appears to have been written for a Constantinopolitan audience,[62] provides a reply to the allegations expressed by the Palaiologan party through George Akropolites, Michael VIII's faithful civil servant. In Akropolites' History Arsenios is portrayed as an undistinguished monk who was chosen patriarch in 1254 as a last-minute thought of the emperor Theodore II Laskaris when the latter was pressed for time.[63] But, according to the encomium, Arsenios was the son of a Kamatere, a family which produced 'those who had power with emperors'. He was not unknown in powerful circles for he had been suggested as a candidate for the patriarchal throne of Jerusalem in the reign of John Batatzes.[64] As for his election as patriarch of Constantinople, no mortal had a hand in this; he was God's choice. The election was conducted by opening the Bible at random in the name of each candidate and reading the first passage on the page. The reading for Arsenios was thought to be the most auspicious;[65] thus, he had the stamp of divine approval.

For the author of the encomium, hagiography of Arsenios is connected with pro-Laskarid and ultimately, anti-Palaiologan sentiments. Theodore Laskaris and his father John Batatzes both have God-given wisdom. Theodore who 'legally succeeded his father, by the vote of God, not the vote of men',[66] was 'wise' because he understood signs from heaven. The author gives two examples of Theodore's abilities in this area which distinguish him from others, especially Michael Palaiologos.[67] Arsenios' encomiast implies that Michael's lack of understanding indicates his lack of *parrēsia.*

The views expressed by the encomiast who combines eulogy of Arsenios with pro-Laskarid sentiments need not be considered idiosyncratic. Evidence exists for a

---

61. cod. Patmiacus 366, ff 430ᵛ-434. On the authorship of this work see P. Magdalino, 'Byzantine Churches of Selymbria', *DOP* 32 (1978), 315 n.47. I wish to thank Fr Chrysostomos, the librarian of the monastery of St John the Theologian, Patmos, for allowing me to consult the manuscript. Nikolopoulos ('Akolouthia', 368) has announced his intention to publish the encomium in the forthcoming volume of *EEBS*.
62. cod. Patmiacus 366, f 430ᵛ: 'Arsenios the shepherd and leader of this great city, I mean Constantinople'.
63. Akropolites, ed. Heisenberg (Leipzig 1903), 106.6-107.13.
64. cod. Patmiacus, 366, f 431ʳ; 433ʳ.
65. cod. Patmiacus 366, f 433ᵛ.
66. cod. Patmiacus 366, f 433ʳ.
67. cod. Patmiacus 366, f 433ᵛ; 434ʳ.

much earlier source for these sentiments in the early Palaiologan period. Theodore Skoutariotes, bishop of Cyzicus (1277-82) gives expression to the same pro-Laskarid and Arsenite feelings in his paraphrase of Akropolites' History, written in the last quarter of the thirteenth century.[68] He knew the patriarch Arsenios[69] and Theodore II[70] personally and shows his admiration for them as well as John Batatzes. In these passages he departs from the text of Akropolites' History, the source of his work. For example, Skoutariotes provides long eulogies of Batatzes and Theodore II where Akropolites is either parsimonious in his praise or liberal with his criticism.[71] On the other hand, when Akropolites is effusive on the subject of Michael VIII's virtues, Skoutariotes is silent.[72]

Furthermore, Skoutariotes' work contains material in common with the encomium of Arsenios which is not found elsewhere. A notable example is the story of Arsenios' election as patriarch which only these two sources present as having been conducted by choosing readings from the Bible.[73] However, differences in the works with respect to biographical details[74] make it impossible to consider Skoutariotes' work the source of the encomium. The latter must have had other Arsenite literature to draw on, perhaps a *vita*.

The author of the encomium, writing so much later than Skoutariotes, was free to go beyond him in using Arsenios and Theodore II as symbols of the right order which existed in pre-Palaiologan days when emperors knew their place. According to Arsenios' encomiast, the emperor Theodore was 'obedient to the patriarch, doing everything according to his wishes, yielding the state to the Church'. This is only proper:

---

68. The authorship of the *Synopsis Chronikē* (ed. K.N. Sathas, *Mesaiōnikē Bibliothēkē*, viii [Paris 1894]) was attributed to Theodore Skoutariotes by Heisenberg in *BZ* 5 (1896), 182-5; idem, *Analekta* (Munich 1901), 12-16. This attribution was questioned by A.P. Kazhdan in *Izvestiia na Instituta za Istoriia* 14-15 (1964), 529-30.

69. *Synopsis*, ed. Sathas, 549. 28ff; Heisenberg, *Additamentum ad Georgii Acropolitae Historiam* 301. 1ff.

70. *Synopsis*, ed. Sathas, 535.20-536.12.

71. *Synopsis*, ed. Sathas, 506-9; 535-6; Heisenberg, *Additamentum* 33 (284-8); 52 (296-8).

72. Compare *Synopsis*, ed. Sathas, 497, 25-6; 527.29-528.1 with Akropolites, ed. Heisenberg 84. 4-6; 136. 26ff. for the passages favourable to Michael Palaiologos which the *Synopsis* omits.

73. cod. Patmiacus 366, f 433ᵛ; *Synopsis*, ed. Sathas, 510. 1-26; Heisenberg. *Additamentum*, 288ff.

74. The author of the encomium gives no surname for Arsenios, but refers to his father's Christian name (Theodore) and his mother's full name (Eirene Kamatere): cod. Patmiacus 366, f 341; Skoutariotes (*Synopsis*, ed. Sathas, 509; *Additamentum*, 290. 1-4) calls Arsenios' father Alexios Autoreianos. Skoutariotes claims that Arsenios was chosen as an ambassador to the pope in Batatzes' reign (*Synopsis*, ed. Sathas, 511. 10-11; *Additamentum*, 290. 11-13), whereas the encomium states that the civil and ecclesiastical hierarchy wanted Arsenios to be patriarch of Jerusalem (cod. Patmiacus 366, f 433ʳ). Skoutariotes says that there were four candidates for the patriarchal throne in 1254 (*Synopsis*, ed. Sathas, 510. 1-26; *Additamentum* 289), the encomium mentions three (cod. Patmiacus 366, f 433ʳ).

for the anointer is greater than the anointed, the one who blesses greater than the blessed one [. . .]. It is all necessary that the emperor, blessed and anointed, should be under the patriarch, as he is in need of grace.[75]

The author of the encomium, writing at a time when the Church had taken the lead from the failing state, uses Arsenios to make a statement about the superiority of the patriarchal position. But it is not only in encomia that Arsenios was a symbol for the Church which had emerged stronger from the crisis of the thirteenth century. Almost every aspect of Arsenios' recognition as a saint demonstrates the triumph of the Church over the Palaiologoi: his reinstatement in Hagia Sophia, the office celebrating him as a champion of the truth, his perfectly preserved body a source of healing. Even in the late fourteenth century, the time of the composition of the encomium, anyone could see with his own eyes that Arsenios had been blessed and his opponent damned. Philotheos, the metropolitan of Selymbria who is probably the author of the encomium, commented that the body of the emperor Michael lay in Selymbria in the monastery of Christ Saviour, 'all bloated' because of his heterodoxy and because of the excommunication which 'the most holy patriarch Arsenios pronounced against him'.[76] Michael never received proper burial rites; his corpse was left near the place of his death, 'a plaything and laughing-stock even to his own children'.[77] Agallianos, writing in the fifteenth century, invites anyone who has doubts about the sanctity of Arsenios and the damnation of Michael to 'judge for himself [. . .] put them [the corpses] side by side [. . .] and tell me with conscience which is the excommunicate and which the saint. But this is obvious even to a blind person'.[78]

If Agallianos and others before him attributed Michael's eternal damnation to the power of Arsenios' excommunication, they also acknowledged the part played by Michael's declaration of Union with the Church of Rome.[79] The latter came to be the dominant issue of his reign and the reason for which his name is missing

75. cod. Patmiacus 366, f 434[v]. The manuscript is unfortunately incomplete and stops here. See Blemmydes' comment on Theodore II's attitude toward Church-state relations: A. Heisenberg, *Nicephori Blemmydae Curriculum Vitae et Carmina* (Leipzig 1896), 42. 5-7.

76. See P. Magdalino, 'Byzantine Churches of Selymbria', 314-15 and n. 46. Compare Philotheos' comment on the reasons for Michael's bloated state with that of the fourteenth century unionist Kalekas: *PG* 152. 211A.

77. Theodore Agallianos in Dositheos of Jerusalem, *Tomos Charas*, 626; Pachymeres, ii. 107-8; Gregoras i. 159. 17-24.

78. Dositheos of Jerusalem, *Tomos Charas*, 627. Agallianos uses the word *tympanias* to describe Michael's corpse. On this term see Du Cange, *Glossarium ad Scriptores mediae et infimae Graecitatis* (Lyons 1688), 1621; also D.M. Nicol, 'The Byzantine Reaction to the Second Council of Lyons, 1274', *Studies in Church History* 7 (1971), 137-8.

79. Philotheos of Selymbria names Michael's 'heterodoxy' first and Arsenios' excommunication second, as the reasons for the emperor's bloated state: Magdalino, 'Byzantine Churches of Selymbria', 314-15. For reactions against the Union see also D.J. Geanakoplos, *Emperor Michael Palaeologus,* 237ff; idem, 'A Greek Libellus against Religious Union with Rome after the Council of Lyons (1274)', *Interaction of the 'Sibling' Byzantine and Western Cultures in the Middle Ages and Italian Renaissance (330-1600)* (New Haven-London 1976), 156-170; D.M. Nicol, 'The Byzantine Reaction to the Second Council of Lyons, 1274', 113-46.

from the commemorative list of emperors in the Synodikon for the Sunday of Orthodoxy.[80] Those who suffered persecution for opposing union were restored and honoured after his death in the reign of Andronikos II.[81] The patriarch Joseph and the monk Meletios are the most celebrated cases.[82]

Patriarch Joseph

Although the Arsenites considered Joseph's position as patriarch uncanonical,[83] they could not denounce him for supporting Michael VIII on the question of union. The patriarch resigned in 1275 over this issue, having made a statement of his faith.[84] Andronikos II restored Joseph to the patriarchal throne in 1282[85] but the patriarch, unable to carry on because of ill health, resigned a few months later just before his death.[86]

Laurent has stated that Joseph was 'canonised' by the patriarch Gregory II, his successor, soon after his death, by synodal act.[87] Although the act does not survive, it is mentioned in the chrysobull of 1310 which Andronikos II issued to announce a resolution of the Arsenite schism. In this document Andronikos refers to the earlier proclamation (anakēryxis) of the Church which he was forced to revoke to meet the requirements of the Arsenites. The anakēryxis stated that Joseph was 'equal in name to the others who had not resigned, the same in faith and the same as those who died while on the throne in similar struggles and conditions'.[88]

What was the exact nature of the proclamation which Andronikos had revoked under pressure from the Arsenites? Contemporaries stated that the Arsenites complained about 'the mnēmosynon of Joseph', or 'the annual commemoration of Joseph as patriarch in the Church'.[89] They therefore give the impression that the

80. J. Gouillard, 'Le Synodikon de l'Orthodoxie: édition et commentaire', TM 2 (1967), 97, (812-15 and n. 327); also 30 and 261. See, by contrast, the attention accorded to John Batatzes and his son Theodore II: 97 (810-13); 258.

81. Pachymeres, ii. 17-19; Gregoras, i. 160; D.M. Nicol, 'The Byzantine Reaction to the Second Council of Lyons, 1274', 132-9.

82. See also the Lives of Athonite monks who were martyrs for the cause of orthodoxy: F. Halkin, BHG³, 223; M. Živojmović, 'Sveta Gora i Lionska Unija', Sbornik Radova Vizantoloskog Instituta 18 (1978), 141-53.

83. According to the Arsenites he had usurped the patriarchal throne from an unjustly deposed patriarch and he had been excommunicated by Arsenios before he came to the patriarchal throne: see Arsenios, 'Testament', PG 140. See also the arguments put forth by the Josephite John Cheilas, metropolitan of Ephesus: J. Darrouzès, Documents inédits d'ecclésiologie byzantine (AOC 10 [1966]), 91ff; 385. 11; V. Laurent, 'L'excommunication du patriarche Joseph Ier par son prédécesseur Arsène', BZ 30 (1929-30), 489-96; idem., 'La fin du schisme Arsénite', 240, 257-60.

84. V. Laurent and J. Darrouzès, Dossier grec de l'Union de Lyon (1273-1277) (AOC 16 [1976]), 88-90; 509-17; Pachymeres, i. 399. 5-7; ii. 35-6; Laurent, Regestes iv, N. 1408.

85. Pachymeres, ii. 18; Laurent, 'La chronologie des patriarches de Constantinople au XIIIᵉ s. (1208-1309)', 145-6.

86. Pachymeres, ii. 37.10; 38.1; 38.16-18.

87. Laurent, Regestes iv, N. 1461: 1283; idem., 'La fin du schisme Arsénite, 257-60.

88. Laurent, 'La fin du schisme Arsénite', 299.78-300.101.

89. Pachymeres, ii. 82.14-17; Cheilas in Darrouzès, Documents inédits, 375.

synodal proclamation had to do with the inclusion of Joseph's name in the list of patriarchs read once a year on the Sunday of Orthodoxy.[90] The recording of a patriarch's name in the *Synodikon* was routine, except in cases such as Joseph's where resignation was involved.[91] A synodal decision was necessary to reinstate the patriarch 'equal to the others who had not resigned'. Needless to say, Andronikos II, crowned emperor by Joseph in 1272, would have been anxious to secure the canonical standing of this patriarch.[92] The Arsenites, however, could not countenance the commemoration of a man whom they claimed had been excommunicated by Arsenios.[93] Perhaps it was to appease the Arsenites on this matter that Andronikos allowed the relic of Arsenios to be translated to Constantinople in 1284.[94]

The synodal proclamation appears to have had no other object than to place Joseph among the ranks of those who were guardians of orthodoxy. But Laurent claims that the *anakēryxis* was a declaration of Joseph's sanctity as well.[95] He bases this opinion mainly on a letter of a supporter of Joseph, the monk Methodios, to the patriarch Gregory, written sometime in the years 1286-8.[96] In this letter Methodios refers to the patriarch Joseph as 'among the Confessors'.[97] Laurent infers that when Joseph was reinstated in the list of patriarchs, he was acclaimed an *homologētēs* or confessor. There are other, later references to Joseph the Confessor as well.[98] Certainly the epithet was appropriate in view of his defense of orthodoxy against Michael VIII's Union.

But if Joseph was proclaimed an *homologētēs* when he was reinstated one would expect to find him mentioned as such in the *Synodikon* to which he was once again restored sometime after 1310.[99] The *Synodikon* of Constantinople in its edited form bears no trace of the epithet. Only the *Synodikon* of Lacedaemonia refers to Joseph as the New Confessor but this special mention — out of keeping with the rest

90. See Pachymeres, i. 399.6, where *mnēmosynon* is used to indicate the mention of a name in the diptychs. See Cheilas for use of the word *anakēryxis* to refer to commemoration of a name in the Synodikon: Darrouzès, *Documents inédits,* 382.8. See Gouillard, 'Le Synodikon', 11, 253; Beck, *Kirche,* 155.

91. Gouillard, 'Le Synodikon', 261. On 'resignation' see Cyril of Alexandria in G.A. Rhalles and M. Potles, *Syntagma tōn theiōn kai hierōn kanonōn* (Athens 1852-9), iv. 359-60.

92. Laurent, 'La fin du schisme Arsénite', 240.

93. Pachymeres, ii. 467. 11-468.8; also see n.83 above.

94. Pachymeres, ii. 82.14-17: complaint of Joseph's *mnēmosynon;* Pachymeres, ii. 83.8-12: Andronikos agrees to the translation of the relic.

95. Laurent, 'La fin du schisme Arsénite', 257; idem., *Regestes* iv. N. 1461.

96. Laurent-Darrouzès, *Dossier grec,* 91-2; 519-27; esp. 525.1-22.

97. Laurent-Darrouzès, op.cit., 525, 7-8.

98. Nikephoros Kallistos Xanthopoulos, 'Diēgēsis peri tōn episkopōn Byzantiou kai tōn Patriarchōn panton Kōnstantinoupoleōs', *PG* 147. 568. This work was written in the first quarter of the fourteenth century: see Beck, *Kirche,* 705.

99. Gouillard 'Le Synodikon', 105 (895). Gouillard (261) suggests that Joseph's name was added to the Synodikon after 1320, with the return of Theoleptos of Philadelphia to Constantinople. See Laurent, 'Les crises religieuses à Byzance. Le schisme antiarsénite du Métropolite de Philadelphie Théolepte (+ c.1324)', *REB* 18 (1960), 45-54.

of the entries in the list of patriarchs — is rendered even more suspicious by the appearance of the epithet next to Arsenios' name as well.[100]

Therefore, although there is evidence that Joseph was honoured as a confessor, it is not clear how the epithet came to be attached to his name. Furthermore, Joseph's reputation as a saint seems to stand on this acclamation alone. For, as Laurent has remarked, no office for Joseph has survived nor, indeed, is there any evidence of a cult.[101] The testimony of Agallianos, the fifteenth-century patriarchal functionary, would seem to be conclusive evidence on this subject. In his 'Dialogue against the Latins' Agallianos lists John Batatzes, John IV Laskaris, Arsenios and Meletios, the other *homologētēs* of the period, as saints with a reputation for working miracles.[102] But he is silent with regard to Joseph, whom he surely would have included because of his anti-Latin position if only a cult had existed. Joseph, in fact, is the only one of the thirteenth-century saints discussed here for whom there is no evidence of popular veneration. His elevation to the status of confessor, one of the categories of sainthood, appears to have been completely controlled by the civil and ecclesiastical hierarchies. But what is perhaps even more noteworthy is the fact that his name was at some time introduced into the calendar of the patriarchate; he is commemorated today on 30 October.[103] It is ironic that the Arsenites, who won in 1310, lost in the long run.

Meletios the Confessor

For Meletios the Confessor (1209-86) there is much more direct evidence and an altogether fuller 'dossier'. Meletios suffered exile twice under Michael VIII, as well as mutilation for his anti-Union stand. He entered into open conflict with the court from the time of Joseph's deposition. After Michael's death he played a large part in the restoration of the churches to Orthodoxy.[104] In addition to his Life, written by Makarios, metropolitan of Philadelphia,[105] Agallianos gives an account of his persecution and the subsequent recognition of his sanctity. According to him, Meletios' corpse, like that of Arsenios, remained uncorrupted and was a source of miracles.[106] Agallianos also gives a full account of the manner in which Meletios' sanctity was recognised. The patriarch Esaias (1323-34) convened a synod which

100. R.J.H. Jenkins and C. Mango, 'A Synodicon of Antioch and Lacedaemonia', *DOP* 15 (1961), 230. For the date of the entry see Gouillard, 'Le Synodikon', 277-8 and n.170.

101. Laurent, *Regestes* iv, N. 1461 Crit.

102. Dositheos of Jerusalem, *Tomos Charas*, 622, 625.

103. S. Eustratiades, *Hagiologion tēs Orthodoxes Ekklēsias* (Athens, n.d.), s.v. 30 October. The date does not correspond to Joseph's date of death (March: Pachymeres, ii. 38.16) and since there is no evidence of a cult, the October date is puzzling.

104. Pachymeres i. 462.15ff; 489. 2-5; ii. 17.3-10; Nicol, 'The Second Council of Lyons', 132-5. L. Petit, *DTC* 10. 536-8; Laurent-Darrouzès, *Dossier grec*, 104-12. On Meletios' anti-Latin works see A. Argyriou, 'Remarques sur quelques listes grecques enumérant les hérésies latines', *ByzF* 4 (1972), 23-4; also Laurent-Darrouzès, *Dossier grec*, 554-63.

105. S Lauriotes, *Grēgorios ho Palamas* 5 (1921), 582-6; 609-24; *Ho Athos* (1928), 9-11.

106. Dositheos of Jerusalem, *Tomos Charas*, 617ff, 622, 625, 626, 633.

examined the evidence for miracles and voted to 'honour him and celebrate him as a true saint'.[107] Agallianos claims that from that time on his memory was celebrated in the monastery of St Lazaros in Constantinople on 19 January of every year.[108] He is still commemorated in the Greek Orthodox Church today.[109]

A revival of interest in saints

The five men discussed above, who practically monopolised the title of saint in the early Palaiologan period, constitute an important group for the history of Byzantine saints and sainthood. They represent the beginning of a revival in the interest in saints after a long period in which saints were little in evidence and hagiography almost non-existent. For, as has been remarked, the years of the Latin occupation (1204-61) and even the twelfth century were not prosperous times for saints. The five early Palaiologan cases can therefore help us to understand why it was that saints enjoyed a revival.

As should have become clear from the above exposition of the saints' lives, the story of their recognition, veneration, and later use by ecclesiastical writers cannot be separated from the 'sins' of Michael Palaiologos, his usurpation of imperial power from the Laskaris family and his union with Rome. Had the empire's affairs prospered in his reign and in those of his descendants our five saints might never have received the attention which they did. But instead, the relative peace and prosperity which the Laskarids brought to Asia Minor was completely destroyed in the last quarter of the thirteenth century.

It was precisely at this time that a revived interest in saints takes place: the writing of hagiography begins again to assume its former importance[110] and there is evidence for the veneration of our saints. This is also the period of the Church's assumption of a position of leadership. The correspondence of the patriarch Athanasios (1289-93; 1303-9) illustrates to what extent the Church took over from the state.[111] Athanasios himself is perhaps the first example of the return of the ascetic to his former position of authority and importance in society.[112] In the early Palaiologan period, then, people turned to substitute leaders, be they former imperial and ecclesiastical figures[113] or contemporary holy men, to fill the void created by the Palaiologan failure.

107. ibid., 626, 633. J. Darrouzès, *Les regestes des actes du patriarcat de Constantinople* v (Paris 1977), N. 2132 (? 1327).

108. Dositheos of Jerusalem, *Tomos Charas*, 626. According to Pachymeres, at the time of his writing (c. 1307), Meletios was considered a saint and his relic lay in the monastery of St Lazaros (ii. 17. 8-9); see also Janin, *La géographie* 1.iii. 298.

109. S. Eustratiades, *Hagiologion*, s.v. 19 January.

110. See Beck, n.3. above.

111. See A.-M. Maffry Talbot, *The Correspondence of Athanasius I, passim;* idem., 'The Patriarch Athanasius (1289-1293; 1303-1309) and the Church', *DOP* 27 (1973), 13-28; D.M. Nicol, *Church and Society*, 11-12, 29.

112. Pachymeres, ii. 107-9; Maffry Talbot, *Correspondence*, Introduction.

113. St Theodora of Arta, wife of the ruler of Epiros, Michael II, is another example of a 'dynastic' rather than ascetic saint from the thirteenth century. Like our five saints,

Methods of canonisation

A discussion of the saints of this period must include a reference to the way in which sanctity was recognised in the Orthodox Church. The early Palaiologan period is a crucial time with respect to this question for it has been remarked that the late thirteenth and the fourteenth century saw a change in the way sanctity was recognised, a change brought about, it would seem, by contact with the Latin Church in the course of the thirteenth century.[114] The period provides several examples of canonisation by synodal decree,[115] with a greater emphasis on bureaucracy and an insistence on the evidence of miracles — elements which closely resemble the canonisation procedure of the Western Church from the eleventh century.[116]

The three best known cases in which this procedure was used are those of Meletios (d.1286), the patriarch Athanasios (d.c.1315), and Gregory Palamas (d.1359). We are fortunate in possessing detailed descriptions for Palamas and Meletios: by the patriarch Philotheos (1353-4; 1368-76) in his *Tomos* of 1368 and by Theodore Agallianos, in his 'Dialogue against the Latins' written in the 1440s. According to Philotheos, members of the ecclesiastical hierarchy collected written testimony from those who had experienced miraculous cures through contact with Palamas' relic. The synod then made a decision with regard to Palamas' sanctity. Although Philotheos does not give details with regard to the patriarch Athanasios' case, he claims that a similar procedure was used.[117] Theodore Agallianos states that testimony for the miraculous powers of Meletios' relic was put to a 'great and exacting test'.[118] Comparison of this evidence with a contemporary Western example, the canonisation of Louis IX of France, for which witnesses' testimony

asceticism was not the dominant element in her veneration as a saint. Rather, her leadership qualities were more important in the formation of her cult. For her thirteenth-century Life by the monk Job see A. Moustoxides, *Hellēnomnemōn* 1-12 (1843-54), 42-3; also *PG* 127. 904ff. On the author see L. Vranoussis, *Chronika tēs Epeirou* i. (Ioannina 1962), 49-54; E. Trapp, W. Rainer, H.-V. Beyer, *Prosopographisches Lexikon der Palaiologenzeit* i.4 (Vienna 1980), 92 n.7959.

114. No systematic treatment of the subject exists. There are only scattered references. Beck (*Kirche*, 274) and P. Joannou (*LThK*, s.v. 'Heilig', 92) note a change in the late Byzantine period, without commenting on its origin. A. Alibizatos ('He Anagnorisis tōn hagiōn en tē orthodoxē ekklēsia', *Theologia* 19 (1941-8), 37-41) attributes the change to Western influence. See also the suggestion at the end of the paper by J. Munitiz, 'Self-Canonisation', below.

115. Joseph (1283): Laurent *Regestes* iv, N. 1461; idem., 'La fin du schisme Arsénite', 257-60, 290 n.1, 300. Meletios (c.1327): Darrouzès, *Regestes* v, N. 2132. Athanasios (before 1368): Darrouzès, *Regestes* v, N. 2540, refers to Athanasios' case but does not give him a separate entry. Athanasios' canonisation will be discussed by Professor A.-M. Maffry Talbot in her forthcoming publication of the *logos* on the translation of Athanasios' relics. Palamas (1368): Darrouzès, *Regestes* v, N. 2540, 2430.

116. *Dictionnaire de spiritualité* ii, s.v. 'canonisation', 77-85; P. Delooz, *Sociologie et canonisations* (La Haye 1969), 24-32. This book provides a clear exposition of canonisation in the West since the schism.

117. Philotheos, 'Tomus contra Prochorum Cydonium', *PG* 151. 711-12.

118. Dositheos of Jerusalem, *Tomos Charas,* 633; Darrouzès, *Regestes* v, N. 2132.

has survived, shows the same insistence on investigation of miracles.[119] Although no comparable 'dossier' survives for the Byzantine saints, the *logos* on the translation of Athanasios' relics, with its catalogue of cures and circumstantial details of the name, profession and hometown of each pilgrim, reads like a dossier of evidence for canonisation.[120]

These examples illustrate a procedure for the recognition of sanctity which appears to differ greatly from what is known of Byzantine practice in earlier periods. For it is generally accepted that recognition of sanctity in the earlier period consisted of the consent and acclamation of a local community. A cult would develop around the physical remains of a person which would have some or all of the following elements: veneration of the relic and miracles, translation of the relic, writing of an *akolouthia* and *vita*, painting of an icon of the saint, celebration of the saint's memory on the anniversary of his or her death. The name and feast day of the saint would be recorded in the calendar of the local church or monastery with which he was associated.[121]

By contrast, the cases of the three Palaiologan saints seem to indicate a much more formal and structured practice, with the stamp of patriarchal and synodal approval an essential element in the recognition of sanctity. This apparent difference is even reflected in the terminology used to describe the practices. Some use the word 'canonisation' only to refer to cases in which there was a synodal decision on the matter;[122] for others canonisation describes the recognition of sanctity, be it by a local community through its veneration and writing of an office and *vita*, or by the ecclesiastical hierarchy through its issue of a formal statement.[123] The confusion in terminology is further aggravated by expressions such as 'official canonisation' in contrast to 'popular veneration', a usage implying that a person is not properly considered a saint until there has been a synodal pronouncement on the matter.

It is necessary, therefore, to ascertain what part patriarchal and synodal approval played in the recognition of sanctity. Was it in fact a new element introduced to Byzantine practice late in the history of the empire and, furthermore, was this approval the *sine qua non* of sanctity?

Philotheos' *Tomos* of 1368 clearly states what function the synodal decision had in the cases of Palamas and Athanasios. According to the patriarch, both men

119. See H.-F. Delaborde, 'Fragments de l'enquête faite à Saint-Denis en 1282 en vue de la canonisation. de saint-Louis', *Mémoires de la société de l'histoire de Paris et de l'île de France* xiii (1896), 1-71.

120. I am indebted to Professor A.-M. Maffry Talbot for sharing with me the results of her work on the *logos*.

121. See Beck, *Kirche*, 274; *Dictionnaire de spiritualité* ii. 77-85. K.M. Ringrose, 'Monks and Society in Iconoclastic Byzantium', *Byzantium Studies/Études Byzantines* 6 (1979), 135 n.12; Alibizatos, *Theologia* 19 (1941-8), 21ff.

122. See P. Joannou in *LThK*, 92.

123. Laurent, 'La fin du schisme Arsénite', 259 and n.6; idem., *Regestes* iv, N. 1461; Ševčenko, 'Notes on Stephen', 173.

enjoyed considerable veneration from their followers in Constantinopolitan monasteries and on Athos before the synodal decisions.[124] Philotheos emphasises the point that anyone who wishes is free to celebrate the memory of Palamas without any hindrance but he is not celebrated in the Great Church or in any other church elsewhere until the holy synod has proclaimed on this matter. According to Philotheos 'this is common practice with regard to the saints whom God glorifies'.[125] He gives the example of Athanasios who for many years after his death was venerated by the monks of his monastery in Constantinople. On the Sunday of Orthodoxy each year his icon was carried to Hagia Sophia in a great procession, 'but after the holy synod pronounced on this, he was celebrated also in the Great Church'.[126]

Philotheos' statement on the significance of the synodal decision with regard to sainthood is as explicit as one could hope. The patriarch and synod do not reserve the right to confer recognition of sanctity. This can take place with the tacit consent of the Church, 'as is the case with many other men and women saints whose relics lie in many monasteries in the capital and are celebrated by anyone who wishes, although the Church has never pronounced on this'.[127] The synodal decision is merely a means of widening the area of a saint's veneration, of promoting veneration beyond its original local community limits. It is not so much a question of 'official' versus 'popular' veneration as it is one of 'local' versus 'Constantinopolitan' recognition. In fact, the synodal decision may always have been the means by which a saint's name and feast day were entered into the calendar of Hagia Sophia. The lack of evidence from earlier periods makes it difficult to know for certain. But it is clear that in the Palaiologan period the synodal decision conferred a wider sphere of veneration to a saint.

This wider recognition was of particular significance for men and women who played important roles in ecclesiastical controversies in the capital, as was the case with Palamas, Athanasios and Meletios. Their followers would be especially anxious to see that the object of their veneration received more attention. So it was that Philotheos and his predecessor on the patriarchal throne, Kallistos (1350-3; 1355-63), both ardent supporters of Palamas, made efforts to collect testimony to miracles worked by his relic.[128] The insertion of Palamas' name and feast day into the calendar of Hagia Sophia was a means of giving recognition to the doctrines he espoused. Similar reasons could have been at work in the case of Athanasios' wider recognition.[129] As far as Meletios is concerned, his importance as an opponent to

---

124. *PG* 151. 711-12; Palamas in the monastery of the Akataleptos and at Laura, Athanasios at Xerolophos.
125. *PG* 151. 711D, 712A.
126. *PG* 151. 712A.
127. *PG* 151. 712B.
128. *PG* 151. 711CD; Darrouzès, *Regestes* v. N. 2430, 2540.
129. Professor A.-M. Maffry Talbot, in her forthcoming publication of the *logos* on the translation of the relics, suggests several links between Athanasios and Palamites.

Michael VIII's union with Rome is clear. The significance of a synodal decision in the patriarchate of Esias (1323-34), at a time when Andronikos II was making tentative efforts at union with Rome, speaks for itself.[130]

The significance of miracles

The central role which these men played in Constantinople during their lives is also perhaps significant for understanding why their canonisation by synod placed such emphasis on proof of miracles. The more well-known and controversial the figure, the more care might have to be exercised in spreading his veneration by entering his feast day into the calendar of Hagia Sophia. Opponents and enemies would have to be convinced. Philotheos says that he first began to collect evidence of Palamas' miracles because of those who had their doubts and were not entirely convinced by the reports of miracles.[131]

The insistence on proof of miracles may have owed its importance in the Palaiologan period to yet another factor. The 'Dialogue against the Latins' by Agallianos can provide some insight into the question. In this work, written in the 1440s when the churches in Constantinople were staffed by Uniate clergy,[132] Agallianos discusses whom the Eastern and Western Churches considered saints and why. The saints of the Western Church are not, in his opinion, true saints for they have been designated saints by men, not by God. The Western Church bestows sainthood on men without God's approval, that is, without evidence of miracles.[133] The Orthodox Church, on the other hand, has a great number of miracle-workers, an indication that God's grace is with them and not with the Latins. Among the post-schism saints named by Agallianos are Batatzes, John Laskaris, Arsenios, Meletios and Athanasios. He discusses the cases of Arsenios and Meletios in detail, for their uncorrupted bodies were a sign of sanctity. Apparently, however, some people dared to attribute their incorruptibility to the pope's excommunication. Agallianos argues that this allegation is ridiculous because the pope's excommunication has no force.[134]

Agallianos' apologia for Byzantine saints gives an indication of the climate which discussions on Union may have created. Although he was writing a long time after our saints, it is possible to see that preparations for Union in the thirteenth century could also have been an occasion for defining how the Churches stood with regard

130. Darrouzès, *Regestes* v. N. 2132, suggests a date sometime before 1327 for the synodal decision. Laiou, *Constantinople and the Latins*, 326ff, dates Andronikos II's unionist attempts to 1324-7.

131. *PG* 151. 711B.

132. Dositheos of Jerusalem, *Tomos Charas*, 610.

133. Dositheos of Jerusalem, op.cit., 621-2, 627.

134. Dositheos of Jerusalem, op.cit., 621-2, 624-5. Further proof of the Latins' lack of God's grace, according to Agallianös (622), is the fact that relics of Byzantine saints taken to the West ceased to perform miracles there. For a similar statement made by Joseph Bryennios in the fifteenth century see H. Delehaye, 'Les Actes de S. Barbarus', *AnalBoll* 29 (1910), 286.

to saints recognised since the schism. We should perhaps see the emphasis on proof of miracles in this context. It was not a question of the Eastern Church's adoption of Western methods of recognising sanctity. Rather, the Orthodox Church needed to exercise more caution in the face of internal and external pressures. This is particularly understandable in the late thirteenth and fourteenth centuries with the ecclesiastical controversies of the Arsenite schism, Union and Hesychasm.

However, in the final analysis, it is not possible to be certain whether insistence on proof of miracles was in fact more marked in the Palaiologan period than earlier. The evidence which exists is limited and basically relates to Athanasios, Palamas, and Meletios.[135] Had it not been for the controversial nature of their careers we might never have learned of the manner in which their sanctity was recognised by the holy synod.

135. A reference to proof of miracles is made by the patriarch John Kalekas (1339) to the metropolitan of Russia, concerning Peter of Kiev's relic: Darrouzès, *Regestes* v, N. 2192.

Sainteté et Pouvoir

EVELYNE PATLAGEAN

SAINTETÉ et pouvoir, ce sont les pouvoirs du saint, et aussi leur articulation aux formes du pouvoir social et politique. Je voudrais poser cette double question dans la perspective d'une recherche sur les rapports entre la société, le pourvoir, et les récits justificatifs de ce dernier dans l'histoire de Byzance aux IXe-XIe siècles.[1] Mon dossier sera constitué d'une trentaine de personnages dont l'existence se place au cours de cette période, de même que, sauf exception, la rédaction de leur Vie. Voici d'abord leur liste, incomplète et provisoire,[2] mais dont auraient été écartés, en tout état de cause, tant l'Italie byzantine que les saints trop exclusivement illustrés par le combat pour les images, par exemple Joannikios.[3]

Désignation	Date(s)	Date et auteur de la Vie	Le plus ancien manuscrit connu
HOMMES			
Philarète le Miséricordieux	792	821/22: le moine Nikétas, son petit-fils et fils spirituel[4]	Genuens. 34, XIe s.
Nikephoros de Medikion	813	entre 824 et 837[5]: le moine Theosteriktos (?)	Monac. 366, fin du IXe s.
Platon de Sakkoudion	814	entre 814 et 826: Théodore Stoudite, son neveu et fils spirituels[6]	Vat. 1660, A. 916

1. Voir pour une époque antérieure les observations de L. Cracco Ruggini, 'Potere e carismi in età imperiale', *Studi Storici* 1979 (3), 585-607.
2. Classement chronologique. Une date unique est celle du décès. Pour chaque Vie, la rédaction et le manuscrit relevés sont les plus anciens à ma connaissance: mais mon tableau est entièrement tributaire des éditions existantes. Deux références vont de soi: *Bibliotheca Hagiographica Graeca* 3e éd. par F. Halkin (Bruxelles 1957) (cité ci-après comme *BHG*³); *Auctarium BHG* par le même (Bruxelles 1969); H.G. Beck, *Kirche und theologische Literatur im byzantinischen Reich* (München 1959).
3. Série étudiée par I. Ševčenko, 'Hagiography of the Iconoclast period' in A. Bryer, J. Herrin, ed., *Iconoclasm* (Birmingham 1977), 113-31.
4. M.-H. Fourmy, M. Leroy, 'La Vie de S. Philarète', *Byzantion* 9 (1934), 85-170.
5. Ed. F. Halkin, *AnalBoll* 78 (1960), 401-25.
6. *PG* 99. 804-49.

Théophane le Confesseur	817	avant 847: le patriarche Méthode[7]	
Théodore Stoudite	826	Vie B; un moine contemporain. Vie A: Théodore Daphnopatès (?)[8]	Vat. 1669 (Cryptof.), Xe s. Monac. 467, XIe s.
Nicéphore (le patriarche)	829	peu après: Ignatios préposé au trésor de la Grande Église[9]	Vat. 1809, Xe s.
Pierre d'Atroa	773-837	vers 847: le moine Sabas[10]	Marc. 583, entre 950 et 1000
Makarios de Peleketè	mort entre 829 et 842	son successeur Sabas[11]	Paris. 548, XIe s.
Nicolas Stoudite[12]	868		Paris. 1452, Xe s.
Pierre l'Athonite	milieu du IXe s.	Xe s.[13]	Ath. Lavra D 79, début du XIIe s.
Ignatios (le patriarche)	877	entre 901 et 912: Niketas David Paphlago[14]	Vat. 1452, XVIe s.
Constantin de Synnada[15]	sous Basile I[e]	après la mort de de Basile: un moine	Med. Laur. IX 14, XIe s.
Evaristos Stoudite[16]	819-97		Paris. 1171, Xe s.

7. *Zapiski Russkoi Akademii nauk po ist.-fil. otd.* VIIIe sér. xiii.4 (1918), 1-40. Sur les autres Vies, cf. *BHG*[3]. 1788-91.

8. Vie B (*BHG*[3]. 1754): *PG* 99. 233-328. Vie A (*BHG*[3]. 1755): *PG* 99. 113-232. Cf. C. Thomas, *Theodor von Studion und sein Zeitalter* (Inaug. Diss. Leipzig 1892). 'Si Daphnopatès est vraiment l'auteur de la Vie A [...] il s'est contenté d'une retouche légère de sa source, car l'orateur parle un peu partout comme un moine studite' (Théodore Daphnopatès, *Correspondance,* éd. J. Darrouzès et L.G. Westerink [Paris 1978], 5-6). Une Vie C (*BHG*[3]. 1755d) serait due à un moine stoudite du IXe siècle, elle se rencontre dans le manuscrit 520 du Musée Rumjanzev, du XIIIe siècle, provenant du Mont Athos, cf. V. Latyshev, *VizVrem* 21 (1912), 258-304.

9. Ed. De Boor, *Nicephori opuscula historica* (Leipzig 1880), 139-217. Cf. P.J. Alexander, *The Patriarch Nicephorus of Constantinople. Ecclesiastical Policy and Image Worship in the Byzantine Empire* (Oxford 1958).

10. *La Vie merveilleuse de saint Pierre d'Atroa (+837)* éd. V. Laurent (Bruxelles 1956).

11. Ed. Van den Gheyn, *AnalBoll* 16 (1897), 142-63.

12. *PG* 105. 863-925.

13. Ed. K. Lake, *The Early Days of Monasticism on Mount Athos* (Oxford 1909), 18-39 (datation du manuscrit, 9). Cf. D. Papachryssanthou, 'La Vie ancienne de saint Pierre l'Athonite. Date, composition et valeur historique', *AnalBoll* 92 (1974), 19-61.

14. *PG* 105. 488-574. La date suivant R.H. Jenkins, 'A note on Nicetas David Paphlago and the Vita Ignatii', *DOP* 19 (1965), 241-7.

15. *ActaSS* Nov. IV, 657-69. Constantin, né juif, se trouve chrétien à la suite d'un signe de croix dont il a signé sa bouche après un bâillement, suivant l'usage populaire. Sans préjuger de l'authenticité du personnage, il est tentant de rapprocher son exemplarité du décret de conversion obligatoire pris par Basile I[e], cf. A. Sharf, *Byzantine Jewry from Justinian to the Fourth Crusade* (Londres 1971), 82 et s.

16. Ed. Van de Vorst, *AnalBoll* 41 (1923), 295-325.

Euthymios le jeune	898	après 905: Basile archevêque de Thessalonique (né vers 860)[17]	Mosq. Syn. B. 387, XIe s. (?)
Demetrianos évêque de Chytri[18]	IXe-Xe s.		Sinait. 789, XIIe s. (composite)
Blaise d'Amorion	entre 909 et 912	un contemporain, moine stoudite[19]	Paris. 1491, Xe s.
Euthymios (le patriarche)	917	un moine de son monastère de Psama-thia[20]	Berol. f. 55, A. 1080-1100.
Nikephoros de Milet	enfant sous Romain Ie	après 976[21]	Paris. 1188, XIIIe s.
Luc le jeune	953	avant 962[22]	Sinait. 514, Xe s.
Paul le jeune	955	après 975: un moine du mont Latros[23]	Paris. 1490, XIe s.
Luc le stylite	879-979	en 980-5: un témoin oculaire[24]	Paris. 1458, XIe s.
Michel Maleïnos[25]	894-961		Athon. Lavra D79, début du XIIe s.
André le Fou Volontaire	?	fin IXe-déb. Xe s.[26]	Fgmt onciale Xe s. dans le Monac. 443, XIVe s.
Basile le Nouveau[27]	actif après 959	1. un contemporain	1. Paris 1547, A. 1286[28] 2. Athon. Ivir. 478, XIIIe s.[29]

17. Ed. L. Petit, *ROChr* 8 (1903), 168-205. Cf. D. Papachryssanthou, *Actes du Prôtaton* (Paris 1975), intr., 22-31.
18. Ed. H. Grégoire, *BZ* 16 (1907), 217-37.
19. *ActaSS* Nov. IV, 657-69.
20. Ed. P. Karlin-Hayter, *Vita Euthymii patriarchae CP* (Bruxelles 1970).
21. Ed. H. Delehaye in: Th. Wiegand, *Der Latmos (MILET* iii.1) (Berlin 1913), 157-71. Cf. J. Gouillard, *Annuaire École pr. Htes Études, Sc. relig.* (1975-6), 348-9.
22. *PG* 111. 441-80, complété par E. Martini, *AnalBoll* 13 (1894), 81-121.
23. Ed. Delehaye, in: Wiegand, *Der Latmos* (op.cit., n.21), 105-35, repris d'une première publication dans *AnalBoll* 11 (1892), 5-74 et 136-82, où il signale trois manuscrits du XIe siècle. Sur l'auteur, cf. H. Delehaye, 'La Vie de saint Paul le jeune († 955) et la chronologie de Métaphraste' (1893), *Mélanges d'hagiographie grecque et latine* (Bruxelles 1966), 84-116.
24. Ed. F. Vanderstuyf, *PO* xi.2 (1914), 189-287. La chronologie est acceptée par H. Delehaye, *Les saints stylites* (Bruxelles 1923), lxxxvi-ci.
25. Ed. L. Petit, *ROChr* 7 (1902), 549-68. Sur le manuscrit, ci-dessus n.13.
26. *PG* 111. 625-888: seule édition couramment accessible pour une tradition complexe, cf. *BHG*3 115z-117k, et S. Murray, *A Study of the Life of Andreas, the Fool for the Sake of Christ* (Borna-Leipzig 1910). La date de composition suivant S. Murray, et J. Grosdidier de Matons, 'Les thèmes d'édification dans la Vie d'André Salos', *TM* 4 (1970), 277-328. C. Mango pense que le noyau de l'oeuvre remonte au VIIe siècle (communication verbale). Je suivrai pour ma part S. Murray, en raison des préoccupations de l'oeuvre que nous connaissons, cf. E. Patlagean, 'Byzance et son autre monde. Observations sur quelques

Nikon 'Repentez-vouz'[30]	998	après 1025	Athon. Kutlum. 210, A. 1630
Athanase de Lavra	vers 1001	avant 1025, et même 1010: moine de Lavra	Mosq. Syn. Bibl. 398, XIe s. (prov. de Lavra)[31]
Syméon le Nouveau Théologien	949-1022	après 1052 (ou plutôt 1054): Niketas Stethatos[32]	Paris. 1610 et Paris. Coisl. 292, XIVe s.

FEMMES

Irène abbesse de Chrysobalanton[33]	sous Michel III	après l'avènement de Basile I[e]	Laur. plut. 10 cod. 31, XVe s.
Athanasia d'Egine	IXe s.		Vat. 1660, A. 916[34]
Marie la jeune[35]	vers 902	après 1025	Vat. 800, XIVe- XVe s. Ath. Lavra K 81, XIVe s.
Theodora de Thessalonique[36]	812-92	894: un clerc local	Mosq. 159 b XIIIe s.
Theodora (impératrice)[37]	867	source de 'Georges le Moine continué'	Londin. B.M. Add. 2870, A. 1111

récits', *Faire Croire au Moyen Age* (Table ronde de l'École française de Rome et de l'Université de Padoue 1979, sous presse).

27. Cf. H. Grégoire, P. Orgels, 'L'invasion hongroise dans la "Vie de s. Basile le jeune",' *Byzantion* 24 (1954), 147-56.

28. *ActaSS* Mart. III, 3e éd. Suppl. 20-32: complété d'après les ms. Mosq. Syn. Bibl. 249 (XVIIIe s.) et 250 (XIVe s.) par A. Veselovskii, *Sbornik otdel. russkago iazyka i slovesnosti imp. Akademii nauk* 46 (1890) et 53 (1892), Prilozheniia. A noter que la Vie circule en Russie dès le XIIe siècle.

29. Larges extraits éd. par S.G. Vilinskii, *Zapiski novorossiiskago universiteta* 7 (Odessa 1911), 5-142.

30. Ed. S. Lampros, *Neos Hellēnōmnemōn* 3 (1906), 131-222, 256. Sur la date de rédaction, cf. J. Gouillard, *Annuaire Ecole pr. Htes Études, Sc. relig.* 85 (1976-7), 368-9 ('une cinquantaine d'années après').

31. Ed. I. Pomialovskii, *Zhitie prep. Afanasiia* (S. Pétersbourg 1895). Voir O. Lemerle, 'La Vie ancienne de saint Athanase l'Athonite composée au début du XIe siècle par Athanase de Lavra', *Millénaire du Mont Athos, 963-1963* (Chevetogne 1963), i.59-100.

32. Nicétas Stéthatos, *Vie de Syméon le Nouveau Théologien (949-1022)*, éd. I. Hausherr et G. Horn (OC 12 [1928]). Le personnage a été éclairé par l'importante publication de ses oeuvres dans la collection Sources chrétiennes; voir notamment l'introduction de B. Krivochéine dans Syméon le Nouveau Théologien, *Catéchèses,* éd. B. Krivochéine et J. Paramelle (Paris 1963-6), i.

33. *ActaSS* Jul. VI, 602-34.

34. *BHG*[3]. 180, et *Auctarium* 180b. La Vie (Vatic. 1660, 211[v]-228) demeurait inédite en 1969, et connue à travers le Synaxaire de Constantinople (*ActaSS* Propyl. Novembris), 611.46-614.

35. *ActaSS* Nov. IV, 692-705.

36. Ed. F. Kurtz, *Zapiski imp. Akad. nauk. po ist.-fil. otd.* VIIIe sér, vi. 1 (1902), 1-49, cf. *BHG*[3]. 1738. L'édition signalée par *BHG*[3]. 1737 ne m'a pas été accessible.

37. Ed. W. Regel, *Analecta byzantino-russica* 2 (S. Pétersbourg 1898), 1-19.

Theophano (impératrice)[38]	893	Xe s.: laic ami de sa famille	Laurent. Conv. soppr. B 1 Camaldoli 1214, XIVe s.
Thomaïs de Lesbos[39]		sous Romain II	ibid.

Les Vies et la société

Les questions posées en commençant concernent d'une part le contenu des oeuvres, de l'autre leur diffusion effective, difficile à saisir parce que masquée à nos yeux par la facilité commune de l'imprimé. Le contenu ne peut se comprendre sans référence aux modèles établis antérieurement. La transition culturelle des IVe-VIIe siècles avait posé en effet les lois des récits hagiographiques.[40] Dans le cadre d'une fidélité formelle, les oeuvres des IXe-XIe siècles présentent des modifications indicatrices du changement qui s'est fait dans la société et dans la culture. Pourtant, au regard du répertoire antérieur, on n'observe parmi les motifs employés ni disparition ni invention véritable. Mais le dosage est assez différent pour conduire en fin de compte à l'impression d'une hagiographie devenue différente, tout comme la société où le saint remplit sa fonction. Car la société byzantine a changé. Les pouvoirs de la sainteté, les rapports de celle-ci avec les pouvoirs politiques et sociaux ont changé en conséquence.

La Vie, dossier des preuves

Tout récit hagiographique est en premier lieu une illustration des pouvoirs du saint, et donc un dossier des preuves de sa sainteté. Celle-ci est parfois annoncée dès le début de la Vie. Le motif de la mère exaucée, comme Anna, après une longue stérilité, se trouve dans la Vie de Pierre d'Atroa, que nous verrons constamment fidèle au modèle ancien. Ailleurs, ce sont des signes à la naissance. La sage-femme voit une marque sur Constantin de Synnada. Un prêtre reçoit une vision relative à Makarios de Peleketè. La venue au monde de Theophano, sainte et impératrice, est marquée par une apparition de Marie à sa mère, mais aussi par le présage d'un aigle. Le thème de la sagesse précoce, qui rend le héros plus proche du vieillard que de l'enfant, se développe, d'autant mieux que l'insistance sur les études se fait plus grande.[41] Les miracles de la mort et de la sépulture en revanche restent fidèles à la

---

38. Ed. E. Kurtz, 'Zwei griechischen Texte über die Hl. Theophano, die Germählin Kaisers Leo VI', *Zapiski* (cit. ci-dessus, n.36) VIIIe sér. iii. 2 (1898), 1-24.

39. *ActaSS* Nov. IV, 234-42.

40. Cf. l'étude classique de P.R.L. Brown, 'The Rise and Function of the Holy Man in Late Antiquity', 61 (1971), 80-101. E. Patlagean, 'Ancienne hagiographie byzantine et histoire sociale', *Annales ESC* (1968), 106-26. En général, S. Boesch Gajano, *Agiografia altomedioevale* (Bologne 1976), 7-48, et M. Van Uytfanghe, 'Les avatars de l'hagiologie. A propos d'un ouvrage récent sur saint Séverin du Norique', *Francia* 5 (1977), 639-71.

41. P. Lemerle, *Le premier humanisme byzantin. Notes et remarques sur enseignement et culture à Byzance* (Paris 1971), 242 et s., utilise notamment la Vie de Nikephoros de Milet. Voir aussi A. Moffatt, 'Schooling in the Iconoclast centuries', *Iconoclasm*, op.cit., 85-92.

tradition bien établie: prévision du moment par le saint, odeur de sainteté, onguent curatif suintant du tombeau, ou de l'image. Ce dernier motif s'est affirmé depuis la fin du VIe siècle, en même temps que le rôle des images elles-mêmes dans la pratique religieuse.[42] Tombeau et image ont en réalité un rôle premier dans la séquence hagiographique, puisqu'ils sont au point de départ du culte, dont le récit écrit est en quelque sorte le commentaire. A cet égard, le récit de la sépulture et de la translation de la moniale Theodora de Thessalonique doit être signalé pour son intérêt exceptionnel.[43]

Le plan ancien développait longuement la prouesse ascétique inséparable de la retraite au désert, pour passer ensuite aux pouvoirs thaumaturgiques qui en étaient la récompense. Mais l'aboutissement et l'encadrement monastiques de ce modèle forment déjà la leçon proposée par les Vies des moines de Palestine, composées au milieu du VIe siècle par Cyrille de Scythopolis;[44] déjà le 'désert' y est interprété comme le lieu de déplacements fondateurs. Il en va de même dans les Vies des anciens stylites.[45] Et l'observation est encore plus vraie des Vies de notre époque. Seule la Vie de Pierre d'Atroa en effet conserve vraiment le motif traditionnel de l'ascèse initiale au désert, près d'un solitaire qui s'empresse d'ailleurs de lui faire donner la prêtrise. Il manque en revanche dans celles de Makarios de Peleketè ou Nikephoros de Medikion, qui deviennent pourtant des higoumènes comme lui. Pour Constantin de Synnada, Euthymios le jeune, Paul le jeune, Michel Maleïnos, la prouesse ascétique suit l'entrée au monastère. Elle déborde parfois l'autorité des higoumènes. Les difficultés qui naissent entre ceux-ci et Constantin de Synnada, Paul le jeune, ou Luc le jeune, signifient peut-être la tension entre la tradition de la retraite dans la solitude et l'actualité de l'encadrement monastique. Le réseau des monastères de l'Olympe de Bithynie et de la péninsule athonite est balisé par les déplacements ascétiques, comme celui du désert palestinien d'antan, bien que sur des distances sans doute plus grandes. L'hagiographie athonite en particulier montre bien que le monastère est la fin du récit, autrement dit le point de départ de sa production. L'obscur Pierre l'Athonite procure une référence délibérément théorique.[46] Mais la Vie d'Athanase de Lavra atteste la répression de l'indépendance des solitaires par son héros.[47]

42. E. Kitzinger, 'The Cult of Images in the period before Iconoclasm', *DOP* 8 (1954), 85-150; P.R.L. Brown, 'A Dark-Age Crisis: Aspects of the Iconoclastic Controversy', *EHR* 346 (1973), 1-34; Averil Cameron, 'Images of Authority: Elites and Icons in late sixth-century Byzantium', *Past and Present* 84 (1979), 3-35.
43. Par le clerc Gregorios auteur de la Vie, éd. Kurtz (cit. ci-dessus, n.36), 37-49 (*BHG*^{3}. 1739).
44. Kyrillos von Skythopolis, éd. E. Schwartz, *TU* 49.2 (1939).
45. H. Delehaye, *Les saints stylites* (Bruxelles 1923).
46. Cf. Papachryssanthou, 'Vie ancienne de saint Pierre l'Athonite [. . .]', *AnalBoll* 92 (1974).
47. Ch. 159, dont on note le ton acerbe; ch. 161-2: ralliement de l'ermite Nicéphore le Calabrais, dit le Nu.

Ce qu'il advient du modèle ancien

Il est des catégories où l'association du désert et de l'ascèse ne trouvent pas de place, et où la présence du monastère est aléatoire. Ce sont celles du laïcat et de la ville, elles-mêmes diversement combinées. Philarète est éprouvé comme Job, et c'est assez: le cloître et la prêtrise son absents de son histoire. Luc le Stylite se coupe les cheveux auprès d'un maître en ascèse, et reçoit même la prêtrise tout en continuant d'assurer son service militaire; puis il paît des pourceaux, séjourne dans une grotte, et enfin monte sur une colonne, en province puis à Constantinople, ou plus exactement près de Chalcédoine. Il est vrai que sa sépulture se trouve au monastère de Bassianos. Pour Basile le Nouveau et André le Fou Volontaire, la sainteté constitue une donnée initiale de la narration. Et ce sont des marginaux au regard de l'Église établie. L'association de l'ascèse au désert fait également défaut dans la sainteté féminine, dont l'hagiographie se développe alors,[48] si ce n'est le rappel schématique d'un modèle ancien dans la Vie de Théoctiste de Lesbos.[49] Marie la jeune et Thomaïs de Lesbos sont éprouvées par le mariage même, avant d'entrer au monastère. Les autres accèdent à la sainteté par le cloître, qu'elles aient été mariées ou non, à l'exception de Theophano, dont l'ascèse individuelle sert à interpréter en fait ce que son hagiographe ne dit pas, mais qui était notoire, son abandon par Léon VI. Theodora de Thessalonique devient sainte par la vertu spécifiquement monastique de l'obéissance. Enfin, et surtout, la conquête de la sainteté au désert n'a pas de rôle dans les Vies des patriarches de Constantinople, Nicéphore et Ignatios,[50] et dans la série des Vies stoudites, où elle n'apporte qu'une référence initiale, à propos de Platon, et du jeune Théodore. Il est vrai que les épreuves des confesseurs la remplacent pour Théodore et Nicolas. Mais le monastère de Stoudios est en fait au coeur de la capitale, et cette position même est significative. L'élan original du monachisme citadin, aussi bien que les réticences et les interdictions qu'il avait suscitées,[51] sont désormais du passé, tout comme l'illustration individuelle de l'anachorète, même si la ville demeure un pôle négatif dans le discours monastique sur la sainteté. L'Église des moines a vaincu, et nul ne revendique cette victoire plus haut que les Stoudites. Le monastère est désormais suffisant, capable de contenir l'ascèse dans ses murs et dans sa discipline. Quand un autre type de sainteté se lève à l'aube du XIe siècle avec Syméon le Nouveau Théologien, dans lequel la révélation est primordiale, son berceau est encore le Stoudiou. Et lorsque Syméon devient higoumène de S. Mamas, il ne cesse pas de se proclamer héritier de la tradition stoudite. Confirmation de cette tendance, les saints moines reçoivent pratiquement tous la prêtrise, ce qui n'est pas sans précédent, certes: la sainteté s'intègre plus que

48. Cf. E. Patlagean, 'L'histoire de la femme déguisée en moine et l'évolution de la sainteté féminine à Byzance', *StM* 17.2 (1976), 597-623.
49. *ActaSS* Nov. IV, 224-33, cf. *BHG*3 1723-26b. H. Delehaye, 'La Vie de sainte Théoctiste de Lesbos' (1924), *Mélanges* (1966), 299-306.
50. La Vie d'Euthymios est mutilée au début et à la fin.
51. Cf. G. Dagron, 'Les moines et la ville. Le monachisme à Constantinople jusqu'au concile de Chalcédoine (451)', *TM* 4 (1970), 229-76.

jamais tant à la communauté monastique qu'à l'Église instituée tout entière. Rédigée en majeure partie par des moines, et pour l'illustration de l'Église monastique, l'hagiographie que nous lisons les renvoyait en un jeu de miroirs à leur propre image. En somme, si la mort et la sépulture du saint donnent lieu à des développements fidèles à la tradition, le modèle ancien de conquête de la sainteté apparaît en revanche quelque peu érodé et modifié.

Les miracles

Qu'en est-il du répertoire des miracles? A première lecture, il paraît inchangé dans ses grandes lignes: guérisons, par des opérations diverses, de personnes souvent nommées, à tous les niveaux sociaux; médiations protectrices lors d'un incendie ou d'une tempête; miracles de subsistance et de résurrection; multiples faits de voyance. Le saint agit pendant sa vie, ou après sa mort, à son tombeau. l'efficacité de ses apparitions et de ses images peintes se vérifie dans l'une et l'autre situation. A mieux regarder pourtant, les proportions du modèle se sont peut-être modifiées, elles aussi, depuis l'époque où il avait été calqué sur le récit évangélique.

Il n'est pas possible de procéder ici à une comparaison systématique avec ce dernier, et avec l'hagiographie ancienne. Mais elle mettrait en lumière les variations d'un récit à l'autre: selon le lieu, capitale, ville de province, monastère isolé; selon la position du saint; selon l'objet central du récit, et la part faite, en particulier, aux relations entre le saint et le pouvoir. On peut noter en général que l'inventaire des maladies n'est plus aussi riche, que les miracles de subsistance et de résurrection n'ont plus la même place, et que la voyance acquiert au contraire une importance sans précédent, dans les rapports du saint avec le commun et avec le pouvoir. Il suffit d'observer l'éclat donné à toutes les formes de voyance dans la définition de la sainteté présentée par Nikétas Stethatos, hagiographe de Syméon le Nouveau Théologien, mais aussi moine et prêtre stoudite au milieu du XIe siècle.[52] Enfin, le saint vivant fait à l'occasion fonction de médiateur entre les fidèles et un autre saint, en fait à un niveau de culte tout différent. Constantin de Synnada intercède ainsi auprès de S. Nicolas et de S. Spyridon, Makarios de Peleketè après de S. Elie: le fait est significatif d'un système de représentations religieuses suffisamment élaboré pour que nous distinguions, sous une étiquette commune, entre les personnages du théâtre sacré, et des hommes ou des femmes qui ont effectivement vécu aux IXe-XIe siècles, en même temps que les auteurs qui ont composé leurs Vies. En un mot, la vieille classification bollandiste était en quelque manière celle des Byzantins eux-mêmes, et il convient en conséquence d'en conserver un usage que l'on verra plus loin.

Tel est le canevas hagiographique de ces récits, qu'il était nécéssaire de situer, au moins sommairement, dans leur tradition. Le pouvoir de la sainteté y est, comme toujours, exposé doublement. Il est démontré dans l'histoire même du saint. Mais de plus, ou à vrai dire en premier lieu, la production même de l'oeuvre hagiographique

---

52. Éd. citée ci-dessus, n.32, xxxiv-xxxv.

proclame et manifeste une association avec le pouvoir en question, l'auteur n'étant à cet égard qu'un porte-parole.

Comment agit le saint

Le saint agit par sa présence corporelle. Ce thème s'épanouit déjà dans la Vie de Syméon Stylite le jeune, mort en 592.[53] Mais il prend beaucoup de relief dans certaines de nos Vies. L'hagiographe d'Euthymios le jeune montre la foule se pressant sur son passage dans les rues de Thessalonique, et cherchant à le toucher. Le clerc Gregorios décrit le corps de Theodora lors de sa translation avec une précision frappante. Paul le jeune enfin reçoit le patrice Photios, envoyé auprès de lui par Constantin VII, avec mission de rapporter exactement ses traits et ses attitudes; et aussi un moine, chargé de la même tâche par le pape. En pareil cas le saint vivant n'est pas loin de sa propre icône, et l'on rapprochera en effet de ces épisodes celui où Nikon 'Repentez-vous' pose pour la sienne, commandée par Jean Malakinos. Mais la question nous entrainerait trop loin. Le saint agit aussi par sa parôle, qui est un 'franc parler' (*parrēsía*): à ce privilège antique, déjà reconnu à l'éloquence sacrée et à la sainteté de l'Antiquité tardive,[54] au modèle du prophète biblique,[55] s'ajoutent des traits qui sont précisément de l'époque. La sainteté et la revendication de dire le droit s'épaulent en effet réciproquement dans le monachisme stoudite. La Vie de Théodore fait une place indiscutablement plus grande à la rupture de son premier mariage par Constantin VI qu'à l'attentat par lequel Irène prive ensuite celui-ci de la vue et du trône.

En particulier, l'époque développe de façon frappante le personnage du directeur de conscience, le 'père spirituel', dont l'autorité sur moines et laïcs s'exerce par le dire et le faire dire, associés à la voyance.[56] Le 'père spirituel' voit l'avenir, et la veuve Danielis apprend ainsi la grandeur future de Basile le Macédonien.[57] Mais il lit aussi dans les coeurs, et peut ainsi contraindre à l'aveu, comme le fait Pierre d'Atroa. Tel document de Lavra, que l'on peut dater de 1016, montre les effets patrimoniaux possibles de la paternité spirituelle.[58] La Vie du patriarche Euthymios confère à celui-ci, dans ce rôle, un ascendant sur Léon VI; le récit exprime un programme monastique; l'historiographie ne le confirme pas. Syméon le Stoudite,

---

53. *Vie ancienne de Syméon Stylite le jeune (La)*, éd. P. Van den Ven (Bruxelles 1962-70).

54. Cf. G. Scarpat, *Parrhesia. Storia del termine e delle sue traduzioni in latino* (Brescia 1964), qui s'arrête malheureusement au seuil des emplois byzantins.

55. Observation de Charlotte Roueché.

56. I. Hausherr, *Direction spirituelle en Orient autrefois* (Rome 1955) n'est pas une étude historique. Celle-ci reste à faire pour Byzance, comme l'a souligné R. Morris, 'The Powerful and the Poor in Tenth-Century Byzantium', *Past and Present* 73 (1976), 16 et n.53. Voir les suggestions de P. Legendre, *L'amour du censeur. Essai sur l'ordre dogmatique* (Paris 1974) (à partir du droit canon occidental, ainsi 143-64 sur l'aveu).

57. *Vita Basilii* in: Theophanes Continuatus, *Chronographia* éd. I. Bekker (Bonn 1838), 227.

58. *Actes de Lavra* i, éd. P. Lemerle, A. Guillou, N. Svoronos et D. Papachryssanthou (Paris 1970), n°20: donation de la veuve et moniale Glykeria à son 'père spirituel', le moine Eustratios, et à 'sa fraternité'.

père spirituel du Nouveau Théologien, marque l'accomplissement de cette fonction en milieu monastique, comme en témoigne la conception absolue qu'il s'en fait.[59] Tout aussi absolue, la dévotion que le Nouveau Théologien lui voue après sa mort vaut à ce dernier d'être convoqué devant le patriarche et le synode, pour un débat où s'affrontent deux modes de reconnaisance de la sainteté (ch. 81-2 et s.).

Les lieux des miracles eux aussi sont semblables, et en fin de compte différents, au regard des modèles hagiographiques. Ils assurent l'autorité du saint dans le monastère qu'il dirige: les moines qui s'y soumettent sont secourus, les récalcitrants frappés. Les Vies de Pierre d'Atroa, Michel Maleïnos, Athanase de Lavra contiennent de telles leçons. On retrouve aussi les villageois, qui montent vers Paul le jeune lorsque la sécheresse les afflige, tandis que Theodora accorde ses bienfaits aux citadins de Thessalonique, et Luc le Stylite à ceux de Constantinople. Pourtant, la lecture des Vies de cette époque donne dans l'ensemble une image sociale autre que celle des Ve-VIe siècles, où la sainteté villageoise et la densité des villages ressortaient dans la Syrie de Théodoret de Cyr, la Lycie de Nicolas de Sion, ou la Paphlagonie de Théodore de Sykéôn.[60] Si l'on pouvait enfermer en une seule formule la multiplicité des oeuvres, on dirait qu'elles dessinent autrement le territoire du saint et de la sainteté, qu'elles le situent dans une société dont la stratification est alors à la fois stabilisée et fortement marquée. Certes, Pierre d'Atroa, Constantin de Synnada ou Paul le jeune, voire Theodora défunte dans Thessalonique, ou Luc sur sa colonne à la porte de la capitale, demeurent fidèles au type du *holy man* de l'Antiquité tardive, devant qui défilent les détresses de toute condition. La plupart des saints toutefois semblent enclos par les récits dans un lieu social plus resserré, où le populaire n'apparaît au mieux qu'en certaines occasions. On se presse ainsi sur le passage d'Euthymios le jeune lorsqu'il descend à Thessalonique. Mais où est la foule dans les Vies de Stoudites, ou dans celles des patriarches de Constantinople? Le saint est bien souvent l'interlocuteur de l'élite dirigeante. Basile le Nouveau circule ainsi à Constantinople non seulement dans la famille de l'empereur Romain I[e] Lécapène, mais dans les maisons aristocratiques que l'auteur de la Vie 1 connaissait manifestement de près. Athanase de Lavra est lié avec les Phokas, avant que Nikephoros Phokas n'arrive au trône. Dans sa province de Lacédémone, Nikon 'Repentez-vous' est présenté par l'auteur de sa Vie comme proche des grandes familles locales; il sème son récit de noms lignagers illustres, Apokaukos, Malakinos, Choirosphaktès.[61]

Nikon est également au fait des affaires impériales du moment, la tentative de Bardas Skleros.[62] Et l'intervention des saints au niveau social et politique alors le

---

59. *Vie de Syméon le Nouveau Théologien*, éd. citée ci-dessus n.32, xlix-1.
60. Les indications ci-après sur l'Antiquité tardive d'après E. Patlagean, *Pauvreté économique et pauvreté sociale à Byzance, 4e-7e siècle* (Paris-La Haye 1977), où l'on trouvera justifications et références.
61. Cf. A. Bon, *Le Péloponnèse byzantin, des origines à 1204* (Paris 1951); et surtout, A.P. Kazhdan, *Sotsial'nyi sostav gospodstvuiushchego klassa Vizantii XI-XIIIvv.* (Moscou 1974).
62. Cf. W. Seibt, *Die Skleroi, Eine prosopographische-sigillographische Studie* (Vienne 1976), 29-58. Voir aussi M. Canard, *Histoire de la dynastie des H'amdanides de Jazira et de Syrie* (Alger 1951), 715 et s.

plus élevé n'est pas sans rapport avec l'importance primordiale prise par la voyance dans la demande qui leur est adressée. Demande accrue de la société entière, sans aucun doute. L'autre monde en particulier intéresse et inquiète: Basile le Nouveau et André le Fou révèlent sa configuration, et le sort que l'on y peut attendre; André connaît même celui des individus à l'occasion. Mais les récits hagiographiques rapportent surtout une demande spécifique des grands d'ici-bas. Paul le jeune déconseille en vain à Constantin VII une expédition en Crète, qui se solde en effet par un désastre (949). Basile prédit la naissance de Romain II, et voit de la capitale une expédition hongroise s'engloutir dans le Danube. Nikon sait l'issue de l'entreprise de Skleros. Et Syméon le Nouveau Théologien ici encore est singulier.

La position sociale du saint

Nous pouvons maintenant dessiner la position sociale du saint. Si les récits de sainteté affirment pour la plupart l'équation entre sainteté et monachisme, ils n'expriment plus l'essor économique et social des monastères, comme au VIe siècle, mais l'affirmation politique d'un monachisme plus codifié et plus savant, au sein d'une société dont le trait décisif semble n'être plus l'abondance humaine, mais la stratification sociale, au sein d'une Église dont il revendique la direction et l'encadrement. Revendication installée dans la capitale par les Stoudites au début du IXe siècle, et reprise par le Mont Athos avec les débuts de Lavra en 963. Qui plus est l'hagiographie du temps démontre la supériorité du monachisme sur l'épiscopat. Certes, le débat n'est pas neuf, et on peut déjà l'observer à l'âge d'or de l'épiscopat d'Orient, aux IVe-Ve siècles.[63] Mais les évêques se faisaient alors eux-mêmes hagiographes à l'occasion, comme Théodoret de Cyr,[64] tandis que leurs discours funèbres représentaient une contribution extérieure au récit hagiographique.[65]

Aux IXe-XIe siècles un tel épiscopat ne se fait pas entendre. Les moines sont une majorité écrasante dans la colonne des auteurs que nous avons dressée en commençant. Parmi les saints eux-mêmes, les rares évêques sont d'origine monastique comme Demetrianos de Chytri. Platon refuse de quitter son couvent pour le siège de Nicomédie. Nikephoros quitte au contraire le sien, Milet, pour revêtir l'habit de moine, 'ayant déposé en faveur de la gloire la plus grande et la plus élevée celle qui était la plus modeste' (ch. 14). La même leçon est évidemment proposée dans les Vies des patriarches venus du monastère, Nicéphore, Ignatios, Euthymios. Réciproquement, l'absence d'une Vie de Photios ne saurait surprendre, bien qu'il arrive à certaines hagiographies de le mentionner avec faveur, ainsi la Vie d'Euthymios le jeune par Basile archevêque de Thessalonique (ch. 12). L'ascendant

63. A.J. Festugière, *Antioche païenne et chrétienne. Libanios, Chrysostome et les moines de Syrie* (Paris 1959).

64. Théodoret de Cyr, *Histoire des moines de Syrie*, éd. P. Canivet et A. Leroy-Molinghen (SC 234, 257 [1977, 1979]).

65. P. ex. Grégoire de Nazianze, *Discours funèbre en l'honneur de son frère Césaire et de Basile de Césarée*, éd. F. Boulenger (Paris 1908). Grégoire de Nysse, 'Vie de Macrine', *Gregorii Nysseni opera*, dir. W. Jaegar, viii. 1 (Leiden 1952), 347-414.

du modèle monastique sur le laïcat impérial lui-même est illustré par la Vie d'Athanase, qui fait état de l'attirance que ce modèle aurait exercé sur Nicéphore II Phokas: le motif de l'empereur-moine s'esquisse. Au terme de la période en revanche, la sainteté de Syméon le Nouveau Théologien, éclatant au sein du cloître, et confortée par la référence à un père spirituel défunt, ouvre en fait un autre chapitre dans l'histoire des rapports entre la sainteté et l'Église des moines.

Le contexte social des saints est indiqué soigneusement, et plus précisément qu'à l'époque précédente. Une bonne partie d'entre eux se place assez haut dans l'échelle sociale de ce temps, où les dénivellations ne cessent de se creuser, où le niveau supérieur tend à se constituer de lignages attentifs à leurs alliances, et forts de leurs patrimoines, et de leur illustration militaire ou civile; où la capitale est, au surplus, au coeur de toutes les fortunes.[66] On relève d'abord, pour les hommes, les activités exercées avant de quitter le monde. Haute fonction publique dans la capitale, voire dans l'entourage même de l'empereur, pour un Platon de Sakkoudion, élevé par son oncle et employé avec lui dans les finances impériales. Pour un patriarche Nicéphore, fils de fonctionnaire, lui-même *a secretis*. Pour un Syméon le Nouveau Théologien, introduit à la cour par un oncle paternel, et membre du Sénat avec la dignité de spatharocubiculaire. D'autres futurs saints sont attachés à de grandes familles de la capitale. Evariste le Stoudite est 'en service' dans la maison de Bryennios,[67] et l'accompagne dans une ambassade auprès des Bulgares, Nikephoros de Milet, castré tout enfant en vue d'une carrière pour laquelle on l'envoie faire ses études à Constantinople, devient l'administrateur du *magistros* Mosellès,[68] son 'patron', Euthymios le jeune et Luc le stylite sont fils de 'maisons militaires'.[69] Le chroniqueur Théophane et Paul le jeune, qui n'auront pas de carrière dans le monde, sont orphelins de père, le premier d'un écuyer favori de Constantin V, le second d'un *comes* de la force maritime.

Mais l'Église offre elle-même une carrière à des individus et à des fratries. Elle absorbe la famille de Théodore Stoudite: son oncle maternel Platon fonde le monastère de Sakkoudion sur un bien de famille, son frère occupe le siège important de Thessalonique, sa mère finit moniale, lui-même joue le rôle que l'on sait à la tête du grand monastère rouvert dans la capitale. Son compagnon et successeur, Nicolas,

---

66. L'aristocratie de cette époque attend encore une étude générale. On en trouve des éléments dans: H.C. Beck, 'Byzantinische Gefolgschaftswesen', SB Bayer Phil. Hist. K1 (1965), H. 5; G. Ostrogorsky, 'Observations on the Aristocracy in Byzantium', *DOP* 25 (1971), 3-32; A.P. Kazhdan, *Sotsial'nyi sostav*, op.cit. (n.61); E. Patlagean, ' "Economie paysanne" et "féodalité byzantine".' *Annales ESC* (1975), 371-96; H. Ahrweiler, 'Recherches sur la société byzantine au XIe siècle: nouvelles hiérarchies et nouvelles solidarités', *TM* 6 (1976), 99-124; R. Morris, 'The Powerful and the Poor', *Past and Present* 73 (1976), 3-27. Liste non exhaustive.

67. Sur ce personnage, et sur le lignage Bryennios, cf. Nicéphore Bryennois, *Histoire*, éd. P. Gautier (Bruxelles 1975), 11-13.

68. Sur le lignage Musele (Moushegh), P. Charanis, *The Armenians in the Byzantine Empire* (Lisbonne 1963), 22, 25, 40-1.

69. Essai d'appréciation sociale dans E. Patlagean, ' "Economie paysanne" et "féodalité byzantine",' cit. ci-dessus, n.66.

entre au monastère de Stoudios sous les auspices d'un oncle paternel, Théophane, avant d'y être rejoint par son frère Titos, venu après lui de Crète. Paul le jeune suit son frère aîné. Euthymios le jeune entraîne après lui dans le monachisme sa mère, ses soeurs sa femme, et fonde pour sa parentèle, sur un terrain qu'il achète, un couvent double que dirigent son petit-fils et sa petite-fille. Familles du coup privées d'avenir, dira-t-on. En fait, il faudrait pouvoir les situer dans la parentèle plus vaste, où un Théodore Stoudite se trouvait le cousin germain de Théodotè, la compagne de Constantin VI.[70] On verrait sans doute alors l'entrée au monastère comme une pièce des stratégies lignagères qu'en fait nous embrassons malheureusement mal. La mort prématurée d'un père semble intervenir fréquemment: Théophane le Confesseur, Makarios de Peleketè, Nicolas le Stoudite, Euthymios le jeune, Paul le jeune, Athanase de Lavra, et le patriarche Ignatios tout le premier, fils de Michel I[e]; la chute de ce dernier, il est vrai, l'écarte du monde tout enfant. La mention d'un oncle moine vient souvent s'ajouter.

Famille et lignage

Ceci conduit à un autre aspect de la physionomie sociale des saints, et cette fois-ci des saintes également, leur position dans ces réseaux de la parenté, par le sang ou le baptême, de l'alliance, et de l'amitié contractuelle, horizontale ou verticale, qui constituent la véritable armature sociale de Byzance à l'époque. Cette position est toujours indiquée dans les récits hagiographiques, ce qui autorise une lecture à double entrée: références aristocratiques pour le saint, illustration de familles ou de lignages par leur mention dans de tels récits, et en rapport avec la sainteté. La relation peut être un simple point de départ. Ainsi en va-t-il pour Evariste le Stoudite, dont le père est avec l'épouse de Bryennios dans une relation d' 'issus de cousins'. Pour Athanase de Lavra' dont une amie d'enfance épouse le fils du stratège Zephinezer,[71] ce qui introduit Athanase auprès des Phokas. D'un autre côté l'histoire entière de Philarète est une entreprise généalogique, motivée par le mariage de sa petite-fille Marie avec Constantin VI, et confiée à son petit-fils et filleul Niketas. S'il faut en croire ce dernier son grand-père l'aurait à cet effet voué à l'habit dès l'enfance.

La tradition manuscrite est à cet égard éloquente.[72] Le cod. Genuens. 34, du XIe siècle, proche de l'original sinon copié sur le manuscrit même de l'auteur, se termine par le tableau de la famille, et ne comporte pas de prologue de type hagiographique. La version du Paris. 1510, en date de 1162, présente une langue normalisée, et ajoute un prologue, tandis qu'elle supprime le nom de l'auteur, et les détails qu'il donne sur lui-même. Enfin, dès le Vat. Palat. 17, du XIe siècle, apparaît une version de caractère rhétorique. où le tableau de la famille est supprimé. On

---

70. Vie A (*PG* 99.136): 'parente' (*syngenis*); Vie B (*PG* 99.253): 'cousine' (*exadelphe*).;

71. Cf. P. Lemerle, 'Vie ancienne de saint Athanase' (cité dessus, n.31), 90-1 et n.91. Il pourrait s'agir de Théodore Zoufinezer, beau-frère (frère de l'épouse) de Jean Garidas (Leo Grammaticus, éd. J. Bekker [Bonn 1842], 299).

72. Cf. l'éd. cit. ci-dessus, n.4.

voit bien, en ces trois étapes, la réduction d'une hagiographie familiale à une forme commune. Au coeur de l'aristocratie, la Vie de Michel Maleïnos s'ouvre par un éloge magnifique de son lignage, qui fait place à Bardas Phokas, époux de sa soeur, et père de Nicéphore II. L'auteur n'oublie pas de rappeler que ce lignage (*genos*) comptait déjà un saint, Eudokimos de Charsianon.[73] La famille d'Irène abbesse de Chrysobalanton est louée sans être nommée. L'hagiographe précise toutefois qu'elle avait concouru pour le mariage impérial − comme Marie petite-fille de Philarète − et que sa soeur avait épousé le César Bardas, oncle de Michel III. L'hagiographe de l'impératrice Theophano, épouse de Léon VI, est un familier des Martinakioi, dont celle-ci est issue. Il ne manque pas de les célébrer, et de rappeler leur vocation impériale.[74] Marie épouse de Constantin VI, l'épouse de Bardas Phokas, la belle-soeur du César Bardas, L'impératrice Theophano femme de Léon VI, la série suggère que le récit hagiographique pouvait avoir une fonction d'illustration complémentaire, par exemple pour le côté féminin d'un arbre généalogique. A l'extérieur des parentèles d'autre part, les fleurs données par l'hagiographe de Basile le Nouveau aux Gongylioi, ou par celui de Nikon à Michel Choirosphaktès, sont une parure à deux fins, l'illustration du saint lui-même, et de ses interlocuteurs aristocratiques. En somme, on arrive à la question générale, et en fait initiale: à qui et à quoi sert le récit de la sainteté?

Pouvoir posthume du saint

On découvre sans difficulté dans les Vies une église ou un monastère qui tirent du récit sur le pouvoir d'un saint la justification de leur pouvoir présent sur les fidèles, étayé par des miracles posthumes, ou tout simplement par une fête commémorative. Leur place dans les Vies va du récit de fondation à la mention de sépulture, en passant par des associations diverses, mais ils ne font pas défaut. Pourtant, les saints dont on examine ici les Vies n'inspirent pas le vocables des églises, à l'exception de Luc le jeune et de Theophano.[75] Ceux-ci sont empruntés à un autre niveau du culte, celui du théâtre sacré, où le saint peut jouer d'ailleurs, on l'a vu, le rôle de médiateur. Leur choix et leur rapport avec les saints contemporains constitueraient l'objet d'une autre histoire.[76] En revanche, leurs images, présentées aux

73. *BHG*[3] 606-7 (sous Théophile).

74. Prédiction faite sur un personnage de ce nom, peut-être apparenté à Théophile, Genesios. iii.15 (*Josephi Genesii Regum libri quattuor,* éd. Lesmueller-Werner et Thurn [Berlin-New York 1978], 49). Sur la parenté possible avec cette famille d'Eudokia Ingerina, mère de Léon VI, voir C. Mango, 'Eudocia Ingerina, the Normans and the Macedonian dynasty' *ZVI* 14-15 (1973), 17-27.

75. On dispose à ce jour de R. Janin, *La géographie ecclésiastique de l'Empire byzantin* 1: *Le siège de Constantinople et le patriarcat oecuménique* iii. *Les églises et les monastères* (Paris 1969); R. Janin, *Les églises et les monastères des grands centres byzantins (Bithynie. Hellespont, Latros, Galèsios, Trébizonde, Athènes, Thessalonique)*, rev. p. J. Darrouzès (Paris 1975).

76. P. ex. le cas de S. Elie dans la dévotion de Basile I[e] et dans l'hagiographie de l'époque appelle une étude, cf. la position du problème d'origine du culte chrétien en Grèce dans l'étude importante de S. Georgoudi, 'Sant'Elia in Grecia', StMSR 39 (1968), 293-319.

fidèles et suppliées par eux, jouaient un grand rôle dans le culte qu'ils inspiraient. Il en reste à vrai dire surtout les mentions hagiographiques, tandis que les icônes conservées pour la même époque se réfèrent au niveau où sont pris les vocables, par exemple S. Michel ou S. Théodore. Pour nous demeure donc en fait un matériel écrit, mentions liturgiques d'une part, récits hagiographiques de l'autre. Le problème de la production historique de ces derniers doit donc être posé au rebours de notre lecture.

L'étape la plus proche de la vie du saint et des débuts du culte était sans doute une transmission orale.[77] La Vie de Theodora de Thessalonique fait explicitement allusion à des entretiens narratifs de moines à son tombeau. Et il est aisé d'entendre ainsi le développement hagiographique habituel sur la diffusion des mérites du saint et l'étendue croissante de sa réputation. A un autre niveau social de la culture, Basil I[e] qui se fait lire des Vies d'hommes illustres et des exhortations spirituelles, 's'informe par le menu' des hommes qui se sont distingués par la 'règle de vie' (*politeia*) la meilleure selon les critères d'en haut.[78] Les Vies des saint alimentent au surplus pour leur part le goût vif de l'époque pour les biographies.[79] Cette étape orale a pu ne pas se produite toujours. La Vie du patriarche Ignatios par exemple relève d'une production de type historiographique. En milieu monastique, c'est-à-dire dans la majorité des cas, les auteurs des récits font état d'une injonction du saint lui-même, ou de son successeur à la tête du monastère. Il faudrait étudier sous cet angle l'echaînement des biographies stoudites.[80] Quoi qu'il en soit de la variété des cas, on peut admettre qu'un récit hagiographique est toujours pour une part la fixation écrite d'un ensemble de récits de circulation orale.

On observe alors que, dans la liste incomplète présentée ici, le décès, la composition de la Vie première, et le plus ancient manuscrit connu de celle-ci tiennent pour la plupart des saints dans l'espace d'un siècle. Il faudrait pousser plus loin l'étude, et commenter la provenance de ce manuscrit, son niveau de langue et sa graphie, enfin sa catégorie et son contenu. Les manuscrits véhiculent en effet des ensembles, dont la constitution n'est pas fortuite, ni toujours fondée sur le seul calendrier. Par exemple le Paris. 1547 réunit la Vie de Basile le Nouveau (26 Mars) et celle d'André le Fou (28 Mai), sans doute en raison d'un choix thématique, avec deux autres. La Vie de Theophano, dont la mention liturgique est pourtant précoce, on le verra, ne nous est plus connue avant un recueil d'hagiographie féminine du XIVe siècle: que s'est-il passé dans l'intervalle? Même question pour la Vie de Syméon le Nouveau Théologien, dont deux manuscrits du XIVe siècle sont aujourd'hui nos premiers témoins. Compte tenu des pertes possibles, on voudrait

77. Pour tout ce qui suit, définitions générales dans Beck, *Kirche und theologische Literatur,* cit. ci-dessus n.1, 246-53 ('Die liturgischen Bücher des byzant. Ritus') et 267-75 ('Hagiographie').

78. *Vita Basilii,* ed. cit. ci-dessus n.57, 314.

79. P.J. Alexander, 'Secular Biography at Byzantium', *Speculum* 15 (1940), 194-209.

80. Voir les suggestions de M. Sot, 'Historiographie épiscopale et modèle familial en Occident au IXe siècle', *Annales ESC* (1978), 433-49.

comprendre ce que le nombre total de manuscrits conservés d'une Vie, et leur ventilation chronologique, enseignent sur sa diffusion.[81]

Reconnaissance publique de la sainteté

L'audience des récits hagiographiques était au surplus multipliée par la lecture faite devant un public de moines ou de fidèles. La reconnaissance publique de la sainteté, d'autre part, se fait par l'inscription dans la liturgie. Et nous observons tout d'abord qu'à l'exception de Luc le jeune nos personnages sont absents du Ménologe classique dit du Métaphraste, composé dans la seconde moitié du Xe siècle,[82] et dont les choix ne descendent guère au-delà du second iconoclasme. Considérons ensuite le Ménologe dit de Basile II,[83] et quatre éditions du calendrier officiel de la capitale, le Synaxaire de la Grande Eglise.[84] Nous en tirons le tableau suivant:

Saint	H	P	Fa	Mén.Bas.	S
Philarète			x	x	x
Nikephoros de Medikion	x				x
Théophane	x	x			x
Théodore Stoudite	x	x	x	x	x
Nicéphore (le patriarche)	x	x			x
Pierre d'Atroa			x		x
Nicolas Stoudite			x		x
Ignatios (le patriarche)	x	x	x	x	x
Constantin de Synnada			x		x
Evariste Stoudite			x		x
Euthymios le jeune			x		
Luc le jeune			x		x
Paul le jeune			x		x
Luc le stylite			x		x
Theodora de Thessalonique			x		x
Theodora (impératrice)				x	x
Theophano (imperatrice)	x		x	x	x
Thomaïs de Lesbos			x		

81. Problème de méthode posé dans *Byzantine Books and Bookmen* (Dumbarton Oaks 1975), surtout par N. Wilson ('Books and Readers in Byzantium', 1-15), et déjà abordé par A. Ehrhard, *Uberlieferung und Bestand der hagiogr. u. homilet. Literatur der griechischen Kirche von den Anfängen bis zum Ende des 16. Jhdts* i.2 (Leipzig 1938).

82. D'après la reconstruction d'A. Ehrhard, op.cit. (n.81). Cf. J. Gouillard, 'Syméon logothète et magistros surnommé le Métaphraste', *DTC* xiv.2 (1941), 2959-71. Luc le jeune figure au demeurant dans la reconstitution plus restrictive proposée par H. Delehaye, 'Les ménologes grecs', *AnalBoll* 16 (1897), 311-29. A noter que la Vie de Paul le jeune est insérée dans le Ménologe métaphrastique de Décembre par le Paris. 1490.

83. *Il Menologio di Basilio II (Cod. Vaticano greco 1613)*, éd. P. Franchi de' Cavalieri (Turin 1907).

84. Cf. J. Mateos, *Le Typikon de la Grande Eglise. Manuscrit Sainte-Croix nº 40, Xe siècle. 1. Le cycle des douze mois* (Rome 1962), Introduction, iii-xix, qui donne les précisions suivantes: H. (Hierosol. S. Crucis 40), Synaxaire de Septembre à Août, écrit et utilisé dans la capitale; la date serait 950-9. P. (Patm. 266), Synaxaire de Septembere a Août, provenant du monastère de S. Sabas, composé à la fin du IXe ou au début du Xe siècle. Fa (Paris. 1590), Synaxaire de Septembre à Février, écrit dans un monastère proche de

On voit que le calendrier officiel est en retrait des récits de sainteté inspirés par les hommes et les femmes des IXe-XIe siècles. Quelques personnages occupent une position forte, aisément explicable: Théodore Stoudite et le patriarche Ignatios, champions du parti moine, ou Theophano, dont la sainteté est une cause impériale. La discordance entre liturgie et hagiographie d'une même époque est significative. Le saint contemporain est effectivement proclamé par le récit de la sainteté et de son pouvoir, mis par écrit dans des recueils qui ne sont pas sans un rapport direct avec le calendrier liturgique. Pourtant, la liturgie la plus officielle ne suit guère: nos personnages n'y pénètrent que plus tard. Il conviendrait alors de mieux saisir la liberté plurielle de reconnaître, de déclarer, et d'honorer des saints.

L'exemple capital de Syméon le Nouveau Théologien en indique les limites. Il est convoqué en effet, on s'en souvient, devant le synode, en raison du culte qu'il a établi pour son père spirituel, Syméon Stoudite. L'autorité s'est émue du reste tardivement. La confrontation rapportée par Niketas Stethatos montre bien que le grief n'est pas simplement d'avoir inauguré un culte de saint, mais de le pratiquer dans le cadre d'une sainteté dissidente, extérieure à toute autorité disciplinaire et canonique [85] On pourrait en conclure, réciproquement, que l'Eglise laissait instaurer les saintetés qui reconnaissaient implicitement les normes d'une telle autorité, sans qu'il y eût pour autant procédure officielle de canonisation. Pareil dispositif rendrait bien compte du pouvoir social du saint à cette époque, dans sa diversité. Il avait toujours été bon d'avoir un saint à l'origine d'un monastère, et ceci demeurait, dans un monachisme distribué autrement que par le passé. Mais la haute société des IXe-XIe siècles trouva qu'il était bon aussi d'avoir un saint dans son lignage, ou parmi ses amitiés.

L'hagiographie et les récits du pouvoir impérial

Il faut ajouter à cela que le récit du pouvoir impérial semble de son côté emprunter en certains cas une dimension hagiographique. Je ne fais pas allusion ici à la Vie d'Athanase, et à la vocation monastique trahie qu'elle prête à Nicéphore II Phokas, mais à des motifs que l'on trouve dans l'historiographie de la même époque.

Tout d'abord, la Vie de Basile I^e, telle que l'a voulue son petit-fils Constantin VII. Les signes de son élection se conforment à la tradition antique, lorsqu'un aigle plane sur son sommeil d'enfant. comme à la tradition scripturaire et chrétienne, avec les visions qui avertissent de sa destinée sa mère ou d'autres.[86] Alors, qui emprunte à

Jérusalem. Le manuscrit S (Berolin. Phillipp. 1622) a été écrit aux XIIe-XIIIe siècles dans un couvent de la capitale, cf. H. Delehaye, 'Le Synaxaire de Sirmond', *AnalBoll* 14 (1895), 396-434, et son édition critique du Synaxaire de la Grande Eglise, *ActaSS*. Propyl. Novembris (1902). Je laisse de côté l'indication supplémentaire du rang dans la notice.

85. J. Gouillard, 'Syméon le jeune, le théologien ou le Nouveau Théologien', *DTC* xiv.2 (1941), 2941-59. J. Darrouzès, introd. à son éd. de Syméon le Nouveau Théologien, *Traités théologiques et éthiques* (SC 122 [1966]), 23-37 ('La doctrine').
86. Étude fondamentale de G. Moravcsik, 'Sagen und Legenden über Kaiser Basileios I', *DOP* 15 (1961), 59-126.

qui? La question est sans objet. Dans les deux cas, l'éloge en forme de biographie utilise les mêmes arguments.

Un autre cas, et moins notoire, est au moins aussi intéressant. Il touche le noeud à la fois politique et hisoriographique du Xe siècle, le meurtre de Nicéphore II Phokas par Jean Tzimiskès − son neveu, l'amant de son épouse Theophano, veuve de Romain II l'empereur précédent, enfin, par ce meurtre, son successeur. La loi de l'historiographie, qui est celle même du pouvoir impérial à Byzance, veut que la victoire désigne constamment l'élu, en place de celui que la défaite, au contraire disqualifie. Dans le cas présent, les circonstances notoires rendaient également difficile de plaider l'élection de Jean Tzimiskès, et la disqualification de Nicéphore. Léon Diacre, compagnon et historiographe de Tzimiskès, choisit une solution dont l'un des éléments est un portrait hagiographique de Tzimiskès devenu empereur: dévotion à Marie, bienfaisance, soins aux lépreux.[87] On pourrait suggérer aussi que, dans toute la tradition, Nicéphore reçoit en fin de compte la mort d'un martyr.

Le montrer m'entrainerait ici trop loin. Pourtant, la confrontation des récits justificatifs de pouvoir à Byzance aux IXe-XIe siècles, hagiographie ou historiographie, est indispensable. Elle permet de comprendre que, dans cette période d'apogée où la théorie et la symbolique des pouvoirs achèvent leur maturation séculaire, le pouvoir est unique.

87. Leo Diaconus, *Historia*, éd. C.B. Hase (Bonn 1828), vi.3 et 5, *passim;* cf. index s.v. 'S. Maria'.

The Holy Fool

LENNART RYDÉN

T HE holy fool is a person who serves God under the guise of foolishness. In principle, the disguise is not discovered until the fool is dead. Then he or she becomes a saint. If the holy fool happens to be recognised earlier he runs away, or else commits an act that is so foolish that the rent in his disguise is repaired.

Palladios

The first time we meet a holy fool in Greek literature is in Palladios' *Lausiac History*,[1] which was finished around 420. Palladios says that in a convent at Tabennisi in Egypt there was a nun who pretended to be possessed by a demon and to be a fool. She lived like an outcast, stayed in the kitchen, did all the dirty work, ate only crumbs and what she could scrape out from the pots and pans after her fellow-nuns' meals. Instead of a nun's cowl she had a rag on her head. The other nuns called her a *sale,* for this was the word, Palladios says, which they used for women who were afflicted by demons (*paschousai*). And since she was supposed to be a *salē* they beat her and humiliated her. But she did not react or even complain. One day a holy man found out, through the intervention of an angel, that the *salē* was in fact a saint, more holy than himself. Now the nuns repented having treated her so cruelly and started to venerate her. But their veneration was too much for her and she disappeared. According to Palladios, this woman put into practice the word of the apostle, 'If any one among you thinks that he is wise in this age, let him become a fool that he may become wise' (1 Cor. 3:18).

In this short legend we already meet several characteristic features of the Byzantine holy fool, the incognito, the self-abasement, the bad treatment, the moral lesson. We also meet the word *salos*, which was to become the technical term of the Byzantine holy fool. And we meet the reference to the first letter to the Corinthians.

What does this reference mean? There is no indication that the *salē* at Tabennisi thought she was wise in this age and that she therefore had to become a fool in order to become wise. St Paul himself did not behave like a fool, nor did he recom-

---

1. Ch. 34; ed. C. Butler (*Texts and Studies*, ed. J.A. Robinson, vi.2 [Cambridge 1904]), 98-100. Cf. J. Grosdidier de Matons, 'Les thèmes d'édification dans la Vie d'André Salos', *TM* 4 (1970), 277-328, esp. 283-5; W. Bousset, 'Der verborgene Heilige', *ARw* 21 (1922), 1-17.

2. Cf. *Dictionnaire de spiritualité* v, s.v. 'Folie de la croix', 646 (A. Derville).

mend the Corinthians to make fools of themselves. It is true that he said, 'We are fools for Christ's sake' (4:10) and 'The foolishness of God is wiser than men' (1:25). But what he had in mind was in essence that the Christian message is a matter of belief, not of reason and speculation. This was also how the Fathers understood the text of the Bible (so John Chrysostom, Basil the Great, and Theodoret).[2] Moreover, the foolishness of St Paul was sincere, whereas the holy fool is an actor, who feigns madness on purpose.

This difference is in line with the fact that the Greek technical term for a holy fool is *salos*, not *mōros*, which is in the New Testament. The etymology of *salos* is doubtful. It is supposed to come from the Syriac translation of the first letter to the Corinthians.[3] If this is true, the holy fool was born in Syria, and his spiritual father was St Paul. But the similarity between *salos* and *sakla*, the Syriac equivalent of *mōros*, is not very striking,[4] and there does not seem to be any other convincing Syriac etymology. This reminds us of the fact that when the word *salos* appears for the first time it is in a story from Egypt, not in a story connected with Syria. So it may be that the quotation from St Paul does not so much show where the idea of holy foolishness came from, as how the hagiographers understood and defended it. At any rate it seems clear that St Paul's words themselves would not have been enough to make certain Christians serve God under the mask of madness. The rise of monasticism was certainly a necessary prerequisite.

Evagrios and Symeon Salos

The church historian Evagrios, who wrote at Antioch toward the end of the sixth century, describes a group of ascetics that look like holy fools, although they are not so called. Having described the life of the monks in the monasteries around Jerusalem in the reign of Theodosius II he then describes the so-called *boskoi*, the grass-eaters.[5] These ascetics do not eat bread but live on wild herbs and plants. They have no home but roam about the mountains singing the glory of God. At last the grass-eaters become just like animals. Then Evagrios goes on to say that some of these hermits, presumably the grass-eaters, leave the desert and return to civilization. They do not interrupt their ascetic life but continue to go naked, except for a loincloth, they continue to fast, to do genuflections, to say prayers, and they also heal the sick. On top of that they pretend to be mad, doing things that would normally be incompatible with asceticism, like eating openly and associating with women, even bathing with them. All this is possible because in the desert they have acquired *apatheia*, a complete insensibility and lack of desire or, if you like, a complete self-control.

3.   Ibid., s.v. 'Fous pour le Christ en Orient', 753 (T. Špidlík).
4.   Professor F. Rundgren, Uppsala, has kindly informed me that the etymology *salos‹sakla* is out of the qeustion. Cf. M.A. Guillaumont as quoted by Grosdidier de Matons, *TM* 4 (1970), 279 n.7.
5.   *The Ecclesiatical History* i. 21, ed. J. Bidez and L. Parmentier, 30-3.

According to Evagrios, this is the highest form of ascetic life, a final step that few hermits are able to take. By taking this step they free themselves of their last human weakness, their *kenodoxia,* their vainglory or vanity. Evagrios does not mention that they are badly treated and humiliated, but this is probably understood. Nor does he expressly quote the first letter to the Corinthians — this would have been alien to his literary style. But as he attaches so much importance to the *kenodoxia,* this may be *his* way of referring to St Paul.

Evagrios does not mention any name at this stage (first half of the fifth century). But later on, as he comes to the reign of Justinian I, he describes Symeon Salos in a way that is reminiscent of this passage.[6] Symeon lived at Emesa in Syria. Most of the time, says Evagrios, he lived by himself. No one knew when he worshipped God or how he did it. When he appeared in the street he seemed completely mad. Sometimes when he was hungry he went into a tavern and helped himself. If anyone made obeisance to him he seemed offended and fled.

Evagrios also reproduces three anecdotes about Symeon. The first is about a girl who became pregnant and put the blame on Symeon. At first, Symeon did not object. On the contrary, he even pretended to be ashamed of what he had done. But when the time came for her confinement the child could not be born until the girl had revealed the name of the real father. The second is about a harlot. Symeon visited her in such a way that everybody thought that he had made love to her. But in reality Symeon had only brought her food, since he knew that she was starving. In the third Symeon predicts an earthquake. He took a whip, went to the agora and slashed the columns there — not all, but most of them. At the same time he said, 'Stand up, you will dance!' Then the earthquake came and many columns fell. But some remained upright, and these were exactly those columns that Symeon had slashed.

These anecdotes demonstrate Symeon's power over nature, his secret kindness and his prophetic gift. But we are not told how he had reached the perfection that enabled him to perform miracles.

The passage ends with the remark that Symeon also did many other extraordinary things, but to tell them all would demand a separate book. This book was actually written, not by Evagrios but by Leontios, who was bishop of Neapolis in Cyprus in the middle of the seventh century.[7]

Leontios and Symeon Salos

Leontios not only tells the stories about Symeon for which Evagrios had no room, he also gives him a background. And in doing so he seems to combine the two passages in Evagrios' history which I have just summarised. At any rate he

6. Ibid., iv.34, 180-4.
7. Ed. L. Rydén, *Das Leben des hl. Narren Symeon von Leontios von Neapolis* (Uppsala 1963), reprinted with minor changes in *Léontios de Néapolis, Vie de Syméon le Fou et Vie de Jean de Chypre,* ed. A.J. Festugière in collaboration with L. Rydén (Paris 1974). The page numbers of the Uppsala edition are given in the inner margin of the Paris edition.

presents Symeon the holy fool as the perfect fruit of a long development. Step by step, Symeon has cut the ties with the world, and after 30 years as a *boskos*, a grass-eater, he has acquired complete *apatheia*. He can return to the world without risk. He can even dance with the show-girls at the theatre and let them touch him without being sexually aroused. This does not mean that he stops living as an ascetic. He continues to fast, to keep awake all night, to pray. But he does it secretly. To the citizens of Emesa he appears as a fornicator, a glutton, a drunkard, a fool, an epileptic, and is treated accordingly.

But why does he return to the world? Evidently not just in order to fight his *kenodoxia*, his vainglory, as did the ascetics described by Evagrios. Leontios does not even mention the word. No, Symeon's aim is more altruistic. As he decided to leave the desert he said to his fellow-*boskos* John, 'What use is it to stay here in the desert? Here we can save ourselves only. Come, let us save others as well!'[8] And later on John, who did not dare to leave the desert, admitted that when he died, he would receive only one heavenly crown, the crown of endurance in the desert, whereas Symeon would receive as many crowns as the number of souls he had saved.[9] This implies that Symeon, as Leontios sees him, is not primarily interested in healing the sick and helping the poor. What he wants to do is to save men from their sins and rescue them from the attacks of the demons. In the words of Leontios

> The whole aim of this all-wise Symeon was this. First to save souls, either through visitations which he brought about in an absurd or ingenious way, or through wonders, which he performed foolishly, or through instructions which he gave while playing the fool. Second, to keep his virtue secret, lest he become the object of praise and honour.[10]

The visitations and wonders may be exemplified by the following two stories. Once Symeon wanted to save the soul of a certain juggler. So he went to the theatre, made the sign of the cross on a little stone and, without anyone noticing it, he threw the stone on the juggler's right arm. The arm was paralysed and the juggler could not finish his act. In the following night when he was asleep Symeon appeared to him in the guise of a monk with a wreath on his head and said, 'If you do not swear that you will never more appear on the stage, your arm will not become sound again'. The juggler dreamt that he promised, and when he woke up his arm was healed. He also told his story to others, but he could not tell who the monk was that had appeared to him during the night.[11] Another time Symeon and a number of beggars were warming themselves in a glassblower's shop. The glassblower was a Jew. 'Do you want a good laugh?' Symeon asked the beggars. 'For every glass the glassblower makes I will make the sign of the cross, and the glass will break'. In this way the glassblower broke seven glasses in succession. When the beggars told

8. Rydén, *Das Leben*, 142. 14-16.
9. Rydén, *Das Leben*, 166. 23-7.
10. Rydén, *Das Leben*, 157. 12-16.
11. Rydén, *Das Leben*, 150. 7-19.

him that it was Symeon's fault he threw him out of his shop. But Symeon said, 'You son of a bitch, until you make the sign of the cross on your forehead you will break everything'. The Jew broke thirteen more glasses in succession. Then he gave up and became a Christian.[12]

Symeon did everything, says Leontios in another passage, under the guise of foolishness and indecency. Sometimes he pretended to be lame, sometimes he jumped and bounced, sometimes he dragged himself along on his buttocks like a cripple, sometimes he tripped people up so that they fell. When the new moon appeared he stared at the sky and fell to the ground, trembling like an epileptic. He also made proclamations, as it were. This is the best method, he said, for those who feign foolishness for the sake of Christ. For in this way he could denounce sinners and stop them from sinning. He could send them punishments. He could make predictions, while people thought that he was one of those who proclaim and prophesy under the influence of demons.[13] Thus Symeon exposed some as thieves, others as fornicators, still others as perjurers or as evaders of communion.[14]

When Symeon died the citizens of Emesa woke up as if they had been asleep and told each other of all the wonderful things that Symeon had performed. Now it was clear to all that he had played the fool for the sake of Christ. But even before, there had been some doubt about the genuineness of Symeon's folly. Once a man had said, 'Perhaps he is simulating'.[15] And another time some had thought that he was a saint, while others had said that he must have been inspired by Satan, since he was insane.[16]

Insane people were supposed to be possessed by demons, and the demons were supposed to speak through the mouth of their victims. Hence the insane sometimes seemed to possess supernatural knowledge. On the other hand, spiritual men who had received the power of the Holy Ghost also knew things that were hidden to ordinary men, and they sometimes also behaved in a strange way. Here was an area of uncertainty which the holy fool could exploit; here was a kind of no man's land between the realm of the angels and the realm of the demons where the holy fool could operate. Moreover, the uncertainty how to judge the fool made it possible to ascribe to him supernatural power. Wonderful stories were invented and attached to him. Then the hagiographer collected the narrative material and formed it according to biblical models and legendary patterns. In this case Leontios presented the holy fool as an unusually ingenious imitator of Christ and defended him with the same skill as he defended the icons against the Jews.[17]

12. Rydén, *Das Leben*, 163. 7-15.
13. Rydén, *Das Leben*, 155. 19-156.4.
14. Rydén, *Das Leben*, 162. 17-19.
15. Rydén, *Das Leben*, 148. 7-8.
16. Rydén, *Das Leben*, 152. 3-4..
17. Leontios' skill as a defender of icons was noted by N.H. Baynes in his paper 'The Icons Before Iconoclasm', *Byzantine Studies and Other Essays* (London 1955), 226-39.

Occasional and dubious folly

With the loss of Egypt, Palestine and Syria, Byzantine asceticism lost something of its impetus and freshness. Holy fools of the calibre of Symeon Salos did not appear any more. Instead we meet pious men who behave like fools for short periods and for special reasons. Basil the Younger, who is supposed to have lived at Constantinople in the tenth century, was such a part-time holy fool.[18] Symeon Eulabes, the teacher of Symeon the New Theologian, was another.[19] In the New Theologian's own monastery at Constantinople there was a monk from the West who did penance in the way of a holy fool.[20] Cyril of Phileas, who died in 1110, also on occasion played the holy fool.[21] At about the same time a young Greek called Nicholas went about in South Italy crying, *Kyrie eleēson* like a fool.[22]

But behind these and other relatively well known cases there must have been a number of anonymous holy fools of a more doubtful sincerity. Symeon the New Theologian warns against them in one of his instructions (No. 28):

> Those who have been enlightened by the Holy Ghost have the power of dis-
> crimination, but the judgment of those who do not have the light of the
> Spirit is bad. They accept those who fast with vanity but condemn those who
> eat with humility. Those who fast with humility they regard as hypocrites,
> but those who eat greedily they consider simple and natural. They even enjoy
> eating in their company, for then they can satisfy their own desires. Those
> who feign that they are fools, cracking jokes and speaking nonsense at the
> wrong moment, those who behave improperly and make people laugh, these
> they revere as being free from desire and holy, thinking that they try to con-
> ceal their virtue and their lack of desire through such behaviour. At the same
> time they disdain and neglect those who live in piety, virtue and the simplicity
> of their heart and are truly holy, as if they were ordinary men.[23]

So far Symeon the New Theologian. In the latter half of the eleventh century Kekaumenos gives the following advice:

> Do not play with a fool. He will insult you and maybe pull at your beard.
> Imagine how shameful that would be. And if you let him run away, everybody
> will laugh, but if you beat him, you will be blamed and reviled by everybody.
> The same will happen to you with regard to those who *pretend* to be fools. I
> recommend you to have pity on them and to be generous, but you should not

18. *BHG*³ 264; cf. L. Rydén, 'A Note on Some References to the Church of St. Anastasia in Constantinople in the 10th Century', *Byzantion* 44 (1974), 198-201, esp. 198 n.2.

19. See. I. Rosenthal-Kamarinea, 'Symeon Studites, ein hl. Narr', *Akten des XI. internationale Byzantinistenkongresses München 1958*, ed. F. Dölger and H.-G. Beck (Munich 1960), 515-20.

20. See I. Hausherr, *Un grand mystique byzantin. Vie de Syméon le Nouveau Théologien* (OC 12 [1928]), 68-78.

21. É. Sargologos, ed., *Vie de S. Cyrille le Philéote* (SubsHag 39 [1964]), esp. ch. 15, 86-7.

22. See H.-G. Beck, *Theodoros Metochites, Die Krise des byzantinischen Weltbildes im 14. Jahrhundert* (Munich 1952), 96-8.

23. Syméon le Nouveau Théologien, *Catéchèses*, ed. B. Krivochéine, tr. J. Paramelle (Paris 1963-5), iii. 156-8.

play and laugh with them. This is no use. I have seen people laugh and play with such a person until they killed him with their pranks. No, you should neither outrage nor beat a *salos*, whoever it is. Listen to him, whatever he says; do not despise him, he may be trying to outwit you with his folly.[24]

Like Symeon the New Theologian, Kekaumenos does not seem to have liked the holy fools. At least he does not seem to have found them interesting. They were poor fellows. Their way of life was dangerous. You should be kind to them. But you should take care, lest you might be involved in a joke unworthy of a gentleman.

In comparison with Symeon Salos, the Middle Byzantine holy fool seems to have been colourless and impotent, evidently because he lived in a different society and there was no Leontios who had the ambition to extol him and give him teeth and muscles.

The late Byzantine fool

In the fourteenth century hagiography was stimulated by the hesychastic movement and the opposition it provoked. Thus the hesychastic patriarch Philotheos Kokkinos wrote quite a number of *vitae*. Among them there is a long Life of St Sabas the Younger.[25] Sabas was born in Thessalonica. After school he spent seven years on Mount Athos. After that he lived the life of an itinerant ascetic. He visited Cyprus, Palestine, Crete, Euboea, and the Pelopponnese. He died at Constantinople, probably in 1348.[26]

Sabas practised asceticism in three ways: he was naked, he was silent, and he pretended to be a fool.[27] Especially during his stay in Cyprus he practised foolishness for the sake of Christ. His foolishness was not of the aggressive kind. Unlike Symeon Salos he did not perform indecent or provocative acts. His folly manifested itself mainly through silence. People thought he was stupid rather than mad. Philotheos himself says that Sabas is not like other holy fools. He says that there are those who play the fool without sufficient preparation. These people are mistaken. Instead of mocking the world and the demons, they let the world and the demons make fun of them. They do not *play* the fool, they *are* fools.[28] If you want to become a fool for Christ's sake, you must be alert, and in order to be alert you must keep silent.[29]

A.-J. Festugière, who has drawn attention to Sabas as a late Byzantine holy fool, thinks that this is a veiled criticism of the classical holy fools Symeon and

24. *Strategicon,* ed. B. Wassiliewsky and V. Jernstedt (R.P. Amsterdam 1965), 63.18-28; ed. G.G. Litavrin (Moscow 1972), 246.13-23; tr. H.-G. Beck, *Vademecum des byzantinischen Aristokraten* (Graz 1964), 111-12.
25. Ed. A. Papadopoulos-Kerameus, *Analekta Hierosolymitikēs Stachyologias* 5 (St Petersburg 1898), 190-359.
26. See A.J. Festugière's essay in *Vie de Syméon le Fou* (n.7, above), pp.223-49. See also D.M. Nicol, *Church and Society in the Last Centuries of Byzantium* (Cambridge 1979), 44-5.
27. ibid., 238.
28. Papadopoulos-Kerameus, *Analekta,* 221. 14-19.
29. ibid., 235.28ff.

Andreas. This seems unlikely. I would rather think that Philotheos had in mind those dilettantish holy fools that Symeon the New Theologian disliked so much. Neither Symeon nor Andreas had started to play the fool until they were ready for it. And there is a passage in the Life of Sabas in which the devil says to Sabas, 'Why did you abandon the usual way of the Fathers and try this unbeaten track? Only one or two have reached their goal on this road'.[30] Who should these 'one or two' be, if not Symeon and Andreas?

A fictitious fool and his impact

I mentioned Andreas Salos. He is a special case, since he is a fictitious saint. He is supposed to have lived in the fifth century and the author of his Life wants us to believe that he was an eyewitness. But in reality the author lived several centuries later, in my view in the tenth century.[31] Why this mystification? Apparently because the author had something to say that he thought he could best express through the medium of an ancient *salos*. He seems to have lived in an atmosphere of eschatological expectation. He thought that his own time was like the time of Noah: people were happy-go-lucky, but soon the flood would come and carry them all away. This message he put into the mouth of a holy fool: the world is blind, but the holy fool knew what would come about centuries ago. The author obviously did not like high-brow theology. Through the holy fool he could convey his own less subtle, more graphic teaching.

We do not know how the Life of Andreas Salos was received as it first appeared. We only know that it was successful in the long run. As time went on Andreas and his teaching became very popular, especially in Russia, where he gained many imitators. The Russian holy fools are somewhat different from the Byzantine *saloi*, particularly in their attitude toward society.[32] But the holy fools of Russia are outside the frame of this brief paper.[33]

30. ibid., 229.5-8.
31. See L. Rydèn, 'The Date of the *Life of Andreas Salos*', DOP 32 (1978), 127-55.
32. For an introduction to the holy fools in Russia, see G.P. Fedotov, *The Russian Religious Mind* ii (Cambridge, Mass., 1966), 316-43, and Chr. Walter, 'Dwazen om Christus' wil', *Het Christelijk Oosten* 27 (1975), 252-65, esp. 257-63. For recent studies of the Russian tales of holy fools, see Natalie Challis and H.W. Dewey, 'Divine Folly in Old Kievan Literature: The Tale of Isaac the Cave Dweller', *SIEEJ* 22 (1978), 255-64, esp. 252 n.1.
33. A slightly enlarged version of this paper is to appear in Swedish in *Religion och Bibel* 39 (1980). [Since this article went to press, a noteworthy study of Folly for Christ has been published by John Saward: *Perfect Fools* (Oxford 1980)].

THE LIFE AS GENRE

The 'Low Level' Saint's Life in the Early Byzantine World *

ROBERT BROWNING

B Y 'low level' saints' lives I mean the lives of saints whose activity is largely among relatively humble people, who have few connections with persons of power and influence, and who are not — except quite incidentally — members of the hierarchy of the Church. Such lives are generally composed in an unpretentious style and in a language little affected by classicising tendencies. Like all early Byzantine hagiographical texts they may be rewritten in more classicising and prestigious style in the tenth century. But both the language and style and the content of the original versions suggest that these lives were composed with a popular audience or readership in mind. The common features which they display — and they are many — may throw some light on how the Byzantine 'man in the street' saw holy men and what he expected of them.

It must be emphasised that we are not concerned with the saint as he was but with the saint as he was perceived by the average members of the society within which he passed his life. The mode of his perception is determined in large measure by a whole structure of shared concepts which formed part of the common man's view of the world.

There are 'low level' lives of 'dead' saints like St George or Sts Kosmas and Damianos. But they present problems of their own. We shall concentrate in the present paper on lives of saints written by persons who knew them in their lives or who had direct access of those who knew them. The stylites, from Symeon in the fifth century to Lazaros the Galesiote in the first half of the eleventh are typical examples.[1] So too are such saints as Theodore of Sykeon in the late sixth and early seventh century,[2] Peter of Atroa in the early ninth century,[3] Luke of Stiris[4] and

---

* In addition to the sources and secondary studies referred to in connection with particular passages, I have derived much help from the following recent publications: Evelyne Patlagean, 'Ancienne hagiographie byzantine et histoire sociale', *Annales ESC* (1968), 106-24; P.R.L. Brown, 'The Rise and Function of the Holy Man in Late Antiquity', *JRS* 61 (1971), 80-101; A. Meredith, 'Asceticism — Christian and Greek', *JThS* 27 (1976), 313-22; Julia Seiber, *Early Byzantine Urban Saints* [British Archaeological Reports, Supplementary Series 37] (London 1977).

1. Cf. H. Delehaye, *Les saints stylites* (SubsHag 14 [1923]); P. van den Ven, ed., *La Vie ancienne de S. Syméon Stylite le Jeune* (Brussels 1962).

2. Cf. A.-J. Festugière, *Vie de Théodore de Sykéon* (Brussels 1970).

3. Cf. V. Laurent, *Vie de S. Pierre d'Atroa* (Brussels 1956).

4. Cf. Vita Lucae, *PG* 111. 441-80.

Nikon Metanoeite in the tenth.[5] It springs to the eye that none of these saints lived in or was connected with Constantinople or with any of the other great cities of the empire. The 'popular' saint belongs to a provincial, and largely to a rural, environment.

Freedom from ordinary needs

What are the common features which the lives of all or most of these saints display? First and foremost, the holy man is one who withdraws from society, its bonds, its constraints, and its rewards. These he sees as irrelevant to his overriding purpose of approaching more closely to God. So he leaves the city of his birth and takes flight to the desert or the mountains; or he isolates himself upon a pillar or in a cave. He abandons the city for the desert. Yet the city follows him. His powers cause a structured society to grow up around him. Often it at first takes the form of a monastic community of men who share his desire to withdraw from the world. But soon a large settlement springs up around the holy man, with churches, accommodation for pilgrims, permanent habitations, and the rest, sometimes surrounded by a wall. Examples are Qal'at Sem'ân, north-west of Aleppo, and the complex of structures on the Admirable Mountain west of Antioch. Occasionally the holy man is incorporated into the hierarchy of the Church, but in general against his will and often only temporarily. An example is Theodore of Sykeon in Bithynia. For though the holy man may live in society, he is not of it, and he constantly distances himself from the manner of life of ordinary people, even those among whom he dwells. There is always a certain tension between the purposes of the saint and those of his followers, since in his person two different worlds overlap.

The holy man does not share the needs of ordinary people. Apart from the rejection of sexual relations, which is common to all ascetics, he has no need of many other things which are essential to the average man and the object of most of his striving. First of all food. Symeon Stylites was reported neither to eat nor to drink. Six centuries later and a thousand miles distant, Lazaros the Galesiote ate only once a week. Symeon the Younger tried to dispense with food altogether and finally succeeded in doing so, save that an angel brought him a kind of rice pudding every Sunday.[6] It is probably futile to speculate whether this last item of information is a rationalisation by Symeon's biographer or a final proof of the saint's holiness. If the holy man does eat — and most of them, most of the time, do — then he avoids cooked food, which is the mark of civilisation, of assertion of human control over a potentially hostile nature.[7] It is almost as if the hagiographers had read Lévi-Strauss. Symeon the Younger from his earliest childhood would eat nothing

5. Cf. S. Lambros, 'Ho Bios tou Nikōnos tou Metanoeitē', *Neos Hellēnomnēmōn* 3 (1906), 131-228.
6. *Vie de S. Syméon le Jeune* 256 (van den Ven, 222).
7. *Vie de S. Syméon le Jeune* 3 (van den Ven, 5).

Anonymous stylite. Stone relief.
Hama Museum, Syria, c. 5th-6th century.
Photo: C. Mango.

119

'prepared'. Peter of Atroa ate only raw vegetables — no meat, cheese, bread, oil or wine, the staples of ordinary diet.[8]

Sleep was another need of the ordinary man with which the saint could dispense. All of them often pass long periods without sleep, in prayer or in psalmody. The monks in the monastery which grew up around the holy man would wake in the night to hear him singing or praying without remission. The stylites did not lie down, except in extreme old age.[9] If they slept at all, they slept on their feet, perhaps leaning on the rail which surrounded their lofty platform.

The saint had no need for shelter. He had no house, but lived in the open or in some natural cavity such as a cave or a hollow tree. Some of the stylites seem to have had no shelter at all; they could be seen in all weathers standing in the open, a visible testimony of their special status. Others had a kind of awning or hut constructed over their platform, with a window through which they could look and communicate with their followers or with visitors.[10] Alypios in the sixth century at first had a tent on top of his pillar, but later demolished it and spent the rest of his very long life in the open.[11] None of the stylites used fire, an essential amenity in the life of ordinary men.

Similarly the saints have no need of clothing. Not merely do they usually have little and poor clothing, usually only a single garment, often a hair shirt. But they may pass long periods of complete nudity. Symeon the Younger as a child often gave away his only garment to a poor companion.[12] In later life he once spent eight months naked on top of his pillar.[13] If the holy man did have clothing, it was not as that of other men. It was often a *trichinon sticharion* or a *sakkos*. And it was imbued with the superhuman powers of its wearer. The sweat-rag of the saint or a few threads from the fringe of his *sticharion* could be the instrument of miraculous cures at a distance.

Lastly, the saint did not, as ordinary men do, require the support of a family. His path to holiness regularly begins with his running away from his family in childhood, and often disappearing for a long period. Luke of Styris is picked up by the Byzantine police as an absconding minor the first time he runs away, given a thrashing, and returned to his mother.[14] But later he succeeds in disappearing without trace, though in fact he had not gone far away. Symeon the Younger, as soon as he was baptised at the age of two, began to repeat constantly the words, 'I have a father and I have not a father; I have a mother and I have not a mother'.[15] (What

8. *Vie de S. Pierre d'Atroa* 11 (Laurent, 97). On abstinence from 'prepared' food cf. Athanasius, *Vita Antonii* 7.
9. Cf. Delehaye, *Les saints stylites,* clv.
10. Cf. Delehaye, op.cit., clvi-clx.
11. *Vita S. Alypii* 15 (Delehaye, op.cit., 159).
12. *Vie de Syméon le Jeune* 30 (van den Ven, 30).
13. *Vie de Syméon le Jeune* 77 (van den Ven, 65).
14. *Vita S. Lucae Iunioris, PG* 111. 445n.
15. *Vie de S. Syméon le Jeune* 5 (van den Ven, 7).

with this and his finickyness about food, he must have been an exasperating child!) Luke the Stylite came of a family that was comfortably off. But he took no part in administering or conserving the family property, and gave away as much of it as he could to the poor.[16] The holy man does not depend on his family to define his position in society. He is alone in his confrontation with metaphysical forces.

However there is a curious ambivalence in the attitude of many of the hagiographers, which suggests a certain mistrust of the complete loner. Once they have established their special status of holiness many saints are reported to have maintained friendly and even close links with their female relations. Symeon the Younger was in constant contact with his mother, who acted as a kind of public relations officer for him. Finally she attained a somewhat bland and nebulous sainthood. Alypios in Paphlagonia was in close contact with his mother until her death.[17] Theodore of Sykeon, once his holiness was established, maintained touch with his mother and his grandmother. It was the latter who saw to it that he took the necessary minimum of food during his exploits of asceticism.[18] It is striking that no saint has much to do with his father, who is usually rather vaguely outlined and often dies when the future saint is still a child. Have we here a reflection of Oedipal jealousy? Or of the tension between the generations which marked a society organised for the transmission of wealth rather than the creation of wealth, to which many anecdotes, particularly in the *Philogelos,* bear witness?[19]

Extraordinary powers

The counterpart of the saint's freedom from ordinary needs is his possession of extraordinary powers. The very nature of his life calls for extreme powers of endurance and resistance to fatigue and hunger. He nearly always has a precocious development. Indeed few saints seem to have had any real childhood. Their intellectual and spiritual powers are not those of children. Theodore of Sykeon learnt the whole Psalter by heart 'in a few days'.[20] Other future saints practise the extremes of asceticism at an age when most children are preoccupied with play. All holy men possess the power of prophecy, which they may exercise on an imperial as well as on a local scale. Theodore of Sykeon foretells the death of the emperor Maurice.[21] Akin to prophecy is clairvoyance, both as the ability to know of distant events and as that of reading the thoughts and feelings of men. Both types of clairvoyance are too common in the saints' lives under discussion to need illustration.

Perhaps the commonest manifestation of holiness is the healing power of the saint. He deals with every physical and mental affliction from constipation to leprosy, cancer and gangrene. Usually he works by touch, often accompanied by

16. *Vita S. Lucae Stylitae* 5, 7 (Delehaye, *Les saints stylites,* 200, 202).
17. *Vita S. Alypii* 15, 19 (Delehaye, op.cit., 159-60, 162-3).
18. *Vie de Théodore de Sykéôn* 32, 33.
19. Cf. *Philogelos,* ed. A. Eberhard (Berlin 1869), Nos. 13, 24, 38.
20. *Vie de Théodore de Sykéôn* 13.
21. ibid., 119.

prayer. Sometimes prayer alone suffices. Sometimes the holy man works his cure at a distance by sending to the patient something which has been in contact with his person. Occasionally he makes a miraculous personal appearance at a distance. In the accounts of these healings illness is as a rule treated as of demonic origin; but there are many exceptions to this rule. Often the healing offered by the saint is contrasted with that of orthodox doctors. It is instantaneous, while theirs is slow, it is painless while theirs involves much discomfort or the agony of surgery without an anaesthetic, and so on. But sometimes there seems to be a tacit demarcation agreement between the holy man and the doctor, who send one another suitable patients. A case in point is the Life of Theodore of Sykeon.[22] It is striking how many of the patients treated by holy men appear to be suffering from some kind of hysterical paralysis. Were such conditions really so common in the early Byzantine world? And if so, why?

The extreme case of healing power is the resurrection of the dead. Many holy men do on occasion restore the dead to life, for example Symeon the Younger[23] or Peter of Atroa.[24] But those restored to life are always special cases – children, persons killed by a sudden accident, persons dying in mortal sin, and so forth. The saint's healing powers are always available to the sick, but only very rarely to the dead. For death is a normal part of life and not the work of demons, as is disease. It belongs to the natural order.

The holy man's life is a continual struggle with demons. Ordinary men and women knew that they were surrounded by demons. But the saint could see and hear them, and sometimes make them briefly visible and audible to others. Often he engages in long dialogues with demons. His victory is never in doubt. Presumably if he failed to overcome a demon he would not be a truly holy man.

The forces of nature are subject to him. He regularly diverts storms, arrests both floods and droughts, causes swarms of locusts to depart or to die. He has power over wild beasts too, and engages in ever-victorious confrontations with everything from snakes to lions.

He regularly has visions or hallucinations, which are quite different from the dreams of ordinary men. Symeon the Younger has a series of apocalyptic visions while wide awake.[25] Peter of Atroa sees both Christ and the Virgin Mary.[26] Sometimes the visions are of events in far distant places. In addition to the ability to see things at a distance, the saint sometimes has the power of bilocation. Symeon the Younger, who never quitted his pillar, was often seen and heard in other places.[27] Peter of Atroa made similar visits at a distance.[28] It is sometimes difficult to distin-

22. ibid., 145.
23. *Vie de S. Syméon le Jeune* 129 (van den Ven, 117-22).
24. *Vie de S. Pierre d'Atroa* 22 (Laurent, 119).
25. *Vie de S. Syméon le Jeune* 29, 66 (van den Ven, 29, 57-9).
26. *Vie de S. Pierre d'Atroa* 4 (Laurent, 75).
27. *Vie de S. Syméon le Jeune* 91 (van den Ven, 71).
28. *Vie de S. Pierre d'Atroa* 41 (Laurent, 155-7).

guish between the holy man's perception of himself as visiting distant places and other people's perception of him elsewhere than where he was known to be. The saint could sometimes become invisible. Peter of Atroa several times evades his iconoclast enemies by passing unseen through their midst.[29] Sometimes he posseses indestructibility which goes beyond mere endurance of extremes of weather and fatigue. A stylite in Asia Minor entered a fire which was burning in a fire-place in order to refute heretics.[30] The third Symeon the Stylite — whose date is uncertain — was struck by lightning without suffering any ill effects.[31] And no stylite ever fell from his pillar, overcome by dizziness or fatigue.

Miraculous provision of food is one of the exploits regularly recurring in these saints' lives. Symeon the Younger fills the granary of his monastery when it is empty and the monks are in despair.[32] Luke the Stylite provides a miraculous catch for the fishermen of the Bosphorus.[33]

The saint is always aware of the powers which distinguish him from other men, and punishes those who question either their existence or their origin. The punishment is often surprisingly severe. Paralysis or serious illness are the most usual forms, and the saint grants relief only when the sceptic repents of his doubts. Occasionally he is given no opportunity of repentance. Symeon the Younger punished a *scholastikos* (lawyer or merely intellectual?) of Antioch who cast doubt on the divine origin of his powers by causing him to suffer a fatal seizure in a public place in the company of two *illoustrioi* (holders of the highest offices of state).[34]

Lastly, the holy man enjoys longevity, in spite of his exhausting life style. Daniel the Stylite lived to 84, Lazaros the Galesiote to 86, Theodoulos the Stylite to 90. Luke the Stylite was more than 100 years old when he died. Michael, a Stylite in Mesopotamia, was 105. Theodore of Edessa knew a stylite reputed to have spent ninety-five years on his column. Alypios lived to the age of 120.[35]

Several different strands can be traced in the life of the 'low-level' saint as perceived by his followers and contemporaries. The most obvious is the imitation of the Gospel story. The healings, the miraculous provision of food, the restoration to life of the dead, the dialogues with demons, the apocalyptic visions, perhaps the close maternal links and slight role of the father, all recall the life of Christ, which provided a model or framework within which the life of the holy man could be organised. But there are many recurring motifs and structural features in these saint's lives which have no Gospel parallels. The most important will be reserved for separate discussion. In the meantime it is evident that invisibility, invulnerability, and longevity fall outside the Gospel framework and recall rather the pagan aretalogy.

29. ibid., 66 (Laurent, 195).
30. Cf. F. Nau, *ROChr* 7 (1902), 605.
31. Joannis Moschi, *Pratum spirituale* 57.
32. *Vie de S. Syméon le Jeune* 122 (van den Ven, 100-3).
33. *Vita S. Lucae Stylitae* 16 (Delehaye, *Les saints stylites,* 212).
34. *Vie de S. Syméon le Jeune* 224 (van den Ven, 194-6).
35. Delehaye, op.cit., *passim.*

The precocious development of the future saint also has pagan precedents — the infant Herakles strangling the snakes in his cradle and the infant Achilles in Pindar (*Nem.* iii. 43ff) are two parallels which spring to mind. Bilocation and clairvoyance are typical marks of the shaman, who, like the saint, acquires his powers by withdrawal from society and returns to it in a new status.[36] The cultural amalgam of late antiquity and the early Byzantine period provided more than enough models and patterns out of which the humble and oppressed could construct a fantasy of life rising above the physical and social constraints to which they were subject, a fantasy which perhaps enabled them the more easily to endure the harshness and drabness of their everyday life. Perhaps for some of his contemporaries the holy man played a role not unlike that of Superman, both in the Nietzschean and in the Hollywood sense of the word, reminding them, if only in an exaggerated and sometimes superficial way, of the range and power which, if God will, human ability can attain.

The path to sanctity

How did the holy man establish his sainthood and gain his superhuman powers? Withdrawal from society is always involved. Usually it is physical withdrawal to the desert or the mountains, or to the aerial regions. Sometimes it is social withdrawal, as when the saint feigns madness and is so freed from the normal restraints and tabus.[37] Self-imposed hardships are also both a path to holiness and a demonstration of it, and are to be seen as a form of withdrawal; the saint seeks out that which other men avoid. Many saints begin by wrapping cords tightly round their bodies until they cut into their flesh. Others voluntarily accept the chains which awaited a humble member of society if he fell into debt or offended those in authority. Theodore of Sykeon wore heavy iron chains and passed a long period in an iron cage.[38] Symeon the Elder loaded his body with chains.[39] So did Luke the Stylite and Lazaros the Galesiote.[40] These apparently perverse choices of what most men avoid were unquestioningly accepted as evidence of holiness.

36. Cf. E.R. Dodds, *The Greeks and the Irrational* (Berkeley 1951), 140-3, 160 (bibliography).
37. Cf. E. Benz, 'Heilige Narrheit', *Kyrios* 3 (1938), 1-55; J. Saward, 'The Fool for Christ's Sake in Monasticism, East and West', *Theology and Prayer*, ed. A.M. Allchin [*Studies Supplementary to Sobornost* 3] (London 1975); L. Rydén, *Das Leben des hl. Narren Symeon von Leontios von Neapolis* (Uppsala 1963); S. Murray, *A Study of the Life of Andreas, the Fool for the Sake of Christ* (Borna-Leipzig 1910).
38. *Vie de Théodore de Sykéôn* 28.
39. Theodoret, *Historia religiosa* 26.10.
40. *Vita S. Lucae Stylitae* 5 (Delehaye, *Les saints stylites*, 200); Delehaye, op.cit., cx.

OPPOSITE
Irons worn by an ascetic (sidērophoros), *displayed at Xenophontos, Athos*
Photo: Robert Byron (by courtesy of the Courtauld Institute of Art)

It is striking how often the acquisition of sanctity involves a kind of substitute death. Often the young man passes months or years in an enclosed or subterranean space resembling a grave. Symeon the Stylite lived in an abandoned water-tank, Alypios in an old tomb,[41] St John of Rila in tenth-century Bulgaria lived for many years in a hollow oak-tree which recalled a coffin.[42] Theodore of Sykeon excavated a *spēlaion skoteinon* under the altar of a church and lived there for some months. Later he hollowed out another *spēlaion* under a rock in a remote place and remained there, unknown to all but one disciple, for two years.[43] When his grandmother and mother found him, his head was covered in dried blood (*ichōr*) and full of worms, his bones were laid bare, and none could stand near him because of the stench. In the words of his biographer, 'he looked like a corpse'. The point could not be made more clearly. Theodore was as it were a man risen from the dead. His holiness needed no further proof, and the local bishop at once ordained him reader, sub-deacon, deacon, and priest. The evil smell resulting from the holy man's self-mortification is mentioned again and again in the lives as evidence that he has passed beyond the normal human state and gained superhuman powers. It clearly symbolises the smell of death. But the stench of holiness soon turns into its apparent opposite, the fragrance of holiness. Once his sainthood is established the saint's body and all that is in contact with it distil an exquisite and unearthly perfume, like that which flows from the relics of dead saints and martyrs.

So the saint is perceived not merely as one who enjoys all the powers which the humble do not possess – a kind of Superman. He is also seen as one who has passed beyond the human condition although he continues to sojourn among his fellow men. He is beyond sin and beyond the power of evil, and has regained the primeval innocence of man before the fall. He is a living reminder of the victory of life over death and of good over evil, and one that is local, visible, and tangible. He has died and been born again. But his rebirth is the beginning and not the end of his earthly career. In this respect the pattern of the saint's life is very different from that of the life of Christ.

Not all 'low-level' saints display clearly all the characteristics that have been enumerated. But all show some of them, and many show all of them.

Social and political status

Human weakness and vanity play their part in the perception of the saint. Naturally he is a man without possessions. But his poverty is usually chosen, not inherited. His parents are often respectable, sometimes substantial citizens. The parents of Luke the Stylite owned a considerable estate – perhaps including a *stratiōtikon ktēma*, since his father was a soldier. As a young man Luke distributed

41. Theodoret, *Historia religiosa* 26.6.
42. J. Ivanov, 'Zhitiia na sv. Ivana Rilskii', *GodSof* 31.13 (1936), 28.
43. *Vie de Théodore de Sykeôn* 16, 19, 20-1.

his property to the poor, then worked for two years as a swineherd.[44] Theodore of Sykeon, though the son of a barmaid and prostitute, was somehow related to leading members of his local community − protiktores, as they are called[45] − and his unknown father was reputed to be a person of more than local importance.[46] This emphasis on the economic and social position which the saint abandons in his search for holiness is partly ethical; poverty is not a moral category unless it is voluntary. But it probably also contains an element of social snobbery. The man who embodies so many of the dreams and aspirations of the group must not be in origin a nobody, a landless, homeless, rootless outsider.

Though essentially a local figure, linked closely with a particular region and often with a particular spot, the saint sometimes displays his powers at an imperial level. He prophesies the death or accession of emperors, warns them, is consulted by them. This is not all fantasy. Daniel the Stylite, who is perhaps not quite a low-level saint, was really consulted by several emperors − presumably through an interpreter, since the saint never troubled to learn a word of Greek. Theodore of Sykeon, living and working in a region through which a main military road passed, may well have actually visited Constantinople and become acquainted with persons of power and influence including three emperors; after all, he was a bishop, however reluctant. But in most cases the imperial and metropolitan connections of the holy man must have been a reflection in fantasy of the common man's eagerness to have influence with the highest authority, an eagerness which cohabited uneasily with an anxiety to keep out of the way of authority in general.

The counter-hero of the dispossessed

The popular saint appears as the direct antithesis of the ideal citizen of classical antiquity. He is a rural, not an urban figure. He lacks military prowess, he has no public career, he is equally devoid of physical strength and beauty and of intellectual distinction. Yet it may be unwise to take him as evidence for a complete abandonment of traditional ideals . Perhaps he displays a kind of reflection of the ideal man of classical urban culture, but a reflection in a distorting mirror. His prowess is in the unceasing war against demons and the powers of evil. He follows a career which takes him out of this world and into the next by a regular progression of triumphs over human constraints. He possesses moral strength and spiritual beauty, often manifested in a kind of glowing aura surrounding his person. And though he may not read books, he has the power to read men's minds and hearts − *dioratikotēs.*[47] He is perhaps to be seen as the counter-hero of the dispossessed and of those to whom the high urban culture of Late Antiquity had nothing to offer.

44. *Vita S. Lucae Stylitae* 5 (Delehaye, 206).

45. *Vie de Théodore de Sykéon* 25.

46. ibid., 3; he was a forrmer circus acrobat who had become an imperial *apocrisiarius* under Justinian. Was he perhaps a protégé of Theodora?

47. Cf. A.-J. Festugière, *Vie de Théodore de Sykéon,* ii. 218.

The Saint as a Symbol

MICHEL VAN ESBROECK

Translated by Michael Breck

I T may at first seem redundant to refer to a saint as a symbol. Do we not chose saints as intercessors and models? I present this essay as *The Saint as a Symbol* simply for lack of a better title. In order to justify this title, we must first examine the historical complexity which the adjective "symbolical" is meant to convey. Our goal is to uncover the historical role of a group of typically hagiographic legends which were appropriately listed by Fr Delahaye among the epic passion narratives.[1] These passion narratives are connected to one another through unexpected details that crop up in each of them. In the style of apologias, fables or even political caricatures, they illustrate the empire's destiny in its conversion to Christianity. Their protagonists are endowed with a symbolic function that extends far beyond the rather nebulous identity of the most prominent of characters.

The development of these legends is actually rooted in the Judeo-hellenistic world, in the various accounts of the Maccabean Passion and the story of Joseph and Asaneth. Their apex was clearly achieved by the fifth century. The central characters bear the names St Sophia, St Irene, St Christina and St Barbara. The fact that these saints are women is an immediate indication of their official origin among the symbols of the community as these appear in the Old Testament. Is the Lord not addressing his more or less faithful spouse? Is the community of Israel not personified as the "daughter of Zion," who comes down from the mount near the holy temple? What I hope this essay will demonstrate, on the basis of specific examples, is that the abundance of daughters or sons of kings in ancient hagiographic writings places these in a special category in which the symbols drawn from the person in question far exceed any discernable historical connections. The saints mentioned above are the mothers of the Rhypsimian saints, of Behnam and Sara, and of many others. These saints represent above all the transformation of a community that is unfaithful to its ancestral place of worship at the moment of its acceptance of Christianity, most often through martyrdom.

It might make more sense to start with ancient representations to arrive at those of the sixth century, nevertheless, it is possible to trace a branch back to its root. In doing so we hope to remain more in line with the theme set forth by this conference,

---

1. H. Delahaye, *Les Passions des martyrs et les genres littéraires* (Bruxelles, 1996), 213-217.

namely the Byzantine saint. It is, after all, in the sixth rather than the first century that Byzantium had become the capital and the bearer of countless examples of saints.

The legends of the martyrs can scarcely be conveyed through a mere summary of their content. The fundamental eloquence of their discourse, the rhetorical opposition within each situation and the abundance of tortures, sufficient to satisfy even the most accomplished sadist, remain the standard backdrop of these narratives. The contrast between the transcendent innocence of the victims bound to their faith and the brutish and diabolical governor is a fundamental element of the genre of which none of these legends is entirely free. But through the presentation of this aggressive and boisterous piety, there is of course the remembrance of what they suffered. The question remains as to whether it is possible, more or less, to pinpoint the date at which these legends first appeared. We believe a certain approximation is possible if we consider the way in which most of these legends are connected to a church or to ancient temples whose own transformations have changed the content of the stories.

However, so as not to mislead the reader by making connections too early on between the rather free accounts of creative imagination and the solid ground of history, we must pay special attention to the legends themselves, with their temporal *aura* and their eternal message: purity triumphing over vulgarity, the righteous, through death, trampling down the iniquity of his wicked judge.

The Passion of Sophia

Lady Sophia of the gentry of Sallustia, among the highest of nobility, is swayed by her three daughters in whom a fervent desire for martyrdom is at work. Thus Antiochus, the prefect of the city, informs Emperor Hadrian of the harmful effects of their propaganda: they encourage abstinence from food and drink and lead house wives away from their conjugal duties.

Hadrian summons them and is immediately struck by the transparent beauty of the three young girls. First, he asks Sophia her name. "Christian," she replies. She then reveals herself to be of Italian nobility, come to Rome to offer to God the fruit which he has given her. Thus the location of the story is given. Sophia exhorts her daughters with all the visceral eloquence of a loving mother: "Hear me and be steadfast! Woe to me! Take from me the sin that surrounds me." The young girls answer: "Have no fear that we will yield to our weakness. Give joyously of the fruit of your womb!"

The Emperor then offers these admirable young girls to be the pride of their mother by making a sacrifice to the gods. Because of their royal lineage he would adopt them as his own daughters. If not, they would be tortured and thrown to the dogs. But all three reply: "God will welcome us as his children, and our way is toward heaven. Bring on the tortures!" So the Emperor learns from Sophia: the eldest, Pistis, is twelve, the second, Elpis, is ten, and the last, little Agape, is only seven. The Emperor asks them again to sacrifice to Artemis, the goddess of beauty. But Pistis answers: "Shall we abandon Christ for inanimate idols and dumb stones?"

129

She then suffers four tortures: first, twelve men undress and scourge her, but she remains unscathed. Then her breasts are cut, but only milk issues from them. The people are scandalized and grumble. She is then places for three days on a red hot grill where she hovers like a ship on a quiet sea. A vat is then filled with oil, wax and pitch, but these all turn to ice the moment Pistis is thrown in. So the Emperor decrees that her head be cut off. Immediately she exhorts her sisters: "You have sucked the same milk as I have! May God remember Elpis and Agape." Her mother then reminds her that she gave her of her milk. Pistis prays to God to send down the worst afflictions on Hadrian. She is then put to death.

So Hadrian turns to Elpis and asks her to make a sacrifice to Artemis, but she says: "I am Pistis' sister and I have sucked the same milk!" She too suffers four tortures. First, ten men wear themselves out trying to beat her; then come the burning embers on which she is able to walk comfortably, all the while invoking on the Emperor a curse of relentless worms. She is then suspended on a tree and skinned with metal brushes; the pieces falling to the ground give off a sweet smell. Finally, a cauldron is filled with pitch, wax, grease and resin, but just when the saint is thrown in, the cauldron shatters, injuring several people. And so she is condemned to the sword. She embraces her mother and the body of Pistis and advises Agape not to follow the iniquitous tyrant.

After the execution, Sophia says to her youngest daughter: "My hope for you is a crown worthy of those of your two sisters!" Thus Hadrian turns to the little one, but she responds immediately: "We were all nourished by the same breast!" And for her part, Sophia asks her to hold fast to the witness from above. Again four tortures are prescribed. Like a roaring lion, Hadrian first orders reeds and brushes to be used together, followed by scourging with the reeds. He then has a furnace heated for three days and says: "Simply say: 'Artemis is Great.'" Agape answers: "You have lost all hope of life!" When the furnace is opened, the flames stretch far and wide, sixty cubits, and six thousand people are swept away. The fire reaches the Emperor himself who barely escapes with his life. He then sends *protectores* to judge Agape's fate. But they see three men in white protecting the girl in the midst of the flames. She is then brought out and her body is pierced with red hot skewers. Only then is the beheading carried out. Agape prays God, asking that after three days Sophia might receive the grace to join them. Sophia expresses her joy and embraces the three bodies.

Three days later, she travels eighteen miles from Rome to fulfill the rites of burial with spices. No sooner have the prayers ended that she falls dead upon her daughters' tomb; and the women that were with her lay her beside her daughters.

Hadrian is struck with an incurable illness: the Emperor's flesh and his legs are consumed by worms, his joints fail and he cries out: "I know that this is the result of the prayers of those three innocent and pure girls!" After his death, his flesh disappears and his bones are dispersed and are no more.

This is, in short, the exact content of the legend. It would be a mistake to

Martyrdom of St Sophia and her children. From the Menologian of Symeon Metaphrastes.

embellish it with a romantic backdrop, full of wailing and cries. The scriptural allusions guide the hagiographer's pen, while the superiority of Christ from above over the prince from below is sketched out with the precision of an architectural drawing. This type of literary icon is atemporal in its essence. It does not lend itself even to an approximate dating nor to corroboration. Yet, without straying from the solid ground of the story itself, I propose a comparison with another Sophia, who is better situated amongst no less evanescent characters, though closer to history.

Another Sophia

Listen to the story of Lady Sophia, the virtuous. There was once a patrician in the court of Honorius and of Arcadius. His name was Theognostus, and his wife Theodora was devoted to him. They were rich but had no children. Furthermore, the emperor, who was also their parent, sent them to see the patriarch, John Chrysostom. The patriarch anointed them with water and oil from the lamp in the sanctuary. Nine months later, they gave birth to the blessed Sophia. Everyone rejoiced in the occasion. When she turned five, her parents built her a high chamber, full of precious stones, of ivory thrones and of beds of gold. In the middle was a cross of gold so she could pray. Later on, one of the patricians, Castor, asked for her hand in marriage, and they had three children, Stephen, Paul and Marc. The emperor ordered that Stephen be seated to his right and Paul to his left. When Castor, Theognostus and Theodora died, Sophia remained alone and began thinking:

> Great wealth does not keep death at bay. Think of your soul, your turn will come. If I remain a widow, I will be remarried because of my three children. God will despise me and I will be humiliated before my parents and my husband. But if I enter a convent, my inward parts will burn and my children will come burn the convent because of me!

So she took counsel with John Chrysostom. But the saint could only repeat for her the words of the gospel: "If you gain the whole world, and lose your soul…" That night Sophia remained prostrate before the golden cross in the room, beseeching the Lord and the Virgin. Then a blinding light appeared in the window. A resplendent woman said to her: "I am the Virgin Mary, the mother of light. If you wish to please God, he will not call you in this city. Arise and follow me, I will have you speak to my son."

The next day Sophia was still prostrate before her cross and did not know where she was. The Mount of Olives and the convent of the community of Euphemia rose up before her. The Abbess Euphemia had seen angels several times, both at Golgotha and at the Anastasis. An angel told her that the Virgin and her son had come to her convent and that at her door lay the chosen creature. She found Sophia in front of her golden cross, unaware of her surroundings. Opening her eyes, she was bewildered at the sight of a hill and mountains. Chrysis, a nun from Constantinople, recognized

Sophia who explained that a cloud had brought her from one capital to another. For fear of the emperor's wrath, Patriarch Theodore was notified. He sent letters of explanation to Arcadius, but three months went by before their arrival.

Meanwhile, the children, deprived of their mother, ran to the emperor in amazement. A wicked man told them he had seen Sophia in the cell of Patriarch John. So the children went there. The saint received them in their distress and with their accusations but could offer no more than his sympathy. But the angel of the Lord told him that a letter of explanation would arrive from Jerusalem three months hence. While at the convent, Sophia deprived herself of all food save a few grains moistened with water on Saturdays. When Arcadius received the letters, he noted that no one can rebel against the decisions of our Lord and admired the way in which the cloud had carried Sophia. But the three children decided to undertake their voyage. It lasted six months. From the eleventh of Touba, an exhausted Sophia fell ill. The virgin appeared to her and said: "You will come to rest with me, but you will see your three sons before your death. They will take your body to Constantinople and place it in the golden pavilion. They will make your house into a church at your sons' request, and it will forever be the emperor's main church." At dawn, on the twenty-first of Touba, the sons arrived surrounded by soldiers. Though these soldiers did not enter the convent, the monastics were greatly troubled at the sight of them. The patriarch entered alone with the three youths. When her sons saw their mother in such a woeful state, they shed many tears. But she thanked the Lord. Sophia taught them wisdom and gave up the spirit the twenty-first of Touba. When her body was venerated it effected miracles and healings. Once it was brought back to Constantinople, it was placed in the golden pavilion which John consecrated in the name of the Father, and of the Son and of the Holy Spirit. But it was called Saint Sophia, the name it bears to this day. It is the metropolitan church where the emperor still hears the liturgy.

In recounting these legends, we have purposely refrained from obscuring the living message with an excess of references. Just in hearing them, I believe that anyone with a grasp of Byzantine history will have detected more than a simple harmony, an orchestration of every detail into a truly symphonic resonance. But before striking a full chord, let us first examine the basic elements of these introductory poems.

The Manuscripts

Sophia, the mother of Pistis, Elpis and Agape, came to us through a fifth-century manuscript[2] and another dated 708.[3] Its later Greek forms had made such changes to

2. BM Add MSS 17204; cf. W. Wright, *Catalogue of the Syriac Manuscripts of the British Museum* (London, 1872), iii. 1081. Agnes Smith-Lewis uses this exceptional testimony in her "Select Narratives of Holy Women," *Studia Sinaitica* (London, 1900), 218-41. The end of the codex is missing.
3. Although the subtitle of the work reads 778 (n. 2): From the Syro-Antiochene or Sinai Palimpsest as written above the *Old Syriac Gospels by John the Stylite of Berth Marî Qanûn in A.D. 778*. H. H.

the language and style that the editor refused to produce a critical edition except as three joint publications. [4] Many Latin adaptation exist as well, one of which includes a long episode out of Milano, connected with the character of Palladius, who is also present in the Greek texts but only in a secondary role.[5] The Syriac text on which we have based this summary of our story is the only one to mention the gentry of Sallustia, and makes no reference to Palladius. The Syriac codex is sufficiently ancient to ensure that this is the older form of the story.

As for Sophia, the mother of Stephen, Paul and Marc, the source is an Arabic witness from the Coptic, Jacobite Synaxarion, the Paris codex 4869, a seventeenth-century copy that was restored in the nineteenth century.[6] An attentive reader will have noted the response to the preceding story, though it is developed from a monophysite perspective in a Coptic milieu.

The historical context of the first Sophia

The legend itself came about in Constantinople where the marvelous basilica of Saint Sophia is located. On the Latin side, the indications of the worship were studied by H. I. Marrou. This worship is confirmed by scrolls from Monza and in an inscription from North Africa, near Constantine, from the end of the sixth century.[7] But the Latin legends are based on the Greek model.[8] Just the Greek names of the young girls, which have led in our day to such common names as Vera, Nadejda or Nadine, and Liubov, are explained in the Latin versions as well as in the Syriac texts

The Latins have nevertheless introduced an interesting element by combining the feast of Sophia with that of the Maccabees on August first.[9] The Roman topography is referred to in terms too vague to allow us precisely to situate the eighteen miles that separated the young girls' tomb from the place of their ordeal in the city. The fourth book of Maccabees, occasionally attributed to Joseph, is generally considered to be a first-century work.[10] It is the very type of Judeo-hellenistic legends and the model for all Christian passion narratives. Like many texts drawn from the same milieu, such as the book of Enoch or the Testaments of the Patriarchs, there are Christian interpolations in more than one version. One of these is preserved in Arabic and Georgian and

Hussmann in 'Die syrischen Handschriften des Sinai-Klosters. Herkunft und Schreiber,' *OKS* 24 (1975), 298, showed the MS sin. 30 to date back to 708.

4. F. Halkin, *Légendes grecques de 'martyres romaines'* (Bruxelles, 1973), 179-228.

5. B. Mombritius, *Sanctuarium seu Vitae Sanctorum* (Paris, 1910), 374-80 (*BHL* 2966).

6. G. Troupeau, *Catalogue des manuscrits arabes. Première partie: Manuscrits chrétiens* (Paris, 1974), ii. 49-50. Ed. J. Forget, *Synaxarium Alexandrinum* (Paris, 1905), 391-99; and R. Basset, PO II (1905), 639-53.

7. H. I. Marrou, "Dame Sagesse et ses trois filles," *Mélanges offerts à Mademoiselle Christine Mohrmann* (Utrecht-Anvers, 1963), 177-83.

8. F. Halkin, *Légendes grecques*, 182-85.

9. "Martyrologium Romanum," *Propylaeum ad Acta Sanctorum Decembris* (Bruxelles, 1940), 318.

10. Cf. *BHG³*. 1006; and A. Dupont-Sommer, *Le IVè livre de Macchabées* (Paris, 1939).

presents an interesting change in the perception of the function that such accounts might have served in the first centuries.

The mother of the seven Maccabees is usually presented as the eighth Shamûnit in Syraic and Arabic versions. However, the name Shamûnit also means Ogdoad. The Arabic-Georgian version of this legend has the mother speaking to each son before he is tortured. To the first she says: "You are the first day of creation. In you light is created," and so on for each of the seven sons and the seven days until the day of rest and the Ogdoad herself.[11] This mother implicitly plays the role of creative Wisdom founded on seven pillars. Like Sophia and her daughters, Shamûnit, with each son, does not spare the fruit of her womb. From this presentation arises the purpose of the Maccabean Passion as a corrective to gnostic speculations in which Sophia is enthroned beyond the limits of the Ogdoad, facing the seven creative elders, children of Ialdabaoth.[12] The cosmic story of Lady Wisdom, incarnate within history through persecutions, already has its place in August first. This Judeo-Christian source becomes completely Christian by creating Lady Wisdom herself, a female Holy Spirit, giving birth to the three godly virtues at work within the Church. These were indeed put to death during the anti-Christian persecutions of the nascent Church. But why in Rome?

At the time of the persecutions, Byzantium was not yet the capital of the empire. A legend arising in Greek lands had to validate its position by drawing the setting for its martyrdoms from the ancient capital. Where else could one set such a universal destiny? An why under Emperor Hadrian? Edessa had its three martyrs: Gurias, Samonas and Habib, under Diocletian. Antioch celebrated Babylas and the three youths under Numerien. Byzantium needed something better and older, yet without diminishing the glory of the period under Nero which held the relics of Saints Peter and Paul. Thus the new capital, so conscious of acquiring the mark of nobility, achieves a nobility worthy of its universal prestige, in the East as in the West.[13]

The question remains whether it was necessary to resort to a fifth-century Syriac witness in order to date the legend of Saint Sophia to the fourth century. There are several such documents that date at least as far back.[14] There are two characteristics we would like to emphasize here: the death of the tyrant is brought about by the curses pronounced at every torture by each of the young martyrs. The execution is then recounted with a level of detail that can also be found in related legends, such as

11. Georgian Sinaitic MS 62 fol. 120-9; and Tbilissi A-95 fol. 482-91; both from the end of the tenth century.

12. On all of these themes, with extensive commentary, one may read F. Sagnard, *Extraits de Théodote* (SC 23 [1948]), 23-5 (la mère et la Sagesse).

13. Cf., on this theme, the entire book of G. Dagron, *Naissance d'une Capitale, Constantinople et ses institutions de 330 à 451* (Paris, 1974); and concerning the churches of Saint Sophia and Saint Irene, 392, 297-401.

14. H. Delahaye, *Les Passions*, 166-69. The panegyrists relied on earlier texts.

that in which the roman monastic, Saint Rhypsimy, wishes on Tiridate that he be transformed into a beast of the field much like Nebuchadnezzar. After the ordeal, Tiridate is indeed changed into a wild boar, while his entire court takes to wandering among the thickets, their snout in the grass and grunting in the mud.[13] The death of Hadrian is reminiscent of the harsh details with which Lactantius, early in the fourth century, stigmatized Diocletian's death, describing powerless physicians applying cooked meat to the imperial back side in an attempt to attract worms whose sole interest was the royal flesh.[14] Until that time, the disintegration of the tyrant's bones was a direct reflection of the complete disappearance of the dragons fought by the likes of Theodore, Gregory the Thaumaturge or Saint George. A sixth-century, leather writing surface already bore an engraving of Diocletian's head beneath the spear of Philotheos of Antioch.[15]

The Monophysite setting of the second Sophia

We assume, therefore, that a monophysite reader around the year 500, under Emperor Anastasius, could easily have come to the same reading as we have in studying the fate of Saint Sophia of Constantinople. Would he not have had, at that time, every means to express the ultimate distortions that would arise within their faith? And yet in the fifth century this faith was shaken in ways that fully justify the account of Sophia of Jerusalem.

In the days of Arcadius, under John Chrysostom, the faith had not yet suffered the vile rejection of the title *Theotokos* for the Virgin Mary, and Constantinople had not yet strayed into the subtle distinctions between two different natures for Christ. It is in this setting that Sophia was born, in spite of her parents' barrenness and with the special blessing of the prestigious John Chrysostom. Fittingly, she is brought into the world in the immediate entourage of the imperial family. She enters into a holy marriage which produces exceptional children: three candidates naturally destined for managing the affairs of the empire. But after the passing of her parents and her husband, faced with the need to remarry, she remains perplexed. How could she submit to another master after having known this orthodox Byzantium in all its glory? How could she risk bringing a new father to her children? Surrounded by a luxury which she rejects, Sophia remains lost. Between the call of God and the rights of her children, she is unable to make sense of her situation. And so the Lord and the Theotokos clearly show her the way. God does not call her in this city that will lose its orthodoxy. In Jerusalem, Sophia sheds her doubts and gains eternal life. After a period of nine months, a period of rebirth in Byzantium, her own children come to recognize her. Patriarch Theodore, undoubtedly the anti-patriarch Theodosius who refused to recognize Juvenaly of Jerusalem upon his return from Chalcedon in 452, expresses

13. M. van Esbroeck, "Un nouveau témoin de l'Agathange," *REArm* 8 (1971), 130 and 133.
14. Lactantius, *De mortibus persecutorum*, ed. J. Moreau (SC 39 [1954]), 115-16.
15. H. Omont in *Bulletin de la Société des Antiquaires de France* (1898), 330-32.

himself clearly in a letter to the emperor.[16] Wisdom is henceforth widowed from all that kept her in Constantinople: the fruit of her womb kept her from the way of the Lord. That is made clear to her by the Theotokos herself. In Jerusalem the faith remains intact and the Lord himself effects the transfer needed to preserve it. The children's last farewell to their dying mother offers an attractive antithesis to Sophia's final farewell to the bodies of her three daughters on the hill near Rome. The first cried before her dead children, the second lays dying before her tearful children. The first offers up earthly fruit to a heavenly calling, while the second offers a heavenly calling to her earthly fruit. Henceforth, orthodoxy originates in Jerusalem; and Saint Sophia of Constantinople is no longer justified by her roots in the world of fourth-century Rome, but through the jerusalemite preservation in the fertile soil of the true doctrine of the Holy City.

We must note that it is on January sixth, during the feast of the Lord's birth and baptism, that Sophia is taken ill, while it is during the Copt's marian feast of the Dormition, on January 16, that she is taken from her tearful children. In a Coptic homily dedicated to Macarius of Tkoou, a signer at Ephesus and at the "robber council" of 449, we learn that on the 21st of Touba (i.e., January 16), the monophysites gathered at the church of the Dormition in the valley of Josaphat, at the feast of the Mount of Olives. They were there to voice a loud protest in opposition to Chalcedon; so much so that Juvenaly, who had recently returned, sent in the troops, and Paul, one of the spokesmen for the monophysites, was shamefully put to death by the Byzantine militia.[17] The soldiers accompanying Sophia's children are equally worrisome to the monks in Jerusalem. Obviously the liturgical reading for Sophia of Jerusalem has been kept on the same date. Everything down to the means of a cloud to carry the apostles to the Dormition has influenced the supernatural means by which Sophia traveled instantly from Constantinople to Jerusalem.

Furthermore, at the beginning of the Dormition, on August 8, in Jerusalem, a church of Saint Sophia was inaugurated where Pilate's house had stood, between Holy Zion and the Temple.[18] Of course this new Saint Sophia represents the Wisdom that inspired Jesus' response to Pilate. It may as well formalize the later refusal to accept Saint Sophia of Constantinople as a legitimate representative of the monophysite faith. It is highly unlikely that the account as it appears in the Synaxarion would have had the Theotokos herself referring to the removal of Sophia's remains to Constantinople at a

16. E. Honigman, "Juvenal de Jérusalem," *DOP* 5 (1950), 247-57, especially 249-50.

17. A panagyric on Macarius of Tkoou, attributed to Dioscorus, ed. E. Amélineau. "Monuments pour servir à l'histoire de l'Egypte chrétienne au IVè et Vè siècles," *Mémoires publiés par la mission archéologique française du Caire* 4 (Paris 1888), 124-26.

18. G. Garitte, *Le calendrier palestino-grégorien du Sinaïticus 34* (Bruxelles, 1958), 296-98. We must note that the inscription for August 7 and 8 corresponds to the Assumption of the Virgin in the Coptic system, in which there are 206 days between the 21st of Tobi and the 16th of Mesore, or August 9. This cannot be mere coincidence as it explains the Arabic legend of Saint Sophia.

time when a church of Saint Sophia was built in Jerusalem itself. This is why one can imagine the legend to have taken place only at the time when the rivalry between the two cities had somewhat subsided, that is primarily under the reign of Anastasius. At that moment, what could have been more tasteful and prophetic that to represent the prefiguration of Constantinople's return to the true worship of the Trinity under the mythically long-lived personality of John Chrysostom? Because the Theotokos announced that young Sophia's Golden Pavilion would be turned into a church of the Son of God; a church which John Chrysostom actually dedicated to the Father, to the Son and to the Holy Spirit. But the account remains logical if we consider that is dates back to a time when, in Antioch, people were singing "One of the Trinity, have mercy on us!" Nevertheless, its advent, as well as the relics of the saint, place the church of "Saint Sophia" prior to Justinian's famous dome. Justinian himself could not have enjoyed the support of the monophysites. His clashes with the church of Jerusalem are flagrant.[21] It is at this time that a Saint Sophia could have been built in Jerusalem. But under Anastasius, we can really say that Sophia's children, Stephen—whose relics were discovered in 415—Paul and Marc continue, in the Byzantine capital, the legitimate line of Arcadius and of John Chrysostom, worthy venerators of the Theotokos and of true Wisdom.

Those for whom the reading of these legends seems too haphazard may benefit from a study of certain precedents. The particular genre of these symbolic saints began to blossom as of the fourth century. We noted that, much like Saint Christina, Sophia's daughters successfully cursed their vile persecutor. Like Barbara, Christina and Irene, the daughter of Theognostos and Theodora is enclosed in a golden room from the age of five, awaiting the most worthy suitor. The story of Saint Irene shares with that of Saint Sophia the prestige of the patronage of one of the greatest churches in Constantinople.

The Legend of Irene

Here is a brief summary of the main events recounted in the legend of Irene. Although they appear in the Syriac codex of 708,[22] though the Greek text has come down to us in a more complete form.

The Passion of Saint Irene recounts the eventful path toward religious peace, via the persecutions under Lycinius, as well as under Numerian, Severus and others. These persecutors of old evolved in various cities of the Near East. Little Irene, who through her name, Penelope, was dedicated to faith in the true God, was presumably born in the 621st year of the Seleucids, or 310 A.D. The date is a good estimate for the period of religious peace in the East. When she was six years old, her father,

21. M. van Esbroeck, "La lettre de l'empereur Justinien sur l'Annonciation et La Noël en 561," *AnalBoll* 86 (1968), 352-71.
22. Agnes Smith-Lewis, *Select Narratives*, 123-194; *BHG*³ 953; ed. A. Wirth, *Danae in christlichen Legenden* (Vienna, 1892), 116-48.

Lycinius, shut her in a golden tower, in Meggido or Maximianopolis. She was converted by a vision: the Apostle Timothy came to give her the rite of baptism. The last test of peace came within the walls of Nisibia, where the great king Sapor captured her and killed her. But she rose again and, much like Noah's dove, got the Persian waters to recede from the city. This legendary episode is reminiscent of the role attributed to James of Nisibia and to Noah's ark when the city was under siege in 350.[21] Irene was then carried on a cloud, like a second Sophia, to the city of Ephesus. Once there, she laid down alive in a casket, asking those who would close her in it to open it after four days. Once they did this, they found that the body had disappeared.

In 356, Emperor Constantine, who had achieved peace in the East as in the West, had Timothy's relics brought from Ephesus.[22] The tomb in Ephesus, where the Apostle to Saint Irene had lain, would remain empty. Around the same time, the emperor was considerably enlarging the church of Saint Irene in the capital, using Saint Sophia as a model: Wisdom and Peace being closely related. While Constantine had simply built the church of Peace, the name became Saint Irene.[23] The border cities of Constantine or Calinicos, where the cult of Irene is observed, represent the outer limits of Peace over against the persecutor. It is inconceivable that such a logical account could have come about after Julian the Apostate, whose apostasy poses a tremendous problem in the area of symbolic legends. It seems that even after the dreadful siege of Anida, in 359, the story of Saint Irene would have had to include the account and aftermath of that city. This is why it seems necessary for us to place this legend in the middle of the fourth century.

The complementary accounts of Christine and Barbara

The legend of Irene did not appear out of nowhere. Before Irene there was an ideal means of representing the conversion of a whole city, along with its temple, to Christianity. It is best illustrated in the complementary stories of Christine and Barbara. The Passion of Christine was best preserved in its Georgian version, from which one passage coincides with a fifth- or sixth-century papyrus fragment.[24] The Passion of Christine takes place in Tyre, under Hadrian. The first persecutor was Christine Urbanos' own father, chastised through her curses while she was yet alive, followed by two other tyrants, Dios and Julian. The latter may have been inspired by the Apostate. While Irene was converting her father, Lycinius, before being pursued by the lords of that region, Urbanos falls prey to his sadistic paganism. Christine is baptized by an angel in the sea within the city of Tyre.

21. Cf. *AnalBoll* 86 (1968), 408-10; and P. Peeters, "La légende de Jacques de Nisibe," *AnalBoll* 38 (1920), 295-312.

22. H. Delahaye, *Mélanges d'hagiographie grecque et latine* (Bruxelles, 1966), 407-13.

23. Socrates, *Hist. Eccl.* i.16 and ii.16; *BHG*[3]. 1472; PG 104.121A.

24. K. Kekelidze, "Ujvelesi redakcia Kristines martvilobisa" in *Etiudebi jveli kartuli literaturis istoriidan* 3 (Tblissi, 1955), 178-96.

The legend of Saint Barbara follows approximately the same scheme. Barbara is locked up in a golden tower by her father, in Heliopolis. This Heliopolis, referred to as Cairo, Baalbek, Mambidj or Sinope, is in any case the sacred city, the quintessential pagan temple. She is converted by Christ, her true spouse, and thus suffers martyrdom for her faith. The symbolism of the tower itself, its architecture, its astral significance, are deserving of elaboration that goes beyond our current scope.

It will be sufficient for us to note that the names of these two saints themselves include the symbol of their deep significance: it is truly the barbarian, Barbara, who becomes Christian, Christine. It is the very archetype of the conversion of an ancient cult, replaced with Christianity. But why would the awareness of the change be expressed in such a way? Here again, we are referred back to the well-known Judeo-hellenistic account of Joseph and Asaneth.[25] Many details make the relationship undeniable. Asaneth is called a "city of refuge" (*polis kataphuges*) by the angel who appears to her; Barbara receives the same name. Heliopolis is the city where Potiphar locks Asaneth up in a tower; Heliopolis, near Sinope, is the city of Barbara, in present-day Turkey.

The radical symbolism of the narratives

On the level of the radical symbolism of these narratives is the fact that the story of Joseph and Asaneth is intended to illustrate the passage of the Egyptian religion to that of the God of Abraham. It is the quintessential conversion story. Nevertheless, the Jewish Halakhah, a semi-juridical element, seems to have had the same function at the time of its advent among Christian communities. What was possible in going from paganism to Judaism would necessarily be so in going from Judaism to Christianity: we might add, to support this point, that this Judeo-hellenistic form sounds a bit like Saint Paul's major argument, namely that it is not necessary for a pagan, when converting to Christ, to pass through Judaism. This may be the innermost core of the symbol within these legends of converted saints. And yet, throughout the empire there existed temples that accepted the Christian faith and whose stones served to build churches. Here again, the symbolic saints were the ideal expression of what was, at that time, the reality of the events.

It may be, however, that the choice of a saint "as a symbol" is insufficient to describe the reality and the function of a legend whose closest parallel in the contemporary world would most likely be found among political caricatures.

---

25. For an overview of the dependence of these three legends on that of Joseph and Asaneth: M. Philolenko, *Joseph et Asaneth* (Leiden, 1968), 110-17.

St Polychronius and his Companions – but which Polychronius?[1]

ANNA CRABBE

A T an interval of some thirty years, Delehaye published martyrdoms of two, apparently distinct, saints Polychronius, one in Latin and one in Greek.[2] In certain details both documents are unusual, not to say implausible. The Latin Passion of Polychronius, bishop of Babylon, and his companions is prefixed to the extended Passion of Sixtus and Laurence (in its germ belonging to the fourth century) and is the most obviously independent of several accretions. Delehaye showed that the rest of this final version was compiled with a higher regard for the exigencies of the martyrological calendar than for historicity.[3] The whole probably dates from the very late fifth or early sixth century.[4]

The Latin version

The Latin Polychronius narrative may be detached with little damage to the more commonly related sequence at one of two possible points,[5] and I offer here a somewhat polyglot summary of its content:

1) 'Orta tempestate sub Decio multi christianorum necati sunt. Praesidente in urbe Roma Galba, pergit Decius ad Persas. Cum bellum urgeret Persarum, veniens in civitatem, quae cognominatur Pontica, sedet in eadem; bello tamen urgebatur. Ascendit autem Decius in montem Medorum; et facto conflictu pugnae cum militia Romana, fecit victoriam et interfecit Persarum multitudinem; et obtinuit civitates has: Babyloniam, Hyrcaniam, Corduliam (Corduene[6]), Assyriam'. A persecution follows: 'invenit *in civitate Babylonia episcopum nomine Polychronium, cum presbyteris Parmenio, Elima,*

---

1. I would like to thank Mr O.P. Nicholson for reading a draft of this paper and offering many helpful suggestions.

2. *Passio Polochronii Parmenii Abdon et Sennes Xysti Felicissimi et Agapeti et Laurentii et aliorum sanctorum mense Aug die X* in 'Recherches sur le legendier romain', *AnalBoll* 51 (1933), 72-98, and *'Neophytou presbyterou monachou kai egkleistou synoptikon enkōmion eis ton hagion hieromartyra Polychronion'* in 'Saints de Chypre', *AnalBoll* 26 (1907), 175-8.

3. *AnalBoll* 51. 40, 66-71.

4. *AnalBoll* 51. 71.

5. This was frequently the case. The break came either at paragraph 7 or after paragraph 10. Apart from the brief mention in 7 of Sixtus's imprisonment in a persecution begun at Rome on the arrival of Decius and Valerian, paragraphs 11-35 (beginning *eodem tempore Decius Caesar et Valerianus praefectus*) are quite independent of the earlier marytrdoms.

6. *AnalBoll* 51. 37.

Chrisotelo et *diaconibus his: Luca et Muco . . .*'. They are imprisoned for refusing to sacrifice to idols: 'aedificavit [Decius] in eadem civitate templum Saturno'. He then writes a letter 'illustro et magnifico viro Turgio Apollonio Valeriano praefecto', bidding him mount a purge of Christians 'in urbe' before completing the construction of his Babylonian temple to Saturn.

2) Further interrogation of a silent Polychronius and a loquacious Parmenius results in the loss of Parmenius's tongue but not of his powers of speech. Polychronius' martyrdom follows. 'Eadem hora dimisit [Decius] corpus eius ante templum et ambulavit *in civitatem Cordulam 13 kal. Mart.*[7] Eadem nocte venerunt *duo subreguli* qui erant occulte Christiani et rapuerunt corpus eius et sepelierunt ante muros Babiloniae'. Decius takes the remaining prisoners off with him to Corduene.

3) Parmenius and his companions are martyred: 'qui cum decollati fuissent, iactaverunt corpora eorum in publica via ita ut custodirentur, ne quis eos sepeliret. Tunc audientes *subreguli, viri religiosi Abdon et Sennes,* venerunt noctem et collegerunt corpora sanctorum *presbyterorum Parmenii et Elimas et Chrysoteli et diaconorum Lucae et Muci* et sepelirent in praedio suo *iuxta civitatem Cordulam 10 kal. Mai*'.[8]

4) Decius extends his Christian witchhunt throughout the whole of Persia; he arrests and interrogates *Abdon and Sennes.*

5) '*Olympiadis et Maximus,* nobilissimi viri' are betrayed and arrested. This pair is martyred by grid-iron[9] under the supervision of one Vitellius Anisius, vicarius: 'Et iussit Vitellius Anisius ut corpora eorum canibus reliquerent'. The dogs refuse to touch them. 'Post quinque vero dies venientes *quidam Christiani ex genere Abdon et Sennes nobiles* colligerunt pretiosa eorum'.

6-10) Four months after Galba's death, Decius arrives in Rome together with Valerian, and with Abdon and Sennes in his train. Sixtus and his clergy are arrested in a general persecution. Abdon and Sennes, still '*subreguli Christiani*', and 'ornati ex auro et lapide', are led before the senate, where their sumptuous appearance makes no little stir. Decius loses his nerve at this point; but Valerian's attempts to make them sacrifice *deo Soli* in the amphitheatre meet with no success, nor can lions and bears (in somewhat short supply due to a miraculous rash of deaths the previous night) be persuaded to eat them, so gladiators finish them off. 'Et iactaverunt eos *ante symulacrum Solis iuxta*

---

7. *Mart. Hieron.* (*ActaSS* Nov. II.ii) Feb. 17, *additamenta* (Echternach codex only): *in Babilonia Policroni.*

8. *Mart. Hieron.* Apr. 22 ff. (Echternach codex only): *in Cordua civitate Parmeni et Elimae, Crisoli presbb. et diaconorum Lucii et Mucii.*

9. Here possibly borrowed from the passion of Laurence to follow later in the account (para. 28). On its genesis there see *AnalBoll* 51.55-8.

theatrum; et iacuerunt corpora ad exemplum Christianorum tribus diebus'. Happily a Roman – 'Quirinus, Christianus subdiaconus' – is found to perform the usual offices of burial on their account, placing them 'in arca plumbea in domo suo, tertio kal. Aug.'.[10] They lie forgotten for many years, but miraculously reveal their own whereabouts in the halcyon days after Constantine's conversion 'et translata sunt in cymeterium Pontiani'.

11 to end)   There follow at length the martyrdoms of Sixtus, Hippolytus, Laurence and others ending with the death of Cyrilla (purportedly Decius' daughter) under Claudius II.

Delehaye's assessment

Delehaye viewed Abdon and Sennes as the only characters in this somewhat repetitive fable with any claim to concrete reality.[11] They appear in the Roman ferial of the *Chronographus* of 354.[12] Their deposition on 30 July runs in all branches of the Hieronymian Martyrology; a sixth-century painting in the Pontian cemetery portrays them in full Persian fig; and in the eighth, pope Hadrian restored their church near the amphitheatre, the supposed scene of their martyrdom.[13] Thus, the Bollandist concluded, they are the pivot by which Polychronius and company are attached to the somewhat more respectable Roman passions: the rest of the little account has neither foundation nor antiquity. Its characters occur only in the Echternach Codex of the Hieronymian and should be relegated to the *additamenta* as deriving entirely from the charming fiction before us.[14] Abdon and Sennes were not *subreguli* at all. Far from being Persian princelings, they were probably Roman slaves whose semitic-sounding names set the whole affair in train.

These scathing comments on the passion of the bishop of Babylon have no small justification. The whole is a repetitious patchwork of hagiographical common-place. Decius never set foot in Persia. If Valerian's unhappy Persian experience is here reflected in the name of Decius's *praefectus*, it has undergone a sea change and the reader may well also wonder where he came by the appellation Turgius Apollonius. On the face of it the topography is as imaginative as the chronology and any link with putative *acta vera et sincera* seems remote indeed. Of Polychronius' immediate companions Delehaye writes

> Il n'a certainement pas voulu les faire passer pour des martyres de Rome. En les faisant enterrer dans des endroits obscurs d'un pays lointain, il montre assez qu'il ne sait rien

10. *Mart. Hieron.* (all codd.) Jul. 30: Abdon et Sennen.
11. *AnalBoll* 51. 37-8.
12. *MHG AA ix chron. min. sac.* I.i (1896) xii (71): *III kal. Aug. Abdos et Semnes in Pontiani quod est ad ursum piliatum.* If the information in the Passion were correct, this would place the *translatio* between 325 and 337. However if the assumption of editors that the *depositio martyrum* of the *Chronographus* is contemporary with the first recension of the list of pontiffs, 336 is the latest possible date. See Duchesne, *Lib. Pontif.* 1.vii. 10-12.
13. Delehaye ad *Mart. Hieron.* Jul. 30 n.1 (*ActaSS.* Nov. II.ii.405).
14. See Duchesne, *ActaSS* Nov. II.i.ix.

de leur église d'origine. L'hagiographe qui, dès la première page de son oeuvre s'est montrer capable d'inventer tant des choses a bien pu trouver des noms de martyres destinés à faire escorte aux saints Abdon et Sennen, reputés Perses d'origine.[15]

Elsewhere, however, he is at pains to emphasise that the compiler's unaided imagination is capable of inventing nothing.[16] Rather his contribution has lain in the efficient dovetailing of subsequent events at Rome with the dénouement of Abdon and Sennes' sufferings, and in the monotonous articulation of alternating martyrdom and burial, itself a familiar conceit, slightly alleviated by the equally derivative motif of the martyrological travelogue.

Some details salvaged

I am not alone in feeling that Delehaye's dismissal of the topographical details is too cavalier and this is true also of the onomastic information. To take the first point, Fiey[17] has made a good case for linking the mention of five 'civitates' with the successes of Galerius' Persian campaign; and the name Cordula, identified by both scholars as Corduene, which figures consistently in the Galerian list,[18] is sufficiently *recherché* to evade the most inventive ignorance of a Roman hagiographer. *Pace* Delehaye the 'mons Medorum' presents no problem[19] and even the 'civitas quae cognominatur Pontica' is susceptible of some explanation.[20] In addition some explanation of the names of the companions is at least desirable. Even if the compiler's powers of invention are slight, he must have found them somewhere.

However I do not share Fiey's confidence that the historical scenario and the name of the persecuting emperor can be laid bare in a single operation. In the light of the five provinces, he argues that Decius here actually is Galerius hiding behind the cognomen Dacius. This is highly unlikely or at most only part of the truth.[21]

15. *AnalBoll* 51.37.
16. Despite the judgments on supporting casts (*AnalBoll* 51.37 and 69ff), the general tenor of Delehaye's discussion demonstrates that at every turn the compiler must run to the calendars for his dramatis personae.
17. 'Notes d'hagiographie syriaque', *OrSyr* xi.2 (1966), 141-3.
18. Petr. Patr. *fg*.14 = *FHG* iv.188ff; Amm. Marc.xxv.7, 9. See J.W. Eadie, *The Breviarium of Festus* (London 1967), 148. It is however the only one of the five found in the list in the Passion.
19. The Median mountains are on the Armenian route to Persia. See Aurelius Victor, *Caes.* 39. 34: *per Armeniam in hostes contendit [Galerius] qua ferme sola seu facilior vicendi via est.*
20. Fiey, op.cit. (n.17, above), 141, suggests a Roman station Ad Pontum on the Tigris (cf. *Tab. Peutingeriana* 20). Alternatively, in view of the possible associations of the 'historical' frame with Valerian as well as Galerius (discussed below) one might assume a link with the Pontic province and Valerian's troubles on that frontier, an episode described by Zosimus (i.32-6) immediately before his account of the Persian disaster of 256-7. *Civitas* here is no obstacle; the other five examples all refer to provinces.
21. *Pace* Fiey, op.cit. (n.17 above) 143 with n.22, Galerius' Dacian origins are not likely to be relevant. The title, which would in any case be *Dacicus*, would record some military achievement rather than a place of origin. After Trajan's initial successes in that area, it is recorded for several other emperors, including Gallienus (*RE* s.v. 'Dacicus'). It is not found

It works well for the initial setback and the subsequent victory over five provinces of the first paragraph; Galerius is also satsifactory as a persecuting emperor, albeit not in Persia. But the trip to Rome will not do and in fact there is another sequence of historical events from half a century earlier interwoven with the Galerian story that dominates the rest of the confection.

This depends on the assumption that Decius is Decius, both persecuting emperor in his own right, and predecessor of Valerian. His place in the story arises from these two facts and the chronology underlying the subsequent Roman martyrdoms is that of the period of Valerian's reign. As Fiey recognizes[22] the Galba 'praesidens in urbe Roma' whose death results in the precipitate return of (Decius and) Valerian to Rome is a shadowy memory of the emperor Gallus.[23] The 'Claudius rex' who succeeds on the death of (Decius and) Valerian is Claudius Gothicus,[24] albeit eight years of Gallienus' reign have been sunk without trace. If Galerius' Persian successes were remarkable, Valerian's misfortunes there were hardly less striking.[25] Both emperors would in popular imagination have been inseparable from the idea of Persia and at some stage a compiler, perhaps the final one, has telescoped many years of Persian-Roman relations. We are faced with that mixture of precisely remembered detail and '1066 and All That' which is the stock in trade of romancing hagiography. As yet, there is no evidence that either the reign of Galerius or that of Valerian has anything to do with an original account of Polychronius and his companions. If Babylon and Corduene figured there as the scenes of the action all the rest may be subsequent addition by a Roman hagiographer.

Fiey rightly rejects the Greek names of Polychronius' companions as a bar to the theory that they were originally Persian martyrs, likewise their absence from all eastern accounts concerning Persian martyrdom, although he does not pursue the consequences of such an argument. However, even leaving Abdon and Sennes out of account, not all the rest have straightforward Greek names. Elimas ($Ἐλυμᾶς$)if not Persian, certainly emanates from the east; so also does the form Lucas ($Λουκᾶς$) and there are possible grounds for believing that Mucius was not originally $ΜΟΥϰιΟϹ$, the standard Greek transliteration of the Roman name. but $ΜῶϰιΟϹ$, which has associations in approximately the right area.[26]

---

for Galerius, who in this region confines himself to the cognomen *Sarmaticus* (*RE* xiv.2. 2520, 2523, 2525).

22. Fiey, op.cit. (n.17 above), 143.
23. Zos. i.38-9.
24. *Pass. Polochronii* 34-5, *AnalBoll* 51.98. See Zos. i.41.
25. Zos. i.36; Aurelius Victor 32.
26. Apart from the shadowy figure of St Mocius (honoured at Constantinople) about whom we know almost nothing (Delehaye, *AnalBoll* 31 [1912], 163-87, 225-32), see Soz. *HE* ii.13 for a Mōkios among the bishops of the Sapor persecutions.

The Greek texts

For the Greek life of a martyr Polychronius, to which we must now turn, we depend on the summaries of the Synaxaria and on an encomium from that curious collection of improving hagiography put together in the twelfth century by Neophytos of Cyrpus.[27] I summarise Neophytos' version as the fuller, giving additions and variants from the Synaxaria in round, and passages in Neophytos not there closely paralleled in square, brackets:

1) Polychronius is the son of a farmer (add Synax.: ὁ δὲ τούτου πατὴρ Βαρδάνιος) in the eparchy Γαμφάνης οὕτω καλουμένης (Synax. Sirm.: τῆς Γαμφανήτιδος; v.11.: [Mv] Γαμφανίτου [Ba] Γανφάνητος. His father teaches him τὰ [ἱερὰ] γράμματα and sends him to pasture the cattle. He fulfils his task with prayer and fasting: [νηστείας καὶ προσευχῆς ἐργάτης ἦν δοκιμώτατος]. When he is in need of water, he receives a miraculous spring through prayer.

2) Famous for the miracle, he sets out τῇ βασιλίδι τῶν πολέων (Synax.: πρὸς τὴν βασιλεύουσαν) [with the following vine-dressing companions: Παρμένιος, Πολυτέλειος, Ἐλυμᾶς Μώκιος, Χρυσοτελῆς, Μάξιμος, Λουκᾶς, Ἄβδιος, Σέμνιος and Ὀλυμπάδιος, οὓς καὶ συναθλητὰς ὕστερον ἔσχεν ὑπὲρ Χριστοῦ μαρτυρῶν. He proves the best vine-dresser and, despite his efforts, incapable of disguising his ἔνθεος πολιτεία.] He eats a little every two or three days. ὁ κύριος τοῦ ἀμπελῶνος (Synax. Ba: *sic*; Synax.Sirm.: ὁ ἐργοδότης), αἰδεσθεὶς τὴν ἀρετὴν τοῦ ἀνδρος, equips him with money for the road and sends him home (Synax. Sirm.: ὑπὲρ ἐμοῦ εὐχόμενος), but keeps his hoe, which works miracles. Polychronius goes home, builds a chapel, εὐκτήριον οἶκον δομησάμενος (Synax.: ἐκκλησίαν κατασκευάσας) and prays.

3) Later he is made priest (add. Synax. Sirm.: ἐν τῇ κατὰ Νίκαιαν συνόδῳ εὑρέθεις ἀναγνώστης ὤν, δέχεται τὸ τοῦ διακόνου καὶ πρεσβυτέρου ἀξίωμα; Ba: τὸ τοῦ πρεσβυτέρου ἀξίωμα δέχεται) and offers τὰς ἀναιμάκτους θυσίας. [Some say that he later became a bishop: εἰς τὸν τῆς ἀρχιεροσύνης θρόνῳ ἀνακεκομίσθαι].

4) After the death of Constantine [οἱ θεομάχοι καὶ δυσσεβεῖς βασιλεῖς run amok] οἱ ἔξαρχοι τῶν αἰρέσεων (Synax. Ba: *sic*; Synax. Sirm.: ἡ τοῦ Ἀρείου αἵρεσις) perse-

27. See n.2 above.

cute the orthodox. Polychronius and his συνάθλοι, after many tortures,[28] suffer martyrdom by decapitation. Polychronius' memory is celebrated on 7 October [and 17 February': δηλονότι ἡ μὲν τῆς αὐτῶν μαρτυρίας καί τελειωσέως, ἡ δὲ ἕτερα ἡ σεπτὴ ἀνακομιδή τῶν ἱερῶν καί θείων λειψάνων αὐτῶν].

6) [Neophytos concludes with pious reflection and biblical allegories of his martyr's career] .

Problems of the Greek

Fiey notes the importance of the coincidence of the names of the companions[29] and Polychronius' episcopal elevation. In a footnote[30] he admits that the expression *tē basilidi tōn poleōn*, which for Neophytos means Constantinople, might in a hypothetical Syriac original have described Seleucia-Ctesiphon. The rest he dismisses rather as Delehaye had done the Latin:

> Ce qui compte ici, c'est qu'une liste des noms de martyres, incluant Abdon et Sennen, soit parvenue jusqu'à Chypre on ne sait comment. Très visiblement la liste arriva sans la légende, puisque Néophyte le Reclus prit grand peine pour habiller l'énumération d'une histoire purement fantaisiste. En soi, l'existence de cette liste en dehors de la légende est une présomption en faveur de son authenticité.[31]

The Greek texts raise too many problems to be dealt with so lightly. That Neophytos did not invent the legend himself[32] is clear from a comparison between his encomium and the two earlier Synaxary texts printed by Delehaye. I have listed sufficient divergencies between Delehaye's chief codex, Cod. Sirm., and Cod. Ba to show that Neophytos was working chiefly from an exemplar which was fuller than Ba's summary, but very close to it. Where all three versions make the same point the verbal parallels are closest between Neophytos and Ba. On the other hand, only the Sirm. mentions the attendance at Nicaea and the precise nature of the heresy,

28. *Cod. Sirm,* informs us that the saint was found τῷ θυσιαστηρίῳ, παριστάμενον and put to the sword on the spot. According to Ba, ἐν ἥ (sc. ἐκκλησίᾳ) θεῷ τὰς ἀναιμάκτους θυσίας προσφέρων ἀναίρεται.

29. Fiey, op.cit. (n.17 above), 141. See also 143 n.23. *Pace* Fiey, Neophytos does not follow the legend in replacing Primulus and Tudianus by the simple Polyteleios, thereby reducing the number of companions from eleven to ten. The Latin life has only nine companions; Πολυτελειος in the Greek is an extra. It is a conflation of Πολυχρόνιος and Χρυσοτελῆς in Neophytos's source. Primulus and Tu[r]dianus, who follow the list of companions on 22 April in the Hieronymian, appear in all branches, not merely in the Echternach codex. On their quite independent identity, see Delehaye ad loc, *ActaSS* Nov. II.ii.

30. Fiey, op.cit. (n.17 above), 141, n.13.

31. Fiey, op.cit., 141.

32. His reasons for choosing it are clear enough. There are some distinct parallels with his own early career. See P. Peeters. 'Vie et Ouvrages de Néophyte le Reclus', *Echos d'Orient* ii (1898-9), 237-68, and more recently P. Tsiknopolou, 'Ho agios Neophytos ho egkleistēs' in *Byzantion* 37 (1967), 313-28.

points we should not have expected Neophytos to omit had he met them. The scene in the presbytery, also missing from Neophytos, is more strikingly depicted in Sirm. than in Ba, although the phrase *anaimaktous thysias,* which is taken up by Neophytos in paragraph 3 occurs at this point in Ba and nowhere in Sirm.[33]

Three further points indicate Neophytos' familiarity with a further variant version, the supporting cast of companions, the elevation to the episcopate and the date of the second feast, 17 February, which figures nowhere in the Greek calendar. Prima facie, these details are sufficient to capsize Fiey's argument for an ultimate and independent Persian source for both Greek and Latin Polychronius. Since the Synaxaria ignore the companions, so, one might argue, did Neophytos' source. Instead he found them in a Greek version of the Latin life and patched them into a quite different Greek life about an ascetic Polychronius martyred after the death of Constantine. The *tines* who say he became a bishop are none other than the compiler(s) of the Latin life; if Greek they are independent of the Synaxary sources so far established. The same holds for the two festivals. Neophytos' language might indicate that their explanation is his own and that he had found 17 February in the Latin acts.

This hypothesis is, in the last analysis, irrefutable, but it is not necessarily true. Negative points first. There are a number of Greek translations of the martyrdom of Sixtus and Laurence and the tale reached the Synaxaria. But there are no traces of a Greek *incipit* that would necessarily imply that Polychronius came too.[34] Rather the indications are that the translation was widespread in the east long before the Persian passion was selotaped on at the start. In addition the absence of companions from a Synaxary notice is not an insuperable barrier and can be paralleled elsewhere. The episcopate may just have been omitted as irrelevant.

Hardly more positive is the calendar evidence. Delehaye's edition of the Hieronymian has demonstrated how frequently saints of the Roman calendar slip from one month to another, reappearing on, say, the identical Ides of the relevant months. The tendency in the Greek calendar for saints to shift within a month or about the year to days with the same final figure is no less marked. The Greek calendar and Neophytos concur in 7 October for the martyrdom. Neophytos has 17 February for the *anakomidē*. The Latin Passion gives both on this date and the Echternach codex of the Hieronymian, probably drawing on the Passion, only the martyrdom. It is however a curious coincidence, if coincidence it be, that in one codex of

---

33. The phrase is however so common that this may be sheer coincidence.
34. See *BHG*[2]. 976-8b and *Auctarium* 976-7C. Several Greek manuscripts begin the saga with Abdon and Sennes on their arrival in Rome from Persia. This is true of Mosq. 162 – see Halkin, *Inedits byzantins* (SubsHag 38 [1963]), 286-300 [=*BHG*[2] *Auct.* 977c] – which bears signs of being a rhetorical paraphase of the Latin and omits the deaths in Persia of Olympiades and Maximus. See also P. Franchi de' Cavalieri, *Note agiografiche* vi = ST 33 (1920), 170 n.3. on cod. Vat. 1761 f126[v] (where Abdon and Sennes seem to be Persian) with 'Agiographica', ST 19 (1908), 120. The synaxaria are familiar only with translations that do not include Abdon and Sennes. On the special circumstances attaching to these two, see below.

the Synaxaria 17 February (the rest give 16 February) is shared by Marouthas of Martyropolis (Maipherqat), who is there said to have died on the anniversary of the founding of his great necropolis for the Persian martyrs, and by those martyrs themselves.[35] Finally, for what it is worth, a reference to Polychronius and his father (plus a stray Hermogenes from a different group of martyrs) appears on 27 January.[36]

It emerges from this confusion of 'sevens' that Neophytos had more than a simple list of names as Fiey suggested. Since he also had the 17 February date, the same two possibilities remain, either some very limited pilfering from a Greek version of the Latin Passion for purposes of embellishment or access to a Greek tradition deriving from the Syriac independently of the Latin and guaranteeing the authenticity of, at the very least, the names of the companions, the episcopate of Polychronius and the February date. Marouthas and his martyrs on 16-17 February give just a hint that the latter might be true, but so far *non liquet*.

The Greek texts offer the nearest approximation to positive and straightforward evidence we are likely to get, one patronymic and one toponym. Like the names of five of Polychronius's companions, Ἐλυμᾶς, Ἄβδιος and Σέμνιος (Abdon and Sennes), Λουκᾶς and possibly Μώκιος [37], the name Βαρδάνιος points at the very least towards Syria, possibly towards Persia or Mesopotamia. What of the ἐπαρχία Γαμφάνητος or Γαμφανήτιδος? It is certainly not to be found on Cyprus. It is an eparchy, which limits the field considerably, ruling out Asia Minor and Pontus completely, where we would expect the name of town or village as well, or would anyway have heard of the eparchy. Again we are directed towards Persia and Mesopotamia and a plausible and interesting candidate offers itself. Γαμφάνητις may be simply a slight mis-spelling of Gauzanitis, that area lying south of Mygdonia, midway between Corduene and Babylon,[38] in other words between the two principal theatres of the Latin account.

It would be a rare coincidence that gave the world two separate Polychronii, born, ordained and martyred in the same remote area and only half a millenium or so later attached the companions of one to the other after a literary circuit of half the Mediterranean world. The truth as we shall see may indeed be very strange, but there is a case that we are considering only one Polychronius and two very distant descendants of a literary tradition that diverged almost at its source. That the legend at Rome concentrates on the passion is comprehensible in view of Roman hagiographical traditions and the rest of the work of which it forms part; that Neophytos has little time for the companions in martyrdom would be equally

35. *Synax CP* Feb. 16. 2 and 3 (461), Feb. 17 (Ba, 469.62).
36. *Synax CP* 425.39.
37. See n.26 above.
38. Ptolem. *Geogr.* v.18 (97). See *RE* s. 'Gauzanitis'.

understandable if the story first caught his fancy because of similarities between his own early career and that of its protagonist.[39]

Suspending sceptical disbelief for a moment, what might then be original to each account? *Pace* Fiey, the career of the Greek Polychronius may not be pure fiction. It is compatible with many biographies from the same area. The stress on the young man's asceticism is characteristic and can be paralleled in its details.[40] Such privations enjoyed a particular vogue in the future refuge of Nestorianism. Attendance at Nicaea and the emphasis on the golden age of Constantine have some ring of plausibility. Jacob of Nisibis and the suffragans of Seleucia-Ctesiphon need not have attended Nicaea unescorted. Whether or not it is actually true, it was the sort of claim made of several bishops in that area.[41] If Mesopotamia was hardly the central area of post-Constantinian Arian persecutions, the tradition of Jacob's hostility towards Arius and the rash of martyrdoms resulting from Sapor II's successive incursions during the period might suffice to account for a conflation of this sort in the Greek.

A Persian location

For it is to Persian persecutions, probably those of Sapor, and not either to Arians or to ungodly emperors that we must assign Polychronius and his friends if we are to accept a common source for the two versions, although as we shall see this theory presents some very grave difficulties. The degree of subsequent historical distortion in each tradition is both a stumbling block to such a thesis and, in a sense, precisely what we should expect if the tradition really was divided almost from the start. Roman persecution of Christians is out of the question in Persia in either tradition. On the other hand attempts to assess what might be definitely Persian and original in the Latin account are fraught with difficulty. We may start by putting down to Latin adaptation all references to Roman emperors and Roman persecution of Christians as a late expansion of the ideas 'king', 'Persia' and 'Christian persecution' in an environment ill-informed on the more remote foreign affairs of the first half of the fourth century. Three of the five *civitates*, as suggested above, may be dispensed with as attaching to a Roman emperor, so also the other geographical information,[42] but Babylon and Corduene are of more interest as precisely the areas where Persian persecution of Christians did take place.[43]

Another major problem is that accounts of persecution at Rome in general bear a marked resemblance in certain details to the acts of Persian martyrs.[44]

39. Delehaye, *AnalBoll* 51.274-7.
40. See for example Johann Georg Ernst Hoffman, *Auszüge syrischen Akten persischer Martyren* [= Abh KM vii.3] (Leipzig 1880), 17, 20, 28, 65, 68 for Polychronius' early career. For the miracles see 17, 20; and for building activities 20, 30, 48, 76.
41. See E. Honigmann, 'La liste originale des pères de Nicée', *Byzantion* 14 (1939) 62-5.
42. The *mons Medorum* and the supposed route followed.
43. See for example Soz. *HE* ii. 9-15.
44. J. Labourt, *Le Christianisme dans l'Empire Perse sous la dynastie Sassanide* (224-632) (Paris 1904), 51-63.

The stress on the clerical status of Persian martyrs is indeed historical,[45] but may only appear here because a similar stress on the clergy of Sixtus, equally historical, forms part of the same work of hagiography. Likewise in the martyrdom of Abdon and Sennes the request to sacrifice *deo Soli* and the account of the statue of the Sun outside the Colosseum certainly refers to the converted Colossus of Nero,[46] yet the same stress on sun-worship is a natural feature of Persian martyrdoms.[47] The same applies to the stress on burials, as a vital element in the cult of martyrs. Thus the whole thing with the exception of Babylon, Corduene and possibly Abdon and Sennes might on a sceptical view be a tissue of successive Roman inventions.

Abdon and Sennes

Abdon and Sennes, although undoubtedly Persian, pose their own problems, both in their date and in the fact that they have apparently at least one other existence independent of the passions under discussion. The name Abdon (or Abdas or Abdias) is common and can be paralleled from other lists of Persian martyrdoms.[48] The same is less true of Sennes. Although the combination is not found in the extensive, albeit not comprehensive, Syriac list of the year 411,[49] it does appear in two other places.

In the Apocryphal Acts of Sts Simon and Jude,[50] one Abdias, who purports to be a Palestinian disciple of those apostles, is consecrated and left as bishop in Babylon. The apostles make their way to the city of Suanir and lodge at the house of a disciple Sennes who subsequently shares their martyrdom there. Material of this kind is notoriously difficult to assess. Scholars are agreed that this apocryphal collection as a whole should be assigned to the late sixth or early seventh century; at the same time, certain strands within it, particularly details of names and places, however distorted, may reflect material of an earlier date. Whatever we are to make of the claim that the Acts of Simon and Jude passed from a Hebrew to a Greek to a Latin redaction,[51] it is difficult to explain how the Latin Acts of Polychronius

45. For Sapor persecutions see Soz. *HE* ii.13, also the disposition of the Persian martyrs in the list of 411 given by the Syraic Breviary (ed. Wright, *ActaSS* Nov. II.i.lxiii-lxv). For Jazdegerd, see Hoffman, op.cit. (n.40 above), 34.

46. See S.B. Platner and T. Ashby, *A Topographical Dictionary of Ancient Rome* (London 1929), 130, sv. 'Colossus Neronis'.

47. For martyrs asked to worship sun, moon and fire, see Hoffman op.cit. (n.40 above), 24, 29. Further, *Synax, CP* Mart. 29.1 (sun, fire and water), Apr. 9.3, 17.3 (sun and fire).

48. For example Soz. *HE* xii.13 and see *Synax CP*, Index nominum.

49. See n.45 above. The name Σενοῆς is found on its own as a companion of the Persian martyr Mil[l]es at *Synax CP* Nov. 13.2 (cf. *BHO* 772-4).

50. J.O. Fabricius, *Codex Apocryphus Novi Testamenti* (Hamburg 1719), 628-63. See M.R. James *The Apocryphal New Testament* (Oxford 1924), 438ff for a summary of the content of these Acts.

51. The list, Abdias to Craton to (Julius) Africanus has all the marks of a very late forgery. R.A. Lipsius, *Die apocryphen Apostelgeschichte und Apostellegenden* (Braunschweig 1883-90), II.ii.170-2, reckoned that the whole collection, book 6 of which concerns the Acts of Simon and Jude, dated from the sixth or early seventh century (see M.R. James, *The Apocryphal New Testament,* 438), but that these particular books might contain material running back to the fourth or fifth century.

could be entirely responsible for two such disparate legends about Abdon and Sennes, even if the two names are still linked with Persia and Babylon. Were this certainly the case, the variant Semnes for Sennes recorded by Fabricius[52] might indicate decisively that Neophytos had taken his list of companions from a Greek translation of a copy of the Latin passion of Polychronius which contained the same error. As we shall see, however, the place name Suanir gives some reason for doubting this.

The second appearance of Abdon and Sennes ought also, apparently, to be excluded from the discussion on grounds of chronology. Here they belong to the fifth century and died in Jazdegerd's persecution of the 420s. Among the likely associates of Marouthas of Maiferqat was one Abdas, a bishop, probably in Sousiane. According to Theodoret, he was martyred for burning a fire temple in an excess of Christian zeal and then proving troublesome about its restoration. Two high-ranking Persian sympathisers, Hormisdas, 'one of the foremost men among the Persians' and *Souēnēs*, 'lord of a thousand slaves', are stripped of their rank and possessions, and finally a deacon Benjamin is murdered.[53] It would be pleasing if we could simply say that in *Abdias* and *Souēnēs* we meet the now familiar Abdon and Sennes, whilst Hormisdas and, once more, *Souēnēs* make a creditable pair of christianising *subreguli*. I do not think it possible to escape the conclusion that Theodoret's account influenced in some measure the portraits of Abdon and Sennes in the Latin Acts. But given that Theodoret represents these as Jazdegerd rather than Sapor martyrs, there is an insuperable chronological obstacle to such an identification. Abdon and Sennes, as I have said, appear in the Roman ferial of the *Chronographus* of 354. That is to say, their cult had arrived at Rome, if it did not originate there, long before the fifth century persecutions had begun.

The Latin Passion apart, there are some strong similarities between this account and the Apocryphal Acts described above, most notably the appearance of Abdas as a bishop and Sennes (or *Souēnēs*) as a layman. In addition the likeness of the place name Suanir or Suanis in those Acts to the form in Theodoret may not be coincidental.[54] Probably the Acts of Simon and Jude draw at several removes on the story we know from Theodoret. It is also likely that they have been influenced in some respects by the Latin Acts of Polychronius, so that in their present form I think it unlikely that they predate the sixth century.[55]

52. Fabricius, op.cit., (n.50 above), 631n.
53. Theodoret. *HE* v.38 (39). The story is well-attested elsewhere. See *Synax. CP* Oct. 17 (145-8) where there is a reading Σουῑνης (further, Sept. 5 [17-58], Mart. 31 [573-6] for Abdas and Benjamin only). Niceph. Call. (*PG* 46. 11, 13-20) gives Σαῆνης, i.e. Sahin for Σουῆνης, see also Mich. Syr. viii.3-4. The Armenian Life is of particular importance; see P. Peeters. *AnalBoll* 28 (1909), 399-415. For the year see 408-9. The Synaxary date of 17 October is perhaps of interest in view of the confusion of sevens and seventeens already remarked.
54. Lipsius, op.cit. (n.51 above), iii.144, follows Tillemont and Gutschmid in linking Suanir with the tribe of the Suani (*RE* s.v. 'Suanoi') in northern Colchis and connecting it with the tradition that the grave of Simon Zelotes lay in the region of the Bosphorus (cf. *Mart. Hieron.* Oct. 28). Nevertheless the similarity of the names here is suggestive.

An insoluble enigma

What effect does this extremely confusing evidence have on the relationship between the two Polychronii and their companions in martyrdom? The result is a virtually insoluble enigma. Short of redating the *Chronographus* and the well-supported Theodoret tradition, none of the several possible reconstructions accounts very satisfactorily for the evidence. The simplest approach is to say that Theodoret's story is irrelevant, which will allow the Latin life and Neophytos to represent two strands of one original tradition as first suggested. Yet the coincidence of names and status in Theodoret is too strong to be ignored.

Another and still less plausible approach is to accept a very early date for the material contained in the Acts of Simon and Jude and argue from that that not only Theodoret but also the Armenian Acts of Abdas and the related texts have updated a much earlier tradition of Abdon and Sennes dating from anywhere between the apostolic age and the fourth-century persecutions, losing Polychronius and the rest of his companions somewhere along the way with a remarkable degree of consistency. This might be tidy but clearly will not do.

In the end, it seems we must return to Delehaye's original contention that Abdon and Sennes are separate from the rest of the list and received early reverence at Rome. Even so, as far as the Latin Acts are concerned this leaves us with two separate pairs of Abdon and Sennes, that of the *Chronographus* and the Hieronymian, who *pace* Delehaye may well be of Persian origin,[56] and the couple from Theodoret who actually provided most of the trappings of the Latin life. We must then be content to remain in ignorance as to how that tradition reached Rome.

It will then be clear that the companions of Polychronius in Neophytos came from a Greek version of the Latin Passion, as was indicated by the manner of their inclusion when compared with the Synaxary versions. This will mean that more than one version of the Latin life was made, since most of the Greek translations do not include Polychronius and the first five companions. However the case for the identity of the two Polychronii still stands and with it the possibility that at least the first five companions (rather less plausibly Olympiades and Maximus) belonged originally with him. They were preserved only in the Latin tradition, whence by a curious fluke Neophytos borrowed them centuries later together with the extraneous Abdon and Sennes. It is not difficult to see why the compiler of the Latin acts, if he had two martyrological texts at his disposal, both of them relating to Persia and Mesopotamia should have conflated the two, less easy to accept that he invented the first set from scratch, without any names to go on.

55. Note particularly a like stress on the temple of the sun and the status of the god in both, though in the Acts of Simon and Jude he has a chariot and there is a comparable statue of the moon as well.

56. *BHL* 7 may have stressed their Persian origin more than the usual text. It is not clear whether the Passion of Sixtus, Laurence and Hippolytus mentioned by P. Franchi de'Cavalieri (*Note agiografiche* 9 = ST 175 [1953] 42n.*) and still unpublished included Abdon and Sennes – probably not. The rhetorical embellishments of the Greek text mentioned above n.34, make it very difficult to estimate what his original Latin source looked like.

Were this correct, we should then have an explanation of the curious coincidence of date which I mentioned above whereby 17 February is given for Polychronius in the Latin Passion and hence also the Hieronymian, but is allotted in some texts of the Greek Synaxaria to Marouthas' martyrs of Martyropolis. It must remain conjecture, but there is indeed a faint chance that one Polychronius, perhaps a bishop in Mesopotamia, was martyred with a small group of companions in his church in the course of the Sapor persecutions of the fourth century, that their bones were among those subsequently collected by Marouthas and buried at Martyropolis and finally that enough of the story reached Rome to find a place in an epic passion whose literary history is of greater than usual complexity. As with much hagiography such a solution is neither clean nor tidy. It is merely one attempt to reconcile a mass of conflicting evidence. Had Franchi de' Cavalieri lived to complete the great study of the Passions of Sixtus and Laurence which he planned,[57] he might have been able to tell us the answer.

57. P. Franchi de'Cavalieri, loc.cit. (n.56 above).

The Acta Sanctorum *and Bollandist Methodology*

FLOR VAN OMMESLAEGHE

1: *The* Acta Sanctorum

THREE and a half centuries have elapsed since Fr John Bollandus (1596-1665), after whom the publishers of the *Acta Sanctorum* are called Bollandists, assumed the task of editing the Lives of Saints *quotquot toto orbe coluntur.* He was not the initiator of the project, however: it had been introduced to the world of scholars in 1607 by another Jesuit, Fr Heribert Rosweyde, a Dutchman, who in 1603 had planned an edition of Lives of the Saints for every day of the year, excerpted from manuscripts preserved in the libraries of the Low Countries (the Netherlands, Belgium and Luxemburg of the present day). In a small booklet published at Antwerp by Plantin in 1607, Rosweyde unfolds his plan, which provides for eighteen volumes: three devoted to the feasts of our Lord and the Virgin Mary, as well as to other major feasts; twelve volumes for the saints celebrated in the twelve months of the year; and three volumes containing explanatory notes and indexes.

For various reasons, Rosweyde's project was never carried out. After his death, Bollandus was appointed by his superiors to decide whether the plan was to be put into execution. Not only did Bollandus offer an affirmative opinion: he also modified the original project in a way that was bound to be decisive for the elaboration of Bollandist methodology. His most important innovation was. that he would take in account not only saints known by written Lives, but also those merely mentioned in other works or known by a short biographical note, by a celebration recorded in a martyrology, by a monument or even solely by their popular celebrity (*sola populi fama*). Together with his first fellow, Godfrey Henschenius (1600-81), who joined him in 1635, he decided that the *Acta* should be preceded by an introductory note on the age and the mutual relations of the documents and on their historical value. The texts were to be equipped with a continuous annotation, whereas Fr Rosweyde had intended to collect all his commentary in one of the last volumes.

The first two volumes of *Acta*, those of January, were issued in 1643. Many of the principles set forth in the introduction are still applicable in our days, though in the course of the centuries, under the influence of such eminent Bollandists as Daniel Papebroch (1628-1714) and, in more recent times, Hippolyte Delehaye (1859-1941) and Paul Peeters (1870-1950), some rules have been modified.

The most noteworthy principle of Bollandus and Henschenius was, undoubtedly, that equal importance should be given to non-literary and to literary evidence, and that even patently non-historical, legendary sources deserve to be taken into consideration.

Since 1643 the *Acta Sanctorum* have developed into a series of 68 in folio volumes containing the Lives of Saints celebrated from 1 January to 10 November. Some limitations of Bollandus' programme have been overcome. The founder of the Acta, for example, only intended publication of Latin texts or translations. The first few pages printed in Greek characters are to be found in the *Acta* of March, volume 1. Since then, not only have Greek texts been welcomed, but also texts in various languages of the Near East and of the Celtic world. It may now be asked whether documents in various vernacular languages should not be taken into consideration.

The 68 volumes of *Acta* are not all equal in quality. In his history of the work of the Bollandists, Fr Hippolyte Delehaye deplores (*inter alia*) that the 18th-century Bollandists were not entirely faithful to the principles of their predecessors: they summarised *vitae* which deserved to be published in full, they indulged in polemics. In later times, after the suppression of the Society of Jesus (1773), they were forced to work precipitately and in bad conditions. The first Bollandists after the revival of their Society in 1837 had lost contact with their own traditions and, what was worse, they were tied to a strict time schedule, imposing on them the publication of new volumes on fixed dates. Nevertheless, it may be said that the last issued volumes are of the same quality as those composed in the best times of the Society of Bollandists.

Since 1882, the collection of *Acta Sanctorum* is completed by a periodical, *Analecta Bollandiana,* and a series of monographs, *Subsidia hagiographica.* In the periodical new results of research, text-editions, critical studies and a bibliographical review are published, which enables today's Bollandists to maintain a fruitful dialogue with scholars throughout the world. The *Subsidia* bring out catalogues of hagiographical manuscripts preserved in important libraries, repertories such as the different *Bibliothecae hagiographicae*, text-editions, as well as more theoretical work. Fr Delehaye's outstanding treatises on hagiographical method, on which we will rely in the following pages, all came out in the *Subsidia.*

2: *Bollandist methodology*

To expound the methodology of the Bollandists is an almost super-human task: indeed it is hardly possible to speak of a proper Bollandist methodology. More correct would it be to say that research in the field of hagiography involves some

OPPOSITE
Title page of Heribert Rosweyde's prospectus Fasti Sanctorum,
*published at Antwerp in 1607. From the original (College Saint Michel,
Brussels), by courtesy of the Société des Bollandistes.*

FASTI
SANCTORVM
QVORVM VITÆ
IN BELGICIS BIBLIOTHECIS
MANVSCRIPTÆ.

Item

Aǎa Præfidalia SS. Martyrum
Tharaci, Probi, & Andronici :

Nunc primùm integrè edita.

Collecǎore
HERIBERTO ROS-WEYDO
Vltraiecǎino, è Societate I E S V.

ANTVERPIÆ,
Ex OFFICINA PLANTINIANA,
Apud Ioannem Moretum.
M. DC. VII.

peculiar applications of historical methods. As Fr Delehaye says in his book *Cinq leçons sur la méthode hagiographique* (1934):

> Critical hagiography is a branch of the science of history. Its methods are not different from those which apply to any historical subject. The study of the documents, the search for evidence are its essential parts. But, as is the case in all particular branches of science, it has its own way of proceeding, dictated by the particularity of its object and of the documents taken into consideration.

Dealing with the subject of hagiographical methodology, we will, consequently, develop our statement under three headings: (a) the proper object of hagiography; (b) the research of evidence; and (c) the interpretation of evidence.

(a) The object of hagiography

The proper object of hagiography is, as the word implies, the saint, the person venerated by Christian people as an heroic example of Christian life. Such persons were, first of all, the martyrs, in other words those who fulfilled to the letter the word of Luke 21: 12-13: 'They will lay hands on you and persecute you, delivering you up to the synagogues and prisons, and you will be brought before kings and governors for my name's sake. This will be for you a time to bear testimony'. In later times, ascetics — desert fathers — were assimilated to these primeval heroes. After them, founders of local churches, missionaries and others were promoted to what is called 'the honour of the altars'. It is important to remember that there is a close relation between the veneration of the saints and the documents considered in hagiography. The difference between a saint and another historical person is that the saint becomes important, in the case of a martyr, from the day of his death; in other cases from the last years of his life. There is little chance that historical reports would have been made of his genealogy, his breeding or the events of his early life. It seldom occurs even that his contemporaries' have recorded how he 'bore testimony before kings and governors'. In a few cases (such as St Cyprian) we have an account based on so called *acta proconsularia*. Sometimes we possess an eye-witness report on how a martyr died (as in the *Martyrium Polycarpi*). In the case of Cyprian, we are even more fortunate, for we possess the whole range of hagiographical documents related to him. But these are exceptional cases.

The veneration of saints did not start from documents, but from practice. The author of the *Martyrium Polycarpi*, which took place in the year 167, concludes that the church of Smyrna will commemorate the martyrdom of her bishop every year on his *dies natalis* — on the day of his death, that is. This practice became general: the faithful of a certain church used to gather at the grave of 'their'

OPPOSITE

Title page of the first volume of Acta Sanctorum, *published by Jean Bolland at Anvers in 1643. Reproduced from an anastatic print provided by courtesy of the Société des Bollandistes.*

saint to celebrate the eucharist. The site was signalled by some monument: a ledger-stone, a small construction, a chapel or even a basilica. In the course of the celebration, the local bishop or another bishop or priest, invited for the occasion, pronounced the eulogy of the saint. Some of these sermons or panegyrics were preserved among the works of church fathers such as St John Chrysostom. But not all martyrs and venerated saints were so fortunate: of some no more persisted than the tradition of a celebration and a funeral monument. In the case of those for whom contemporary documents were lacking, substitutes were composed in later times on no larger base than a few historical data, on memories, or on nothing more than the fact that the saint was buried or that some of his relics were venerated on a particular spot and that his feast was celebrated. The rest was freely supplied by a willing hagiographer, on whom was imposed the ungrateful task of glorifying his hero, of proving that he was a real saint and of pleasing his audience. In later times it even happened that documents devoid of any evidential value were taken for authentic historical sources and provided the basis for a veneration.

(b) The research of evidence

From this short outline history of the veneration of saints it may be seen that the range of documents considered in hagiography is very diversified. They may be divided into documents which testify to the existence of a veneration, and those which relate a martyrdom, a saintly life, a series of miracles worked during the life and after the death of a saint.

To the first category (which in accordance with Fr Delehaye we call liturgical evidence) belong, in the first place, some archaeological and epigraphic documents. In this respect, little has been done in the field of hagiography. However Fr Delehaye collected a great amount of epigraphic evidence in his book *Les origines du culte des martyrs* (1912), which, notwithstanding the fact that it requires a thorough revision and completion so many years after its publication, remains one of the most required of *Subsidia hagiographica*. A certain number of articles on the same subject by Fr F. Halkin were published in Variorum Reprints under the title: *Inscriptions grecques relatives à l'hagiographie* (1973).

Other documents belonging to this category are: local calendars, of which a few are preserved (the Roman *Depositio martyrum*, dating from the fourth century, being the oldest). More recent documents are the well-known martyrologies, which require very careful handling. It is fortunate that in the *Acta Sanctorum* the *Commentarius in martyrologium Hieronymianum* (1931), the *Synaxarium Ecclesiae Constantinopolitanae* (1902) and the *Martyrologium Romanum scholiis historicis instructum* (1940) have all been published.

The second category in hagiographic evidence are the literary documents. They are preserved in innumerable manuscripts in libraries throughout the world. Comparing our times to those of the first Bollandists we may congratulate ourselves. Fr Rosweyde contented himself with what he occasionally discovered in the libraries of his country. But Henschenius and Papebroch started the search of manuscripts in foreign libraries. From 22 July 1660 till 21 December 1662 they undertook a journey which brought them through Germany, Switzerland, Italy, Rome and France. Their aim was to collect unknown Lives in the most important libraries. We now have at our disposal catalogues of most of the manuscript libraries in the world. In *Subsidia hagiographica* and in *Analecta Bollandiana* the Bollandists have brought out a number of catalogues of hagiographical manuscripts preserved in the various libraries of Europe. But the work is not finished.

Most useful in the research of literary documents concerning the saints are the different *Bibliothecae hagiographicae*. These are alphabetical listings of the saints with a survey of all the ancient literary works on their lives, the translations of their relics, and their miracles. The first of these repertories, the *Bibliotheca hagiographica graeca*, was made by Delehaye in 1895; the *Bibliotheca hagiographica latina* came out in 1898-1901; a Supplement was brought out in 1911. The *Bibliotheca hagiographica orientalis*, a work of Fr Paul Peeters, followed in 1910. An entirely reworked edition of the *Bibliotheca hagiographica graeca* [*BHG*³] in three volumes was published by Halkin in 1957; a complementary volume, called *Auctarium* came out in 1969. A thorough revision of the Supplement to the *Bibliotheca hagiographica latina* is on the stocks.

(c) The interpretation of evidence

The genuine historical work begins with the reading and interpretation of the evidence. The proper characteristics of the texts related to the veneration of the saints determine some definite methodological rules which it would be too elaborate to explain here in full. Some of them were formulated from the very beginnings of the *Acta Sanctorum*; others were established in the course of the work. For that reason, every Bollandist speaking on hagiographical methodology must feel grateful to his predecessors and masters. Among these, one of the most distinguished is Fr Hippolyte Delehaye, author of such remarkable works as: *Les Passions des martyrs et les genres littéraires* (1921); *Sanctus. Essai sur le culte des saints dans l'antiquité* (1927); *Les origines du culte des martyrs* (1912); and *Cinq leçons sur la méthode hagiographique* (1934). From the words of this master, let us gather a few principles which may guide us in dealing with hagiography.

For the scholar who wants to place a venerated saint in his historical context, the decisive evidence is *liturgical evidence* which permits the celebration of a saint to be fixed on a particular day (usually his *dies natalis*) and in a definite place. This is what Fr Delehaye calls the 'hagiographical co-ordinates' *(les coordonnées hagiographiques)*, which are to be determined by non-literary sources. Archaeological and epigraphical evidence may help to establish the place; in determining the day of a celebration we must rely on a thorough examination of the local calendars. Here Fr Delehaye gives a solemn warning to scholars who rely on those general martyrologies which uncritically assembled different calendars. He especially mentions in this context the so-called *Martyrologium Romanum* edited by Cardinal

Baronius. In this respect, the commentary on the Roman Martyrology, published as the *Propylaeum ad Acta Decembris* will be of the greatest help.

Unfortunately, the results of 'liturgical evidence' are limited. They give us an answer to the question whether a person who is venerated as a saint ever did exist. But they do not tell more about those individuals with whom we sometimes feel particularly related and who may have exerted a long-lasting influence on our personal or national history.

Literary documents on the saints may do so, but they present their own peculiarities. We can mention the difficulties in the field of textual criticism only in passing. The Lives of Saints were not copied as carefully as classical texts: the personal devotion of the copyist might intervene in order to embellish an ancient text; a copy might be summarised, amplified, contaminated or entirely rewritten.

One of the tasks of the scholar in hagiography will be to determine the historical value of a given document. From the very beginnings, the Bollandists adopted the rule that an edition of the *acta* of a saint should be preceded by an introduction in which the authorship, date and prosopography of the documents would be discussed. It was also (as we read in the introduction to the first volume of the *Acta Ianuarii*) Bollandus' intention to point out what was to be retained as historical, and what was not.

As a result of his own study and experience, Fr Delehaye made an inventory of different literary genres with their own characteristics. He distinguishes first of all *acta proconsularia* and eye-witness reports, which are first-rate documents. Further he distinguishes panegyrics, that is sermons pronounced at a saint's celebration. As regards epic passions, he argued that some may contain a few reliable elements, which may be traced back to eye-witnesses, while other ones are merely fictitious documents, composed in order to provide with *Acta* a saint who was only attested by liturgical evidence. Other documents are mere fiction, originally intended as a kind of novel with Christian inspiration and developing topics of Christian doctrine or life. The scholar who is dealing with literary evidence on a saint will have to make a thorough investigation on the genre of the documents which he is considering.

As a last rule of methodology, and by way of conclusion, we would like to draw attention to a principle which was very dear to Fr Delehaye, a principle aiming at the general disposition of people dealing with history in general and hagiography in particular. This outstanding scholar, who was far from being a romantic, never ceased to recommend a sound criticism, equally averse to 'conservatism' and 'hypercriticism'. This kind of criticism dictated the Bollandists' attitude towards the legends of the saints. On the one hand, they gave them a place in the *Acta Sanctorum*, for though these documents do not yield any valuable historical information on the saint himself, they may inform us about the history of saints' veneration in general or the way Christians saw their heroes, examples and intercessors. On the other hand, the editors of the *Acta Sanctorum* never failed to warn against ill-founded or erroneous practices in the veneration of saints. It is the sincere hope of today's Bollandists that in the future they may render the same services to the Christian world and that, in collaboration with scholars the world over, they may perpetuate the tradition of generosity and the humane qualities which so honourably characterised their founders and predecessors.

Self-Canonisation: the 'Partial Account' of Nikephoros Blemmydes

JOSEPH A. MUNITZ

T HE first thing to be said about the twin autobiographies of Blemmydes is that they are extremely difficult to understand. When, four years ago, I first tried to read them, I found page after page that was either unintelligible, or at least obscure to a baffling degree. It was somewhat of a consolation to discover some years later that I was not the only one to have difficulties: in his *BZ* (1897) review of the *editio princeps* (by August Heisenberg in 1896), Edmund Kurtz pointed out that the editor has clearly misunderstood numerous passages, and that the text as printed is often punctuated in a way that effectively blocks a correct grasp of its meaning. In my opinion his scathing review was too harsh. Heisenberg had to work with a single manuscript, the Monacensis 225, which is an excellent scholarly copy but packed with more than its fair share of abbreviations. The simple fact is that this Greek text is very difficult. It badly needs a new edition: (i) with improved punctuation; (ii) with the help of a second manuscript, Holkham graecus 71 (another excellent scholarly copy), now in the Bodleian Library, which will help to fill the occasional omissions of the Monacensis (like all scribes, he has been misled by *homoioteleuta*); (iii) with an English translation, which will provide at least an Aunt Sally for future interpretations. Such an edition is now considerably advanced.

The enigmatic author

The second problem arises however when one tries to enter the thought world of Blemmydes and asks: 'What makes him tick? What sort of a person was he? What is his autobiographical work intended to do?' Here, it is not only the Greek that is difficult; it is rather that one enters a Byzantine labyrinth of culture and thought patterns, so alien from our own. I would like to suggest that a possible thread to guide us is to view Blemmydes' work as belonging to the realm of hagiography. I realize that there are other possibilities: Professor Ihor Ševčenko has suggested here in Birmingham that new light can be thrown on these autobiographies if they are seen as revealing the world of a neurotic. My own suggestion does not claim to be very original. Heisenberg himself applied the term 'hagiography' to the twin works. Krumbacher, dropping the clerical tone, spoke of them as an example of *Autopanēgyrikos*, but Hunger has returned to the hagiographical aspect in his short reference to these works. The longest modern account of them that I know is that by the German scholar Georg Misch in his history of

164

autobiography. He refers repeatedly to a latent contradiction in Blemmydes' Accounts. On the one hand they are so personal and idiosyncratic; on the other hand, the sharp critical bent of Blemmydes' mind is blinkered by recurring Byzantine thought patterns, legends of the saints and belief in demons.

We can begin by asking why Blemmydes wanted to write these two accounts of his life. I suspect that his *point de départ* may seem to us very banal: he begins his first Account by saying that he was 66 years old; 'Having completed six and ten times six years since my birth' (1.1).[1] This strange circumlocution is not just verbiage: Blemmydes is extremely concise, or rather elliptical, in his style. We must remember that any Byzantine scholar, familiar with the works of Maximos the Confessor (e.g. *Qu. ad Thalassium* 49 schol. 19 and accompanying text),[2] will realize that six is a special number: *drastikos te kai teleios* (*activus atque perfectus* translates John Scotus). Blemmydes had arrived at a critical year of his life, comparable to his 28th year when he entered the church hierarchy as a deacon (7.15; 22.26-7), and to his 38th year when he was ordained a priest and clothed in the full monastic habit (22.25-6). Numbers are important for Blemmydes. Now that he is 66 he has reached full maturity: and he wants to give an account of a complete life.

But at once other motives appear: and here we have to distinguish. There are the conscious, declared, motives. But there are also the unconscious drives, never explicitly recognised by the subject, though possibly more influential than the former. The declared motives are: 'I have wanted to set up as a monument my profession of faith in the Helper, the Saviour [. . .] (that is God)' (1.4-5):

> May my effort be an encouragement for my companions (for whom I am much concerned), a reason for loving God, and an instigation to place the search for him above preoccupation for food, breath, and life; also a sort of defence and a consolation among necessary sufferings (1.9-14).

Here there is reference to the community for which Blemmydes was responsible, and to the dangers which he foresaw threatening them.

At this point the background has to be filled in: between 1241 and 1248 Blemmydes supervised the construction of a monastery dedicated to 'God Who Is' situated in barren country not far from Ephesus (72-4). He had already been *hēgoumenos* of another monastery for more than ten years. The titles found after his name at the beginning of his Accounts are those of 'monk, priest and founder'. His fears for his community were not unjustified and shortly after his death (as Pachymeres relates)[3] his monastery was confiscated, despite all the measures taken to ensure its financial security and independence (74.3-9).

The Accounts then are linked in their conscious motivation to the monastery founded by Blemmydes. They were written for his disciples — a 'monument'

1. References in the text give the page and usually the line in A. Heisenberg's edition of Blemmydes (1896).
2. *PG* 90.464 C 2-3; CChr SG7, 377.124.
3. Pachymeres (Bonn ed., 1839), i.342.

(*stēle*) engraved with his profession of faith in God, to serve as an encouragement and a defence (1.4).

Blemmydes as would-be saint

What sort of a man did Blemmydes want his disciples to remember? It seems to me pretty clear that Blemmydes was convinced deep down that he was a saint. The signs are the following:

1.   A list of miraculous events connected with his boyhood. Admittedly Blemmydes is the first to point out that in themselves, these premonitions are worthless. But a Byzantine saint does not have a 'normal' childhood. Blemmydes' mother has visions (angels clothe him) (53.15-19); he refuses to be suckled by anyone but his mother (milk from someone else would be 'conterfeit nourishment') (53.22-5); he never uses bad language, never tells a lie, never kisses a woman and 'throws stones with all his might at anyone who jokingly talks to him of marriage' (54.1-7). He likes going to church, and in his games he plays at being a cleric (54.7-10).

2.   Blemmydes is insistent that his worldly scholarship is worthless, and that his true learning (concerned with divine things) is that of a saint. He began to study thus as a lad, continued with the study of scripture ('especially at night', he notes, while he was busy with what we would call university studies at Nicaea), and continued throughout his life (6.9-13). Here his great pre-occupation is to establish not so much his cleverness, as his orthodoxy. This explains the long accounts of his discussions with the Latins (63-70, 74-80) and the Armenians (80-3), and his refutation of the charge of heresy brought against him in 1254 over a sermon involving christology (83-7). When he refers to his Paraphrase of the Psalms, he notes that he wrote them 'not from second-hand knowledge, but from the experience of one who sings the Psalms: thus I set up chanting monuments [. . .] to the glory of God' (88.5-8).

3.   Apart from his unshakeable orthodoxy, there are the miracles: the signs sent by God to distinguish his particular friend. Here one could draw up a very long list, but the problem is that events which most people would regard as fortuitous coincidences, are for Blemmydes miraculous happenings. Thus the timely departure of a girl friend when he was about 23 (she had designs on him, more than vice versa, but he was clearly shaken) (3-4), or the fact that he was not sea-sick on the boat taking him to Palestine (28.13-21), are for him divine interventions. It is not surprising that he, like Anna Komnena before him, regards a sword getting stuck in its scabbard as a clear miracle (40.4-20)., and even more so if in another case the sword emerges and cuts his garment, but fails to wound him (17.18-18.3). Actual miracles of curing are more difficult to find, but we must remember that Blemmydes had been trained as a doctor for seven years. Thus he attributes the curing

166

of Kosmas (whose nose had been mutilated) to his own nursing mother rather than to divine powers (23.29-24.6). However, when Blemmydes had been crushed under the overhang of his house (a place, he candidly tells us, that was being used as a privy), he describes his recovery as a miracle (37.16-25).

4. The miracles, of course, and the earlier legendary elements, along with Blemmydes' orthodoxy, all add up to drive home his peculiar relation with God. He is convinced that there is a special relation in his regard. One might have expected signs of mystical experience. But Blemmydes is reticent. He hints that his refusal to visit his parents on their death beds brought him inner joy: 'The blessings then unexpectedly received surpassed many times over the inheritance I had expected; the man who is worthy of gifts from above enters into possession of goods that surpass all measure' (71.28-31). He also hints that his study of scripture filled his heart and not just his mind, as when he spoke of John the Evangelist (83.30-84.1). A vigorous life of prayer underlies and explains much in the Partial Accounts: he can turn to God and demand guidance at difficult moments, such as the renunciation of the patriarchate (42.12; 44.28-9), or the refusal to grant indulgences to the epileptic Theodore Laskaris (47.25-48.6).

5. There remains another paragraph that could be extended indefinitely: for Blemmydes, his life, like that of any saint, is a continual war with the devil. The latter is constantly inspiring people to plot against him. He admits that he was accused of the following crimes: unnatural vice (8.17, 10.3-5, 11.13-14), misappropriation of funds (29.26-9), criticism of the emperor (31.22-4), euthanasia (32.18-21), hoarding up wealth (34.15-16), harsh and insulting conduct with the marchioness of Frigga (40.23), pride (11.5), magic (40.14-15), heresy, both Manichean (32.20-1) and Arian (84.4-6), and blatant madness. All these are dismissed, and he describes in detail the grisly end reserved for most, if not all, of the people who acted against him (31.1-16; 91.26-7).

6. A saint enjoys the company of saints. The few friends whom Blemmydes claims to have are men like the patriarch Germanos II and bishop Manasses; they are presented as men of outstanding sanctity.[5] Similarly, although Blemmydes tells us that two of his students conceived a violent hatred for him (29.13-17), and two of his monks (Kosmas and Gabriel) turned against him, on the other hand both John Vatatzes and his son respected him greatly (41.8-11; 50.5), and people were willing to ask him for favours (for example the mother of Drimys, who had tried to kill him) (50.14-17). Thus he would insist on his deep and genuine friendliness, and also on his concern for other Christians (46.23-30).

4.   *Alexiad* IX.vii.5 (ed. Leib ii.177.1-15).
5.   Ed. Heisenberg, 6.28-9; 7.17-18; 22.10-16; 74.24.

7.   Blemmydes is willing to admit his faults: it is *in spite* of what he knows himself to be, rather than in reward for his virtues, that God (referred to with names of touching intimacy as the Saviour, Helper, Doctor, Tutor, Lord, and Father)[6] continues to love him. The great virtues that he has tried to cultivate result from an uncompromising attachment to God's will, and a horror of false adulation. As he remarks, 'My own Tutor had successfully impressed on me that during all my life I should hold in abhorrence any word or deed undertaken for the sake of harmful adulation. So it is that most people criticise me as boorish and uncompromising' (60.10-14). He would claim to have carried fidelity to his inner vision to heroic lengths.

Preparations for a case

This list could be extended. But Blemmydes' own conviction is sufficiently clear already. Is it conceivable then that he believed in the possibility of his own canonisation?   The first reaction may be to reject such a notion as self-contradictory – as of course it is, in its most literal sense. But if we look a little further, the idea may seem less absurd.

Blemmydes was probably aware that in the thirteenth century the Roman attitude to canonisation was changing. Professor Vauchez (now at Rouen) has studied the acts of canonisation that exist in the Roman archives, and shown a marked increase in centralisation, formalisation, and the insistence on bureaucratic paper-work.

Constantinople was not Rome, of course. But chancelleries tend to standardise procedures. Blemmydes could foresee that written proofs would have an even greater weight in the new Rome, the 'Great Church', to which he was proud to belong. As a 'founder' (a title which he may well have given to himself), he could expect a certain *cultus*. The monument he wished to bequeath to his monastery fits into a general pattern, which points in one direction. Blemmydes does his best to supply his side of the picture, while fully acknowledging that devil's advocates would not be lacking. No doubt it is to his satanic majesty that he would attribute the turn of events which led to the destruction of his monastery, to the loss of his Typikon, and to the modern picture of him not as a saint, but as a cantankerous neurotic.

---

6.   Ed. Heisenberg, 26.5; 37.21; 38.1; 50.12; 51.25.

THE SAINT IN CULT AND ART

The Traffic in Relics: some Late Roman Evidence

E.D. HUNT

AS the controversial monk Pelagius was defending his views before a synod of bishops in Palestine in December 415, news arrived of miraculous events at the village of Caphargamala in the neighbourhood of Jerusalem.[1] Impelled by a series of dream-visions of the New Testament rabbi Gamaliel, the local presbyter Lucianus had unearthed three burials – of Gamaliel himself, his fellow-rabbi Nicodemus, and (the real prize) of the first Christian martyr, St Stephen (whose place of burial had been unknown since the time of his death). The bishop of Jerusalem and others hurried to the scene to preside over the revelation of Stephen's remains: Lucianus (to whose first-hand account we owe our knowledge of these events) describes the fragrance that filled the air as the tomb was opened, such that 'we thought we were in paradise'. In this heady atmosphere seventy-three people (it is asserted) were cured of sundry ailments, before the martyr's body was solemnly laid to rest in the great basilica on Mount Sion in Jerusalem, on his feast-day of 26 December.[2]

The interment of Stephen's remains in Jerusalem is far from the last word in the story. For, after his rediscovery, the first martyr was to become one of the most widely-travelled of Christian saints. According to a fifth-century sermon in praise of Stephen (attributed to bishop Basil of Seleucia) '*every place* is glorified and hallowed by your remains; your protection shines out over *all the earth*'.[3] Certainly it was not long before some of the relics reached Constantinople and the pious court of Theodosius II and his sister Pulcheria.[4] The saint made a journey even further afield by the hand of the Spanish presbyter Orosius, on his return to Augustine in north Africa after the vindication of Pelagius by the Palestinian bishops;[5] through this channel of distribution relics of Stephen were circulated among Christian congregations in Africa, where he effected miraculous cures and

1. For a recent summary of the political background, see J.N.D. Kelly, *Jerome: his life, writings and controversies* (London 1975), 317ff.
2. The text of the *Epistula Luciani* (Avitus' Latin translation of the presbyter's account) is to be found in *PL* 41.807ff.
3. Basil Seleuc. *Orat.* 42 (*PG* 85. 469).
4. Theoph. *Chronographia,* s.a. 420 (ed. de Boor, 86-7): a fragment of Stephen's right hand in return for Theodosius' gift of a gilded cross for Golgotha.
5. For Orosius as the bearer of the relics, see *Ep. Aviti, PL* 41. 805-8.

was believed to intervene in the life of the community in a variety of ways to alleviate day-to-day hardships (whether the consequences of nature or the Roman government).[6] Orosius, unable to reach his native Spain, also deposited relics of Stephen on the island of Minorca, where the saint inspired the local congregation to an onslaught against their neighbouring Jewish population, and achieved a mass conversion.[7]

The distribution of relics

The widespread distribution of Stephen's relics, and the miraculous achievements associated with them, illustrate what has become a 'fact of life' in the Christian Roman empire of the early fifth century. Christian saints escape from their tombs to become the possession of congregations far and wide.[8] Churches denied traditions associating them with apostles and martyrs could acquire such pedigree by the import of relics, to lend authority and prestige: by such means, as is familiar, the city of Constantinople sought to make up for its lack of Christian history.[9] In the era of St Ambrose, new churches were dedicated at Milan and elsewhere in northern Italy over the shrines of apostolic relics which had become the prize of eastern pilgrimages.[10] So Gaudentius, bishop of Brescia, housed relics which he had himself acquired on such a journey;[11] while the Holy Land pilgrim Silvia (whom tradition also associates with Brescia) is said to have promised her friends in the West that she would return with the remains of 'many martyrs from the East'.[12] This traffic was predominantly, but not exclusively, from east to west — there was a 'counter-flow', for instance, in the sample of the remains of the three Christian missionaries martyred in 397 by the pagans of the Val di Non which was sent to John Chrysostom in Constantinople;[13] or the Roman relics of Peter and Paul which Theodosius I's praetorian prefect Fl. Rufinus (brother-in-law, incidentally, of the pilgrim Silvia) transported to grace his new church across the Bosphorus at Chalcedon.[14] Clearly there was already a considerable

6. For the arrival of the relics in Africa, see Augustine, *Serm.* 317-8 (*PL* 38. 1435ff.), and the record of miraculous cures in *Civ. Dei* xxii.8. For incidents at Uzalis, *De Miraculis S. Stephani* (*PL* 41. 833ff.).

7. The events are described in the Letter of Severus, bishop of Minorca, *PL* 41. 821ff.

8. The classic study remains H. Delehaye, *Les origines du culte des martyrs* (SubsHag 20 [1933]), esp.ch.8 'Développements du culte des martyrs'. Cf. A. Grabar, *Martyrium, Recherches sur le culte de reliques et l'art chrétien antique* (Paris 1946), and B. Kötting, *Die frühchristliche Reliquienkult und die Bestattung im Kirchengebäude* (Cologne-Opladen 1965).

9. E.g. Philostorgius, *HE* iii.2 (Andrew, Luke, Timothy); cf. Jerome, *Chron.* (ed. Helm) *s.a.* 356, with G. Dagron, *Naissance d'une capitale* (Paris 1974), 409.

10. See E.D. Hunt, 'St Silvia of Aquitaine', *JTS* 23 (1972), 370-1.

11. Gaudentius, *Tract.* xvii. 14ff. (ed. Glueck, CSEL 68).

12. Paul. Nol. *Ep.* 31.1. On Brescia, see *JTS* 23 (1972), 362ff. and P. Devos, 'Silvie la sainte pèlerine II', *AnalBoll* 92 (1974), 321ff.

13. Vigil. Trident. *Ep.* 2 (*PL* 13. 552ff.).

14. Callinicus, *Vita Hypatii,* 66 (ed. Bartelink [SC 177], 98); on Rufinus, see John Matthews, *Western Aristocracies and Imperial Court* (Oxford 1975), 134ff.

The protomartyr Stephen.
Mosaic formerly in the church of the Archangel Michael, Kiev (now at St Sophia, Kiev).

array of saintly relics in circulation before the emergence of St Stephen in 415. One final example befits a symposium on the Byzantine saint: chief among the remains which Gaudentius carried back to Brescia were those of the Forty Martyrs of Sebaste, which he had acquired from the family of bishop Basil at Caesarea – both Basil and Gregory of Nyssa, in their sermons on these martyrs, acclaim the ubiquity of the soldier-saints: 'they are offered hospitality in many places, and adorn many lands'.[15]

Concern about translations

It is not self-evident why this distribution and proliferation of relics should have arisen in the later fourth century, especially in view of the long-standing assumptions of antiquity about not interfering with the dead in their tombs. Laws continued to be issued in the late empire reaffirming the traditional prohibitions against tampering with the dead,[16] and in 386 this was specifically applied to the martyrs; in a law addressed to the eastern praetorian prefect Theodosius ordered 'no person shall transfer a buried body to another place [by the time of Justinian's Code the clause 'except with the permission of the emperor' is added]; no person shall sell the relics of a martyr; no person shall traffic in them [. . .]'.[17] Not only the powers of the state were marshalled to preserve the body in peace; on occasions the saints themselves communicated their wish not to be disturbed. As early as 259, at Tarragona in Spain, bishop Fructuosus made a *post mortem* appearance to prevent the separation of his ashes and to secure proper burial;[18] while, in their so-called 'Testament', the Forty Martyrs leave specific directions against any division of their remains.[19] Delehaye long ago observed a difference of practice here between East and West, and that Western Christendom (far less richly endowed with tombs of apostles and martyrs) was reluctant to sanction the disturbance of precious remains: the Roman Church in the time of Gregory the Great was still affirming that the saints' bodies were inviolable (though promoting sacred objects which had had contact with the remains as substitute relics).[20] Not long before the bishop of Jerusalem was enthusiastically transferring Stephen's newly-discovered relics into the basilica on Mount Sion, Exsuperius, bishop of Toulouse in Aquitania, had reluctantly contemplated the removal of the body of the local martyr Saturninus to a new church – he needed to be reassured by a dream, and by imperial authorisation.[21] But if Ambrose's energetic

15. The story of the Forty Martyrs (its first appearance in the West) is the theme of Gaudentius, *Tract*. xvii (loc.cit); cf. Basil Caesar. at *PG* 31. 521, and Greg.Nys. at *PG* 46. 784.
16. *CTh* ix.17, *passim;* e.g. ix.17.4 (356): 'nothing has been derogated from that punishment which is known to have been imposed on violators of tombs'.
17. *CTh* ix.17.7, with *CJ* iii.44.14.
18. *Martyrium Fructuosi*, 6.3 (H. Musurillo, *The acts of the Christian Martyrs* [Oxford 1972], 182).
19. *Testament of the Forty Martyrs*, 1.3 (Musurillo, 354).
20. Delehaye, *Les origines*, 50ff.
21. ibid., 67 (citing the *Acta Saturnini*).

excavations of martyrs' remains are any guide, not all western bishops were so particular in respecting the peace of the dead.[22]

Some church authorities strove at least to *contain* the enthusiasm for relics pervading their congregations. As the shrines and miraculous accomplishments of Stephen proliferated in the African province, Augustine instituted the practice of publicly authenticating and documenting the martyr's achievements, both to give the miracles currency and also to guard against fraudulent claims;[23] he warned against bogus monks going the rounds with relics for sale, alleged to be those of martyrs.[24] Similarly a council at Carthage in 401 had urged congregations against shrines and relics which were not authentic but merely the result of 'dreams and *empty* revelations'.[25] The search for authenticity and the acknowledgement of the possibilities of fraud only emphasise the degree to which the movement of relics was now incorporated into the life of the Church; as does its emergence as a subject of ecclesiastical debate. Jerome's defence of the cult of relics against Vigilantius' attacks on the veneration of mere 'scraps of dust' is perhaps the classic contemporary statement:

> While the devil and the demons wander through the whole world and present them-selves everywhere, are martyrs after the shedding of their blood to be kept out of sight shut up in a coffin from whence they cannot escape?[26]

Later Theodoret was to parade before pagan critics the salutary deeds of martyrs achieved through their scattered remains.[27] One theme is common to all such treatises and sermons – and fundamental to the thinking behind the spread of relics: that the saint is *indivisible* and *omnipresent*, and wherever the smallest portion of his remains is to be found he is there in his entirety. Thus Gaudentius on his fragments of the Forty Martyrs, *'pars ipsa, quam meruimus,* plenitudo *est'*.[28] With such an argument the Church came to terms with the increasing dismemberment of its treasured saints.

22. In addition to Sts Gervasius and Protasius, Ambrose brought to light Sts Vitalis and Agricola, and Sts Nazarius and Celsus; cf. F. Homes Dudden, *The Life and Times of St Ambrose* (Oxford 1935), 316ff., and Delehaye, *Les origines*, 75-80.

23. Cf. Peter Brown, *Augustine of Hippo* (London 1967), 414-5, based on fundamental studies by Delehaye. For the text of a *libellus* documenting authentic cures, see August. *Serm.* 322 (*PL* 38. 1443).

24. August. *De opere monachorum,* 36.

25. Conc. Carthag. 13 Sept 401 (CChr 149, 204) '[. . .] *nulla memoria martyrum probabiliter accipetur, nisi ubi corpus aut aliquae reliquiae sunt aut origo alicuius habitationis vel possessionis vel passionis fidelissima origine traditur'.*

26. Jer. *Contra Vigil.* 6; on the treatise in general, Kelly, *Jerome,* 286ff.

27. Theodoret, *Cure of Pagan Ills,* viii.10-11 (ed. P. Canivet [SC 57]): 'no one grave conceals the bodies of each of them, but they are shared out among towns and villages, which call them saviours of souls and bodies, and doctors, and honour them as founders and protectors [. . .]'.

28. Gaudent. *Tract.* xvii.35-6; cf. Theodoret, loc.cit., with Chromat. Aquilei. (ed. J. Lemarié, SC 164) *Sermon* 26.1 ('*data est portio, ut et vos totum in portione haberetis, et nos nihil de eo quod datum fuerat amitteremus'*), Paul.Nol. *Carm.* 27.440ff., Victricius, below, 179.

The influence of the pagan past

We may wonder, with Vigilantius, what was the attraction for pious individuals and congregations in the possession of these bones and ashes. In some respects it seems to represent only the thinnest Christian veneer veiling the traditional practices of pagan antiquity. When St Makrina, for example, like many others, kept by her her precious fragment of the wood of the Cross, it functioned much as a pagan talisman – a good luck charm to keep misfortune at bay.[29] Superstition knew no religious boundaries. Similarly, relics deposited in churches afforded potent collective protection for congregations, even (of course) whole communities.[30] Yet there was more to this than institutionalised superstition. The saints who were present in diverse places through the mobility of their remains turn out to be late Roman *patroni par excellence;* their intercessions would vanquish the influence of earthly *potentes.* The language of patronage pervades our accounts of the accomplishments of saints and martyrs through their relics: so Gervasius and Protasius in Milan would overwhelm the forces of the Arian court of Valentinian II;[31] so, too, Stephen, in effecting the conversion of the Jews in Minorca, outclassed the worldly standing and aristocratic prestige of the Jewish leaders.[32] The record, furthermore, of Stephen's interventions at Uzalis in north Africa is that of the *patronus communis* of the Christian congregation, behaving as a leading local citizen protecting the interests of his clients in the community.[33] Not for nothing is emphasis placed on the relics representing the physical *praesentia* of the saint in the earthly community – access to his influence and patronage demanded that he be present in their midst, and not confined in a distant (and unknown) grave.

The relics of the Holy Land

The experience of these late Roman congregations may be illuminated by reference to a specific group of relics which came to the fore in the fourth century – those from the holy places of Palestine.[34] St Makrina's fragment was only one of the many pieces of the wood of the Cross scattered, according to bishop Cyril of Jerusalem, all over the Mediterranean world.[35] The enthusiasm to possess a portion of the sacred wood is vividly glimpsed in the story, told to the pilgrim Egeria in

---

29. Greg.Nys. *Vita Macrinae,* 30 (P. Maraval [SC 178], 240ff, with notes). Cf. Jerome, *Comm. in Matt.* iv, 23.5 (CChr 77.212), on the phylacteries carried by *'superstitiosae mulierculae'.*
30. As at Primuliacum: Paul.Nol. *Ep.* 31.1 *'munimentum* praesentis *et pignus aeternae salutis'.*
31. E.g. Ambr. *Ep.* 22.10 *'Tales ego ambio defensores tales milites habeo: hoc est non saeculi milites, sed milites Christi. Nullam talibus invidiam timeo, quorum quo maiora, eo tutiora* patrocinia *sunt'.*
32. At *Ep. Severi* 4 (*PL* 41. 823), the earthly patronage of Theodorus is contrasted with *'patroni Stephani patrocinium';* cf. the *Ep. Aviti, 'ut ipse* [sc. Stephanus] praesens *advocatus et patronus obsequentium sibi petitionibus dignetur assistere* [...]'.
33. *De miraculis S. Stephani,* ii.1 (*PL* 41. 843); cf. P. Brown, *Augustine of Hippo,* 413.
34. For a catalogue of Holy Land relics, see B. Bagatti, 'Eulogie Palestinesi' *OCP* 15 (1949), 126-66.
35. Cyril, *Catecheses,* iv.10, x.19, xiii.4. For *testimonia* of the fragments of the Cross, see A. Frolow, *La relique de la vraie croix* (Paris 1961), 155ff.

Jerusalem, of the worshipper who had bitten off a piece as he knelt down to kiss the relic.[36] As with the remains of apostles and martyrs, so the wood of the Cross came to adorn the foundation of new churches: a martyrium at Tixter in Mauretania, for instance (359), or Sulpicius Severus' new basilica at Primuliacum in Gaul (c.400).[37] A close second in popularity to the True Cross was the earth from the Holy Land on which Christ had walked – St Augustine knew of an ex-official in his diocese who had a lump of Holy Land earth hanging in his bedroom.[38] The favoured quarry for such soil was the spot at the summit of the Mount of Olives said to have borne Christ's last footprints on earth before the Ascension (the footprints, like the True Cross in Jerusalem, were miraculously preserved despite the depradations of the relic-hunters).[39] Another increasingly popular Holy Land relic (or very nearly a relic) was a small flask of oil from the lamps which burned at the Holy Sepulchre – the same variety of memento was favoured by devotees at the shrines of saints.[40]

We are in a position to understand something of the kind of devotion which surrounded the acquisition of these Holy Land relics thanks to the record of the early pilgrims at the holy places in the years after Constantine.[41] There is already a clue in the *ampullae*, the oil-flasks mentioned above: surviving examples are distinguished by the realistic representations of the shrines at the holy places as they appeared to contemporary pilgrims – they give us an idea of what the holy places actually looked like.[42] Pilgrims, we are reminded, went to the Holy Land not just to *be* there, where Christ had been, but also to *see* the evidence of his presence on earth before their eyes.[43] For Jerome, it was the 'eyes of faith' which revealed to the pilgrim Paula the whole biblical scene in all its detail at the sites she visited – the Bethlehem manger and the surrounding characters assembled (even the star shining above), the Cross with Christ hanging upon it, and so on.[44]

36. *It.Eg.* 37.2.
37. Tixter: *MEFR* 10 (1890), 440-68 [=*CIL* viii, suppl.iii, 20600]; cf. similar dedication at Rusguniae, *CIL* viii, 9255 (with J.F. Matthews, *CR* 88 [1974], 104). Primuliacum: Paul. Nol. *Ep.* 31.1.
38. August. *Civ. Dei*, xxii.8 (CChr 48. 820); cf. the Donatists who venerated earth from the Holy Land, id. *Ep.* 52.2.
39. Sulp.Sev. *Chron.* ii.33.8; cf. Paul.Nol. *Ep.* 31.6 (on the Cross) *'detrimenta non sentiat et quasi intacta permaneat'*.
40. On these flasks, cf. Anton. Placent. *Itin.* 20 (CChr 175. 139). Martyr-shrines: Joh.Chrys. *Hom. in Martyres, PG* 50. 665: *'Labe elaion hagion* [. . .]'.
41. For the texts, see *Itineraria et alia geographica* (CChr 175 [1965]), and translations by J.D. Wilkinson, *Egeria's Travels* (London 1971) and *Jerusalem Pilgrims Before the Crusades* (Warminster 1978).
42. See A. Grabar, *Ampoules de Terre Sainte* (Paris 1958). For their use in reconstructing the original building at the Sepulchre, cf. Wilkinson, *Egeria's Travels*, 246ff., and 'The Tomb of Christ', *Levant* 4 (1972), 83-97.
43. Paul.Nol. *Ep.* 49.14 *'non enim alter affectus homines ad Hierosolymam rapit, nisi ut loca, in quibus corporaliter praesens fuit Christus, videant atque contingant* [. . .]'.
44. Jerome, *Ep.* 108.9ff; cf. Kelly, *Jerome*, 118ff., on Paula's 'emotional transports'. For Jerome's more succinct version of his own experience, see *Apol.c.Ruf.* iii.22 *'vidi multa miracula; et quae prius ad me fama pertulerat*, oculorum iudicio *comprobavi'*.

Throughout her travels in the Holy Land hers was an essentially *visual* experience, conjuring up to a vivid imagination the biblical past in the Palestine of the present. The pilgrims' experience was not confined to the New Testament: others, like Egeria, saw (for example) in the Sinai desert the very bush from which the Lord had spoken to Moses out of the fire, or saw in the sand on the shores of the Red Sea the tracks of the Egyptians' chariot wheels disappearing into the waters.[45] The imagination came to be aided not only by the constant reading of the appropriate biblical passages *in situ* but also, in Jerusalem, by the development of a distinctive church liturgy designed to re-enact, in strongly visual terms, the events of Christ's life at the places where they had occurred.[46] Egeria's description of the round of worship in Jerusalem captures the immediacy and visual realism of experiences such as accompanying the bishop from the Mount of Olives into the city on Palm Sunday — a direct echo of Christ's own entry into Jerusalem — or hearing the Passion narratives read at Golgotha on Good Friday: 'you could hardly believe how every single one of them weeps during the three hours, old and young alike, because of the manner in which the Lord suffered for us'.[47]

The characteristic pilgrims' response at the holy sites was thus, with the 'eyes of faith', to recreate the biblical past as a *present reality*; and to come away from the Holy Land with relics from the holy places, wood of the Cross, a portion of earth, was to enable that present reality to be recreated *wherever* the relics might come to rest. The experience of pilgrims in the Holy Land might thus become the experience of congregations far and wide, and of those who had never been anywhere near the holy places. The point is discussed by Paulinus of Nola in a letter he wrote to Sulpicius Severus to accompany a fragment of the Cross which he was sending for the dedication of Sulpicius' new church at Primuliacum.[48] All that Severus will see with the naked eye is a few scraps of wood: but his 'interior eyesight' will be stimulated to behold the whole series of biblical events surrounding the Crucifixion and their implications for belief — he will see 'the whole force of the Cross in this tiny fragment'. Paulinus is sending the relic, he urges, so that Severus may possess the *physical reality* of the faith which he has long adhered to in the spirit. There seems little reason to doubt that Severus' 'interior eyesight' here and the pilgrims' 'eyes of faith' are one and the same; and that, through the medium of the relic of the Cross, the immediacy and vividness of the pilgrims'

45. Burning Bush: *It.Eg.* 4.6ff. *'qui rubus usque in hodie vivet et mittet virgultas'.* Chariot tracks: Pet. Diac. (deriving from Egeria) Y5 (CChr 175. 100-1); Orosius, *Hist.* i.10.17, knew they were still visible.

46. The liturgy is described by Egeria, *It.Eg.* 24ff.; cf. Wilkinson, *Egeria's Travels,* 54ff. The best modern study is A. Renoux's introduction to his edition of the *Armenian Lectionary,* PO 35 (1969). For Bible-reading, cf. *It.Eg.* 4.3 ('[. . .] *ubicumque venissemus, semper ipse locus de libro legeretur'),* 10.7.

47. Palm Sunday: *It.Eg.* 31 (*NB* 31.3 *'sic deducetur episcopus in eo typo quo tunc Dominus deductus est').* Good Friday: ibid. 37.7.

48. Paul.Nol. *Ep.* 31.1ff.; the fragment had been brought from Jerusalem by Paulinus' kinswoman, Melania the elder.

experience is being reproduced far away from the Holy Land. The Cross and its implications are to be as *present* to the community in Aquitania as they are on Golgotha.

The part and the whole

Against this background the ubiquitous presence of the saint or martyr through the distribution of his remains becomes, I believe, less of an abstraction. Picture the scenes described by Jerome, as the remains of the prophet Samuel were transported from Palestine to the court of Arcadius at Constantinople: as the relics made their journey the route was lined by the faithful, linking the Holy Land to the Hellespont (so he asserts) in a unison chorus of acclamation; they were welcoming, not a casket of dust and ashes, but the prophet himself as though he were still among them *'quasi praesentem viventemque'*.[49] The fragmentary relics were the visible testimony of the prophet's continued presence. The same kind of language will be found characterising the devotion to martyrs and their relics. Asterios of Amaseia pictured the tomb of the martyr Phokas as evoking a vision of the saint's life and martyrdom — and he has an explicit parallel with pilgrims at the Holy Land site of Mamre *visualising* the biblical history of Abraham and the patriarchs which the shrine commemorated.[50] Gregory of Nyssa portrays the faithful approaching a casket of relics of the martyr Theodore:

> Those who behold them embrace them *as though the actual living body,* applying all their senses, eyes, mouth and ears; then they pour forth tears for his piety and suffering, and bring forward their supplications to the martyr *as though he were present and complete* [. . .].[51]

Victricius bishop of Rouen, an enthusiastic collector of relics, justifies the practice in similar terms: the physical remains, the 'blood and gore' (*'cruor et limus'*) are what the eye sees; yet through this visual experience the 'eyes of the heart' (another variant of the 'eyes of faith') are opened to apprehend the presence of the saint himself — 'where there is any part, there is the whole' (*'ubi est aliquid, ibi totum est'*).[52] Victricius' relics of saints have the same capability as Sulpicius Severus' fragments of the Cross: to engender the effective presence of the saint in the Christian community which possessed his relics.

The traffic in relics, then, may be seen to have originated from a species of devotion which hankered after physical objects and remains which could be *seen* to embody, for individual and community, the saint and his powers. That there were many whose piety had this concrete, visual propensity may be established from the evidence of pilgrims' reactions to the holy places, and the evident reality, for them, of the biblical past which they commemorated. For the Church at large,

---

49. *C. Vigilant.* 5. For Samuel's arrival in Constantinople, cf. *Chron. Pasch.* s.a. 406 (ed. Dindorf, 569).
50. *Hom.* ix, *PG* 40. 301-4: the worshippers become 'spectators' of the biblical record.
51. *Hom. in S. Theod. PG* 46. 740B.
52. *De Laude Sanctorum,* 10.

the age of the martyrs was past; but that did not mean that their presence could not be revived (on a much more widespread scale than their previous earthly existence (through the circulation of their remains. It may be supposed that St Stephen was as *real* a presence to the Christian community in Minorca or to the congregations in north Africa as were the living holy men of Syria or Egypt — and his impact on local life comparable to theirs.

The Role of the Byzantine Saint in the Development of the Icon Cult

NICHOLAS GENDLE

T HE theology of the icon during the Byzantine iconoclast controversy turns very largely on the image of Christ and its implications for Christian faith and practice. To what extent was it legitimate, or even possible, to depict the human face of God in an art-work? Especially in the second phase of the dispute, the arguments get increasingly channelled into the well-worn tracks of the debate about the relation of the two natures in Christ, and whether the icon of the Saviour does not involve confusing or dividing the natures.

Given the long history of christological controversy, it was perhaps inevitable that any new doctrinal problem should be subsumed under these categories. But were they really relevant to what was vital in the icon cult? Historically speaking, were christological considerations to the forefront, even implicitly, when icons were becoming central foci of Byzantine popular piety from the early fifth century onwards? Or is Peter Brown right in suggesting that the whole debate about christology during inconoclasm is basically a 'red herring'?[1]

Little was said at the second Nicene Council (787) about saints' icons. Icons of saints and angels were merely included in a list of subjects that might properly be represented in religious art, with the explanation, 'The more we see such images, the more we are led to recall with love the persons depicted'.[2] Nonetheless, I should like to suggest that the cult of the early Byzantine saint, and especially the ascetic, is at least as crucial to the emergence of the icon as a quasi-sacramental object of devotion, as is the image of Christ. Indeed, both art-historical and literary evidence suggest that the images of saints were even more important as the real growing-point for the icon as cult object.

Initially, scruples were felt against showing Christ in his human form, and this undoubtedly explains the practice of the second and third centuries of depicting him as a general type, the Good Shepherd or Philosopher, or as Lamb of God.[3]

---

1. P.R.L. Brown, 'A Dark Age Crisis: aspects of the Iconoclastic Controversy', *EHR* 246 (1973), 1-34. Brown argues that the controversy was essentially 'a debate on the position of the holy in Byzantine society'. He connects the role of the icon closely with that of the holy man, and plays down the importance of the christological dimension. For an incisive critique of Brown's article, see P. Henry, 'What was the Iconoclastic Controversy about?', *Church History* 25.i. (1976), 1-16.

2. Mansi, xiii. 377B ff.

3. See P. du Bourguet, *Early Christian Art* (London 1972), 9, 53, 22-3, 30, 171 for 3rd century Roman depictions of Christ as Good Shepherd (mural in the catacomb of

Neither these images, nor New Testament narrative (whether to decorate sarcophagi or walls) were likely to be treated as cult objects; yet fear of idolatory leads to the clear veto of the Council of Elvira (? early 4th century): 'Let that which is worshipped not be painted on walls'.[4] Admittedly, it is not long before Eusebius is to refer to commemorative portraits of Christ, and to the thaumaturgic statue of Christ at Paneas.[5] But early images of Christ of the classic bearded adult type[6] are rare, and references to such images infrequent in our period.

Early images of saints

The earliest positive references to Christian figural art in the fourth century are almost all concerned with martyr-cycles on church walls. Thus Gregory of Nyssa tells us how a certain artist has depicted all the struggles of the martyr Theodore, 'as in a speaking book'.[7] Basil praises the eloquent scenes of the 'victorious conflict' of the martyr Barlaam;[8] and Asterios of Amasea, referring to a painted sequence showing the martyrdom of Euphemia, singles out the capacity of art to render emotions, such as anger or compassion.[9] The images referred to in these texts are not strictly iconic, yet the emphasis, not so much on the didactic value of art,[10] as on its ability to elicit appropriate religious feelings, is significant for the subsequent development of the cult. Even more telling is Gregory Nazianzen's account of how the mere sight of the venerable face of St Polemon in an icon was enough to convert a prostitute: 'She was overcome by the sight, and filled with shame before the holy man depicted, as if he were [still] living'.[11] We see here an early example of an icon acting as a psychological trigger-mechanism of compunction.

According to John Damascene, Chrysostom himself kept an image of St Paul on his desk: 'when he studied the epistles at night, the picture seemed to come alive and speak to him'.[12] If this piece of evidence is reliable, then again we have an

Callixtus), Christ as Orpheus (mural in the cemetery of Domitilla), Christ as True Philosopher (sarcophagi in the Lateran Museum and at the Palazzo S. Severino); and as Lamb of God (cemetery of Sts Peter and Marcellinus).

4. J. Vivier, ed., *Concilios Visigoticos e Hispano-Romanos* (Madrid 1963), 8.
5. *Hist.Eccles.* vii.18.4 (commemorative portraits of Christ) and vii.18.3 (Paneas image).
6. The earliest painted example known to me is from the catacomb of Commodilla, 4th century (du Bourguet, *Early Christian Art*, 123). Later in the same century, we have a bearded Christ enthroned with Peter and Paul in the 'Crypt of the Saints', cemetery of Sts Peter and Marcellinus, Rome (ibid., 171). Images of the key-events of the NT kergyma, especially the Passion, are very rare before the 6th century. Even as late as that century, we read in Gregory of Tours (*de gloria mart.* 23) of a bishop being obliged to veil a painting of Christ on the Cross because the image was causing scandal (*PL* 71. 746).
7. *PG* 66. 739D.
8. *PG* 31. 489.
9. *PG* .50. 335A.
10. See N. Gendle, 'Art as Education in the Early Church', *Oxford Art Journal* iii (1979), 3-8.
11. *PG* 37. 737-8.
12. *PG* 94. 1277C.

early case of the power of the icon to mediate the living presence of the saint. We can surely see in such instances the genesis of the 'potentiated' icon and ex-voto – in Kitzinger's words, 'a means of visualising the invisible, through which love and respect can be conveyed'.[13] Such an attitude to icons may be compared with Gregory of Nyssa's words on contemporary behaviour towards relics: 'Those who behold them embrace them as if the living body itself; they bring [. . .] all their senses into play, and shedding tears of passion, they address to the martyr their prayers of intercession, as if he were alive and present'.[14] In both cases, the same psychological components may be observed: the warm, emotional tone, the need for a palpable, sensual point of contact with the holy person, the tendency to treat icon or relic as some kind of *continuum* with the living saint.

Indeed, by the fifth century, icon and relic may be fused at times into a single spiritually charged object. The 'sacred dust' of ascetics like Symeon the Younger is incorporated into commemorative portraits, and the tokens (*eulogiai*) given by the holy man to visitors may take the form of an *ampulla* or medal (or just a frag-ment of clothing) that has been in physical contact with him.[15]

The use of commemorative portraits of saints may well go back to the third century. The Apocryphon of John describes how a disciple surreptitiously made a portrait of the apostle, much to the latter's disapproval.[16] Even though the story may be fictitious, it could well represent the actual practice of the time. Grabar has published commemorative medallions of Peter and Paul from Rome, which he dates to the third century.[17] One notes that the standard iconography of the saints is already fixed in these images.

Again, we have John Chrysostom's testimony to the eagerness with which the citizens of Antioch acquired commemorative portraits of their beloved bishop Meletios, objects which clearly must have been treated with devotion.[18] Given Eusebius' antipathy to religious art, we can surely take him at his word when he claims to have examined 'portraits of Sts Peter and Paul [. . .] preserved in painting'.[19] He explains these as a seepage of pagan customs into the Church; and indeed, the natural practice of making honorific images of benefactors and patrons (heavenly

13. E. Kitzinger, 'The Cult of Images in the Age before Iconoclasm', *DOP* 7 (1954), 83ff.

14. *PG* 66. 740.

15. *La Vie ancienne de S. Syméon Stylite le Jeune*, ed. P. van den Ven, SubsHag 32.1 (1962), 40-1, 209; and P.J. Alexander, *The Patriarch Nicephorus of Constantinople. Ecclesiastical Policy and Image Worship in the Byzantine Empire* (Oxford 1958), 5.

16. Text in W. Schneemelcher, *Neutestamentliche Apokryphen* (Tübingen 1959) ii.147-8. A late 3rd century date is now generally preferred: cf. J. Breckenridge, 'Apocrypha of Early Christian Portraiture', *BZ* 67 (1974), 101-9.

17. A. Grabar, *Christian Iconography* (Princeton 1970), fig. 166. The medallions are now thought to be late 4th century (M. Sotomayor, *S. Pedro en la iconografía paleocristiana* (Granada 1962), 14ff (also E. Dinkler, 'Die ersten Petrusdarstellungen', *Marburger Jahr-buch für Kunstwissenschaft* xi [1939], 1-80, esp. 9-11).

18. *PG* 50. 516.

19. *Hist. Eccl.* vii. 184.

or otherwise) may well be a point of continuity of early Christian practice with pagan antiquity.

Commemorative portraits, while probably always more common in the East, are not unknown in the West in our period, and here too they are mainly connected with the cult of the saints. Thus, Paulinus of Nola allowed an image of St Martin of Tours to be painted in his baptistery 'for this heavenly soul [. . .] is a worthy object of contemplation for those catechumens laying aside their earthly image in the font'.[20] Augustine records, in passing, images of Sts Peter and Paul and of the stoning of St Stephen in such a way as to suggest at least tolerance[21] – even though in general, his view is that all art is a seductive snare.[22] Perhaps most interesting of the Western patristic references is Hilary's recognition of St Paul in a dream on the strength of his common appearance in images (*cuius me vultum pictura docuerat*).[23] This motif becomes quite common in post-Justinianic hagiography, especially in the recognition of saints in incubatory dreams.[24]

The ascetic and his icon

So far I have mentioned mainly representations of martyrs and apostles. Images of martyrs become increasingly important in the fifth- to seventh-century period; and there are indications of something approaching mass-production of votive mementoes at those *martyria* which were major pilgrimage churches, such as the shrine of St Mamas in Egypt or St Sergios in Syria.[25]

However, of particular importance in the development of the icon as a cult image, able to mediate the presence of the holy man, is devotion to the person of the monastic saint. The ascetic, the spiritual 'star' of the age, was an object of massive popular adulation, and his cult could be extended by commemorative images even in his life-time, and still more so after his death. Already in the fifth century we hear of apotropaic images of St Symeon Stylites nailed above the doors of smiths' workshops in Rome.[26] People often undertook the difficult and tiring trek across the desert merely to look at the ascetic. Late Antique popular piety contained a strong visual element.[27] Thus, in an apothegm of Anthony, when

20. *Ep.* xxxii.2.
21. *PL* 34. 1049.
22. Conf. x. 33.49ff.
23. *PL* 17. 821D.
24. For example *Miracula S. Demetrii* (*PG* 116. 1265ff) and *Mirac. SS. Cosmae et Damiani* 13 (*Kosmas und Damian*, ed. L. Deubner [Leipzig-Berlin 1907], 132ff).
25. See K. Weitzmann, ed., *Age of Spirituality* (New York 1979), 513-55, 564-91; esp. Nos. 497 (icon), 512 (plaque), 514 (pyxis) and 575 (terracotta ampulla), from the shrine of the martyr Menas (all 6th or 7th centuries). No. 522 is an example of a double stone mould (5th century) for the mass-production of lead medallions (like No. 80).
26. Theodoret, *Hist. Relig.* xvi (*PG* 82. 1473A). Cf. a very similar account in the *vita* of the younger Symeon of an Antiochene artisan who set up an ex-voto image of this sixth-century holy man above his workshop (SubsHag 32 [1962], 140ff).
27. Cf. Paula's visualisations of the Nativity and Passion when visiting the Holy Places in the fourth century (Jerome, *Peregrin. S. Paulae*, vi. 20ff).

the slightly bemused holy man asks a silent visitor if he has not something to ask, he receives the reply 'Father, it is enough for me to see your face'.[28]

Such saints' emaciated faces, with their intense, spirit-filled gaze, were reproduced constantly in images by those who sought their subject's intercession and protection.[29] Icons like these provided the growing-point *par excellence* of the potentiated image, a 'two-way door',[30] through which grace might be mediated and prayers conveyed. Standing face to face with the holy man in his image, the early Byzantine believer was provided with a palpable point of encounter with the heavenly world, through which he could directly address his needs to the saint in question and expect equally direct assistance. In this way, the relationship which might be established with the *living* ascetic as 'spiritual physician' could be indefinitely extended in time through his icon. No wonder, then, that (especially in the late sixth and early seventh centuries) we have numerous accounts of individuals always wearing an icon of their favourite saint on their persons.[30]

Art and transfiguration

Finally, one should mention the conviction of Byzantine ascetics that the purpose of their penitential labours was not the mortification of the body, but its transformation. 'If you will, you can become all flame', exclaims Abba Joseph of Panephysis to a disciple, holding up his hands to show fingers which had become 'like ten lamps of fire'.[32] Elsewhere in the *Apophthegmata*, we read of disciples being unable to bear the effulgence of the holy man's face, so refulgent had it become with the light of divinity.[33] Surely here, in the lives of the early monastic saints, we have the basis for an understanding of the icon as the art of transfiguration; an attempt to convey the radiant faces of men who, while still on earth, anticipated the resurrection of the body.[34]

It is the same uncreated light or energy manifest in the Byzantine saint that provides the inner dynamic of a true icon; and this leitmotive, concerning the

28. *Apophth. Patrum* (Alphabetical series), Antonios 27. Cf. account of woman healed by coming to see an icon of St Symeon the Younger: 'for she said, "If only I see his likeness, I shall be saved" ' (SubsHag 32.1 [1962], 98).

29. Some of the most striking surviving examples are from Coptic Egypt, such as the famous Christ and St Menas (Weitzmann, *Age of Spirituality*, No. 497, 6th century); an orant monk (Weitzmann, No. 499, 6th/7th century).

30. *Vita S. Stephani Junioris* (*PG* 100.1113A).

31. For example *Mirac. SS. Cosmae et Damiani* 13 (ed. Deubner, op.cit. [n.24 above], 132. A soldier, Constantine, 'when posted abroad, always took along [...] for his own protection, a representation of the saints in the form of a picture'.

32. *Apophth. Patrum* (alphabetical series), Joseph of Panephysis 7.

33. For example, ibid., Silvanos 12 ('his face and body shining like an angel'), and Arsenios 27 ('he [a disciple] saw the old man entirely like a flame').

34. L. Ouspensky remarks, 'What the icon shows us is precisely the body of a holy man [...] liberated from the corruption of sin, and "participating to a certain degree in the properties of the spiritual body which he is to receive at the resurrection of the righteous". Thus the icon discloses to us the glorified state of the saint, his transfigured and eternal countenance' (*Essai sur la théologie de l'icône dans l'église orthodoxe* [Paris 1960], 209).

185

capacity of matter to become spirit-bearing, is developed into one of St John Damascene's main defences of the icon cult in the early eighth century.[35] At the same time we may see here the religious basis of the abstract, stylised treatment of holy figures in much pre-iconoclast Byzantine art,[36] not least in icons of ascetics. Such images are essentially soul-masks, like the portrait busts of pagan *pneumatikoi* like Plotinus or Isidore.[37]

In stressing the link between the cult of the saints and the development of the icon, I do not wish to minimise the importance of the icon of Christ. There can be no question of disputing the significance of such famous *acheiropoiētai* as the Camuliana image or the Holy Face of Edessa for the religious history of our period.[38] However, it can be no accident that the majority of pre-iconoclast texts dealing with sacred images have to do with depictions of saints. Despite the almost exclusive attention of the iconodule theologians to the icon of Christ and its implications, there can be little doubt, in my view, that historically speaking the connection of the icon-cult with holy men, especially ascetics, is of considerably greater importance than these theological sources might suggest.

35. See *de imag.* ii.8; i.4, 16, 36 (ed. B. Kotter, *Die Schriften des Johannes von Damaskos* [Berlin 1969-], 77-8, 89, 90, 92, 148).

36. For example, the ex-voto mosaics of St Demetrios, Salonica, or the apse mosaic of Sta. Agnese, Rome (all 7th century) (E. Kitzinger, *Byzantine Art in the Making* [Cambridge Mass. 1977], figs. 187-90).

37. See H.P. L'Orange, *Likeness and Icon* (Odense 1973), 32-3 (and figs. 1-6), 91-102 (figs. 8-11). The face of Isidore, according to his biographer, conveyed 'the divine effulgence and illumination which indwelt him' (*Damaskion Bios Isidōrou* 32); and the philosopher-busts of the period, with their abstract features and large staring eyes, offer a remarkable parallel to the description of these sages in pagan hagiographies. Exactly the same traits may be found in icons of Christian holy men, for example in the Bawit icon of St Abraham in Berlin (L'Orange, 101 and fig. 12).

38. See E. Dobschütz, *Christusbilder* (Leipzig 1889), 40ff (Camuliana), and 102ff (Edessa image).

The mass-produced Byzantine Saint

DAVID BUCKTON

Summary

A WELL known class of objects, moulded glass medallions usually with representations in raised relief of saints and indentifying inscriptions in either Greek or Latin, has been the subject of scholarly dispute for some twenty years.[1] Close on two hundred such medallions exist, from about sixty different moulds. In 1959 Hans Wentzel attributed them to thirteenth-century Venice; three years later Marvin Ross dated the Dumbarton Oaks examples to the eleventh, twelfth and thirteenth centuries and argued that Constantinople was the place of their manufacture.

Because of the homogeneity of the group, attempts at localisation based on a division of the medallions into Byzantine and western on the grounds of size, shape, subject, iconography, epigraphy, style or provenance have ultimately failed to convince. A division based on a different criterion has been tried with the largest collection of these objects, in the British Museum, with what appears to be greater success. When the collection was sorted into translucent and opaque medallions, the translucent ones were seen to form a group characterised by Byzantine iconography or Greek inscriptions, or both.

Examined under high magnification, most of the opaque medallions, whether 'Byzantine' or 'western' were seen to comprise the same three colours of glass: an orange-red (Munsell colour reference 10 R 4/8-10), a dark purple (10 RP 2/4) and black. The considerable colour variation apparent to the naked eye was accounted for by the proportions of the colours and the amount of mixing. Only one of the twenty-five opaque medallions in the British Museum did not exhibit at least one of the above colours: a western St Michael which, although clearly in the tradition of the rest of the medallions, must date from the late fourteenth century (fig. 8a).[2] The conservative palette and the consistency of the colours employed

1. Hans Wentzel, 'Das Medaillon mit dem Hl. Theodor und die venezianischen Glaspasten im byzantinischen Stil', *Festschrift für Erich Meyer zum sechzigsten Geburtstag 29, Oktober 1957* (Hamburg 1959), 50-67; M.C. Ross, *Catalogue of the Byzantine and Early Medieval antiquities in the Dumbarton Oaks collection* i (Washington, D.C. 1962), 87-91; Wentzel, 'Zu dem Enkolpion mit dem Hl. Demetrios in Hamburg', *Jahrbuch der Hamburger Kunstsammlungen* 8 (1963), 11-24; Michael Vickers, 'A note on glass medallions in Oxford', *Journal of Glass Studies* 16 (1974), 18-21; David Buckton, in: Hugh Tait (ed.), exh. cat. *The Golden Age of Venetian Glass* (British Museum 1979), 13-15.

2. Buckton (see n.1), 14, A (f).

in the opaque medallions strongly suggest a single glass factory, and to Wentzel's arguments for Venice must be added the evidence for the continuation of the tradition in the west provided by the St Michael medallion and the information that, while extremely rare in Constantinople, orange-red glass is commonplace in Italian mosaics.[3] Since Wentzel's dating is absolutely convincing in the case of the western medallions, the opaque group — including 'Byzantine' examples — can confidently be attributed to thirteenth-century Venice.

The translucent medallions, some of which bear a striking resemblance to Byzantine hardstone cameos of the eleventh and twelfth centuries (figs. 8b, 8c),[4] can now be considered eleventh-, twelfth- and, possibly, thirteenth-century products of a Byzantine factory, the models — literally — for Byzantine medallions of Venetian glass and — less literally — for western medallions of similar type.

Whether actual moulds found their way from Byzantium to Venice or impressions of Byzantine medallions were used as new moulds, the above findings effect a pleasing compromise between the conclusions of Ross, who decided on Constantinople and dated the medallions in the eleventh, twelfth and thirteenth centuries, and Wentzel, who — after considering placing an 'earlier byzantinising' group in Constantinople — attributed the whole *corpus* to thirteenth-century Venice.

---

3. Ernest J.W. Hawkins, 'Further observations on the narthex mosaic in St Sophia at Istanbul', *DOP* 22 (1968), 165. I am greatly indebted to Dr Robin Cormack of the Courtauld Institute of Art for this reference and for his helpful general remarks.

4. See also Wentzel, 1959 (see n.1), 57, figs. 9, 10. I thank Professor Ihor Ševčenko of Harvard and All Souls for his observation that the *delta* of the inscription on the St Demetrios medallions, while perfectly at home in the eleventh and twelfth centuries, would be out of place in the thirteenth.

8a
Moulded glass medallion of
St Michael 21.7 x 16.6 mm
(British Museum,
M & LA S.947).
Drawing: David Goodger.

8b
Carved bloodstone cameo of
St George 40.9 x 28.2 mm
(British Museum,
M & LA 1916, 11-8, 1).
Drawing: Carey Miller.

8c
Moulded glass medallion of
St Demetrios 30.0 x 25.6 mm
(British Museum,
M & LA 70, 11-26, 16).
Drawing: Carey Miller.

189

The Forty in Art

Z.A. GAVRILOVIĆ

Summary

THE paper dealt with the symbolic meaning of the representations of the Forty Martyrs of Sebaste in Byzantine church decoration programmes. It reviewed the arguments put forward by S. Radojčić[1] who had shown that the presence of the busts or figures of the Forty Martyrs painted in the upper region of the building in a number of churches from the eleventh century onward revealed a belief in the prophylactic power of these representations.

The author reinforced Radojčić's arguments[2] and proposed an enquiry into the location of the scenes of the Forty's passion in church decoration schemes.

In a survey of relevant monuments (mentioning among others St Sophia, Ohrid (11th century)[3], the baptistry of St Sophia, Kiev (12th century)[4], and Sopoćani (13th century)[5] the pattern of the location of scenes from the cycle of the Forty Martyrs

1. Svetozar Radojčić, 'Temnićki natpis. Sujeverice srednjovekovnih graditelja o čudotvornoj moći imena i likova sevastijskih mučenika', *Zbornik za likovne umetnosti* 5 (Novi Sad 1969), 1-11.
2. The argument was reinforced by quoting the tradition of the rebuilding of the dome of the Anastasis church in Jerusalem during the time of patriarch Thomas in the 9th century. The patriarch, having seen in a dream the Forty holding the cupola, ordered that forty beams should be inserted at the base of the new roof (H. Vincent and F.M. Abel, *Jérusalem, Recherches de topographie, d'archéologie et d'histoire* ii [Paris 1914], 224, 244).
3. Gordana Babić, *Les chapelles annexes des églises byzantines. Fonction liturgique et programmes iconographiques* (Paris 1969), 117-21, figs. 23, 84, 87.
4. N.L. Okunev, 'Kreshchal'nia Sofiiskogo sobora v Kieve', *Zapiski otdeleniia russkoi i slavianskoi arkheologii Imp. Russkogo Arkheologicheskogo Obshchestva* x (Petrograd 1915), 113-37, fig. 38 and pl. xxii, xxiii.
5. Vojislav J. Djurić, *Sopoćani* (Belgrade 1963), 128-9.

and of Christ's baptism pointed to an ideological parallelism between the passion of the Forty and baptism.

In the author's opinion this parallelism is confirmed by the allusions to baptism in two kontakia for the feast of the Forty Martyrs (9 March) by Romanos the Melode,[6] reflecting and developing the symbolism already present in the homilies to the saints by St Basil and St Gregory of Nyssa.[8] The circumstances of the Forty's death — the water of the freezing lake, the martyrs' nakedness, the light and the crowns descending from the sky, and the symbolism of the number 40 — are used to explain the Forty's passion as a baptism through water and fire. Moreover, the blameless phalanx, finally rewarded, crowned and clothed in white is compared to the spiritual bride of Christ.[9]

In view of such a meaning attached to the passion of the Forty Martyrs, expressed through liturgy, the occurrences of the representations of that event in mid- and late-Byzantine narthex decoration schemes should be understood as components of a general ideological structure in which the illumination of man's soul by Christ's Wisdom through baptism, and the divine inspiration of the emperor (or king), are the dominant theme.[10]

The narthex at Lesnovo (1349)[11] is quoted as an example of such a programme. The throne of glory from the Vision of Ezekiel (north side) placed immediately above the mystical investiture of Dušan (figs. 9a and b), suggests the divine authority of the throne from which the emperor reigns.[12]

On the other hand, according to Byzantine authors the throne from the prophet's vision is the image of the soul which becomes the dwelling place of the Logos, once it has been illuminated by the grace of the Spirit.[13]

6. P. Maas and C.A. Trypanis, *Sancti Romani Melodi Cantica: Cantica genuina* (Oxford (1963), 487-505.
7. *PG* 31. 508-25.
8. *PG* 46. 749-56; 757-72; 773-88.
9. This last image from Romanos (Maas and Trypanis, *Cantica*, 498), is interpreted differently, and in the present author's opinion incorrectly, by Marjorie Carpenter, *Kontakia of Romanos* (Columbia 1973), 283.
10. Cf. Z.A. Gavrilović, 'Divine Wisdom as part of the Byzantine Imperial Ideology. Research into the artistic interpretations of the theme in Medieval Serbia', *Abstracts of papers read at the Fifth Annual Byzantine Studies Conference* (Dumbarton Oaks 1979), 38-9. The full text of the paper is forthcoming in *Zograf* xi (Belgrade).
11. N.L. Okunev, 'Lesnovo', *L'Art Byzantin chez les Slaves: Recueil Th.Uspenskij* i.2 (Paris 1930), 222-63.
12. Cf. E. Ville-Patlagean, 'Une image de Salomon en basileus byzantin', *Revue des études juives*, iv. s.i (cxxi), fasc. 1-2 (1962), 16-17 and 26-7.
13. Werner Jaeger, *Two rediscovered works of Ancient Christian Literature: Gregory of Nyssa and Macarius* (Leiden 1954), 220.

OPPOSITE

The Forty Martyrs of Sebaste. Fresco in the narthex at Lesnovo (west wall), 1349. Photo: G. Millet and T. Velmans (1969).

The theme of the Forty Martyrs represented on the west wall of the Lesnovo narthex (fig. 10) in the immediate proximity of the Vision of Ezekiel and the investiture of Dušan, and on the opposite side of the cycle of St John the Baptist (east wall),[14] is illustrated with the intention of reinforcing the ideology Wisdom-kingship-baptism. The symbolic meaning of this ensemble throws more light on the conception of narthex programmes in general. One perceives that the area preceding the main body of the church is intended as a visual interpretation of the *Basilikē hodos*,[15] the Royal Road onto which the Christian is stepping in the hope of rejoining his Creator. This is in accordance with the liturgical function of the narthex for the period concerned.

14. N.L. Okunev, 'Lesnovo', op.cit., (n.11 above), 262.
15. Expression from the Book of Numbers (20:17) applied to the mystical path of the human soul towards unity with Christ in the Life of Moses by St Gregory of Nyssa (ed. Jean Daniélou, SC1 ter [1968], 20, 300-5). For a detailed analysis of the origin and the use of the term, see F. Tailliez, 'BASILIKE HODOS: Les valeurs d'un terme mystique et le prix de son histoire littérale', *OCP* 13 (1947), 299-354. References to the mystical road of the soul abound in the medieval biographies of the Serbian kings and archbishops; see for instance Domentian, *Život Svetoga Simeona* tr. L. Mirković [Srpska Književna Zadruga xli. 282] (Belgrade 1938), 262-3; 281-3.

OPPOSITE

Martyrdom of St Pamphilos and his companions. Miniature from the Menologion gr.9 f 229ʳ, State Historical Museum, Moscow, 11th century. Photo: V. Likhacheva.

The Iconography of the Byzantine Saint in the Illuminations of the Eleventh and Twelfth Centuries

VERA LIKHACHEVA

Summary

THE eleventh and twelfth centuries in Byzantium were a period of firmly established iconography, created during the preceding centuries. Towards the eleventh century the mode which determined the depiction of a saint was elaborated. Because of its connection with the text, the image of a saint was often more completely and more profoundly expressed in manuscript illuminations than in frescoes, mosaics or in icon painting. The most perfect images of saints are to be found in manuscripts of the Menologia which were executed during this period in the scriptoria of Constantinople. The main principles of depicting a saint and the different technical means by which the image was achieved – examples were given from two Menologia of the State Historical Museum in Moscow (gr. 9 and 183) – are typical not only of the eleventh-twelfth centuries. Though these principles were partially abandoned later, the main difference in the depiction of saints in this period on the one hand and the Palaiologan on the other should be attributed to changes in style.

The Panēgyris *of the Byzantine Saint: a study in the nature of a medieval institution, its origins and fate*

SPEROS VRYONIS Jr

I N this paper there is no attempt to draw up a detailed and complete picture of the *panegyris* itself, an attempt which would have been based on an exhaustive search of all the published texts and which would have followed the events of a theoretical *panēgyris* from the first νυκτεγερσία to the ἀπόλυσις and its termination. Rather I have attempted to draw in broad lines the principal character of the religio-commercial *panēgyris* in Byzantium simply by letting the texts speak for themselves and with a minimum of analysis. By giving the texts a certain sequential ordering I have attempted to show how the Byzantine saints became the heirs to the pagan past and how, having subjected this pagan past to a Christianisation and having given it a Christian meaning, they passed it on to the post-Byzantine life of a portion of the Balkans and Asia Minor.

Though the element of analysis will lag behind that of the presentation of the texts themselves, that analysis is nevertheless there, and in any case a discussion of the *panēgyris* should attempt to convey something of the panēgyric or festive spirit. After all, this festiveness is one of the derivative meanings of *panēgyris* and it is this aspect against which the church fathers often fulminated. Perhaps it will serve as a partial palliative to the scholarly austerity which accompanied so many of the papers on the saints during the past three days and which seemed to threaten us all with sanctification in the snows of Birmingham.

Of the texts which I shall present, all are published and many have been mentioned in connection, specifically, with the *panēgyris*. Some of the texts have not, however, been brought to bear on the subject and in any case I have not seen an arrangement of the texts in such a way as to treat the evolution of the *panēgyris* from the beginning to the end.

The subject is as vast as Byzantine society itself, inasmuch as in its most comprehensive form it deals with religion, economics and society. In the realm of religion scholars are prone to think of the formal, theological, and administrative manifestations of Byzantine religiosity with its rigidly structural dogma, its tightly programmed artistic iconography, and its beautifully decorated churches. The

frequent neglect of the informal manifestations of Byzantine religiosity deprives the historian of proper perspective in evaluating Byzantine religiosity and culture as a whole. The role of hagiolatry in Byzantium can be exaggerated only with the greatest of difficulty for it constituted an institution that cut across social, political, economic, ethnic, and educational strata.

It did so by virtue of the fact that it was basically a local phenomenon, something close and immediate to the lives of those who inhabited a given locality. It existed everywhere and was regulated to the dynamics of a given local society, economic, climatic, geographic, and other local dynamics. A Symeon Metaphrastes might give the cults a 'classicising' literary form and so make them more palatable to an educated clientele, but this does not obscure the fact that the vitality of the saint's cult came from local events and circumstances.

This situation must, of course, be modified to take into account outside factors such as the benevolence of emperors and powerful nobles who often gave benefactions to a saint's cult or helped promote it elsewhere. The economic significance of the saint and his *panēgyris* has, certainly, caught the attention of Byzantinists, though the insufficient evidence (at least as it has been identified to date) does not allow us to ascertain in detail its role in the overall economy of Byzantine society. There can be no doubt that at the social level the saint's cult/*panēgyris* played a very important role in integrating Byzantine society and in giving it common points of reference with Bulgars, Serbs, Russians and others.

Given the undisputed importance of our subject for the religious, economic and social history of Byzantium one would have expected a systematic treatment of it in the scholarly literature, and yet it has not been so treated. P. Koukoules dedicated thirteen pages to the subject in his massive work and the subject has been treated episodically in other works on economic history.[1] Meritorious though these works are there has been no comprehensive treatment. Though many of the salient characteristics are known, we know very little about the specific details of the Byzantine *panēgyris*. There has been no thorough gathering of the data scattered throughout countless texts as to individual *panēgyreis* and though one may assume that most, indeed probably all, saints had their *panēgyreis*, yet we do not know which ones had complex and which had simple *panēgyreis*. The meanings of the word *panēgyris* and of its various forms have not been clearly estabished, and the same holds true of other terms connected with these celebrations.

The term panēgyris

Πανήγυρις is used with several meanings. For instance, in Sozomenus it is employed as the equivalent of Easter,[2] to denote the celebration of imperial decennalia,[3] to indicate a public feast of the martyr Peter in Alexandria,[4] to refer

1. P. Koukoules, *Byzantinōn bios kai politismos* (Athens 1949), iii. 270-82.
2. Sozomenus, *Kirchengeschichte*, ed. J. Bidez (Berlin 1960) (hereafter Sozomenus), 36. 5.
3. Sozomenus 46. 8.
4. Sozomenus 73. 6.

to a gathering of bishops,[5] for a pagan celebration,[6] and finally Sozomenus refers to πανηγύρεις μαρτύρων.[7] On occasion *panēgyris* seems to be the equivalent of a market, as when the emperor promises to supply crusading armies with foodstuffs by holding *panēgyreis*.[8] Some of the Peloponnesian *panēgyreis* mentioned in a chrysobull of the early fourteenth century and of the Antiochene villages mentioned by Libanius may have been of this type.[9] *Panēgyris* could also refer to an encomiastic speech as when the fourteenth-century epistolographer Michael Gabras writes to Andronikos Asanes that the emperor before his death was worthy of πανηγύρεις ... αἱ διὰ λόγων ᾄδουσαι.[10] Nicetas Magistrus charges the patricius and mysticus John with being tongue-tied so that he cannot do deeds and speak freely in public (πανηγύρεις) and gain trophies.[11] Manuel Philes uses the phrases πανυγυρικῶς εὐτρεπίζειν τὸν λόγον, again an association of the word with rhetoric.[12] Evagrios employs *panēgyris* to refer to a marriage celebration.[13] Finally, the term also refers to the joint religio-commercial affairs connected with many of the more famous saints and their shrines: Archangel Michael at Chonae, Eugenios at

5. Sozomenus 87. 23. In addition, the same text utilizes πανήγυρις to denote a large annual celebration commemorating the building of a great church in Jerusalem during the reign of Constantine the Great:

ἐξ ἐκείνου δὲ ἐτήσιον ταύτην τὴν ἑορτήν λαμπρῶς μάλα
ἡ ʽΙεροσολύμων ἐκκλησία, ὡς καὶ μυήσεις ἐν αὐτῇ
τελεῖσθαι, καὶ ὀκτὼ ἡμέρας ἐφεξῆς ἐκκλησιάζειν,
συνιέναι τε πολλοὺς σχεδὸν ἐκ πάσης τῆς ὑφ᾽ ἥλιον, οἱ
καθ᾽ ἱστορίαν τῶν ἱερῶν τόπων πάντοθεν συντρέχουσι
κατὰ τὸν καιρὸν ταύτης τῆς πανηγύρεως.

6. Sozomenus 151, 14: τῇ γὰρ ἐς αὔριον γράμματα τοῦ κρατοῦντος
ἀπεδόθη τοῖς ἄρχουσι παρακελευόμενα μὴ συγχωρεῖν τοὺς
῝Ελληνας τοῖς ναοῖς προσβάλειν μηδὲ τὰς συνήθεις
θρησκείας καὶ πανηγύρεις.
See also *Libanii Opera*, ed. R. Foerster (Leipzig 1903) (Hereafter Libanius) 517-18.

7. Sozomenus, 96. 17.

8. Anna Comnène, *Alexiade*, ed. B. Leib (Paris 1937-45), VII. vi. 6: X. v. 9; X. ix. 9; XIII. vii. 2.

9. F. Miklosich et J. Müller, *Acta et diplomata graeca medii aevi sacra et profana* (Vienna 1860-90), v.167.

10. G. Fatouros, *Die Briefe des Michel Gabras, ca.1290-nach 1350* (Vienna 1973), ii. 384.

11. L.G. Westerink, *Nicétas Magistrus. Lettres d'un exilé. 928-946* (Paris 1973). 67:
γλωττωπέδῃ καθάπερ ἔχεις εἰργμένην οὐδὲ πρὸς ἔργα
παρρησιάζῃ καὶ πανηγύρεις καὶ τρόπαια.

12. E. Miller, *Manuelis Philae Carmina* (Amsterdam 1967), i. 17.

13. J. Bidez and L. Parmentier, *The Ecclesiastical History of Evagrius with the Scholia* (Amsterdam 1964), 227:
καὶ τῆς πόλεως ἑορταζούσης καὶ δημοτελῆ πανήγυριν
ἀγούσης περί τε τὴν πομπὴν καὶ τὴν παστάδα.

Trebizond, Phokas at Sinope, Theodore at Euchaita, John the Theologian at Ephesus, Nicholas at Myra, Spyridon at Triminthous of Cyprus, and Demetrios at Thessalonica.[14] It is clear that the word has a variety of specific meanings, all extensions of its basic meaning which is 'gathering'. Thus πανηγυρίζω, πανηγυρικός, πανηγυριστής can have various specific meanings. We see that πανήγυρις can refer to a strictly religious festival, to a commercial fair, to a religious festival combined with a local fair, to a festive occasion such as a marriage or political celebration, to a gathering of bishops, or even to an encomiastic speech. Obviously it is not the purpose of this communication to exhaust all these and other possible categories, for this would be the subject of a book (to which I hope, eventually, to return). The paper will concentrate primarily on the *panēgyris* as a religio-economic institution, will glance at a few representative examples for which we have textual evidence in an effort to delineate its character, and will refer to purely religious *panēgyreis* only occasionally. Having described the nature of this type of *panēgyris*, an effort will be made to say something about its origin and something about its post-Byzantine existence.

The panēgyris *of St Thekla*

Let us begin with the incidental description of the *panēgyris* of St Thekla at Seleuceia and nearby Dalisandos, composed by an orator in the mid-fifth century. An eyewitness and participant, he places the cult and the *panēgyris* realistically in a milieu where Christianity is freshly and stridently victorious over paganism. Thekla has displaced Sarpedon, Athena, Aphrodite, Zeus, and in expelling them from Seleuceia and the vicinity has turned over the Temple of Zeus to St Paul. Linked with the latter in the Apocryphal Acts, Thekla is closely connected to Paul in the religious life of fifth-century Cilicia. Paul acts as the host of Seleuceians when they journey to Tarsus, and Thekla of Tarsiotes when they come to Seleuceia. The inhabitants of the two cities rival one another in the celebration of the *panēgyris* of Thekla and Paul respectively.[15] The *panēgyris* of Thekla was celebrated on 24 September, seems to have lasted for about one week (that of St Paul at Tarsus was on 29 June), and was well attended.[16] The author relates: 'As the virginal festival approached everyone, and most of all Cilicians, ran and are still running to us, and will so long as there are people, in honour of the martyr and each on behalf of his soul, so that the earth was crowded and the sea was thronged as all came here by demes, by households, by races [...]'.[17] There is mention of a Cypriot boat bringing participants from Cyprus and bringing, very probably,

14. S. Vryonis, *The Decline of Medieval Hellenism in Asia Minor and the Process of Islamization from the Eleventh through the Fifteenth Century* (Berkeley-London 1971) (hereafter Vryonis, *Decline*), 39-41.
15. G. Dagron, *Vie et miracles de Sainte Thecle* (Brussels 1978) (hereafter Dagron), 294-6, 366-8. The saint takes vengeance on the bishop of Tarsus when the latter forbids his flock to attend her *panēgyris*.
16. Dagron, 15, 78, 330-2.
17. Dagron, 368.

commercial wares as well. But there is no mention of any commercial market at the *panēgyris* by our author-orator. It may be that there was none, though it is highly unlikely that a *panēgyris* of one week, and one to which boats came from Cyprus, would have been without its commercial counterpart.[18]

On the eve of the celebration many participants went to the heights of the nearby town, Dalisandos, to witness the miracle of Thekla's sky ride in her chariot, the night of the wake (νυκτεγεροίαν).[19] In this area, which was especially beloved by Thekla, was located her νυμφευτήριον . It was an area thickly wooded, well watered by cold springs, and was ideal for feasting, dancing, jumping, and for cures. There she gave the customary gifts to those in attendance and returned to Seleuceia. Aside from the νυκτεγεροία our author does not give a great many details about the *panēgyris*, but the few that he does give are none the less of some interest. People come to the *panēgyris*, among other things, for cures. The saint has a pool or bath (λουτρῷ) which is efficacious in the curing of eye ailments,[20] she is visited in particular by ailing orators and learned men, to whom she shows special compassion.[21] Among those cured was the author of our text himself who was cured by the martyr of an abcessed ear. The cure, he tells us, came on the eve of a rhetorical contest during the *panēgyris*, the so-called δεικτήριον, in which he was to participate.[22] Finally, there is a description of the last day and the dissolution of the *panēgyris*, when the participants came together for the final religious service.

> On this day all rushed, citizen and foreigner, man, woman, and child, governor and governed, general and soldier, leader of the mob and individual, both young and old, sailor and farmer and everyone simply who was anxious, all rushed to come together, to pray to God, to beseech the Virgin, and having partaken of the holy mysteries to go away blessed and as someone renewed in body and soul.[23] Then they banqueted and set to discussing the wonders of the *panēgyris*. One participant praised its brilliance, another the size of the crowd, yet another the culture of the teachers, and still another the harmony of the psalmody, another the duration of the vigil, and so they continued commenting on the liturgy and prayer, the shoving of the crowd, the shouting, and the quarreling. One man commented on the fact that he was most inspired by a beautiful young woman that he saw during the celebration and was consumed by the thought of having his pleasure with her so that he could only offer prayers to this end. It seems also that at the *apolysis* gifts were given by the servants of the sanctuary to the pious.[24]

Such in brief are the details that the text gives us on the *panēgyris*. It is first of all a religious gathering and one attended by large numbers of people. It may

18. Dagron, 330-2.
19. Dagron, 356.
20. Dagron, 354.
21. Dagron, 399.
22. Dagron, 398, 79.
23. Dagron, 376.
24. Dagron, 378.

have had a commercial aspect but this is nowhere specifically stated. There is the reference to a Cypriot boat, to the quarreling and shoving, and to the fact that the *panēgyris* lasted a while. There is a rhetorical contest, the role of teachers is mentioned, a night long vigil, and also a reference to banqueting, dancing, and merriment. Finally, there are the cures.

John Mauropous, the eleventh-century metropolitan of Euchaïta, refers to the brilliance of the *panēgyris* of St Theodore which brought a great host of people 'from every nation'[25] and which transformed Euchaïta from an untrodden wasteland to a populous city,[26] inhabited and ornamented with markets and stoas. Officials, local inhabitants, and visitors gather there on the occasion of the *panēgyris* to pray, sing, burn incense,[27] offer gifts to the saint, and, finally, to trade.[28] The *panēgyris* of St John the Theologian at Ephesus, as is well known, was not only religious but commerical, and Constantine VI remitted the commercium of its *panēgyris* (100 pounds of gold) to the church of St John in 795.[29]

The panēgyris *of St Demetrios*

In many ways the most specific and detailed description of the religio-commercial *panēgyris* as it existed in Byzantine society is that which the Cappadocian author[30] of the Timarion gives of the *panēgyris* of St Demetrios in Thessalonica during the twelfth century. He relates that he went to the city just before the feast and at the onset of the *panēgyris* he went to the church to render the necessary honour to the saint and then went to the commercial *panēgyris* which had been set up outside the city gates. So it began six days before the feast of St Demetrios and ended on the Monday after the Sunday of the feast.[31] He begins his characterisation and description of the celebration with the following:

> The Demetria are a feast, just as the Panathenaia [were] in Athens and the Panionia among the Milesians. There flow to it not only the indigenous and local throng, but from all sides all possible of the Hellenes everywhere, of the nearby dwelling Mysians and of all nations up to the Danube and Scythia, of Campanians, Italians, Iberians, Lusitanians, and Celts from beyond the Alps. And the ocean sands send, in short, suppliants and spectators to the martyr. So great is his glory in Europe.[32]

25. P. deLagarde and J. Bollig, *Johannis Euchaitarum metropolitae quae supersunt in cod. vaticano graeco 676* (Berlin 1882), 131.
26. ibid., 132.
27. On the use of incense in religious cults during the ancient, Byzantine and Ottoman times in Asia Minor, Vryonis, *Decline*, 40 n.204.
28. ibid., 40.
29. *Theophani Chronographia*, ed. C. de Boor (Leipzig 1883-5), i. 469-70.
30. R. Romano, *Pseudo-Luciano. Timarione. Testo critico, introduzione, traduzione commentario e lessico* (Naples 1974) (hereafter *Timarion*), 25-31, tends to attribute the work to Nicholas Callicles.
31. *Timarion*, 126ff.
32. *Timarion*, 53.

Being a Cappadocian and unfamiliar with the fair, the author went up on the heights and saw an impressive spectacle:

> The arrangement [of the *panēgyris*] was thus. [There were] commercial tents facing one another and set up in parallel rows. As the rows extended over a long distance, they widened an opening and square in the middle with some parallel passages, thus opening up passage to the surge of the crowd. You might say, looking at this density and at the balance of the array, that there were lines from an opposite point flowing afar. Other tents were set up at some point athwart the rows. However they were not long, but grew like very small feet alongside creeping mechanisms.[33]

Having surveyed the symmetrical arrangement of the tents-shops, the author then descended from the heights and came down to the fair itself where he saw: 'Every type, which [is in the form of] textiles and yarns for men and women, and all those that commercial ships bring to the Hellenes from Boeotia, the Peloponnese, and Italy. Also Phoenicia contributes and Egypt, Spain, and the Pillars of Hercules weave the most beautiful of fixtures. Merchants bring these directly from the various lands to former Macedonia and to Thessalonica. The Euxine sends its goods to Byzantium and thence it ornaments the *panēgyris*, many horses and mules bearing the loads from there [. . .]'.[34]

While he was still up in the heights he saw and heard the animals brought for sale.

> And while I was still up on the heights the types and number of the animals amazed me as their loud and confused cry fell extraordinarily upon my ears. [There were] horses whinnying, oxen bellowing, sheep bleating, hogs grunting, and dogs barking [. . .]. These follow their masters when they battle with wolves and thieves. The [*panēgyris*] occurs during three all-night vigils, many priests and many monks being divided into two choirs, they carry out the hymnology to the martyr. The archbishop presides over like some *archideoros* [leader of the feast – a pagan term] arranging the feast properly, ordaining the acts [of the celebrants]. These are all nocturnal and celebrated under light and torch.
>
> 'When the early-born rosy-fingered Dawn appeared', as Homer would say, the governor of the land arrives at the church, advancing with a great bodyguard and brilliance, many horsemen and not a few cavalry elaborated the march and processions.
>
> As the populace was buoyed up in suspense before the entrance awaiting his presence [. . .] they came out with some of the spectacle-lovers of the populace [. . .].
>
> How shall I recount how much of the undistinguished mob, both from the countryside and the city, followed? Its chosen [leaders], a group of clients some might say, made of the procession something wonderful, all in their prime, all in full health, all men and companions of warlike Ares, initiates, beautiful with silken and studded garments, with thick golden hair. Seeing the hair you would have said it more elaborately according to the poet, and their nature [came] from the head. 'He bore crisp curly locks like the hyacinth flower'. They had prancing Arab horses, covered, their feet high in the air, prancing, and let loose, like the air they turned away from the ground. They seemed to be joined to the brilliance round and about, as much as shone on the reins from the gold and silver as they were pleased by the ostentation, [for] they had thickly curled the manes with ornaments. These thus advanced, making their progress with orderly move-

33. *Timarion*, 54.
34. *Timarion*, 54-5.

ment and military pace. After them there was a gap and then the Dux advanced with a calm movement. Eros and muses and graces ran before and about him.

And as this noble one arrived before the sacred sanctuary [and] performed the customary invocation of the martyr, acclamations arose from the crowd, customarily devoted to the leader [. . .] and he ordered the archbishop to appear before him, this too perhaps being prescribed or else customary. Then was maintained, exactly, the office of the festival [. . .] and a very divine psalmody was heard, in rhythm, order, and in artful alterations varying very gracefully. The chanting arose not only from men but also from holy women, in the wing to the left of the altar, after having been divided into two antiphonic choirs, and they offered up the holy to the martyr. And when the spectacle and the offering were concluded as was the custom, we invoked [the saint] as was the custom, and having asked the martyr for a glorious return, we came out from the church together with the populace and the Dux.[35]

Our Cappadocian observer has given a clear and, though incomplete, a detailed description of one of the most important religio-commercial celebrations in Byzantium, the *panēgyris* of St Demetrios in Thessalonica. Present are the religious elements: archbishop, clergy, nuns, liturgy with psalmody and antiphons. There is the participation of the masses not only from the city itself but from all Macedonia. The state is represented by the Dux in his brilliant attire and with his striking retinue of cavalry and infantry, and upon his entry into the church of St Demetrios, it is he who gives the signal to the archbishop for the ceremony to commence. The commercial fair under the saint's sponsorship, which took place in the enormous area outside the walls, brought together merchants, from the Mediterranean world all the way from Gibraltar and Spain, from the Balkans and from other parts of Europe. Our author noted in particular the textile and livestock markets, but undoubtedly the fair abounded in a rich variety of agricultural, craft, and animal products as well.

The distribution of the panēgyris

These short notices and descriptions of the *panēgyreis* of St Thekla at Seleuceia (fifth century), St Theodore at Euchaïta (eleventh century), St John the Theologian at Ephesus (eighth century), and of St Demetrios at Thessalonica (twelfth century) are characteristic of the type of source material available to us for the analysis and study of the Byzantine *panēgyris*. They tell us a number of specific things and activities associated with the Byzantine *panēgyris*, but inasmuch as they are incomplete we can use these sources as negative evidence only with great risk. The fact that these sources do not mention a particular practice is not sufficient evidence for

---

35. *Timarion*, 55-9.

us to conclude that it did not exist in the Byzantine *panēgyris*. The one thing that we can conclude from the accounts of these four *panēgyreis* is the extent to which the *panēgyris* was widespread in Byzantine society. A further and random perusal of Byzantine sources indicates clearly that not only the purely religious *panēgyris*, but also the religio-commercial *panēgyris* was widespread over the entire empire throughout its history. In the earlier period Jerusalem, Antioch and its villages, Gaza, Constantia, and Alexandria featured numerous such festivals,[36] as did also Cyprus during the feast of St Spyridon.[37] Later we see important religio-commercial *panēgyreis* at the feasts of St Eugenios in Trebizond, of St Phokas in Sinope and Charax of Pontus, of St George in Paphlagonia, of Archangel Michael in Chonae and in Nicomedeia.[38] Alongside the *panēgyris* of St Demetrios in Thessalonica we see such celebrations at Stenimachus near Bačkovo,[39] in the area about Mount Athos;[40] and the sources speak of an extensive network of *panēgyreis* in the Peloponnese during the thirteenth and fourteenth centuries.[41] There is also evidence for its existence in southern Italy during the twelfth century, there being mention of a *panēgyris* of St Heliou in the district of Messina.[42] Thus it is clear that not only the purely religious, but also the religio-commercial *panēgyris* constituted an important characteristic of Byzantine society throughout the history of Byzantium and in all of its geographical regions.

Classical roots

The next major topic to which I wish to turn, briefly, is the question of the origin of the *panēgyris*. The author of the Timarion saw the *panēgyris* of St Demetrios as parallel to the celebrations of pagan antiquity: Ἑορτὴ δή ἐστι τὰ Δημήτρια, ὥσπερ ἐν Ἀθήνῃσι Παναθήναια, καὶ Μιλησίοις τὰ Πανιώνια — 'The Demetria are a feast, just as the Panathenaia [were] in Athens and the Panionia among the Milesians'.[43] He uses terms which were also employed by pagan authors in describing the ancient celebrations. First and foremost he employs the term πανήγυρις, then παννύχιος, διανυκτερεύειν, the presiding archbishop is ἀρχιθέωρος.[44] It is obvious from the text that the author is very conversant with classical literature

36. Libanius, i. 517-18. Sozomenus, 87, 196. Evagrius, 110.
37. P.A. Yannopoulos, *La société profane dans l'empire byzantin des VIIe, VIIIe, et IXe siècles* (Louvain 1975), 163.
38. Vryonis, *Decline*, 14-20.
39. S. Kauchtschischvili, *Typicon Gregorii Pacuriani* (Tbilisi 1963), 74-8.
40. A. Soloviev and V. Mošin, *Grčke povelje srpskih vladara* (Belgrade 1936) (hereafter Soloviev-Mošin), 108.
41. Miklosich et Müller, v. 167. D. Zakythinos, *Le despotat grec de Morée* (Athens 1953), ii. 253-4. J. Longnon and P. Topping, *Documents sur le régime des terres dans la principauté de Morée au XIVe siècle* (Paris 1969), 64.
42. A. Guillou, *Les actes grecs de S. Maria de Messina* (Palermo 1963), document No. 9.
43. *Timarion*, 53.
44. ibid., 55, 59.

and so his utilisation of these terms may in part be explained by a classical influence on his style, but this can only be a partial explanation. Again in the miracles of St Thekla we encounter other such terms, ἱερὰ νυκτεγερσία, νυμφευτήριον ,[45] and again our author is an orator who is likely to seek such terms from classical antiquity. Is the similarity between the Byzantine and classical *panēgyris* then the product of a philological archaeism and devoid of any historical substance?

The author of the Timarion is not alone in presuming a classical origin or parallel to the Byzantine *panēgyris*. B. Schmidt in his perceptive study of modern Greek popular culture and that of Greek antiquity also proposed a classical origin for the Greek *panēgyris* as it was observed in the nineteenth century.[46] M. Nilsson in his fundamental history of Greek religion assumes an ancient Greek origin for the *panēgyris* and refers the reader to Schmidt's description. 'Wer eine Panēgyris im heutigen Griechenland gesehen hat, wird lebhaft an die des alten erinnert'.[47] The word *panēgyris* itself seems to have gone through an evolution from meaning simply a large gathering of people to indicating a religious feast at which large numbers gathered, to indicating finally a large religious festival with important commercial and other social activities such as athletic contests.[48] Thus one ancient inscription speaks of θυσίαν καὶ πανήγοριν καὶ ἐκεχειρίαν καὶ ἀγῶνα στεφανίτην .[49] One of the earliest such descriptions is in the Homeric Hymn to Apollo:

> In Delos do you, o Phoebus, most delight your heart; for there the long-robed Ionians gather in your honour with their children and shy wives: mindful they delight you with boxing and dancing and song, so often as they hold their contest. A man would say that they were deathless and unaging if he should then come upon the Ionians so met together. For he would see the graces of them all, and would be pleased in heart gazing at the men and well-girded women, with their swift ships and great wealth.[50]

Many centuries later Strabo, in writing of the *panēgyris* of Delos, says: ἥ τε πανήγυρις ἐμπορικόν τι πρᾶγμα ἐστι .[51]

---

45. Dagron, 79, 356, 368. Grégoire de Nysse, *Vic de sainte Macrine*, ed. P. Maraval (SC 178 [1971]), 248-9:
   τῆς οὖν παννυχίδος περὶ αὐτὴν ἐν ὑμνῳδίαις καθάπερ ἐπὶ μαρτύρων πανηγύρεως τελεσθείσης.

46. B. Schmidt, *Das Volksleben der Neugriechischen und das hellenische Alterthum* (Leipzig 1871), 83-8.

47. M. Nilsson, *Geschichte der griechischen Religion* (Munich 1967), i. 827, 826-81. Also his *Popular Greek Religion* (New York 1947), 13-18, and his *Griechische Feste von relgiöser Bedeutung mit Ausschluss der Attischen* (Stuttgart 1957).

48. For what follows see 'Panēgyris' in *RE*.

49. ibid.

50. This section is from lines 146-55 of the Homeric Hymn to Apollo. The translation is basically that of the Loeb edition, but altered by myself.

51. Strabo, X. 5. 4.

This combination of religious, commercial, and other secular activities was particularly noticeable in the four greatest *panēgyreis* of the pagan Greek world, celebrations which remain par excellence the *panēgyreis* of this ancient world. Both Demosthenes and Pindar refer to the Olympian, Isthmian, Nemean, and Pythian festivals as *panēgyreis*.[52] Dio Chrysostom gives details as to the variety of the participants at the Isthmia and at the temple of Poseidon. There he saw sophists with their students, orators, authors, poets, miracle men, seers, and peddlars.[53] But the term *panēgyris* was also applied to the celebrations of political federations such as the Delia, Panionia, and Pamboeoteia. Though the ancient *panēgyris* had, variously, religious, commercial, athletic, and political characteristics, the basic common denominators seem to have been the assembly of large numbers of people, commercial activity, and the popular flavour to its various manifestations.[54] Individual features common to most *panēgyreis* were the following: oratorical performances to celebrate the occasion, commercial markets, tents to house the merchants and other participants, the great procession to the temple, the sacrificial meal following the procession and the giving of provisions from the income of the deity to the participants.[55] The ancient *panēgyris* provided society not only with religious and economic expression but also with the opportunity for rest and recreation. As Demokritos wrote: βίος ἀνεόρταστος μακρή ὁδὸς ἀπανδόκευτος.[56]

52. Pindar, *Isthmia*, IV. 47-8:
οὐδὲ πανηγυρίων ξυνᾶν ἀπεῖχον
καμπύλον δίφρον.

Demosthenes, *De Corona*, 91::
ἀποστεῖλαι δὲ καὶ θεαρίας εἰς τὰς ἐν τῷ Ἑλλάδι
πανηγύριας, "Ισθμια καὶ Νέμεα καὶ 'Ολύμπια καὶ Πύθια.

53. Dio Chrysostom, viii. 9.
καὶ δὴ καὶ τότε ἦν περὶ τὸν νεὼν τοῦ Ποσειδῶνος
ἀκούειν πολλῶν μὲν σοφιστῶν κακοδαιμόνων βοώντων καὶ
λοιδορουμένων ἀλλήλοις, καὶ τῶν λεγομένων μαθητῶν
ἄλλου ἀλλῷ μαχομένων, πολλῶν δὲ συγραφέων
ἀναγιγνοσκόντων ἀναίσθητα συγγράματα, πολλῶν δε
ποιητῶν ποιήματα ἀδόντων, καὶ τούτους ἐπαινούντων
ἑτέρων, πολλῶν δὲ θαυματοποιῶν θαύματα ἐπιδεικνύντων,
πολλῶν δὲ τερατοσκόπων τέρατα κρινόντων, μυρίων δὲ
ῥητόρων δίκας στρεφόντων, οὐκ ὀλίγων δὲ καπήλων
διακαπηλευόντων ὅτι τύχοιεν ἕκαστος.

54. Nilsson, *Geschichte*, i. 826-7. The author of 'Panēgyris' in *RE* (L. Ziehen) translates *panēgyris* not as *Fest* or *Festversammlung*, but as *Volksfest*.
55. ibid.
56. Diels, *Die Fragmente der Vorsokratiker* (Berlin 1952), i. 191.

Two authors of the Roman imperial period give us brief descriptions of the *panēgyris* as it existed in Asia Minor and Greece. Pausanias describes the *panēgyris* celebrated biannually in honour of Isis at Titheora of Phocis. At the onset of the *panēgyris* the sanctuary was cleared and on the next day the *panēgyris* got under way.

> The merchants made tents of cane and other rough substance. On the last of the three days they celebrate the *panēgyris* in selling slaves and all kinds of livestock, and in addition clothing, silver, and gold. Later at midday they turn to sacrifice. The more prosperous sacrifice both oxen and deer, but those who lack wealth [sacrifice] geese and guinea fowls. They do not allow [the use of] goats and swine in sacrifice.[57]

The description of the celebration at Titheora is terse and yet it includes the three basic elements: a large gathering of people, commercial enterprise, religious litany.

Strabo describes a similar religio-commercial celebration at Comana but he adds an interesting detail:

> Comana is populous and it is a commercial emporium to those [coming] from Armenia. Men and women come together at the time of the procession of the goddess from all sides, from towns and countryside for the celebration. Certain others dwell there permanently in order to pray, performing sacrifices to the goddess. And those who dwell there are luxurious and all their fields have vineyards. And there is a multitude of women who sell their bodies, most of whom are temple prostitutes. The city is in some way a small Corinth. Those who visit and celebrate in the region are numerous, and the merchants and soldiers are completely broke so that such a proverb arose concerning them: 'The trip to Corinth is not for every man'.[58]

Again there is reference to a large gathering, religious worship, and commerce. But the new detail, prostitution, is of considerable interest as we shall see later. Thus the religio-commercial *panēgyris* has a more or less constant kernel from the archaic through the Roman imperial period.

The fourth century

The crucial period between Graeco-Roman antiquity and the Byzantine age is in many respects the fourth century. At that time victorious Christianity came into open contact and conflict with the cultural institutions of the pagan world on the basis of political superiority. According to Libanius the pagan religio-commercial *panēgyris* was in a flourishing state during the fourth century and constituted a fundamental cultural institution in a world that was making the transition from paganism to Christianity. He says of the villages in the vicinity of Antioch:

> These are large, populous villages, more populous than many towns, with craft industries just as in towns, and which set in motion their products to one another through the

---

57. Pausanias, X. 32. 14. To Pausanias the Olympia are still a *panēgyris*, V. 4. 5:
 πανήγυρίν τε ᾿Ολυμπικήν.
58. Strabo, XII. 3. 36.

panēgyris, each [village] demanding in part for itself and [in turn] being asked for [things] [. . .] and they furnish from their surplus and produce what they need, disposing of the former and purchasing the latter. They are more prosperous by far than the merchants on the sea and indeed of the dashing wave, acquiring money with laughter and noise, needing little from the city because of their mutual trade.[59]

In another text Libanius remarks that his contemporaries and compatriots have a large number of old *panēgyreis*, including that of Io. 'In these feasts we shall sing praise to the god being honoured in each one [. . .]'.[60] Finally he gives an account of the procedure of the religious phase of a pagan *panēgyris*.

When *panēgyreis* are about to take place desire comes to men, when they are occurring there is pleasure, and when they have ceased there is remembrance. And again remembrance renders people close to their labours. And remembrance has some utility. He who speaks of *panēgyreis* must also speak of the gods on behalf of whom the holding of the *panēgyreis* has been indicated. As they [*panēgyreis*] approach, men prepare themselves gladly, many of them prepare that from which they will attend the gods. Flocks are brought from the fields and from the field wine and all other things, they clean their clothes and each strives how he might celebrate in every way. The poorer acquire clothing from the rich to adorn themselves. On the arrival of the main day the priests open the sanctuaries and take care of the statues and nothing of those things brought to the common altar is neglected. The towns are full of the masses coming in from the neighboring lands for the ceremonies, some on foot, others by boat. At sunrise and in brilliant attire they gather at the temple to accompany that god whose *panēgyris* is being celebrated. The lord of the household [*despotēs*] goes ahead bringing incense and there follows the servant bringing the sacrificial animal.[61]

Libanius thus indicates that in the fourth century the religio-commercial *panēgyris* of the pagans were thriving and widespread at precisely that time when Christianity was transforming the institutional and cultural life of the ancient world.

The attitude of the church fathers

What was the attitude of the Church toward these religio-commercial *panēgyreis*? The church fathers, on the one hand, assume the existence of the *panēgyris* and refer to it in their sermons by way of simile. St Gregory the Theologian compares life to a *panēgyris* from which one has to take profit, as though life too were a business enterprise.[62] But more often the patristic texts decry the *panēgyris* and warn the faithful against it. St John Chrysostom remarks on the manifold evil of the *panēgyris*. First of all, those who go to a *panēgyris* to buy clothing or oxen must borrow money. Then they have to bear heat, hunger, and thirst to arrive at the *panēgyris*. In the haggling between buyer and seller when the former vows not to buy over a certain price, and the latter not to sell under a minimum price, the buyer and seller often break their vows. Beside this sin he remarks that there is also the danger that what one buys at a *panēgyris* may die before the

59. Libanius, i. 517-8.
60. Libanius, ii. 463-4.
61. Libanius, viii. 538-9.
62. *PG* 37. 930.

purchaser reaches home with it.[63]   A fourth-century text attributed to Clement of Rome warns Christians: 'Panēgyreis and those things carried out in them are to be avoided. A believer must not go to a panēgyris except to buy a slave, to take care of life and to buy certain other things fitting for existence'.[64]

St Basil blames the Christians for having turned the celebrations of the martyrs into panēgyreis or commercial fairs. Thus, instead of praying for one another and of thanking God for blessings, they turn to the affairs of the agora or panēgyris.[65] The raw spirit of financial gain which predominated on these occasions came to be symbolised in Constantinople itself where, we are informed, 'The statue of a swine was raised signifying the noise of the panēgyris, and a barren stele which signified the shamelessness of the buyers and sellers'.[66] A holdover from the pagan panēgyris also seems to have been the presence and activities of prostitutes and the expectation on the part of the male participants in the panēgyris of sexual enjoyment. Chorikios of Ghaza ostentatiously notes that he avoided these feasts 'because courtesans excite lovers and turn them to spending money'. Then a young man coming to the panēgyris will desire to purchase, not some silver or gold object, but the services of a pretty girl.[67] More systematised than all of these is the attack of Asterios of Amseia upon the pagan panēgyris as exemplified in the celebrations of Calends. He asks his flock, why is it that we gather in these annual meetings and feasts? First we meet to honour the martyrs. Then we do so in order to learn something useful, something that we did not previously know, something from Christian dogma. We do so also in order to be inspired to imitate the piety of the martyrs, or to understand some part of the scriptures or to hear some discourse on ethics. But, he continues, the faithful have transferred, thus, all their concerns to the mob of mammon and to absorption with the shops. Some do so in trading and others in buying and become involved in haggling. He then enjoins his flock: 'Transfer, for me, your desire to the Church. Abandon basic and frantic avarice'.[68]

In his 'Discourse against the feast of Calends', Asterios continues his attack on the pagan aspects of the panēgyris. He starts by juxtaposing two feasts which though they occur simultaneously are nevertheless antithetical. 'The one is a [feast] of the pagan mob which gathers greatly the silver of mammon and which drags along, also, other petty trade, that of the market place and the servile [ἀνελεύθερον].[69] The other feast is that of the holy and true religion [. . .]'. In referring to the former, he asks, what is the purpose of such a panēgyris? 'Some answer that "it is a remembrance and festivity of the year" '.[70] Asterios asserts that the transactions

63. *PG* 64. 436.
64. *PG* 1. 752.
65. *PG* 31. 1020.
66. *Scriptores originum Constantinopolitanarum,* ed. T. Preger (Leipzig 1901), 206.
67. Choricius of Ghaza, ed. Foerster-Richtstieg, 255.
68. *PG* 40. 195.
69. *PG* 40. 216.
70. *PG* 40. 217.

and expenses at a *panēgyris* cannot be justified. The true *panēgyreis*, he says, are those of God: that of his birth, that of the Lights, and that of the Resurrection. Any other feast is false. 'For the citizens, rabble, and the jugglers of the theatre [οἱ τῆς ὀρχήστρας θαυματοποιοί] arranging themselves in ranks and bodies and then splitting up, knock on each door and annoy. There they shout greetings and acclamations, and they remain before the gate of the traders until he who is besieged inside, being worn out, brings forth the silver which he has [. . .]'.[71] Furthermore, those who get ready for the *panēgyris* go to great expense and so have to contract loans so 'the *panēgyris* should be called the indigence of men'.[72] According to him the feast teaches children to be greedy, emphasising as it does the commercial instincts. The country people are ridiculed and reviled in word and deed. The common soldiers spend their money, learn evil habits, and don women's clothing during the celebration. Finally the mighty consuls waste and exhaust their great wealth.

It is obvious, thus, that the Church found much in the *panēgyris* to revile, and attempted to restrain the faithful from their ancestral customs. It was permissible for a Christian to purchase the necessities at a *panēgyris*, but he should not abandon prayers for commerce and the attendant frivolities. The temptation of gain, of the painted ladies, and of all the other non-religious occurrences was so great, however, that ultimately the Church had to compromise. There was, after all, the fact that human nature is constant, and further there was the indisputable fact that the Church reaped handsome financial rewards from the *panēgyris* of the martyrs.

Assimilation by the Church

The seventy-sixth canon of the council in Trullo reflects the continuing conflict of ecclesiastical claims and pagan practice in regard to the *panēgyris*. The seventh-century canon reads:

> One must not establish a shop within the sacred enclosures or display foodstuffs or conduct other sales, guarding [thus] the reverence of the church. For our Saviour and God, instructing us by his life in the body, ordered us not to make the house of God a house of commerce. And he threw out the coin of the money-changers and he drove out those who made the sanctuary common. If some one be apprehended in the crime under discussion let him be excommunicated.[73]

But the comments of both Zonaras and Balsamon indicate that as of the twelfth century the prohibitions of canon seventy-six were being violated and that shops were still being set up in the holy precincts of the church on the occasion of the *panēgyris*.

> Take note of this present canon for those who trade in the perfume shops and barber-shops of the most holy Great Church and even more so inside it. Similarly take note

71. *PG* 40. 220.
72. *PG* 40. 220.
73. G.A. Rhalles and M. Potles, *Syntagma tōn Theiōn kai ierōn kanonōn ktl.* (Athens 1852), ii. 480.

of this canon for those who come to the festivals and *panēgyreis* occurring everywhere and who take as an excuse for commercial transactions the worship of the saint being celebrated at that time. Such are deserving of a great punishment. And the great Basil greatly forbids this in his [work on] asceticism. Read the section which writes thus, concerning the commercial transactions in the 'synods', and which says in part these things: 'Since others, having anticipated, corrupted the established custom on the occasion of the saints and instead of praying they make of that period and land a market, a *panēgyris*, and commerce'.[74]

In the fourth century the pagans were still reluctant to abandon their religio-commercial customs. Sozomenus writes: 'Since many populaces and towns throughout the inhabited world had fear and reverence for their fantasies concerning the statues, they turned away from the dogma of the Christians, and they maintained their antiquity, their ancestral customs and *panēgyreis*'.[75] But the process of partial Christianisation of the pagan *panēgyris*, and therefore of its continuity into Christian and Byzantine society are illustrated by a second interesting passage in Sozomenus.

It is necessary also to relate those things which Constantine the emperor decided in regard to the oak of Mamre. This area, which they now call Terebinthus, is fifteen stadia from Hebron in the south and is some two hundred and fifty stadia from Jerusalem. The truth about it is that [here] the Son of God appeared to Abraham and foretold to him the birth of the child, and [here] were sent the angels against the Sodomites. The nearby Palestinians, Phoenicians and Arabs still hold there, in the summer, a brilliant annual *panēgyris*. Very many come there on account of commerce to sell and buy. This feast is very important to all: to the Jews because they boast of the patriarch Abraham, to the pagans because of the visit of the angels, to the Christians because there did reveal himself to the pious man he who in later years [was born] through the Virgin for the salvation of the human race. They honour this land fittingly in their religions. Some pray to the God of all, others beseeching the angels pour libations of wine and incense, and they sacrifice either an ox or a goat or a rooster.[76]

It happened, however, that Constantine's mother-in-law witnessed this *panēgyris* and was so shocked that she denounced it to Constantine himself. The latter wrote a letter to the Palestinian bishops expressing his own shock that the clergy should allow such a holy land to be polluted by libations and sacrifices. So he ordered them to raze the altar, to burn the statues, and to build a church there that would be worthy of the antiquity and reverence of the place. All future pourers of libations and offerers of sacrifices would be subject to severe punishment.[77]

The incident is doubly illuminatory of the rise of the Christian *panēgyris*. First, it shows clearly that there was a stage in which there were *panēgyreis* common to both Christianity on the one hand and to paganism and Judaism on the other hand. Second, we see the next step in the evolution of the Christian *panēgyris* in which the non-Christian *panēgyris* was taken over by the Church, was purified of the more flagrantly pagan features and baptised so to speak.

74. ibid., ii. 483. For government regulation of the *panēgyris* see 1 and P. Zepos, *Jus graeco-romanum* (Athens 1931), i. 271-2.

75. Sozomenus, 56.

76. Sozomenus, 54-5.

77. Sozomenus, 55-6.

Thus the Byzantine *panēgyris* is the pagan *panēgyris* converted and baptised. The pagan-Christian-Jewish *panēgyris* of the Oak of Mamre-Terebinthus is the evolutionary link, in our sources, between the *panēgyreis* of Apollo at Delos, the four great *panēgyreis* of Olympia, Nemea, Isthmia, Delphi, of Isis in Titheora and of the goddess at Comana on the one hand, and the Christian *panēgyreis* of Thekla at Seleuceia, of Theodore at Euchaïta, of St John at Ephesus, and of St Demetrios at Thessalonica. Obviously the pagan *panēgyreis* continued into the fourth century of the Christian era, but gradually they were absorbed into the Christian cycle of martyr celebrations which were themselves transformed by the form of the pagan *panēgyris.*

Late Byzantine panēgyreis

Now it remains for us to examine briefly the fate of the Byzantine religious commercial *panēgyris* in Asia Minor and the Balkans in the later Byzantine period, at which time Byzantine political authority was being replaced by that of Muslim Turks in Anatolia and by that of the Orthodox South Slavs and Catholic Latins in the Balkans. First it should be noted that the Byzantine *panēgyris* was never exclusively limited to internal trade among the Byzantines. Ammianus Marcellinus tells of a fair held early in September during the mid-fourth century at Batme on the Euphrates where goods were brought from India and China.[78] In the Balkans, Priskos relates, one of the clauses of a Byzantino-Hunnic treaty provided that 'the *panēgyreis* should be equal and free of danger for the Romans and Huns'.[79] Finally, the great *panēgyreis* of St Eugenios in Trebizond and of St Demetrios in Thessalonica were frequented by a variety of Muslim, Slavic, and western European peoples, so that Byzantine neighbours knew of and participated in the *panēgyreis* both at the borders and in the hinterlands.[80]

When the Serbs began to expand southward into Byzantine and Bulgarian domains they found the *panēgyris* a firmly established and living institution. In 1300 Stephen Uroš II (Milutin) renewed the rights of the monastery of St George at Servai of Skopje and in so doing regulated the *panēgyris.*[81] This *panēgyris*, celebrated for eight days in early November (around 8 November), had been previously regulated by the Bulgarian ruler Roman. To this *panēgyris* we are told, there came Greeks, Bulgars, Serbs, Latins, Albanians, Vlachs, and all were to pay the *panēgyris* taxes, as was the case at the *panēgyreis* of Tetovo and Gračanica. The

78. Ammianus Marcellinus, XIV. iii. 3.

79. *PG* 113. 705.

80. For the case of a Turkish emir who sent his wife to be cured at the shrine of St Eugenios, see Vryonis, *Decline,* 486. For Macedonia and Thrace, C. Asdracha, *La région des Rhodopes aux XIIIᵉ et XIVᵉ siècles. Étude de géographie historique* (Athens 1976), 112, 221, 222, 224.

81. I should like to thank Mrs Elizabeth Allen of Dumbarton Oaks for having collected most of the references to the South Slav documents and for making them available to me. A. Soloviev, *Odbrani spomenici srpskog prava (od XII do kraja XV veka)* (Belgrade 1926), (hereafter Soloviev, *Odbrani*), 611.

rights to the collection of these taxes were vested in the abbot of the monastery.[82] This text illustrates clearly the continuity of the *panēgyris* from Byzantium to Bulgars and Serbs, it shows the connection between the Church and the merchants, and it underlines its multinational character.

The same Serbian monarch confirmed the regulations previously assured by the Bulgar ruler Roman to the village of Brod and its annual *panēgyris* on 1 September.[83] In a document dated 1321 the Serbian ruler mentions an annual *panegyris* of the Virgin under the jurisdiction of the monastery of Gračanica.[84] Stephen Uroš III (Dečanski) set forth the regulations governing the *panēgyris* of the birth of the Virgin in the region of Prizren, to which both Greeks and Latins went.[85]

But the 'Slavic' *panēgyreis* are most copiously mentioned in the reign of Stephen Dušan, a reign which witnessed the most extensive expansion into former Byzantine lands. This ruler renewed the privileges of the following *panēgyreis*: at the monastery of the Theotokos at Htetovo between 1337-48,[86] at a *metochion* in Prizren of the monastery of St Demetrios at Prilep,[87] St Demetrios at Leskovac,[88] the monastery of the Archangel at Prizren,[89] St George at Stephanitai of Esphigmenou,[90] St George at Zographou on 23-27 April.[91] In this last instance the documentation states that Feofilakt, patriarch of Trnovo, and king John of Trnovo came to Athos originally and established this *panēgyris* of St George. Again this is a reference to a Bulgarian tradition of the *panēgyris*. There are later mentions, in Serbian held lands, of a *panēgyris* of St Petka at the monastery of Ravanica (1381),[92] of St Panteleimon at Debritzi (*c.* 1430)[93] and at Parakina (1452).[94] Thus in a portion of the South Slav lands, we see an adoption and continuation of the Byzantine *panēgyris* by Bulgars and Serbs right down to the beginning of the Ottoman conquests.

In Asia Minor the initial impact of the Seljuk invasions seems to have been disruptive. As a result the *panēgyreis* of St Phokas at Sinope and of St Eugenios at Trebizond were interrupted and halted for a time. Instituted in the reign of Basil I, the *panēgyris* of St Eugenios had brought merchants and travellers from all parts of the Middle East to Trebizond: Arabs, Armenians, Greeks, Russians, Colchians, Jews, Georgians and Circassians. But in the eleventh century the Turkish invasion brought it to a halt. 'At that time there [were] massacres and captures of

---

82. Soloviev, *Odbrani,* 620. J. Jiriček, *Istorija Srba* ed. J. Radonić (Belgrade 1978), 190-1.
83. Soloviev, *Odbrani,* 615.
84. Soloviev, *Odbrani,* 636.
85. Soloviev, *Odbrani,* 640.
86. Soloviev, *Odbrani,* 657.
87. Soloviev, *Odbrani,* 666.
88. Soloviev, *Odbrani,* 671.
89. Soloviev, *Odbrani,* 691.
90. Soloviev-Mošin, 108.
91. ibid., 362.
92. Soloviev, *Odbrani,* 770.
93. Soloviev, *Odbrani,* 335.
94. Soloviev, *Odbrani,* 504.

cities and collections of prisoners and there attended all those things which are grievous to life [. . .]. From that time the memory of the celebration became the victim of deep oblivion, and again this annual celebration forgot the city, as the necessities were lacking'.[95]

By the late thirteenth or early fourteenth century, however, the *panēgyris* was revived and so continued into the Turkish period. The description which Michael Akominatos gives of the *panēgyris* of Chonae in the twelfth century also reflects anomalous conditions imposed by the arrival of the Turks: 'The miracles in the church gave rise to a *panēgyris*, a multitudinous *panēgyris*, about it. It is multitudinous, indeed very multitudinous for it draws, not to exaggerate, all the neighbouring towns, but also in addition the Lydians, Ionians, Carians, Paphlagonians, and Lycians from beyond, and in addition barbarian Iconiotes, in order to buy and sell'.[96] The author goes on to narrate an episode which indicates the troubled and anomalous conditions prevailing in a *panēgyris* on the Byzantine-Seljuk borders.

> Thus because of all these things (and) as the *panēgyris* was full of people from those coming from all around, strife arose among the Romans and barbarians. The great and unarmed [group] of people, inasmuch as the evil broke out suddenly, having nowhere to which they might flee, stampeded, fell into the church [. . .] crying out loudly and trampling one another. Then the barbarians assumed a more dangerous advantage and were about to pursue through the holy gates as our people had given way.[97]

At this point the metropolitan of Chonae appeared before the Turks, was able to halt the pending slaughter, and the *panēgyris* returned to normality.

These two examples indicate that despite the initial destruction wrought by the Seljuk invasions in Asia Minor, the *panēgyris* revived and continued to function in Byzantino-Turkish Anatolia.

In the Peloponnese the system of *panēgyreis* seems to have continued during the Latin and Greek domination. A chrysobull of the fourteenth century refers to the *panēgyris* as a widespread phenomenon in the Peloponnese.[98] In a very interesting passage of the French Chronicle of the Morea we are informed that at the fairs called *panejours* people come from all parts to buy and sell and that they flock there from the lands of both the Byzantine emperor and the Latin prince.

> Si se faisoient les foires que on claime Panejours, les quelles se font au jour de Nuy au demie juyn: auxquels foires venoient la gent de toutes pars pour acheter et pour vendre, tant dou pays de l'empereur comme de cellui dou prince.[99]

Despite the political disintegration of Byzantium in Asia Minor before the Turks, in the Balkans before South Slavs and Latins, the religio-commercial *panēgyris* survived as a vital institution in the internal and external life of these areas.

95. Vryonis, *Decline*, 39-40, 160, 477.
96. S. Lambros, *Michaēl Akominatou ta sōzomena* (Athens 1879), i. 56.
97. ibid., i. 57.
98. D. Zakythinos, *Le despotat grec de Morée* (Athens 1953), ii. 253.
99. ibid.

The effect of Ottoman rule

Now we must proceed to the last major historical period in this exercise by posing the question, what effect did the Ottoman conquests and administration have on the *panēgyreis*? There existed in the fifteenth and sixteenth centuries an Ottoman tax known as *panayir resmi*, or the *panēgyris* tax, just as there had been such a tax in Byzantine and Serbian times. In 1478-9 the monastery of the metropolitan Jacob had an income of 250 akçes from *panēgyreis*; the church of St Nicholas collected 350 akçes from two *panēgyreis*, whereas another monastery had a right to 40 akçes. In addition we see that the Ottoman state gave rights to the taxes from *panēgyreis* in Thessaly and in eastern Macedonia to timariots in the mid-fifteenth century.[100] It is thus obvious that the Ottomans conserved, observed, and taxed this Byzantine institution. Later texts of the Ottoman period indicate that not only did the *panēgyris* survive but it played a very important role in local and larger scale, even in international commerce.

The seventeenth-century Evliya Çelebi describes a very important, indeed what must have been a vast *panēgyris*, even after we allow for his exaggerations, at the site of Doliane in the Kaza of Stroumitza in Macedonia.

It [Doliane] is located on an extended and flat site which has many valleys, trees, boundless pasturage and is covered with narcissus.

It is like a castle, like a great *han* with gates on the four sides and with many upstairs and downstairs rooms of stone. It is the site of a *panēgyris* which prospers and is great. Along its streets, which have been laid out like a chessboard, right and left, are to be found over a thousand shops covered from top to bottom with tiles. It was built by [lacuna] and in the *waqf* of [lacuna].

Above its gates are large sarays, and on the days of the market the officials, *cadis*, and *serdars* remain in the sarays with soldiers, and they administer. There [also] exist secured chambers and storehouses where is placed the sultanic tithe which the emirs collect from the market.

Once a year, at the time of the cherries, 100,000 men from the Ottoman empire. Arabia, Persia, India, Samarkand, Balkh, Bokhara, Egypt, Syria, Iraq, the entire West, and generally from the four corners of the world all the merchants of the land and sea, come together at the *panēgyris* with their boundless merchandise.

Aside from these who enter the market of the bazaar, many thousand tents of different types, shacks, and miserable huts of rags [. . .] are set up on the plains outside. There is set up an army of merchants of the bazaar like the army of Alexander the Great or of Kaihusro or of Darius. This plain fills with a human sea. Many hundreds of thousands loads of merchandise come to the centre and are sold and many thousands of loads of merchandise are purchased. One can even find the milk of the bird [egg], and of man [woman's milk] and of the lion [wine].

On those days of the market all the guilds [connected with] foodstuffs and drinks, bakers, cooks, and tanners, come from all the villages and small towns. Thousands of ships with their wares form an army camp. They shove one another with their shoulder and this pleasant market lasts for forty days and nights [. . .].

All types of goods are sold. Even women openly sell their hidden wares. Many thousands acquire the wealth of Croesus. But many thousands, as a result of their

100. P. Nasturel and N. Beldinceanu, 'Les églises byzantines et la situation économique de Drama, Serres et Zichna aux XIVe et XVe siècles, *Jahrbuch der österreichischen byzantinischen Gesellschaft* xxvii (1978), 281-5.

pleasures and unrestraints find themselves in need of one akçe, one seed, one piece of clothing. There is, in addition, a great sheep market at this celebration. Hundreds of thousands of sheep and goats are sold. Thousands of horses and mules are [also] sold at the horse bazaar; with the exception however that there is no camel market since camels do not exist in Rumeli. There is a market for cows and oxen.

There is also a slave market. Thousands of sun-bright and moon-faced beautiful youths and maidens are sold. They set up a separate market for blacks, black Abyssinians. Immediately forty to fifty thousand people come and purchase blacks because in these lands the black male and female slaves are eagerly sought.

There are markets where all the guilds stay, each one in a separate section. These dwell in the shops and in the numerous stone houses covered with tiles, which resemble a castle, great merchants who have many hundreds of thousands of kurus.

The front of each small shop is like a Chinese temple of idols burdened with ornaments and strewn with pearls, as they display in common view every type of textile: silk, spider-woven, gold brocade, purple, velvet, atlaz, katife, gold stitched silk. In addition one sees rubies, sapphires, emeralds, diamonds, Ceylonese stones, gold stones, peruze, pearls, sards of Yemen, eyes of the sea, cat eyes, fish eyes, and thousands of other types of valuable and choice gems. Every type of rare and expensive ware is sold. For as that *han* is like a fortified castle of the market and a safe area, everyone puts out in the front of his shop his invaluable merchandise.

However the largest part of these great merchants offer their goods at their shops which are to be found in the open market of the rural *panēgyris* and in their tents. Thousands of shops and tents and kiosks are set up in this open space like a labyrinth. There are to be found, in rows, twenty to thirty thousand tents of different types, and from one end to the other tents of kilims. This verdant region with its tents is like a garden of white lillies [. . .].

Aside from the kitchens of the governors, they roast whole sheep and lambs perhaps in a thousand places. There are also more than a thousand coffee houses and shops where they sell ices and taverns. But when someone gets very drunk, surpassing the bounds [of decency] and seeks argument and blows, immediately the *molla* of the city of Serrez, the *çorbaş* of the Janissaries, its emirs, *voevod*, and *mutevelli* hasten there, seize the troublemakers and punish them with blows and a fine. It is a very safe area.

All the sleight of hand artists and acrobats who exist on the surface of the earth are to be found in the squares and tents. Some are magicians, others play with pans; others are tightrope walkers; others cardplayers; some play with shadows, others with receptacles, knives. Some display their strength; others play with strings, fires. Some have puppet theatres, others shadow theatres. Some perform beggary, somersaults. Some play with trays, glasses, bottles, fires, rocks, flasks, cups, crows, swords. Others play with bears, monkeys, goats or donkeys, while others play with clubs [. . .], snakes, card decks, birds, lighted coals, cards, mirrors, plates, balls. In a few words, the famous sleight of hand artists of the whole world, all the vagabonds, and all the good-for-nothings are to be found in this great assembly of people.

In all the tents and the open market there are, from every land, singers, players of kithara, dancers, wrestlers, athletes, archers, brave and handsome youths, honourable and beloved boys of their era, and even female singers. All are to be found in this pleasing bazaar. There takes place a great feast.[101]

The description of the great *panēgyris* of Doliane brings together many of the combined characteristics of the pagan and Byzantine *panēgyris*. There are large numbers of various people present; there are extensive markets; there are extensive

101. V. Demetriades, *He kentrike kai dytike Makedonia kata ton Evligia Tselempe* (Thessalonica 1977), 343-7.

textile and animal markets; there are athletic contests and various amusements. What is lacking is the mention of a saint's feast day. Further there is a central building, obviously a caravansary, which is supported from the income of a *waqf*, probably therefore an Islamic institution around which the *panēgyris* gravitated. Evliya also refers to annual *panēgyris* at Strunga, which lasted ten days and to which supposedly 40,000-50,000 came, and at Moscholouri of Elasson. While travelling in Macedonia Evliya encountered bandits who had recently raided and looted the large *panēgyris* at Moscholouri.[102]

These last two *panēgyreis* are included in the table of the ten principle fairs which de Pouqueville reproduces in his *Voyage dans la Grèce* for the late eighteenth and early nineteenth century.

Table of the Principal Fairs of Rumeli

Indication of Panēgyreis or Fairs	Period of their opening according to the old calendar		Duration Days	Names of provinces in which they took place
Strongia	February	29	15	Macedonia Illyria
Prilep	April	30	25	Cisaxien Macedonia
Moscholouri	May	20	15	Thessaly
Nicopolis	At Ascension		3	Epirus
Mavronoros	July	30	15	Cisaxien Macedonia
Zeïtoun	August	1	8	Thessaly
Pogoniani	August	15	15	Epirus (Jannina)
Vrachori	September	8	8	Aetolia (Thermon)
Pharsala	September	15	8	Thessaly
Mavrovo	November	29	20	Cisaxien Macedonia[103]

We see from this table that Macedonia, Epirus, Thessaly, and Aetolia were the sites of a well-developed network of religio-commercial *panēgyreis* that provided a total of 131 days per year for such occasions. The mention of Strongia and Moscholouri in de Pouqueville's table shows us that we are dealing with a phenomenon that was very tenacious, for they are mentioned two hundred years earlier by Evliya Çelebi. In commenting on these fairs at the beginning of the nineteenth century de Pouqueville delivers himself of his theory on their origins and of a colourful sketch of the participants.

> Les anciens, en appelant les peuples aux fêtes d'Olympie, de l'Isthme, de Némée, de Nicopolis et de Thermus, unissaient à leurs solennités (1) l'exposition des produits des arts (2) et les intérêts du commerce (3). Les Romains, après avoir subjugué les Grecs, substituèrent à ces brillants panégyris condamnés par le christianisme, les foires que Servius Tullius avait instituées, dont un édit rendu par Valens, dans des temps postérieurs, fixa l'ordre et la distribution dans l'étendue de l'empire d'Orient (4). Les révolutions avaient respecté ces institutions; et les Turcs, qui les trouvèrent établis, les maintinrent assez religieusement pour permettre aux peuples de langue différentes

---

102. ibid., 51, 182, 282ff.
103. F.C. de Pouqueville, *Voyage dans la Grèce* (Paris 1820), iii. 457-8.

répandues dans leur vaste empire, de se voir, et de communiquer ensemble à des époques déterminées. Ainsi les Illyriens vendent encore chaque année des armes, des lames de poignards, et la courtellerie, qu'ils tirent des fabriques de Gasco et de Fochia, aux panégyris de la Macédoine. Les Hyperboréens de Baxor, donc les ancêtres envoyaient des présents à Délos; les Bosniaques, successeurs des Triballes; les peuplades de Calcandéren, descendants farouches des Tavasbars, y exposent les laines de leurs troupeaux, les peaux de cerfs et d'ours, produit de leurs chasses, à côté des riches marchandises tirées des bazards d'Andrinople et de Salonique. On y voit les Épirotes de Janina avec leurs boutiques de selleries, et les pistolets montées en argent à l'usage des Schypetars; les Valaques, avec leurs capes; les Thessaliens, fiers des produits des fabriques de Tournovo, et riches de la soie de la Magnésie; des marchands forains, avec des pelleteries de Moscou, des mousselines de Carnate, et des cachemires de l'Inde. D'autres y apportent des cafés de l'Hiémen, des riz d'Égypte, des peaux de lions et de panthères des déserts de l'Afrique; enfin des esclaves de Darfourt, conduits par des negriers (qu'on ne fera jamais renoncer à la traite), arrivent chaque année à ces réunions [...].[104]

The *panēgyreis* of the Christian craftsmen and guildsmen of Thrace and Istanbul have been studied in detail and while they do not seem to have been as extensive or massive as the *panēgyreis* of Macedonia, the connection of economic organisation with religious celebrations is striking. On the occasion of the celebration of the two greatest holidays, Christmas and Easter, the guilds took part and provided dancing and music. Kaisarios Dapontes describes the dance of the guilds at Easter:

οἱ χοροι ἐγίνοντο κατὰ μέρος, τάγματα τάγματα, ἤγουν τὰ κασαπ-ὀγλάνια μὲ τὰ κασαπ-ὀγλάνια, οἱ γουναράδες μὲ τούς γουναράδες καὶ τὰ λοιπὰ τάγματα παρομοίως.[105]

It is not clear whether the religious celebrations of the guildsmen were followed by markets, but the inclusion of music and dance fits the general patterns of the traditional *panēgyris*.

In the Peloponnese the *panēgyris* is very much in evidence in the seventeenth century. According to the report of the Venetian governor Gritti, the Peloponnese held five large annual fairs in 1691. These were at Gastouni in May, at Tripolitza in June, at Saint John and at Tzami in August, and at Kalavryta in September.[106] In the eighteenth century the significance of the large fairs increased as Peloponnesian production was commercialised by French trade. The *panēgyris* of Mistra in

104. ibid., 456-7.

105. E. Vourazele-Marinakou, *Ai en Thrake syntechniai ton Hellenon kata ten Tourkokratian* (Thessalonica 1950), 113; M. Gedeon, 'Peri ton megaloprepesteron en Konstantinou polei teloumenon ierokosmikon panegyreon'. *Laographia* xiii (1951), 236-41.

106. V. Kremmydas, *To emporion tēs Peloponnēsou sto 18 aiōna (1715-1792)· (me basē ta gallika archeia)* (Athens 1972), 320.

OPPOSITE

'Praising the Lord'. Detail of a fresco in the Chapel of the Panagia Koukouzelissa, Great Lavra, Athos, 18th century. Photo: S. Kadas, Mount Athos (1979).

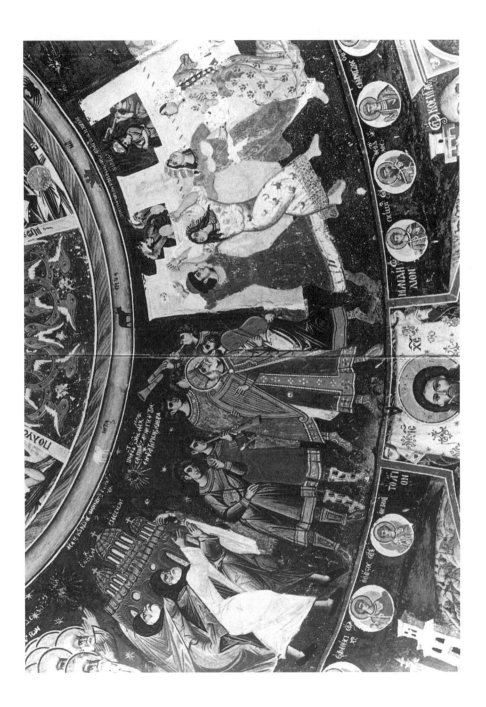

September and that held in the week of Pentecost at Tripolitza acquired particular importance. These *panēgyreis* which now lasted seven instead of fifteen days as had been the case in the seventeenth century, suffered considerably as a result of the Greek risings and Albanian depredations in the decade of the 1770s.

In Thessaly the *panēgyris* of Pharsala mentioned by de Pouqueville, seems to have been the largest and most important in the nineteenth century. It attracted pilgims and merchants from the regions of Greece, Serbia and Bulgaria at the time of the celebrations of the Dormition of the Virgin (15-30 August). But it is a second Thessalian *panēgyris*, that of St Anthony the Young, celebrated in Aghia, which will concern us here. Probably established in the mid-eighteenth century, it was celebrated on 1 September in the nineteenth century. Originally a *panēgyris* of modest proportions, it began to expand in the middle of the century subsequent to the establishment of internal security so that all of Thessaly attended it. The church of St Anthony became relatively rich as the pilgrims donated livestock, money, jewellery, oil and land. The sick were brought to be healed and often the faithful donated themselves or their sons as servants of the church for a set period of time. We possess considerable detail as to the *panēgyris* itself by virtue of a written account left by one of the participants in the affair. Theodore Chatzimichales, the author, was born in Metaxochori of the eparchy of Aghia in 1873, at the age of fourteen graduated from the *scholarcheio* of Aghia and after a brief career as a teacher returned to Aghia in 1889 where he became a farmer and candlemaker. He inherited from his father an interest in and love for his *patrida* and so sought to record the lore of his homeland.[108]

The organisation of the *panēgyris* was carried out with some order and system: not a simple undertaking, as the presence of large numbers of people, commercial goods, and cash presented both the opportunity and incentive for mischief. The local Ottoman authorities enforced order through their Albanian *zaptiehs*, but the actual arrangement for the *panēgyris* itself were made by the *epitropoi* or supervisors of the church. Some fifteen days before the feast they undertook the preparation of fifteen to twenty cisterns in the stream bed (undoubtedly dry at that time of year) of Aghia, and then came to an agreement with the millers and those locally in charge of the disposition of water to drain the water from the mills into the cisterns.[109] The *panēgyris*, honouring St Anthony the Great and St Anthony the Young, began on 1 September, the agreement with the millers for the diversion of the water having been struck on 30 August. Chatzimichales gives a very brief description of the religious side of the *panēgyris*, assuming that these details were so well known to his readers that no detailed account of it was necessary. In the morning the pilgrim went to church, lighting candles in front of the icons of the two saints and there attended the holy Liturgy, sought the saints'

107. ibid., 329-30.
108. T. Chatzimichales, *Ena panēgyri sta chronia tēs sklabias*, ed. J.A. Sakellion (Athens 1975) (hereafter Chatzimichales), 23-7, 53, 90-1.
109. Chatzimichales, 92.

intercession against all danger, and then went out to participate in the secular aspects of the celebration for the rest of the day. Then in the evening and at the signal of the bells he might interrupt his activities to attend Vespers or if he could not or would not do so, he uncovered his head, paused briefly and piously made the sign of the cross three times.[110]

The affair was attended by large numbers from all the villages and towns of Thessaly. There were Greeks, Turks, Vlachs, Sarakatsanoi, Jews, Gypsies, and 'Ethiopians'. The array of tongues spoken at the fair was bewildering and the variety was further emphasized by the infinite variety of local costumes. Hatzimichales describes this in detail. The male Aghiates wore, variously, the *vraka* or *salvari* whereas the inhabitants of Velitsone, Spelion, Keramidi, the Karagounides of Kampos and Maimouli had their own clothing styles; the Vlachs wore white or purple *chupunia*, the Sarakatsanoi white *salvaria*, the Jews of Jannina were bearded and wore the long *anteria,* and the Gypsies were barefooted. The women were distinguished by their headdresses in particular. Those of Aghia wore black *cheperia,* the Athenatiotes yellow, those of Selitsane wore a *burma*, and those of Kampos, Kissovo, Sclethes and the Karagrin all wore distinctive headdresses. The Muslim women wore the *feredje* whereas the Gypsy women wore a yellow *cheperi.*[111]

Finally, the numismatic variety was infinite, as we see from the author's description of the coins which circulated at the fair.

> An abundance and variety of gold, silver, and copper coins of various nations greatly facilitated exchange: Turkish lire, English pounds, Napoleons, Venetian floria, dubloons, pentolira, sfantzika, florins, fterota, shillings, distela, kapikia, colonata, midjidia, akçes, paras, 5 paras, 20 paras (half kuruş), 40 paras (one kuruş) or karantona of weight of 6½ drams, medjedia, mahmutia, metalikia. Only Greek coins were absolutely forbidden.
>
> Those who did not know the actual value of the non-Turkish coins obtained knowledge of it from numismatic specialists among whom the best known then were Euthymines Vatzras, Constantine Tzemeroz, and Anagnostes Chatzimichales, father of the author of this work.[112]

Most impressive in many ways was the livestock market, which lasted for three days and in which the horses, mules, asses, oxen, water buffalo and swine reached the sizable number of 20,000. The animal merchants came from all around but particularly prominent were the Keserli Turks (divided into three groups, according to whether they were selling oxen, horses, or asses), the Karagounides and the Greeks from across the border in Lamia. The presence of such a large number of livestock created a demand for local produce as the animals had to be fed with fodder. The animal market took place in a long area some 270 by 30 paces alongside the grain, swine and yarn markets and the customs house. Here the prospective buyers had room enough to test the speed, stamina, and strength of the animals.[113] Parallel to this area of the animal market and at a distance of 150 metres from it

110. Chatzimichales 105-6.
111. Chatzimichales, 97ff.
112. Chatzimichales, 96-97.
113. Chatzimichales, 92-3.

was the second major area of the market occupied by the merchants, and coffee houses. In the interim space between these two areas and above the town bridge was a third area occupied by women who had brought for sale *velentzes, hramia, skoutia, samaroskoutia, tserepia, kappes, kontokappia, salvaria* and so on.[114]

It was the *epitropoi* of the church who established and maintained the topographical disposition of the various merchants and who arranged the order of precedence among them. The primary position was given to the *chrysikoi*, the jewellers — dealers in gold objects, most important of whom were the jewellers of Selitsane. 'Their jewellery consisted of rings, earrings, bracelets, *tselengia* [gold wings, ornaments for the head], pins, chains, belts with clasps ornamented with *titriri* or *poulais* [. . .]'.[115] Because of the valuable donations which the *chrysikoi* made to the church, the *epitropoi*, on the first day of the *panēgyris*, gave to each *chrysikos*, a ceramic plate of rice and meat previously prepared in a large cauldron of 50 oka capacity. A similar share was given by the church to each pilgrim who gave to the saints a cow, ox, goat, sheep, or olive oil. Then there followed, in order, the sellers of roasted chick peas, the cobblers, the jug sellers from Trnovo who sold vases from Çanak Kale, sellers of wooden vessels and water pitchers, peddlers of mortars for the preparation of *skordalia* (garlic sauce), or baskets, of flasks, of *vistelai*, of wooden flutes, of bells, and of *kiprines*. The wood workers-merchants were primarily from Trnovo and Metsovo. Another important group, the *halvatzides*, had their cooking establishment nearby the cemetery attached to the church and were often frequented by the engaged and newly married. Mention has already been made of the women-merchants of textiles in the large area separating the animal market from the coffee houses. The principal area of textile shops was in the area north of the church where the most important merchants were those from Aghia, Lauria and Trnovo. One could purchase both foreign and local textiles there. The latter included *astari* (lining?), white cloth, *staurolon, ragatziki, phytli*, and *tsikmes*. The merchants of Ampelakia came to buy the *tsikmes* of the villages of Athenata and Petsane which they then sold on the markets of Vienna and Trieste.[116]

Aghia possessed a lively local 'industry' in the tanning of hides, producing some 17,000 annually, and the hide merchants came from Kozane and Jannina to purchase these. The local craft of soap makers specialised in a green soap that was used locally in Larissa, in all the villages of Kampos and in Velestini.[117]

Incomplete though the author's description of the economic aspect of the *panēgyris* undoubtedly is, it nevertheless gives a very clear overall view of it. Of equal interest is his detailed description of the lighter side of the *panēgyris*, an aspect referred to by contemporary authors in their descriptions of the ancient, Byzantine, and post-Byzantine *panēgyris*. Our author writes:

114. Chatzimichales, 95.
115. Chatzimichales, 93.
116. Chatzimichales, 108-10.
117. Chatzimichales, 107-9.

Underneath every plane tree there was a 'symphony' of musical instruments and there gathered male dancers only and not female dancers as this was contrary to the customs of that period. Around the dancers there gathered a circle of curious spectators shoving and pushing so that they get a view of them. This [happened] particularly when wearers of the *foustanella* danced, as their costume was not common among the Aghiotes and because it was impressive because of its Greekness. The dancers [were] Greeks, the dances Greek and the songs Greek.[118]

The musical instruments included the drum (the noise of the drummer Liangkos of Tsaritsane was so thunderous that it could be heard as far as Retsane and Tourkochorion, 1½ and 3 km respectively from Aghia). Aside from the drum and string instruments were to be heard the pipe, flute, bagpipe, and *taipes*. The males spent long hours at such performances, eating lamb roasted on the spit and drinking wine from the great wooden barrels.[119]

Recreation and relaxation at the scenes of eating, drinking, and dancing were accompanied by displays of sports, an aspect mentioned in ancient *panēgyreis*, in Evilya Çelebi, but not in Byzantine authors. It is not known whether the athletic contests existed in the *panēgyreis* of the eighteenth century or whether they were instituted later. At other Thessalian *panēgyreis* there were foot and horse races but at Aghia the *agōnes* consisted primarily of wrestling, boxing and jumping. The games took place on the second day of the *panēgyris* at a special site to the west of the church, and seem to have enjoyed great popularity. The social hierarchy was reflected in the seating arrangement of the spectators. Preference was given to the bishop, *mudir, cadi, kolagan, binbasi,* priests and aghas. The participants in the actual contests included 'Ottomans', Albanians, 'Ethiopians', and Christians, but not Jews. Illustrious Turks and Christians did not themselves compete in the sports arena though the beys and aghas bought 'Ethiopians' and had them trained specifically for athletic contests. The patrons were particularly honoured and esteemed when their athletes were victorious. The victors themselves were rewarded with 2 medjidia, 2 besliks. In addition the *dallal* passed a tray among the spectators for further contributions, and on the return of the victor to his home on horseback he was accompanied all the way by his co-citizens who shared his glory on behalf of their town or village. Chatzimichales goes on to give accounts of famed athletes, both Christian and Muslim, and their encounters at the *panēgyris*. In 1876-8 Aghia and the larger region were caught up in the extraordinary events and anomalies attendant upon the Russo-Turkish war: conscription of the male Turkish population, incursions of Albanian and Ottoman groups and other guerilla groups. The last *agōnas* was celebrated in 1875 and thereafter the celebration was celebrated without games and in general on a more limited scale. But in 1881 the *panēgyris* took place in concurrence with the presence of the Greek army and the union of the area to the kingdom of Greece. The *panēgyris*, because of the recent events, drew very large crowds and continued to be lively until 1892 when the *panēgyris* of Larissa began to eclipse it, together with the fact that the

118. Chatzimichales, 110-15.
119. Chatzimichales, 123-7.

neighbouring areas of Epirus and Macedonia could no longer move freely to the *panēgyris*.

Cultural adaptation

What can one say, by way of conclusion, after the monotonous recitation of these texts? I warned you in the beginning that the analysis would be limited to a few basic observations and to the sequential ordering of the texts and that I would allow the texts to speak for themselves. The principal import of the ordering of the texts is the following. Despite the fact that the Byzantine saints as literary heroes were opposites to the literary heroes of pagan antiquity, they were celebrated in a manner which was, partly, of pagan origin. The *panēgyris*, against which the church fathers declaimed because of its concern with commerce, frivolity, and sin, early became attached to the annual celebration of the saint's cult. Though it included Christian religious ceremony, the *panēgyris* offered Byzantine society that which it has also offered pagan society: recreation and relief from cares; commerce and sex. Thus the Byzantine *panēgyris* represents what anthropologists call cultural adaptation, for it involved the acceptance of a pagan institution re-oriented to the scene of Christian localism; and thus it was passed down into modern times.

OPPOSITE

Panēgyris *of St George at Prinkipo, Princes' Islands, Sea of Marmara (23 April OS 1908). Previously unpublished photograph taken from the glass plate negative of Sir Benjamin Stone. Reproduced by permission of the Sir Benjamin Stone Collection, Birmingham Public Libraries.*

Nino

Gregory the
Illuminator

True Cross

N

Sergios & Bakchos

Orentios

Eugenios

Mandilion

Polyeuktos

Eustratios

Gregory the
Wonderworker

40 Martyrs
Blasios

Kosmas & Damianos
Symeon Stylites

John Baptist

John
the New

Ignatios

Leontios

Jerusalem
True Cross

Basiliskos

Merkourios
& Mamas

George

Phokas

Barnabas

Sinai

Theodore
Tyro

Thekla

Lazaros

Clement

Neophytos

Kallinikos

Hyakinthos

Platon

Amphilochios
Basil

Mark

Archangel
Michael

Menas

John the New

Nikolaos

Anthimos

Tryphon

Euphemia

Theotokos
Andrew

Glykeria

Severos

Antipas

Polykarpos

John Theologos, 7 Sleepers

Christodoulos

Isidoros

Athanasios

Menas
Titos

Sabas
the
Goth

Demetrios

Achilleios

Andrew

Dionysios

Gerasimos

Demetrios

Spyridon

Blasios

HAGIOGEOGRAPHY
OF THE
BYZANTINE WORLD

Domnio

Nikolaos

Anastasia
Chrysogonos

Archangel
Michael

Justus

Mark

Januarius

Agatha

Lucia

Major patrons shrines and

Mark
Theodore

Apollinaris

Peter · Paul

translations

0   100 200 300 400 500 km.

JLD

AAMB

Contributors

Professor Robert Browning, Taught at University College, University of London, since 1947. Since 1965 Professor of Classics at Birkbeck College, University of London. Elected FBA 1978. His publications include *Justinian and Theodora* (1971); *Byzantium and Bulgaria* (1975); *The Emperor Julian* (1976); and *Studies on Byzantine History, Literature and Education* (1977), as well as articles in various learned periodicals.

Professor Anthony Bryer, Director of the Centre of Byzantine Studies in the University of Birmingham. Symposiarch of the Fourteenth Spring Symposium, as of others. Many of his articles are collected in *The Empire of Trebizond and the Pontos* (1980).

Mr David Buckton, Assistant Keeper of Medieval and Later Antiquities at the British Museum, where he is responsible for the Early Christian, Byzantine, Carolingian and Ottonian collections. He has published articles on earthenware, glass, ivory and metal artefacts, and he is currently compiling the corpus of early medieval enamel.

Dr Anna Crabbe, Taught at the University of Oxford 1975-80. At present Lecturer in Classics in The Queen's University, Belfast. She has published *'Ignoscenda quidem:* Catullus 64 and the IVth Georgic', *Classical Quarterly* 27 (1977); and 'Cologne and Sardica', *JThS* 30 (1979). Shortly to appear are articles on Ovid in *Aufstieg und Niedergang den römischen Welt* 31.2 and on Boethius in *Boethian Studies,* ed. M. Gibson (1981). She is working on patristic literature and hagiography for the Lexicon of Greek Personal Names.

The Revd Professor Henry Chadwick, Formerly Regius Professor of Divinity in the University of Oxford (1959-69) and Dean of Christ Church, Oxford (1969-79). At present Regius Professor of Divinity in the University of Cambridge. He is the author of *Early Christian Thought and the Classical Tradition* (1966); *The Early Church* (1967); and *Priscillian of Avila* (1976). He has also published translations of Origen (1953), Lessing (1956) and Hippolitus of Rome (1968).

OPPOSITE
Hagiogeography of the Byzantine world. A map of major patrons, shrines and translations by A.A.M. Bryer and J.L. Dowling.

Professor Han J.W. Drijvers, Professor of Syriac in the State University of Groningen. Among his publications are 'Bardaisan of Edessa', *Studia Semitica Neerlandica* 6 (1966); *Old-Syriac (Edessan) Inscriptions* (1972); 'The Religion of Palmyra', *Iconography of Religions* xv.15 (1976); and 'Cults and Beliefs at Edessa', *EPRO* (1980).

The Revd Professor Michel van Esbroeck SJ, Member of the Society of Bollandists and Professor in the Pontificio Istituto Orientale, Rome. His publications are in the field of the history and hagiography of Eastern (including Caucasian) Christianity.

Mrs Zaga Gavrilović, Associate member of the Centre of Byzantine Studies, University of Birmingham. She has published 'La Résurrection d'Adam. Une réinterpretation', *CahArch* xxvii (1978) and 'The Humiliation of Leo VI the Wise. The mosaic of the Narthex at Saint Sophia, Istanbul', *CahArch* xxviii (1979).

Dr Nicholas Gendle, Since completing his doctorate at Oxford, Dr Gendle has held research fellowships in the Universities of Edinburgh and Washington DC. He is the author of *Icons in Oxford* (1980).

The V Revd Dr Sergei Hackel, Reader in Russian Studies, University of Sussex. He has published *One, of Great Price: The Life of Mother Maria Skobtsova* (1965, revised Russian ed. 1980); *The Poet and the Revolution: Aleksandr Blok's 'The Twelve'* (1975) and a variety of articles in such periodicals as *ECR, Contemporary Literature* and *The Modern Language Review.* Editor of *Sobornost/ECR.*

Mrs Susan Ashbrook Harvey, Research student at the Centre of Byzantine Studies, University of Birmingham, where she is preparing a thesis on John of Ephesus. Her articles include 'Syriac Hagiography: An Emporium of Cultural Influences' in *Horizons in Semitic Studies,* ed. J.H. Eaton (1980) and 'Asceticism in Adversity: An Early Byzantine Experience', *Byzantine and Modern Greek Studies* 6 (1980).

Dr E.D. Hunt, Lecturer in the Department of Classics and Ancient History, University of Durham. Previously (1974-7) Lecturer in the University College of Swansea, University of Wales. Among his articles is 'St Silvia of Aquitaine', *JTS* 23 (1972). His thesis on 'Pilgrims to the Holy Land in the 4th and early 5th centuries AD' is due to be published by the Oxford University Press.

Professor Vera D. Likhacheva, Professor of Russian and Byzantine Art in the Academy of Fine Arts, Leningrad. She is the author of *Khudozhestvennoe nasledie Drevnei Rusi i sovremennost'* (1971) (in collaboration with her father, Academician D.S. Likhachev); *'Iskusstvo knigi. Konstantinopol', XI vek* (1976); *and Vizantiiskaia miniatiura v sobraniiakh Sovetskogo Soiuza* (1977), and a contributor to *VV, DOP, CahArch* and *Byzantinoslavica.*

Dr Ruth Macrides, Tutor in Medieval History at the University of St Andrews. She has published 'What's in the name *Megas Komnenos?',* *Archeion Pontou* 35 (1979) and 'The New Constantine and the New Constantinople — 1261?', *Byzantine and Modern Greek Studies* 6 (1980).

Dr Paul Magdalino, Lecturer in the Department of Medieval History, University of St Andrews. Among his articles are 'Some additions and corrections to the list of Byzantine churches and monasteries in Thessalonica', *REB* 35 (1977); 'Manuel Komnenos and the Great Palace', *Byzantine and Modern Greek Studies* 4 (1978); 'An unpublished pronoia grant of the second half of the fourteenth century', *ZVI* 18 (1978); and 'Byzantine Churches at Selymbria', *DOP* 32 (1978).

Dr Rosemary Morris, Lecturer in Medieval History in the University of Manchester. Joint editor of *Mashrik* (papers of the Eastern Mediterranean Seminar, Manchester), and of the *Bulletin of British Byzantine Studies.* She has published 'The Powerful and the Poor in Tenth-Century Byzantium: Law and Reality', *Past and Present* 73 (1976).

The Revd Dr Joseph A. Munitiz SJ, Engaged on the *Corpus Christianorum Series Graeca* at the Katholieke Universiteit, Leuven. He has published *Theognosti Thesaurus* (1979) and has contributed articles to *ECR, REB, JTS* and *Byzantion.*

The Revd Dr Flor Van Ommeslaeghe SJ, Associate member of the Society of Bollandists (1974) and fellow of the Society (1975). He is engaged on an edition of *Vita S. Iohannis Chrysostomi, a. Martyrio Antiocheno (BHG* 871), and has published articles related to this subject in *AnalBoll.*

Professor Evelyne Patlagean, is Professor at the University of Paris–X (Nanterre), where she teaches the history of Late Antiquity and Byzantium. She is the author of *Pauvreté économique et pauvreté sociale à Byzance,* 4e – 7e siècle (1977) and is a regular contributor to *Annales E.S.C.*

Professor Lennart Rydén, Professor of Byzantine Studies in the University of Uppsala. Previously docent in Ancient Greek Language and Literature (1963-72) and research docent in Byzantine Studies (1973-80). Among his publications are *Das Leben des hl.Narren Symeon von Leontius von Neapolis* (1963) together with *Bemerkungen* (1970); 'Zum Aufbau der Andreas Salos-Apokalypse', *Eranos* 66 (1968); and 'The Date of the *Life of Andreas Salos', DOS* 32 (1978).

Professor Speros Vryonis Jr, Professor of Byzantine and Early Turkish History, and Director of the Gustave E. von Grunebaum Center for Near Eastern Studies in the University of California (Los Angeles). He has published *Byzantium and Europe* (1967); *Byzantium: its internal history and relations with the Muslim World* (1971); and *The Decline of Medieval Hellenism and the Process of Islamization from the Eleventh through the Fifteenth Century* (1971). In addition, he has contributed to a wide range of learned periodicals on Byzantine, Balkan and Ottoman Islamic history.

Index nominum

compiled by NORMAN RUSSELL